AF566918

MIRQATUL-WUSUL
Ilallah-i-war-Rasul

Malfuz of
The Renowned Saint of Gujarat
Shaikh Ahmad Khattu Sarkheji
of Ahmadabad.

Thesis submitted to Gujrat University for the Degree of Ph.D. in Persian University

A Critical Study and Editing
by
Prof. Nisar Ahmad Ansari

KITAB BHAVAN
NEW DELHI-110002

Kitab Bhavan
Publishers, Distributors, Exporters & Importers
1784, Kalan Mahal, Darya Ganj
New Delhi-110002 (India)

Phone : (91-11) 23277392/93, 23274686
Fax : (91-11) 23263383
E-mail : nasri@vsnl.com
Website : www.kitabbhavan.com

Ist Edition ... 2004

ISBN : 81-7151-351-4

Published in India by:
Nusrat Ali Nasri for Kitab Bhavan
1784, Kalan Mahal, Darya Ganj
New Delhi-110002 (India)

Printed in India at:
Lahooti Fine Art Press
Suiwalan, Delhi-110002

Shaikh Ahmed Khattu's tomb, Sarkhej - Ahmedabad

DEDICATION

I feel gratified to dedicate this humble
effort to the sweet memory of
my beloved parents,
father
Muhammad Yusuf Ansari
mother
Hafizabibi Ansari
whose affectionate, love and blessing
I shall always cherish.

CONTENTS

PREFACE

The importance of Malfuz literature compilation of utterances of Saint in their periodical meetings with disciples, followers, visitors, a sort of table talks as primary and very important source of medieval Indian history, particulary religious social, and cultural, has long been recognised. The earliest authentic Malfuz of note, Amir Hasan Sijzi's Fawaidul Fuvad, a compilation of the account of weekly or periodical assemblies of Hazrat Nizamuddin Auliya of Delhi, blazed a new trail in the field of Indo-persian literature. In the wake of which fairly good number of malfuz of celebrated saints came to be complied in Bihar, Deccan and Gujarat, away from Delhi. This is understandable, because the centre of Sufistic instructions has shifted partially to provinces under the benign orders of Hazrat Nizamuddin during his life time and totally after the death of his spiritual successor Hazrat Nasiruddin Muhammad Charagh-i-Delhi. But little attempt has been made to systematically tap this important source of contemporary history with the exception of a few works, published text, or Urdu translations, mostly in the Deccan (Which are fairly well-known) and two Malfuz works of celebrated saints Shaikh Ahmed Khattu Maghribi of Gujarat-available in Urdu translations only- (almost unknown to scholars though published more than half a century ago)[1]. One of the reasons for this is the nonavailability of these works in public libraries and their inaccebility in the private collections of saintly establishment and families. As a result a very valuable source of contemporary history was overlooked and also the contribution of the saints to contemporary life and society was overlooked by modern historians.

Consequently, the services rendered by the saints of Gujarat to its life and society as well as to the cause of Arabic, Persian and Gujari literature has remained a closed-book to the scholars of even Gujarat. And outside Gujrat there's only except the stately account of their contribution to the origin and growth of Urdu language and literature, pieced to gether from two-three works available to them by Moulvi Abdul Haq and Hafiz Mahmud Khan Sherani.

Therefore, when the historical importance of one of the two malfuz works of Shaikh Ahmed Khattu was brought to the notice of the historians through the Khuda Baksh Memorial Lecture, Patna, my teacher of a scholar of eminence, Dr. Ahmed Husain Qureshi, Head, Department of Persian, Gujarat University, Ahmedabad, suggested to me to edit this malfuz viz. Mirqatul Wusul Ilallah-i-War-Rasul for my

Ph.D. Thesis. Accordingly I started the work under his guidance but the cruel hand of death snatched him away from our midst before the work could be completed. Then I sought the guidance of his successor, Professor Dr. B.A.Tirmizi. I am extremely thankful to both of them.

When the work was accepted for the Ph.D. degree in 1999, Professor Muhiyuddin Bombaywala, who has evinced keen interest in the progress of the work and who is taking great pains to project Gujarat's contribution in various spheres, not only suggested that this doctorial thesis, in view of its utmost importance, be made available to scholars and people atlarge, but also took pains to arrange for its publication. My most sincere thanks are due to him. I am also much beholden to Mr. Nusrat Ali of Kitab Bhavan, Delhi for having undertaken its publication and brought it out so well in such a short time.

I consider it my duty to thank the Chairman President and the management of Hazrat Peer Mohammed Shah Dargah Sharif. Trust and Chairman of the Library and Research Centre Committee to permit me to utilise the manuscripts in their library. The authorities of the Gujarat University, Ahmedabad, have been kind enough to permit me to publish this thesis for which I feel highly obliged. Last, but not the least, my cordial thanks are also due, to the great scholar Dr. Z. A. Desai for his suggestions and help in the course of my work. Without his interest and ungrudging help this book might not have seen the light of the day.

The edited text is preceded by an exhaustive introduction, dealing in great details, with the life and teaching of the saint, as also the contents of the book. I earnestly hope that this important contemptory text, furnishing new information on the different aspects of life and society of the people of North India, particularly Rajasthan and Gujarat, in the late 13th century, 14th century will be found useful by the scholars of Indian history as well as general readers.

Prof. Nisar Ahmed Ansari
Ahmadabad

FORWORD

Gujarat, due to its geographical position, has attracted migrants from different walks of life throughout the centuries. Long before the establishment of Muslim rule in north India, the Arabs and Persians had settled down in various parts of Gujarat. With the herald of Muslim rule in Gujarat, it become a center of attraction for the Muslim scholars, poets and saints who flourished under the benevolent establishment of these Muslim rulers. Most of the Sufis who founded their orders in India, including Gujarat, were mostly from Central Asia, Iran or Iraq. But one Abu Ishaq from Maghrib (north-west Africa, a region which included Morocco, Algeria, Tunisia, Syrenaica and Tripolitania) now popularly called Baba Ishaq, fondly decided to settle down permanently at Khattu near Nagaur. He was a great sufi and a spiritual descendent of Abu Madyan Shu'aib bin al-Husain and a friend of the famous Shaikh Ahmad ar Refa'i (d. 1182)

It is so narrated that once a child named Ahmad was playing outside his house when suddenly a dust storm took him to a place away from his house. As he was wandering in search of his house, he fell into the hands of Baba Ishaq Maghribi. Ahamed was about four years old at this juncture of time. Baba Ishaq brought up the child with utmost care and affection. He was also brought to Delhi by the Baba to visit the tombs of the saints of the city where one of Ahmads brothers recognized him. As a result of the affection of Baba Ishaq, Ahmad remained with him till his death in 776/1374-75 at khattu Shaikh Ahmad again came to Delhi and after twelve years of hard ascetic exercises, he went to perform Haj from where he reached Delhi prior to the invasion of Timur. He was imprisoned alongwith forty people in a house by the invading army. Reports of his spiritual powers reached Timur who released him with his forty co-prisoners. Timur later became his devotee and took him to Samarqand. The shaikh left Samarqand to visit khurasan and Mecca and finally returned to Gujarat. All the contemporary rulers of Gujarat were greatly devoted to Shaikh Ahmad Khattu and most of the credit for the foundation of Ahmadabad is given to the Shaikh.

Shaikh Ahmad khattu (d 849/1445) was a sufi of great understanding and achievements. He also penned his observations and fidings about his world of Sufism. It was simply to benefit others who wished to attain union with God, the only cherished goal of a sufi.

This popular and eminent sufi of Gujarat wrote Risalahe-Ahmediyyah fi Manaqibil Mashaikhil Maghrebiyyah in chaste Arabic. In this treatise, the Shaikh gives an account of the Shaikhs of Maghribi order of Sufis founded by Shaikh Abu Madyan Maghribi. This brief treatise shows the command of the Shaikh on writing simple Arabic with literary acumen. Apart from this treatise, there are two different collections of Shaikh Ahmad's malfuzat (discourses). One is Tohfat al-Majalis compiled by Shaikh Mahmud Iraji and thes other is Mirqat al-wusul Ilallah e-war Rasul by Maulana Muhammad who was in counstant attendance upon Shaikh Ahmad for almost three decades. Both of these collections are important to make a comprehensive assessment of the career, personality and teachings of the Shaikh. Similarly both these collections, like the other Malfuz literature, be regarded as one of the most important literary achievements of medieval India.

Mirqat al-wasul is an important work of its kind. Apart from being a primary source of political and social history of Gujarat and Rajasthan, it also furnishes useful material on geography and topography rarely found in other contemporary sources. The glimpses of the cordial relations between the different communities found in Mirqat al-Wasul lead one to realise the relevance of the Sufis to preach universal brotherhood and love. Mirqat ul-wusul also provides interesting and sometimes unique information on literary activities in Gujarat. The Shaikh, himself enjoying a literary taste of high order, has referred to a number of men of letters of his time and their literary and scholarly achievements both in prose and poetry. Some of these informations are hardly found in any other source of that time. This collection of Malfuzat also bear evidence to Shaikh Ahmad's intimate knowledge of the Quran, its exegesis and Hadith.

Prof. Nisarahmad M. Ausari, a known scholar of Persian from Ahmadabad, has critically edited the persian text of Mirqat al-wusul which is now in your hands for the first time in print form.

Prof. Ansari has written a scholarly prologue to this work. He has ably dealt in detail with Maghribi order of the sufis. Its background, history and contribution to sufism as such have been authentically traced by Prof. Ansari. The life and teachings of Baba Ishaq, the founder of the Maghribi order of Sufism in India, have been described with a discerning mind. Similarly the details provided by prof. Ansari about the life and attainments of Sheikh Ahmad khattu, based on different authentic sourcs, throw new light on the personality of Shaikh Ahmed. Since Prof. Ansari has carefully and minutely gone through the text of Mirqat al-wusal, he has been able to draw the required informations to reconstruct in detail the life of the Shaikh and his contribution to sufism in general. Prof. Ansari is also successful in critically editing the text of Mirqat al-wusul. Let it be clear that the text of these Malfuzat is not an ordinary one and hance its critical edition was not an easy job. Mirqat al-wusul mainly deals with sufism and a number of religious matters. The terms relating to both sufism and religion had made the text a bit difficult. But Prof. Ansari has been able to do justice in presenting an authentic and correct text based on the manuscripts available to him.

I express my appreciation for this achievement of Prof. Ansari and hope this work would be received well by the scholars in general and those interested in Sufism in particular.

Prof. S.H. Qasemi
Formerly Head Department
of Persian and Dean
Faculty of Arts,
University of Delhi
Delhi-7

1

PROLOGUE

As has been pointed out by scholars of history, the 14th century is an important period in religious history. There was an affulgence of mystical activities from Multan in the West, to Bengal in the east and the whole of the Deccan plateau in the south where sufis, savants and learned mystics and shaikhs were busy spreading the message of love and universal peace and brotherhood. The first half of the 15th century saw the extention of the sphere of intense sufistic activities to Gujarat and the Deccan. The Sufi establishment, the Khanqahs and Jamaat-Khanas served as hospices for travellers and wayfarers and also as training centres for the novices, resounding with lessons and discussions on theology, mysticism, scholastic philosophy, ethics, morality, etc., at which the saint was the principal speaker and expounder of thoughts and ideas.

The utterances of the saint (*malfuz*) were most covetously taken down by disciples generally with the express and tacit approval of the saint. In this way, a considerable number of saintly sayings came to be compiled in different parts of the country, truthfully recording their discourses and proceedings at these meetings or assemblies which were open to all sections of the society. Thus malfuz literature by its very nature constitutes an important non-political history source on one hand and supplies valuable material for the study of contribution to Persian literature on the other. In no Islamic country perhaps to our knowledge, this branch of theological compilation has been so extensively cultivated as in our country, especially during the pre-Mughal period, particularly in Bihar, Gujarat and Deccan. It was primarily intended to serve as a book of guidance for laymen and as a manual of spiritual instructions or code of behaviour for the disciples in particular. Obviously, the subject- matter of these works centered around the saint concerned who occupied a highly respected position in the society. As a result, they covered all aspects of life of the society at different levels and in all temporal or spiritual matters. It will not be an exageration to say that no branch of medieval literature presents such detailed picture of contemporary society as in the malfuz literature. While they furnish an intimate peep into the social life and behaviour of different sections of the society, they underline varied intensley human qualities of the spiritual guide.

The malfuz works in short enable us to have a picture of society and its different aspects, In them are reflected the moods, aspirations and varied problems of its members, their ways of life and living and likes and dislikes. A striking feature of the study of these works is the revealing information that in certain respects social life and behaviour of medieval society have undergone but little change in essential parts until our times.

It is a known fact that while the malfuz works from Bihar and the Deccan have been published in original as well as some in translation and utilized by scholars and historians for the reconstruction of important aspects of the political, social and cultural history, similar works from Gujarat have remained unnoticed. Here the Chishti, the Suhravardi, the Maghribi, the Qadiri and the Shattari orders have flourished almost from the beginning of the fifteenth century if not earlier and have played an important role in the life of its people. These saintly families, whose members were learned have left treatises on sufistic subjects, as well as collections of sayings and utterances; accounts of their assemblies are also compiled. Most prominent among these are the Suhravardi saintly family of Ahmadabad, descendents of the celebrated fourteenth century saint Sayyid Jalaluddin Husain popularly called Makhdum Jahanian -i-Jahangasht, whose grandson Sayyid Burhanuddin popularly called Qutb-i-Alam was the first to come to Gujarat, The Chishti family of Ahmadabad claiming descent from the sister's son of Hazrat Nasiruddin Mahmud Chiragh-i-Dehli, namely Khwaja Kamaluddin Allama and the Shattari saints, the most prominent of whom is Shah Wajihuddin Alavi, a great scholar and teacher as well. The first two mentioned families have the unique distinction of having had successive six-seven generations of authors and poets whose contribution to learning and literature has remained almost unknown so far. One of the reasons for this is unavailability of these works, which are usually found in the saintly families to which scholars have no access. As a result, only in the case of a couple of such works found in libraries, some study has been made and published in the recent past. For example, an article on one of the two three malfuz works of Shah Wajihuddin, to wit *Bahrul-Haqaiq* was published by Prof. M. Aslam of Punjab University, Lahore. Another malfuz work which has been the chief basis of the article entitled "Shaikh Ahmad Maghribi as a great historical personality of medieval Gujarat" by Prof. Khaliq Ahmad Nizami is the *Tuhfatul Majalis*, a collection of assembly discourses of Shaikh Ahmad Khattu of Sarkhej, compiled by Shaikh Mahmud Iraji. Late Maulavi Sayyid Abu Zafar Nadvi had published the Urdu translation of the *Tuhfatul -Majalis* as early as in 1939. He also discovered a copy of another malfuz of the same saint, called *Mirqatul-Wusul Ilallah-i-war-Rasul* "The ladder facilitating nearness to Allah and the Prophet", the subject of this Thesis, compiled in A.H. 861 (1457 A.D.) or some twelve years after the saint's demise, by Maulana Muhammad, son of Abul-Qasim (or Qasim) who was in constant attendance upon him for full three decades. Its Urdu translation also was published by the late Maulavi Abu Zafar Nadvi Saheb under the title *Sirat-i-Ahmadiya*, "Biography of Ahmad" in or immediately after 1945.

It is this malfuz work which I propose to edit, with introduction highlighting its manifold importance for the political, cultural and social history of western India.

I may humbly say that this has become possible only because, in the words of the celebrated Persian poet Sadi,

تمتع زہر گوشۂ یافتم   زہر خرمنی خوشۂ یافتم

"I received assistance from every nook and corner,
I got an ear of corn out of every harvest"

and have been under obligation of my teachers and friends, to quote, again, the words of the poet Chandra Bhan Barahman,

تمام شکرم از احسان بی نہایت دوست (دوستان)

"I thankful in earnest due to the unbounded grace of friends."

Notes

1. This section is based on Prof. Khaliq Ahmad Nizami's introduction to the *Khairul-Majalis* of Hamid Qalandar (Aligarh 1959), pp.1-2, Doctor Ziyauddin Abdul-Hayy Desai's *Malfuz Literature* et .al. (Patna, 1991), and personal information.

Preface

1. The Hazrat Pir Muhammad Shah Library and Research centre, Ahmadabad under the guidence of it's Hon. Director Prof. Muhiyuddin Bombaywala has brought out new addition of these translation, one of them in that of the present work made by late Moulvi Abu Zafar Nabvi. This Centre has also published the Biographies of the 16th century Gujri poet saint Shah Bahauddin Bajan, and Kazi Mehmud Daryayai.

2

ADVENT OF MUSLIMS IN THE PROVINCE OF GUJARAT[1]

It is generally believed that Sind was the first province of Indian sub-continent to come into contact with Islam. This is open to question. Evidence shows that it was Gujarat which first attracted the attention of Muslim forces in the time of the second pious caliph Hazrat Umar (634-44 A.D.). In A.H. 15 (634 A.D.), a naval expedition was despatched by the governor of Bahrain under his brother Hakam against Thana on the west coast, Next year, Hakam attacked Barus (Broach). These expeditions met with some success, but they were strongly resented by Hazrat Umar who was not in favour of sea expeditions to distant lands. About three quarters of a century was to elapse, before Muhammad bin Qasim conquered Sind in A.H. 93 (712 A.D.). His successor Junaid despatched one of his officers against some parts of Gujarat, like Marmad or Barbad, Mandal, Dhanuj and Barus, Later on, in A.H. 157 (773-74 A.D.), governor Hisham bin Amr invaded the maritime port Gandhar situated at a small distance from Broach. Apart from these sporadic attacks, the Arabs might have made some other raids into parts of Gujarat but they do not appear to have any lasting effect. Similarly, two three centuries later, Mahmud of Ghazna, Muhammad bin Sam better known in Indian history as Shihabuddin Ghori and his freed slave and successor in India, Qutbuddin Aibak carried out expeditions against the rulers of Gujarat, but being more or less like lightning in nature, they failed to establish Muslim rule or authority here. It was only towards the close of the thirteenth century that Ulugh Khan brother and general of Delhi ruler Alauddin Khalji, conquered Gujarat and made it a part of his empire.

But Gujarat had been a visiting place and even home of the Arabs and Muslims before and after the advent of Islam, as is vouchsafed by early Arab geographers and travellers, some of whom had visited western India centuries before the political association of Muslims with Gujarat. The non-Muslim Arabs and later Arab Muslims had been visiting western India, where in Gujarat important sea-ports lay and were carrying on trade and commerce, through these ports which served as the import and export inlets and outlets for the entire country.

The vocation of Arabs and Persians, as sea-faring people carrying on trade brought them into close contact with their Indian counterpart, and since the foreigners also contributed a great share to the coffers of Indian princes, they were treated with respect and consideration and were allowed to enjoy certain privileges which guaranteed to these foreigners partial autonomy. The accounts of the Arab travellers who visited India in the tenth, eleventh and twelfth centuries, furnish ample information concerning the Muslims who had chosen to settle in different parts of Gujarat. The glowing tribute paid by these travellers amply bear out the friendly nature of the commercial and cultural relations that brought the local people who were exclusively Hindus and Muslims into close association with one another. Long before the founders of Muslims rule in north India had trampled upon its rich and fertile plains and later on annexed the province of Gujarat to their empire, the Arabs and Persians had established their settlements in Gujarat not only on the sea coast at places like Ghogha, Bhadreshwar, Cambay, Broach and Sopara, but also in the interior places like Nahrwala-Patan and Junagadh, where these merchants and their families had settled down. The celebrated Arab traveller Masudi, who visited western India speaks of some cities which had Muslim population ten thousand strong, comprising, besides the Muslim settlers from Siraf, Oman, Basra, Baghdad and other places, Muslims born of Indian mothers, known as Bayasira. At that time, the Hunarman of that place was one Abu Said Maruf Ibn Zakariya. A few years before Masudi's visit, another traveller Buzurg ibn Shahryar also found a Muslim, Abbas bin Mahan, performing the duties of Hunarman. In those days of the numerous sea ports of Gujarat the flourishing town of Cambay (Khambhat) occupied an important position as a centre of commercial activities. In the absence of historical data, it would be hazardous to make a surmise with regard to the earliest settlement of the Muslims in this town, but it may be said with certainty that when Masudi visited Cambay in 303 A.H./915 A.D., he found a large number of Muslims who had settled there. Like his predeccessor Sulaiman, Masudi was also impressed by the benevolence and just rule of the local ruler who provided ample opportunities for the Muslims to live in peace and carry on their professions without any hindrance. According to Istakhri, who after Masudi visited this part in 950 A.D., in the cities of the territory from Cambay to Saymur which was under the sway of Balhara, one of the Indian kings, lived a good number of Muslims who were governed by none except a Muslim on behalf of

Balhara; in these cities there were Jami mosques where Friday prayers were offered and Islamic rites and customs were performed and observed publicly. Ibn Hauqal whom Istakhri had met in India, gives some additional details and mentions the towns of Khwaja al-Sarir al-an, Gandhar and Ghogha, where the Muslims, few though they were, would not tolerate the exercise of authority nor the imposition of punishment, nor the testimony of witness except by Muslims. In the cities of Gujarat, the Muslim settlers lived in perfect peace and in case they suffered any injustice at the hands of the local population or others, the just rulers looked into their grievance and got it redressed. For example, the famous Persian author Muhammad Aufi who had visited Cambay in about 1223 A.D. has vividly described at length the justice dispensed by the Chaulukya ruler Siddhraj Jaysinh (1094-1143 A.D.) by ordering the reconstruction of the Jami mosque of Cambay — which was demolished and some eighty Muslims were killed by a section of the Hindu population— in response to the complaint by the Imam of the mosque. Incidentally, it was in the town of Cambay that according to the traditional accounts, the first missionary of Ismaili Bohras, Abdullah, is stated to have arrived from Yemen in southern Arabia in 1067 A.D. Another notable Bohra missionary also, namely Muhammad Ali, was in Cambay and died there in 1137 A.D.; his tomb in the town is held in great respect and veneration by the Bohras.

Long before the Muslims established themselves as the masters of erstwhile capital of Gujarat, Patan, it had been frequently visited by the Arab merchants who were treated with respect and consideration by the ruler and his ministers. Apart from the mercantile class, a number of eminent Sufis also found their way to Patan. Of these sufis who had settled in city and whose tombs still exist today and are visited by Muslim pilgrims from far and wide, one is Haji Hud the illustrious ancestor of the renowned Qadri families of Ahmadabad and Patan, the first to come to Patan; the phrase *Yaluhush- Shams* (The sun shines) gives the date of his arrival, i.e. 454 A.H. (1062-63 A.D.) and the numerical value of the word "Ishqullah" (Love of God) gives the date of his death, viz. 536 A.H. (1141-42 A.D.). Other saints Shaikh Ahmad, generally known as Baba Dehliya and Sayyid Muhammad Barahman are stated to have visited Patan during the reign of Siddhraj Jaysinh. Another saint Shaikh Ahmad Arafati (d.645 A.H./1245-46 A.D.) had selected Patan for popularising the Sufi cult. It was the existence of a considerable elements of the spiritual fraternity in Patan, which led Shaikh Abdul Haq Muhaddis Dehlavi to remark that "The region diffuses the fragrance of love and its desolate places emit light of blessings and saintliness."

Broach also seems to have attracted the attention of the early Muslims, as it was a sea-port for vessels coming from China and Sind. A saint named Baba Raihan inspired with missionary zeal is said to have visited Broach in the tenth century A.D., accompanied by his younger brother and forty followers. All of them are reported to have courted martyrdom. Broach is also mentioned by Masudi, Abu Raihan Biruni, Idrisi, Yaqut and the like. In Rander, now part of Surat city, there is an Arabic inscription on a tomb which shows that a certain sailor of Cambay had died there in 633 A.H. (1236 A.D.). Petlad in Kheda district claims the tomb of a Muslim saint Baba Arjan Shah who died in 633 A.H. (1236 A.D.). According to a modern authority, "The existence of this tomb shows clearly that Islam's influence had permeated the province of Gujarat early in the thirteenth century at a period when it was still ruled by its own Rajput princes."

That even near and around the old (Kohna) Asawal close to which the city of Ahmadabad was founded and which finds mention by Biruni, Idrisi and others as a commercial rich city producing useful articles, Muslims used to live in the eleventh- thirteenth centuries, is testified by epigraphs, which record the construction of mosques, furnishing evidence of a good sized Muslim population in the area. One of these inscriptions states that a mosque was built in 445 A.H. (1035 A.D.), while according to another inscription which was set up at a late date in the fifteenth century, the mosque on which the inscription was set up was reconstructed on the site of an old mosque in 636 A.H. (1238 A.D.), by Malik Haji. The contents of these inscriptions make it abundantly clear that long before the conquest of Gujarat by Alauddin's general, there were Muslims settlements in almost all the parts of Gujarat and they enjoyed perfect peace on account of the benevolent and tolerant attitude of the Hindu Rajas.

Notes

1. This section is mainly based on Prof. M. I. Dar's article "Cultural and Literary activities under the Sultans of Gujarat". Published in the *Journal of the Gujarat Research Society, Bombay,* Vol. 10 (1948), pp.240-57; Elliot and Dowson, *History of India as told by its own Historians*, Vol. I (London, 1867); Ali Muhammad Khan, *Mirat-i-Ahmadi*, Supplement, English Tr. Syed Nawab Ali and C.N.Seddon (Baroda) 1928, pp. 91 ff.

3

GUJARAT UNDER SULTAN OF DELHI AND AS AN INDEPENDENT SULTANS[1]

As stated above, the first Delhi Sultan to annex the fertile region of Gujarat to his vast empire was Alauddin Khalji, who in the very third year of his reign (697 A.H. 1298 A.D.) under his brother Ulugh Khan and the latter's deputy, Nusrat Khan, despatched a well-equipped army to subjugate it. Though the last Chaulukya king Raja Karna offered stubborn resistance to the imperial army, he lost the kingdom and took refuge with Raja Ramdas of Deogir (later Daulatabad) in Deccan. After regaining the lost kingdom for a short while in the wake of the rebellion by the Mongol chiefs in the Delhi Sultan's army, Karna Dev ultimately lost it for ever and the Muslim rule was firmly established in 1304 A.D.

After the final conquest of Gujarat, Alauddin appointed his brother-in-law Alp Khan as the first governor to rule the newly conquired rich province. During his benevolent and efficient rule which lasted for about sixteen years, Alp Khan maintained absolute peace and ushered in an era of prosperity in the province. During his term of governorship, he built the Adina (Friday) mosque, in Nahrwala-Patan, which was in existence till the middle of the 18th century as mentioned in the *Mirat-i-Ahmadi*. After Alp Khan's recall and his being put to death by the orders of ailing Alauddin for no apparent reason in A.H. 716 (1315A.D.), Alp Khan's followers rose in revolt in Gujarat and they slew Kamaluddin Gurg who had been sent by Alauddin to chastise the rebels. Under the short-lived Khalji dynasty, Gujarat in the span of hardly a decade after Alauddin's death fell victim to disorder and saw successive governors like Malik Kamaluddin Gurg, Malik Ainul-Mulk Multani, Malik Dinar entitled Zafar Khan, Malik Husamuddin brother of the Usurper Khusraw Khan, Malik Vahiduddin Quraishi, Tajul-Mulk and Khusraw Khan himself.

Under the Tughluqs, Malik Tajuddin Turk appears to have been appointed the governor of Gujarat by Ghiyasuddin Tughluq Shah (1320-25 A.D.). Then Sharaful-Mulk Alp Khan, the son of the king's tutor Qutlugh Khan was appointed the governor of Gujarat by Sultan Muhammad bin Thughluq (1325-1351 A.D.) in the first year of resuming the reigns of authority. The next governors under the king were Malik Muqbil Telangi entitled Khan Jahan and Shaikh Muizzul-Mulk Muizzuddin bin Alauddin a descendant of Hazrat Shaikh Fariduddin Ganj-i-Shakar Ajhodhani. After him, the governorship was held by Nizamul-Mulk Husain bin Amir Miran who held the post till 762 A.H. (1362 A.D.) and continued to govern during the reign of Firuz Tughluq also (1351-1380 A.D.) It was during Malik Muqbil's tenure of office that disturbances broke out on a wide scale in Gujarat which became the scene of Muhammad bin Tughluq's activities in the province to suppress the rebellion of Malik Taghi.

Some ten years after his succession to the throne, when in 762 AH (1326 A.D.) Firuz Tughluq led an expedition against the ruler of Sind but had to retreat to Gujarat on account of pestilence and scarcity of provisions, he removed Nizamul-Mulk, otherwise described as a capable officer, from governorship of Gujarat for his inability to send supplies to the faminished imperial army in Sind and appointed Zafar Khan Farsi, son-in-law of king Fakhruddin of Sonargaon in Bengal, and a distinguished noble at the court. He was succeeded on his death by his son Darya Khan, who received the title of his father. In 778 A.H. when the junior Zafar Khan was still in to office, Firuz Tughluq, strangely enough, perhaps with a view to replenish the treasury accepted the offer of Shamsuddin Damghani to hold the province of Gujarat with the stipulation that in addition to the usual revenue he would pay forty lakhs of tankas, one hundred elephants, four hundred Abyssinian slaves and one hundred Arabian horses. But as he found it difficult to fulfill the terms of the contract, he adopted harsh measures for the collection of revenue and had to pay with his life for forcible exactions. He was succeeded by Malik Mufrih Sultani, who received the title of Rasti Khan. His long stay in Gujarat from 778 to 794 A.H. (1376 to 1392 A.D.) was partly due to his personal qualities and partly to the chaotic conditions which prevailed in the north, after Firuz Shah's abdication in favour of his son Nasiruddin Muhammad Shah. The new king conferred the title of Sikandar Khan upon Malik Yaqub, the Akhurbeg and made him the governor of Gujarat to which place he repaired with a large body of retainers. Rasti Khan treacherously put him to death and on account of certain compelling reasons, the then king Tughluq Shah, grandson of Sultan Firuz, in 790 A.H. (1388 A.D.) confirmed him in the governorship of Gujarat. Three years later Sultan Muhammad Tughluq II receiving complaints of the highhandedness and oppression of Malik Mufrih Rasti Khan and for other reasons, dispatched Zafar Khan, later on Muzaffar Shah I of

Gujarat in 793 A.H. (1391 A.D.) to supersede Rasti Khan. The latter defying the royal order opposed Zafar Khan and was killed in a battle near Patan on 4th January 1392 A.D.

With the removal of Rasti Khan, who had headed the province for a long period, Zafar Khan devoted his attention to restore order and take measures to bring about the welfare of the province. In the following years he subjugated the insurgents in Khambat, the Raja of Idar, the Khandesh ruler Malik Raja Faruqi etc. and led an expedition to the temple of Somnath.

After the death of Nasiruddin Muhammad Tughluq, in 1395 A.D., the capital city of Delhi was plunged into anarchy and Zafar Khan's son Muhammad who had received the title of Tatar Khan from the late King, finding things going against him, came to his father in Gujarat in 1398 A.D. Zafar Khan refused to be persuaded by his ambitious and intrepid son to proceed to Delhi and carve out for himself an independent sultanate there. About this time, Timur's catastrophic invasion in 1398 shook the very foundation of the tottering Tughluq empire, compelling Nasiruddin Muhammad to seek refuge with Zafar Khan. But the latter showed his reluctance to lead an army to Delhi as desired by the unlucky king Muhammad. In the aftermath of Timur's invasion, provincial governors started asserting their independence. Tatar Khan who enjoyed wide powers under his father and helped him in his campaigns against Idar and other neighbouring areas stressed upon his unwilling father to declare independence and the latter not accepting this suggestion, he imprisoned his father and assumed kingship in 1403 A.D. by having his coronation held in Asawal. However his reign was short termed and he died in the next year, having been allegedly poisoned by his uncle Shams Khan.

Whatever the cause of death of the young and energetic king Muhammad Shah I, officially designated in state records as "Khudaigan-i-Shahid" (Martyred lord), Zafar Khan is reported to have ascended the throne with a heavy heart.

On the death of Zafar Khan, the exact cause of which is also shrouded in mystery, Muhammad Shah I's son Ahmad Shah ascended the throne and very soon earned place amongst the foremost rulers not only of Gujarat but also of India. It was he who laid the foundation of a new capital at a strategic place in the vicinity of Asawal, in central Gujarat at a site which had no habitation whatsoever, and named it Ahmadabad after himself. This town also called "Zainul-Bilad." (Ornament of cities) finds frequent mention in this thesis of doctoral dissertation.

Ahmad Shah I placed the newly established but shaky kingdom of Gujarat, by subjugating turbulent and rebellious elements not only in his own army and family, but in the entire province, on a firm footing and also put the neighboring sultanates of Deccan and Malwa and Rajput princes of southern Rajasthan on the defensive.

The just mighty and able Ahmad Shah I, was succeeded on his death in 846 A.H. (1442 A.D.) by his son Muhammad Shah II (1442-1451 A.D.) who also frequently finds mention in the *Mirqatul-Wusul* as the saint's admirer and disciple. It was during his reign that Shaikh Ahmad Khattu joined the mercy of God in A.H. 849 (1445 A.D.). Muhammad Shah II had visited the saint during his illness. He was asked by Maulana Muhammad bin Qasim, the author of the *Mirqat* who had been the leader of prayer (Imam) of the saint, to lead the funeral prayer.

The saint, as he himself had often remarked in the presence of the author of the *Mirqat* and others, had witnessed the reigns of seven rulers of Delhi (three) and Gujarat (four) who were the admirers or disciples of Baba Ishaq the Shaikh's mentor and adopted father, and the saint himself. The pages of the *Mirqatul Wusul* are replete with the instances and events depicting high regard and respect in which these kings Muhammad bin Tughluq onwards held the two saints. Likewise, their nobleman and high and low officials also by and large were ever ready to carry out the slightest wish of the saint and would consider it a high favour if the saint accepted their Futuh-offering which he was normally reluctant to accept.

It may also be mentioned that even after his death, the saint's tomb complex comprising the mosque, the tomb, the lake, etc. was held in veneration by successive Gujarat sultans. Sultan Mahmud I, famous by his cognomen Begda "with big mustacheos' had not only selected the place for his summer palace, of which the majestic ruins are still a matter of awe and wonder of the visitors, but he also chose the ground on the bank of the lake at the feet of the saint, that is to say the south of the saint's tomb, for his eternal resting place, and that of his consort. At least two more sultans, Muzaffar Shah II son and successor of Mahmud I, and Mahmud Shah III son of Latif Khan and grandson of Muzaffar Shah II, and their consorts one of them, wife of Muzaffar Shah II named Rani Raj Bai are found buried in the same complex. The entire area around the complex was dotted until recently and is, to same extent, still, with graves and fairly large tombs of the noblemen and poets who chose to be buried in the precincts of the saint's mausoleum, even at a later date under the later sultans of Gujarat and the Mughal emperor Akbar who put an end to the sultanate by his victory over Sultan Muzaffar III (1561-73 A.D., 1583-84 A.D.) and finally in 1584 A.D. by his general Mirza *Abdur Rahim Khan Khan-i-Khanan*.

Notes

1. This section is maithe Saintly based on Maulavi Sayyid Abu Zafar Nadvi's *Tarikh-i-Gujarat* in Urdu (Delhi, 1971); Dr. S.C. Misra. Rise of Muslim Power in Gujarat (Delhi, 1982); Prof. M.S. Commissariate, History of Gujarat, Vol. 1 (Bombay 1938); and Rasiklal Parikh and H.G. Shastri ed. Gujarat no Rajakiya Ane Sanskritic Itihas Vol. V, Sultanat Kal, Ahmadabad 1970.

GENEOLOGICAL TABLE OF THE SULTANS OF GUJARAT

Wajih-ul Mulk Tank

1. Muhammad I (Tattar Khan) 1403
2. Muazffar I (Zaffar Khan) 1407-1410
3. Ahmad I 1411-1442
4. Muhammad II 1442-51
5. Qutbudding Ahmad II
6. Daud 1458
7. Mahmud I Begda (Fateh Khan) 1453-1511
8. Muzaffar II (Khalil Khan) 151-1526
9. Sikandar 1526
10. Mahmud II (Nasir Khan) 1526
    Rajim Adil Khan, Ruqayya Faruqi of Khandesh
11. Bahadur Latif Khan 1526-1537
12. Muhammad III
13. Mahmud III 1538-1554
14. Ahmad III 1554-1561
15. Muzaffar III (Nathu or Habib) 1561-1573 and 1583-1584

4

LAYING THE FOUNDATION OF AHMADABAD CITY

Even if his wars and conquest or his most successful reign and administrative system were to be consigned to the niche of oblivion, the title of Ahmad Shah to immortal fame in the pages of Indian history would rest on the foundation of the great city of Ahmadabad on the bank of the river Sabarmati, which he made his new capital and which has maintained through the vicissitudes of almost six hundred years, its position as the metropolis of the province of Gujarat. It was early in 1411 A.D. that the sultan with the advice of his spiritual guide Shaikh Ahmad Khattu of Sarkhej laid the foundation of Ahmadabad in an open and spacious area in the immediate vicinity of the old (as against the later habitation of new) Asawal (Asawal-i-Kuhna) and to the east of the river Sabarmati. The welknown eighteenth century historical work *Mirat-i-Ahmadi* gives the date of the foundation as 3rd day of Zil-Qada 813 A.H. (27th February 1411)[1]. A modern historian Ratnamanirao Bhimrao, Jote, the author of a voluminous corpus on the city named *Amdavad Gujarat-nu-Patnagar*, (Gujarati), consulting an eminent astrologer about the horoscope given by the author of the *Mirat-i-Ahmadi* (who was the last Mughal Diwan of the province and had the entire state archives at his disposal) has come to the conclusion that the horoscope is correct and that the day should be 3rd or 5th of Zil-Qada (27th February or 1st March 1411 AD).[2]

The imposing river-bastion, called the Manek Burj, which stands at the head of the Ellisbridge now named Swami Vivekanand Bridge and measures fifty-three feet in height is said to have been selected for the site of the foundation of the city.[3] However, the transfer of the capital of Gujarat from Anhilvad-Patan, for well about six centuries the seat of government, to a new locality was not to be undertaken without spiritual guidance. Hence, as the tradition goes the Sultan with the aid of the saint Shaikh Ahmad Khattu, invoked the blessings of venerable and mysterious personage the Prophet Khizr, who is identified by some Muslim divines with the Prophet Elijah. His consent was given to build a new city provided that its boundaries were lined by four persons with the name Ahmad who were reputed for their piety and righteousness and who had not missed even a single day's *Sunnat* prayers of Asr. The Sultan and the saint who fulfilled these conditions made half of the number required and the other two found were Malik Ahmad, who is buried at Pathanwada near the Kalupur Gate of the city,[4] and Qazi Ahmad Jodh of Patan, a spiritual successor of the saint.[5]

The tomb of Qazi Ahmad Jodh is still to be seen in the ancient town of Patan where he died in 1437 A.D. It's original building appears to have been rebuilt by a descendent of Qazi Ahmad early in the seventeenth century according to an inscription occurring on the present tomb.[6] The famous Suhravardi saint Hazrat Sayyid Burhanuddin Qutb-i-Alam of Vatva was also invited from Patan, to attend and bless the occasion; he gave his blessing saying احمدآباد آباد باد 'Ahmadabad, prosperous for ever."[7]

These four Ahmads are said to have been helped in the foundation ceremony by twelve Babas or Faqirs. All of them are said to have been disciples directly or indirectly of the famous saint Shaikh Nizamuddin Auliya of Delhi. (d. 1325 A.H.) and their names with details of the place where they lie buried are given by the author of the *Mirat-i-Ahmadi*. Of these Babas, Baba Ali Sher was a majzub, having renounced all wordly effects and concerns and would not put on any clothes, But whenever Shaikh Ahmad Khattu would visit him or pass by his lodgings, he would say (in Gujarati) *Lugdun lavo shara no kot ave chhe* (લુગડું લાવો શરાનો કોટ આવે છે.) "Give me clothes, the bastion of Shara (religious Code) is coming". These twelve Babas are : Baba Khoju, Baba Laddhu, Baba Karamat (all buried at Dholka), Baba Muhammad and Baba Ali Sher (buried at Sarkhej), Baba Tavakkul Nasirabadi (buried at Hajipura on Shahibaug Road, Ahmadabad), Baba Muhammad *alias* Baba Lului (buried near Saptarshi's ara, at the eastern end of Sardar Bridge, Ahmadabad), Baba Ahmad Hankuri Nalband (buried at Khas Bazar to the north of Alif Masjid, Ahmadabad), and Baba Laddha, Baba Dhokal, Baba Kamal Kirmani and Baba Sayyah (buried respectively at Halim's Khadki, in between Delhi gate and Shahpur gate, Ek Minarwali Masjid, Behrampur in Ahmadabad and Viramgam).[8]

Notes

1. Ali Muhammad Khan, *op. cit.*, 215. H. Blochmann, Eng. Tr. *Ain -e- Akbari*, vol. I, 507n. has, on the authority of a comparatively recent work *Khazinatul-Asfiya*, 7th Zil- Qada. The *Tarikh-i-Firishta,* Kanpur 1884, 183 gives the close of the year 815 A.H., while the *Mirat-i-Sikandari* (Baroda, 1958), 37, gives 813 A.H. as the date of foundation.
2. Ratnamani Rao B Jote, *Gujarat-nu-Patnagar, Amdavad* (Ahmadabad, 1928), 784-87.
3. H. G. Briggs, *Cities of Gujarashtra*, 230.
4. Ali Muhammad Khan, *op. cit.*, 3.
5. Ibid., 3, 100.
6. *Epigraphia India Arabic and Persian Supplement* (*EIAPS*), 1997, pp plate. According to this inscription, Junaid son of Faqih and a decendant of Hazrat Qazi Jodh started the construction of the tomb in Shaban 1025 A.H. (1616 A.D.) and completed it in 1026 A.H. (1617 A.D.).
7. Ali Muhammad Khan, *op. cit.*, 25.
8. Ibid., 78-79.

5

SUFISTIC ATTAINMENTS AND CONTRIBUTION OF SHAIKH AHMAD KHATTU TO SUFISTIC PHILOSOPHY

In a letter to Maulana Fakhruddin Zarradi, the esteemed saint Shaikh Nizamudin Auliya says; "The highest purpose and the supreme aim of creating mankind is the love of God. Hence it is incumbent upon every one to free his heart from everything besides God (ماسوی الله) and devote himself exclusively to Him".[1] In other words, a true saint is he who lives for Lord alone. Union with Him is the sole aim of his life. As an early sufi saint Shibli says:

الفقیر مستغنی من دون الله

"The poor (Sufi) is independent of everything other than God".

Shaikh Ahmad Hujviri, better known as Daṭa Ganj Bakhsh, of Lahore, who was the first to explain fully the sufistic terminology in Persian in his magnum opus *Kashful-Mahjub,* and at whose tomb, the celebrated Ajmer saint Khwaja Muinuddin Sijzi Chishti performed Chilla for 40 days, says: "He is above because He has no other object or desire".[2] Likewise, Amir Hasan Sijzi says in the *Fawaidul-Fuad*:

حیات آنست کہ درویش بذکر حق مشغول باشد

"Life (of the Darvish) is only that he is engrossed in meditation of God".[3]

In short, a true Sufi should devote every moment of his life and dedicate every fibre of his being to Him alone. He removes the distinction between "I" and "Not I" and merges his soul in the Absolute.

Gnosis (معرفت) or Union (وصل) with God through it being the cherished ideal of a Sufi, Shaikh Ahmad Khattu strove to achieve it. It was generally believed that prayers and penitence, vigil and fasts could best help a seeker of union with God in the pursuit of his ideal. But there is one essential requisite without which all efforts of the mystic are bound to prove futile. It is "Concentration" (حضور قلب). Therefore, the Sufi masters have laid great emphasis upon the training of heart. They insist upon it, acting according to the Tradition the Holy Prophet, namely "Concentration is of utmost importance in sufistic exercise." The Sarkhej Saint tried to follow this saying in letter and spirit and took up as his goal the attainments and traversing of the supreme stages prescribed by his eminent sufi predecessors, under the instruction of Babu Ishaq, his foster-father and spiritual guide Shaikh Ahmad Khattu had cultivated the spirit of self reliance, independence, courage and magnanimity of heart. The same spirit he infused in his disciples too. After settling down at Sarkhej where actually his spiritual career may be said to start, he rarely left his Khanqah or visited any body; on the contrary, kings and nobles used to come to his Khanqah to see him and seek his advise and blessings.

According to what Shaikh Mahmud Iraji has recorded in his *Tuhfatul-Majalis* at various places, the saint, like Ibnul-Arabi (d. 1241 A.D.), one of the greatest exponents of Sufi philosophy, regarded both nature and man as the mirror reflecting the Supreme Being. "Allah manifests himself in every atom of creation; He is revealed in every intelligible object and is concealed from every intelligence except the intelligence of those who say that the universe is His form and phenomenon (صورت و ہیئت), in as much as it stands in the same relation to phenomenal object as the spirit of the body." Regarding the relation of Allah and man, Shaikh Ahmad is reported to have asserted, "Man is the form of Allah and Allah is the spirit of man:

اِن اللہ خلق آدم علیٰ صورتہٖ

"Allah created man after His own image".

Through man, Allah beholds the objects which he has created.

فَاَحْبَبْتَ اَنَ اُعرِفُ خلَقَا

"I wished to display Myself and that is why I created the universe".

Furthermore, he says, man is the substance of every attribute wherewith he endows Allah; whoever contemplates Allah, contemplates himself. Attainment of union with God through the knowledge of Allah was the only end of man. And complete union of human soul with the supreme soul was not possible as long as the body lasted.

اَلمَوتُ جِسَرٌ یوصِلُ الحَبِیبُ اِلیَ الحَبِیبُ

"Death is the bridge between the friend to the friend".

The saint also says, knowledge is acquired by Faith and Contemplation, in which human reason divests itself of its discursive or reflective faculty. The end of knowledge, according to him, is transcendental consciousness where the phenomenal vanishes in the presence of the actual, which is the stage called in Sufi parlance (فنا فی الله). Only gnosis (معرفت) is not enough. It must lead to the next and highest stage. Ultimate Truth, that is complete Union (وصل) with Divinity, transportation of the whole of man from his baser being to the Unitive state. In this state, the saint says, the mystic through self-annihilation (فنا) resides in eternal Reality with Allah (بقا). The illusion of subject and object having vanished. The sense of individuality dies, law and tend lose their meaning, and the seeker of God, Man joins the friend, God.

The saint also believed in the fundamental Sufi belief that the mystic who sets out upon the path of Union (وصل) through self-annihilation (فنا) needs a spiritual mentor to guide him on the right path. The Pir or Murshid, (پیر یا مرشد) the guide, is the pivot round which the entire life machinery of a Sufi moves. His guides authority is absolute, as the poet Hafiz says:

به می سجاده رنگین کن گرت پیر مغان گوید　　که سالک بی خبر نبود ز راه و رسم منزلها

Shaikh Ahmad Khattu did not merely preach but put into practice what he taught. That is his genuine sufistic achievement; Unlike others who do not practice what they preach, are called pseudo Sufis. Shaikh Ahmad says:

گزشتم من ازین دنیا چه طرفه کارها کردم　　ندانند ناقصان نکته ازین میدان چه گو بردم

I have renounced this world. What wonderful thing I did.

"The imperfect ones do not know of this point, what ball I have carried away from this field."

He also wrote in chaste Arabic, *Risala-i-Ahmadiyya fi Manaqibil-Mashaikhil- Maghribiya* (رساله احمدیه فی مناقب المشائخ المغربیه) a Treatise pertaining to the account of the Shaikhs of the Maghribi order. In this treatise, which as its title suggests, the saint has given a brief account of the Maghribi saints by the Maghribi order founded by Shaikh Abu Madyan Maghribi; It is more like a geneaological tree tracing the spiritual not lineal descent from the Holy Prophet to the author Shaikh Ahmad Khattu himself.[4] This Risala is mentioned twice by the author of the *Mirqat* in his account of the discourses of the saint. One mention is about the dream narrated by the saint in which he saw Hazrat Shaikh Abdul Qadir Jilani, holding a turban and offering one end to him and asking him to hold it. The other mention of the Risala is when Maulana Muhammad Qasim refers to the benefits of repetition of the *Kalima* (First Creed). He says, In the Risala-i-Maghribiya the virtues of reciting the Kalima, which is written by Bandagi Makhdum Pole-star of the time and Shaikh of the world (i.e. Shaikh Ahmad) are mentioned with great emphasis, supported by proofs from the Book of God (Quran and the Traditions (Hadis).

The *Risala*, a small treatise of 47 pages, with 15 lines a page in the modern copy,[5] is in chaste Arabic and shows the saint's command over prose and simple but literary style. In this treatise, the saint has mostly confirmed himself to give briefly notices of the Maghribi saints in the contact of the heirarchy of the Maghribi order or the spiritual genealogical table, *shajara* , as stated above. In the commentary written by one Ismail son of Ibrahim,[6] called *Sharh-i-Risala-i-Ahmadiya*, notes on all the saints mentioned in this genealogical table will be found in their respective places. The said *shajara*—genealogical table is quoted below :

GENEALOGICAL TREE OF THE SAINTS OF THE MAGHRIBI ORDER

1. Hazrat Makhdum Ganj-i-Ahmad Maghribi
2. Babu Ishaq Maghribi
3. Shaikh Muhammad Hajjaj Kimi
4. Shaikh Abul-Abbas Qarashi
5. Shaikh Ali Muhammad Salih
6. Shaikh Abu Madyan Shuaib[7] (the founder of Maghribi order)
7. Shaikh Abu Masud Undlusi
8. Shaikh Abul-Barakat Yamani
9. Shaikh Abul-Fazl Baghdadi
10. Shaikh Imam Ahmad Ghazali
11. Shaikh Abu Bakr Nassaj
12. Shaikh Abul-Qasim Jurjani
13. Shaikh Abu Usman Tarabalasi
14. Shaikh Ali Khatib
15. Shaikh Abi Ali Rudbari
16. Khwaja Junaid Baghdadi
17. Khwaja Abul Hasan Sirri Saqati
18. Khwaja Maruf Karkhi
19. Khwaja Daud Tai

20. Khwaja Habib Ajami
21. Amirul-Muminin Imamul-Mashariq wal-Magharib Hazrat Ali Karramallahu Wajhahu
22. Hazrat Rasul-i-Pak Ahmad Mujtaba Muhammad Mustafa (May God's peace be on all of them).

In olden times, as also today, the term Maghrib Literally (west) was applied to the land situated to the west of Egypt comprising Tarablis, Al Jazair, Tunis, Moracco, etc. Hence the Sufi order which was founded by Shaikh Abu Madyan who belonged to Maghrib is known as Maghribi order.

On the other hand, the Mirgat, by quoting the discourses with the saint and his experiences and discussions with desciples, admirers, visitors learned men Shaikhs and the like helps its readers to have an idea of the saint's teaching and guidance in spiritual matters as well as theological problems. These topics including to same to which reference has been made earlier are *Khalq-i-Afal* (human action, who is responsible ?), man's existence (وجود) being the greatest hindrances in the Realisation of God (لاحجاب الا وجودك) none but your own existence is the curtain (between you and God), meaning of Khaliq "Creator" Voluntary poverty, (Faqr) the hemistich.

احب الصالحين ولست منهم

"I love the holy, but I am not one of them" in a couplet attributed to Imam Abu Hanifa; saying *Qirat* in Namaz prayers loudly or silently (قراة سرى وجهرى) use of palanquin (seeing of God) (ruyat), Renewal of analogies (تجدد امثال) Knowledge of self (عرفانِ نفس) correct meaning of (من عرف نفسه صغرىٰ فى عينه شى) He who knows his self, in his eyes everything becomes too small, etc.[8]

The saint had acquired such mastery over commonly used works on Jurisprudence like *Aqida-i-Hafiziyya, Bazdavi*, etc. that he could not only correct reading of corrupt or incomplete copies, but also solve some such difficult problems as could not be solved by eminent teachers.

Notes

1. Mir Khurd - Siyarul Auliya (Lahore, 1986), 413-14.
2. *Kashful-Mahjub*, Eng. tr. R. Nicholson, London, 19 , 25.
3. *Fawaidul-Fuad* (Urdu Academy, Delhi, 1990).
4. A modern copy of this Risala exists in the Dargah Hazrat Pir Muhammad Shah Library. Some years back, a copy was got made from it for the

library of the Dargah of Hazrat Shaikh Ahmad Khattu at Sarkhej, by that Dargah Committee Chairman the Late Ahmadji Esupji Patel, Advocate. Since then, the copy is untraceable, but the xerox of the copy made is to be found in the library of the Dargah Hazrat Pir Muhammad Shah. Needless to say the copy has quite a few scribal errors.

5. Text, 95, 113.
6. A copy of this commentry also was in the Dargah Hazrat Pir Muhammad Shah Library. A copy was got made for the Sarkhej Dargah Library by Mr. Patel of this manuscript also, which is now not traceable, but a modern copy made by the same scribe in fine Nastaliq writing is there.
7. The celebrated sufi and author Shaikh Muhiyuddin Ibn Arabi refers to him respectfully in his famous works *Futuhat-i-Makkiya* and *Fususul-Hikam*. For a brief biographical notice see, Maulana Jami's *Nafahatul-Uns*, Nawal Kishore ed. 1915.
8. Quite a few of these topics pertain to interpretations of Quranic verses and Hadis or jurisprudence, scholasticism, etc. The saint's views on certain ritual aspects of practical Sufism are to be found in the previously mentioned *Risala-i-Irshad-i-Ahmadiya fi Bayan-i-Iradat-i-Ittqadiya* Treatise on. The Direction of Ahmad in the exposition of the (problem of) discipleship by belief" A worm eaten somewhat damaged copy unique perhaps, of this important work written in Arabic by an anonymous author who was a disciple of Miyan Allauddin son of the saint Ahmad's successor Shaikh Salahuddin, is preserved in the library of the Dargah Hazrat Pir Muhammad Shah Ahmadabad. Descriptive Catalogue of Arabic Persian and Urdu Manuscripts in the Dargah Hazrat Pir Muhammed Shah Library, Vol. IV (Ahmadabad, 1994) No. 1236, awaiting the attention of competent scholar.

Part One

Introduction to the Critical Edition of the Mirqatul-Wusul Ilallah-i-war-Rasul

1

AUTHOR, HIS LIFE AND WORK

The author Maulana Muhammad bin Abul Qasim as he calls himself in his work is almost totally an unknown figure. Except for the contemporary author of the *Tuhfatul-Majalis*, Shaikh Mahmud Iraji and the anonymous near-contemporary author of the *Irshadat-Ahmadiya*, written at the instance of Miyan Alauddin son of Shaikh Salahuddin, Hazrat Shaikh Ahmad Khattu's spiritual successor,[1] he does not find mention any where in other contemporary or later biographical works like *Akhbarul Akhyar*, which however does mention Shaikh Mahmud Iraji.[2] Even none of these too give any worthwhile information about him. While the author of *Irshadat-i-Ahmadiya* does not go beyond mentioning his name and his hometown in connection with an incident showing the saint's fame having spread to far-off Islamic lands, quoted by him on the authority of the *Mirqat*. Shaikh Mahmud Iraji mentions him in his account of four assemblies (Majalis) of the saint; he too however, does not give any valuable information about him except for stating that he had composed a poem in praise of the saint and had recited it in one of the assemblies, and that once he was sent on an errand by the saint to the village Uteliya fearing some harm occurring to his men at the hands of the men of the village Headman. He calls him Maulana Muhammad Qasim.[3]

Even the compiler of the account of the saints of various orders of Gujarat, compiled by Qazi Muhammad. Ruknul-Haq grandson of Maulana Nuruddin incorporated *in toto* by the author of the *Mirat-i-Ahmadi* in the Supplement of that work does not mention him independently, though he devotes a separate notice to Shaikh Muhammad Iraji, author of the *Tuhfatul-Majalis*. However, for his fairly good amount of the account of Shaikh Ahmad Khattu, he relies more upon the *Mirqat* of Maulana Muhammad bin Qasim whom he calls Shaikh Abul-Qasim according to the two printed editions of the *Mirat-i-Ahmedi, Supplement*. It is certain that he had a copy of the *Mirqat* before him when he wrote that account; but it is difficult to say now if in that copy, the author was called Abul-Qasim or Maulana Rukul-Haq misunderstood the sentence in which he gives his name[4] as will be seen later.

The Urdu translator of the *Mirqat*, Maulana Sayyid Abu Zafar Nadvi who attempted a brief life-sketch of the author supplementing it by some particulars from the *Tuhfatul-Majalis*, and correcting it wherever necessary, gives his name as Maulana Muhammad Qasim without the *izafat-i-ibni*, that is taking Muhammad Qasim to be one name only. However, the author's name was not Qasim as Maulana Nadvi says[5] but Muhammad-i-Abil-Qasim i.e. Muhammad son of Qasim (the latter shortened form of Abul-Qasim). The two contemporary and near-contemporary authors mentioned above also give his name as Maulana Muhammad "-i-" (Abul) Qasim presumably with *izafat-i-ibni*. In any case, the author himself says in the prefatory portion of this work:

وبعد فقد قال سمیّ نبی الله ابن کنیتہ صلی الله علیه وسلم عفی عنهم،

"After this (i.e after God's praise and that of the Holy Prophet) says one who is named after the prophet of God (i.e. Muhammad) son of his *kuniya* (i.e. Abul-Qasim), may Gods salutations and peace be upon him.[6]

This portion of the text is not to be found in the modern copy of a now untraceable manuscript made by Sayyid Manzur Husain Alavi, popularly known as Husaini Pir and supplied to the late Maulana Sayyid Abu Zafar Nadvi, from which the Urdu translation *Sirat-i-Ahmadiya* was made. That is why he says he could not determine and find the name despite efforts. It did not strike to him that in the name given by the author of the *Tuhfatul-Majalis*, the *izafat-i-ibni*, Muhammad-i-Qasim—Muhammad son of Qasim—was intended. Shaikh Iraji calls him Muhammad Qasim (Abul-Qasim's shortened form) in three out of four places[7] "but the fact that the author himself intended *izafat-i-ibni* is clearly shown by his calling himself only Muhammad in the *Mirqat* book.[8] In short, there should be absolutely no doubt that the author's name was Muhammad and his father's name was Qasim, a shortened form of Abul-Qasim.

The saint, Hazrat Shaikh Ahmad Khattu in whose constant attendance he was, used to address him, normally not by his name but by the cognomen Mullani.e. Mulla, with the last syllable with nasal intonation, as this word is even pronounced today. To call out at him, if he were not in his presence, he would loudly say, "Mullan."[9] He was addressed by his compeers or even elders by the honorific Maulana. He enjoyed this respect by his nearness to the saint as also being the leader of the saint's prayers *(Pesh Imam),* as he himself relates and is corroborated by Shaikh Muhammad Iraji,[10] "a rival" in the words of Maulana Sayyid Abu Zafar Nadvi.[11] When he proposed Sultan Muhammad II to lead the funeral prayer of the saint, as per the normal custom, the latter said to him, "Maulana Muhammad "-i-" Qasim! You have been the leader-of-prayer in his life-time, now also you lead the prayers."[12] Again, it was he who bathed the saint's body, with Qazi Badh son of Mubarak Walwalji the saint's librarian and scribe (*katib*), pouring water[13] on it.

Not much is known about the author's family. The author, unlike Shaikh Mahmud Iraji, is reticent on this point. That he came from a respectable learned family is apparent from stray references to his relatives like Maulana Khurram, the author's grandfather on mother's side, Maulana Abdus-Salam and Abdur-Rahman, sons of Maulana Khurram, who enjoyed some position under Sultan Ahmad of Gujarat, Qazi Daud son of Abdus-Salam's mother's sister, who was the Qazi of Naraina (in Sawai Madhopur district of Rajasthan) and the like. Among those from this family who find incidental mention by the author is Muhammad Rashid son of Nur Muhammad.[14]

Likewise, from another casual reference made by him to the pestilence of thread-worm in Gujarat, we learn that the author had more than one son and at least one daughter. The author states that one day, his son-in-law came from Modasa and informed him that his elder son had also fallen prey to the disease of thread-worm. The author was naturally greatly upset and obtaining permission of the saint who had assured the son-in-law that they need not worry, set out on foot for Modasa without waiting for a conveyance, which his son-in-law arranged and brought it to him when he had already reached Vasna (about five kilometres from Sarkhej towards Ahmadabad). The author was restless as had no appetite for food or drink until he was told of the saint's assurance. When on his way to Modasa next day, he met Sayyid Nasir son of Sayyid Qasim Nagori, whom the author dared not ask about the condition of his son, the Sayyid gave him good news that his son Miyan Mitthan, had recovered, at the prayers of his maid-servant who prayed for his life, bartering her own life away.[15]

From this, it appears that Maulana Muhammad Qasim's family was residing at Modasa. It can not be said whether the family was in permanent residence there or was staying there temporarily with his son in-law. Very probably, the author had, on coming to Gujarat from Rajasthan, settled down in Modasa also, with other fellow-beings from that state and his son-in-law was also staying there. The mention of a maid servant also corroborates this.[16] It is again difficult to say it his wife was alive at this time or not. In short, one does not have any information about his family beyond the fact that the author was married, had at least two sons of whom Miyan Mitthan was elder and had a married daughter. From lack of any reference to his wife, it may perhaps be surmised that she was not alive at this time and the sons had continued to leave at Modasa with the sister and brother-in-law.

Likewise, not much is known about the early life and education of the author. He must have had his education in his own native place, about which the *Mirqat* does not give any information or at his maternal grandfather's place Didvana in Rajasthan. The only thing we know is his two teacher's names Sayyid Mahmud son of Rukn, a Rasuldar Sayyid and Malik Badh about whom also no information is available.[17] However, the author must have received good education in Arabic, Persian and religious sciences, as is clear from the *Mirqat*. He had a good command over Arabic and good knowledge of Quran, Tafsir, Fiqh and like sciences. He frequently used to take part in the discussions in the saint's assembly along with other learned men and would also pass some remarks or comments which generally met with the approval of the saint, himself a very learned man. The *Mirqat* contains instances of such and other learned comments or remarks passed by him after narrating the discussion. These give an idea of his grasp, understanding, power of reasoning, judiciousness etc. He is also found to be engaged in perusal of scholarly works like the Arabic dictionary *Sihah* of Jauhari or hagiological works like *Khairul-Majalis*.[18] However, he would always behave with restraint and even candidly acknowledge if he could not understand any problem or argument.[19] Likewise, he never hesitated to acknowledge his lack of knowledge about certain things. For example, he frankly admits that he did not know how Shaikh Ahmad returned from the lodging of the two Egyptian princesses in the holy city of Makkah where, impressed by the Shaikh, they had taken him and entertained him.[20]

He had come to Gujarat in the year when Sultan Muhammad I had ascended the throne of Gujarat, that is to say in 806 H. (1403A.D.) in the company of his teacher Malik Badh. [21] This was when Muslims from the Nagor region migrated southwards to Gujarat in the wake of the atrocities committed by Rao Chonda. On his arrival, he went to Sarkhej in the company of his teacher to pay respects to the saint. Nothing is known about his career in Gujarat until 819 H., when on Thursday of the last day of Shaban of that year (22 October 1416 A.D.), he was conferred the cap of wool (*kulah-i-suf*), which the saint wore, as a token of his having been taken into his inner circle of disciples.[22] Before that date too, he must be paying regular visits to the saint. For the next three decades, until the death of the saint in 849 H. (1445 A.D.), as he states more than once in the *Mirqat*, he served the saint, acting also as his Pesh-Imam for some time, presumably after Qazi Abdul-Aziz and Qazi Mansur.[23] During this period, he would also run important errands for the saint. For example, when the Headman of the village Uteliya (in Dholka taluka of Ahmadabad district), which was granted by Sultan Muzaffar I to the saint for the expenses of his Khanqah, was harassing the servants of the saint who went there for purposes related to the produce of the village, the saint always resisted the suggestions of high officials about their intention to teach him a lesson. Ultimately, a nobleman Malik Jalalshah brought the matter to the notice of Sultan Ahmad I who asked him to punish the said Headman immediately. The Malik was to start for Uteliya when the saint having come to know of it immediately sent the author to the Malik asking him to desist from the action as "God had created him not to shed blood of his creatures." [24] On another occasion, in the month of Ramazan, the author was asked to go to Uteliya for some work.[25]

The saint also held a high opinion about the author and expressed his admiration for his sincerity, dedication, knowledge and religiosity. He would also chide him if any occassion arose. For example, when he narrated the story he had read in the *Khairul-Majalis* of a Saint's dying without appointing a spiritual successor, one being appointed by consensus among his disciples, and that one, at some one's objection to this procedure repairing to the grave of the saint and getting it confirmed from the saint in his grave, the Sarkhej Saint chided saying him "Mullan! You are a strict follower of Sharia (Religious Code). How do you give credence to such a story of a voice coming from the grave ?" [26]

Despite his nearness to the saint, the author was always scrupulous in his behaviour and would not step beyond the limit of propriety or discreetness. His utmost devotion and love for the saint was examplary. He was conversant with the saint's temperament, mood, ways, etc. and would not do anything which would go against his wish or displease him in the least. This is best illustrated by the incident that occurred during the fatal illness of the saint. At one stage, the personal attendant of the saint, Talib, produced in the presence of others, a parwana (written order) of the saint stating that when his appointed time came, Mullan i.e. the author, should recite the *Kalima*. In the night of the fourteenth of Shawwal (849H), the saint's condition became very critical, alternately loosing and regaining senses amidst restlessness. After this taking place thrice, and there being considerable delay in regaining sense, some one asked the author why he was not reciting the *Kalima* as desired by the saint. The author out of circumspection and caution, was reluctant, thinking that the saint might been engrossed in meditation and communion with God and kept quiet. Another person, out of good faith, recited loudly the *Kalima* at which the saint opened his eyes and said the person who uttered the *Kalima* should go out.[27]

Notes

1. *Irshadat-i-Ahmadiyya* ms. Hazrat Pir Muhammad Shah Library and Research Centre, No.1316.
2. Abdul Haqq Muhaddis Dehlavi, *Akhbarul-Akhyar fi Asraril-Abrar*, Delhi 1332 A.H. (1914 A.D.), 157. However the name of our author Maulana Muhammad Qasim does occur in the book in the extract quoted from the *Tuhfatul-Majalis* (*Ibid*., 160).
3. *Tuhfatul-Majalis*, ms. Dargah Hazrat Pir Muhammad Shah Library, No. 1231, *Ibid*, Urdu tr. (*TMU*), 55.
4. Ali Muhammad Khan, *op. cit*. (Calcutta), 34; *Ibid*. (Bombay), 22.
5. The Maulana throughout on the title-page as well as in the Introduction calls him Maulana Qasim which is his father's name.
6. Text, p. 1. This is found in the Calcutta manuscript copy only. The copy supplied by Husaini Pir Sahib to the Maulana which is preserved in the Dargah Hazrat Pir Muhammad Shah Library does not have this portion. See the edited text, p. 1.
7. *TM*, 42 b, 46 b, 67 a, 98 b, 99 a, *TMU*, 55, 86, 129. In one place (*TM*, 466 *TMU*, 60), the name is given as Maulana Qasim, which unless a seribal error would make the *Tuhfatul-Majalis*'s authenticity suspect, as Qasim was the name of the father of the author of the *Mirqat*.
8. Text, 33.
9 Text, 112, 122, 133, 234, etc.
10. *TM*, 98b, 99a, *TMU*, 129.
11. *TMU*, 66 n.
12. Shaikh Mahmud Iraji says, he asked Muhammad Qasim to request the Sultan to lead the funeral prayer since as the reigning monarch, it was his previledge (TM.99a, TMU 129).
13. Here also Shaikh Mahmud Iraji claims that he and Muhammad Qasim performed this job. As is well known, normally, only one person performs the actual bathing, other assist him.

14. Text, pp. 33,69,146, etc. The genealogical tree given in the *Sirat-i-Ahmadiya*, p.5, is not correct; it is not in conformity with what Maulana Nadvi himself says.
15. *Ibid*, 154. The *Sirat-i-Ahmadiya*, which otherwise gives a faithful rendering of the text omits the name Miyan Mitthan, probably because. Husaini Pir Saheb's hand copy was not clear at this spot. Obviously Miyan Mitthan seems to have been the pet name of the son.
16. The near contemporary author of the *Irshadat-i-Ahmediya* (*op. cit*, 101a) also calls him Maulana Muhammad Qasim of Modasa. *Mukhbirul-Auliya* of Hazrat Khwaja Rashiduddin Maudud Lala (Xerox copy, Hazrat Pir Muhammad Shah Library and Research Centre, f) also implies that Maulana Muhammad Qasim held from Modasa.
17. Text, 90, 148 The *Mukhbirul Auliya* (loc cit, 409b) used a detailed account of Sayyid Mahmud as also of the highly venerated Rasuldar family whose history is traced from its founder, this account is taken from a Persian treatise on the history of the said family. The author of *Mukhbirul Auliya* quotes the *Mirqat* account of Sayyid Mahmud-i-Rukn's visit to the Sarkhej saint, reciting his Persian quatrain and the saint's suggest him a better word in one place. (f. 373 a).
18. Text, 8, 73, 91, 118, etc.
19. *Ibid.*, 173.
20. *Ibid.*, 183.
21. *Ibdi.*, 148.
22. *Ibid.*, 126.
23. *Ibid.*, 108. On the title page of the *Sirat-i-Ahmadiya*, the author is described as the Pesh-Imam of the Jami mosque of Sarkhej which is not correct.
24. *Ibid.*, 130.
25. *TM.*, 42 b, *TMU*, 55.
26. Text, 233-34.
27. *Ibid.*, 237.

2

MIRQATUL - WUSUL

(A) Whether a Malfuz or a Biographical Work

The popularity of the first authentic malfuz of an Indian saint, Amir Hasan Sijzi's *Fawaidul-Fuad*, a narration of the proceedings of the assemblies of Hazrat Nizamuddin Auliya of Delhi, served as a great impetus to the successors and dedicated disciples of other saints like Hazrat Burhanuddin Gharib of Daulatabad, Makhdum Shaikh Ahmad bin Yahya Maneri of Bihar, Hazrat Sayyid Muhammad Husain Gesudaraz Bandanawaz of Gulbarga etc. to perpetuate and propagate their spiritual masters' sufistic mission by compiling such works or biographies. The *Mirqat* also, as will be seen in its proper place, is one such work, the earliest in Gujarat, compiled by Maulana Muhammad Qasim, who was an attendant of Shaikh Ahmad Khattu of Sarkhej for three decades and his leader-of prayers. However, it does not fall into the category of a pure biography or of an exclusive compilation of the proceedings of the saint's open-house meetings or assemblies taken down faithfully as a true malfuz work like the first mentioned *Fawaidul-Fuad* or the *Khairul-Majalis* or even *Tuhfatul-Majalis,* a collection of assembly proceedings of the Sarkhej saint, compiled by Shaikh Mahmud Iraji.

However, a perusal of the *Mirqat* shows that strictly speaking it cannot be assigned to the category of malfuz only on one hand or purely a biography, on the other. It is chiefly a random and straying account, with many digressions, of the life and spiritual achievements of the saint Shaikh Ahmad Khattu Maghribi, popularly known as Ganjgir Ganjbakhsh. Random in the sense that it does not deal with the subject in the systematic manner of a biography, birth, childhood, education, career, death etc. On the other hand, it is not a malfuz-work, which is compiled by a disciple, noting down faithfully the proceedings of the saint's meeting with his disciples and visitors, on a particular day or any day of the week. He takes notes of everything taking place, in particular the sayings and utterances of the saint in his own words as far as possible and compiles that in a book-form, after sometimes getting it approved by the saint, for the benefit of his fellow-disciples and people at large. In this sense, the *Mirqat* cannot be assigned to the category of a malfuz-work.

In other words, the book falls somewhere between a biography and a malfuz-work. Though the author who spent thirty years in the company of the saint also acting as his leader-of-prayers was fully qualified to compile either a biography or a malfuz-work, it obviously it did not occur to him to undertake any such work during the saint's life-time or immediately thereafter. It was later, after more than a decade that the author was urged by his compeers to undertake such a work as will be presently seen.

However, it is to be noted that the author, Maulana Muhammad Qasim himself, considered his work as a malfuz. For in the introduction to the *Mirqat*, he specifically states that he was called upon by his contemporaries to write down for them the malfuz of the saint.[28] Therefore, while the book, strictly speaking is a biography mainly in the words of the saint himself, it came to be considered as a malfuz right from the beginning. For example, the near contemporary anonymous author of the another work on the teaching of the saint called Irshadat-i-Ahmadiya. (Teachings of Ahmed) also refers to Maulana Muhammad Qasim's work as a malfuz. [29] Likewise, in the account of the saints of Ahmadabad, the *Mirat-i-Ahmadi Supplement*, compiled in circa 1761 A.D., also calls it malfuz.[30]

(B) Why and When Written

As has been stated above, it never struck to Maulana Muhammad Qasim to compile the malfuzat of his spiritual master and mentor Shaikh Ahmad Khattu or write his biography. If he had intended to do so he would have started the work if not during the life-time of the saint, at least immediately after his demise in 849 H. (1445 A.D.). He seems to have been a man of modest nature, resting content with performing his duties as a true disciple and attendant of the saint and his leader-of-prayer. Then one day, لما حتف لی جم غفیر من الاخوان a large number of brothers (fellow-disciples) (والحق لی سم کثیر من الاقران ان کتب الهم ماوهب اِذلیٰ ثلثین عامامن ملفوظات الشیخ الخ) told me and a great multitude of fellow-beings asked me to write down whatever utterances, I had the good fortune of hearing from the Shaikh".[31] But he excused himself telling them that it was a formidable task. Then, (فخرصو ارباب العساکر الکرام و ارباب الدفاتر و الحکا حضرت متحیراو تهیث متفکرًا) "the (Sultan's) venerable army officers and masters of civil offices and officials also insisted; this made me perplexed and set me to think". Ultimately, twelve years after the death of the saint, he strove and worked hard and industriously and did not leave out anything from the pearl-scattering words of the saint. And he also put down as much information about Shaikhul-Mashaikh Shaikh Hazrat Shaikh. Babu Ishaq Maghribi as possible which he had received from Shaikh Ahmad Khattu himself and incorporated it. When the book was completed the author was lying in a state of half-sleep and half wakefulness when he heard the voice of the saint saying, "Baba, has your object been achieved.?" I submitted, "Yes, O blessed Saint ! God be praised, the kindness of God is helpful and your help needed." [32]

The Urdu translator of the *Mirqat* entitled *Sirat-i-Ahmadiya*, Maulana Sayyid Abu Zafar Nadvi, in his exhaustive introduction thereof, after giving the reason for the compilation of the book as stated by the author and described above, suggests another factor also. He seems to think that as the other Malfuzf of the saint, the *Tuhfatul-Majalis* does not contain a full account of the saint, nor is there any arrangement, being a short diary, it did not fulfil the need of those anxious for the saint's full particulars. Therefore they must have pressed Maulana Muhammad Qasim to write his book which could fulfil their aspirations. He goes further and suggests as the real thing which is more important that Shaikh Muhammad Iraji has referred to Maulana Muhammad Qasim in several places in not-so-good terms, which must have been resented by Maulana Muhammad Qasim's followers who must have expressed their desire to him to write the book.[33] There is some force in this argument, but looking to the low-profile approach of Maulana Muhammad Qasim in his own work, it is doubtful if he minded Shaikh Mahmud Iraji's not very good mention of himself in the *Tuhfatul-Majalis.*

In short, the book was completed in 861 H. (1456-57 A.D.) in deference to the wishes of the saint's disciples and admirers from different walks of life, including high officials and dignitaries, and the author spared no pains to make it as comprehensive as possible. To what extent he succeeded will be seen later on.

(C) Arrangement, Sources, Style, Language etc.

I. Arrangement and Scope

When the work attained completion, the author gave it the name *Mirqatul-Wusul ilallah-i war-Rasul* "The ladder of attarining union with Allah and the prophet Muhammad". He divided it into sixteen *Fasls* that is sections or chapters, each under a specific heading indicating the topic narrated or discussed in the respective section or chapter. These Chapters run as follow :

1. Dealing with the childhood (lit. rearing up) of the Shaikh and particulars about his coming to the presence of Babu (Ishaq) and the latter training him in archery, polo, justice, courage, chivalry.
2. Dealing with the good fortune, popularity, greatness, sense of sacrifice, celibacy and highmindedness of Bandagi Makhdum (Shaikh Ahmad)
3. Dealin with the virtues of Bandagi Shaikh Babu Ishaq son of Muhammad, spiritual guide and patron of Bandagi Makhdum.
4. Dealing with the education and instruction of Bandagi Makhdum in various sciences.
5. Dealing with academic discussions which Bandagi Makhdum had with illustrious savants and the former's replies.
6. Dreams which other great men and saints have seen concerning Bandagi Makhdum or have themselves seen him.
7. Devotions, Fasting and sincerity and utmost concentration (*huzur*) in prayers *(namaz)* of Bandagi Makhdum.
8. The concept of Unity of (God) of Bandagi Makhdum and poetic verses he has composed (on the subject) and their appropriateness.
9. Concepts of Bandagi Makhdum which he enjoined upon his disciples, admirers and friends.
10. Bandagi Makhdum's eating little and his asceticism, rigorous exercise and Arabian (Chilla=Forty-days seclusion).
11. Supernatural powers, divination (kashf), miracles and unusual things of Bandagi Makhdum.
12. Sama (Musical assembly) practiced by Bandagi Makhdum Qutb-i-Alam, (Pivot of the world).
13. Bandagi Makhdum Qutb-i-Alam Shaikh Ahmad Maghribi proceeding for Hajj pilgrimage.
14. Hazrat Makhdum proceeding to Samarqand for enjoining upon Timur to do what is good.
15. Return of Hazrat Makhdum from Khurasan, in the time of Muzaffar Shah and coming to Gujarat.
16. The Journey to the Next world of Bandagi Hazrat Shaikh -i-Jahan Qutb-i-Alam, may mercy and forgiveness (of God) be upon him.[34]

The above arrangement of the material is by no means unsatisfactory. However, it is not as perfect as it should be for a biographical work. But as the author's main object was to present and preserve the utterances of the saint for the benefit of fellow-disciples and like interested persons, he compiled these under different heads and topics which form the pivot round which the mission and activities of a saintly person revolves. Learned and erudite as he was in religious sciences and doctrines of sufism, and endowed with poetic talents, the author was evidently not moulded in the role of a writer and therefore he could not put together the ample material he had in a more systematic form. Nevertheless, he did succeed in his attempt to present a somewhat coherent and lively account of the saint, which is authentic coming as it does from and based as it is on the saint's own words. That the narrations of the saint of the events in his own life are true and authentic is corroborated by historical works and inscriptions, as well be seen later, and the author also has recorded these with accuracy and faithfulness. It can be asserted that he has come up to the expectations of his fellow disciples and admirers of the saint by providing them with the very sayings of the saint—whether relating to his own life-events and achievements or his views on topics of sufism or jurisprudence or worldly affairs or the like and also provided them with material that would present to them a lively picture of the saint's life and activities. This despite the fact that he did not keep any work to serve as a model for his maiden attempt. Were it not the case, he would have, as is the wont of writers, made mention in the preface of any such work. Therefore, he laid out his own plan of work, without any guidance and experience and arranged the material that he collected into as systematic and comprehensive coherent account as he could. This is no mean achievement for the author.

However, while the author did give details of the life of the saint from birth to death and of his journeys, his dealings with people around him including sultans, high officials, learned men, sufis, saints, ordinary people etc., the work suffers from certain shortcomings, the foremost of which is that the author is sparing in dates and does not follow a strict chronological order, particularly in his account of the saint's early life. At times, the events are narrated as a flash-back. Also, there is overlapping and though comparatively less, repetition also. For these shortcomings, however, the author may not be wholly responsible. For, the saint himself, narrating the events of his life at an age of eightyone—for Maulana Muhammad Qasim, as seen above,[35] started as the saint's disciple and a constant attendant only in 819 H (1416 A.D.)– might have omitted the dates of the events described by him. Likewise, for the information gathered by the author from the saint's companions also, the same time factor might have been responsible for lack of dates.

While this is a handicap of no mean consequence, it is somewhat mitigated by the fact that quite a few of the events can be approximately dated and a few with a fair amount of exactness, through historical works and inscriptions. The saint who was held in esteem and venerated by at least three Delhi kings, Muhammad bin Tughluq, Firuz Tughlug and Muhammad bin Firuz Tughluq and four Gujarat kings-the first five sultans, and their high officials and noblemen and had met well known saints like Makhdum Jahaniyan Jahangasht Sayyid Jalal Bukhari, and the like, mentions them apropos few events in which the saint also played some part. And such events could be approximately dated through the known dates of these personages from historical works or inscriptions. It is not possible nor perhaps necessary to detail all such instances, but a couple of examples may be cited in support of this view.

As against the events in Gujarat, while going for pilgrimage to the holy cities and later on settling down here in 802 H. (1400 A.D.), the dates or approximate time of most of which is indicated in the *Mirqat*, the dates of the saint's frequent visits from Khattu to Delhi and to places like Didvana, Ladnun, Nagor and Ajmer, in the company of Babu Ishaq or by himself, cannot be so easily approximated from the narrative of the *Mirqat*. However, from the persons, particularly kings and officials mentioned in the events, their dates could be suggested in quite a few cases. The names of the high officials mentioned in these events are the minister Khan Jahan, Malik Raziul-Mulk and his son Malik Haji, Malik Umar Ariz-i-Mamalik of Firuz Tughuq and his son Malik Kamal the Muqta of Hisar-i-Firoza, Islam Khan of Delhi and the neighbourhood, Malik Qutb bin Najam and Malik Khurram Muqtas of Khattu, Malik Yaqub, Sikandar Khan and Darya Khan, governors of Gujarat, Malik Mufrih,[36] governor of Cambay region and Malik Alauddin, Muqaddim of Ladnun. The dates of these officials and saints like Makhdum Jahaniyan Sayyid Jalal Bukhari are known from contemporary historical works like *Tarikh-i-Firuz Shahi*, *Tarikh-i-Mubarak Shahi*, *Tarikh-i-Mahmud Shahi* or later chronicles like *Mirat-i-Sikandari*, *Tarikh-i- Firishta*, etc. The events during the saint's visits to Delhi and other places can be more or less correctly dated to an approximate extent on the basis of their dates in these works. For example, the saint's visit to Delhi in the company of Babu Ishaq, when they met Makhdum Jahaniyan who died in 785 H. (1384 A.D.)[37], must have taken place during the reign of Firuz Tughluq in on about. 775-80 H (1374-79 A.D.). The events of ministers, or other officials like Khan Jahan, Darya Khan, Sikandar Khan, Malik Mufrih, Islam Khan, Malik Umar, Malik Kamal, Malik Khurram etc., can be similarly dated by referring to *Tarikh-i-Mubarak Shahi*, a contemporary work by Yahya Sirhindi. It is not within the scope of this thesis to give details in this regard, and reference to the said work where the exact dates in their career are given may perhaps suffice.[38] However, at least two officials each of Nagor and Ladnun,

Malik Qutbuddin Najam and Malik Alauddin respectively and of Gujarat Malik Khassa and Malik Shaikhan bin Musa, who find frequent mention in the *Mirqat*, are untraceable in these chronicles. But fortunately, their period is known from their inscriptions found at these places, which supply exact dates about them. Malik Qutbuddin, according to his epitaph discovered and published in recent times, died in 791 H. (1389 A.D.), while fighting in a battle with the local non-Muslim insurgents. Thus, the saint Shaikh Ahmad's more than one visit by himself as well as in the company of Babu Ishaq to Nagor must have taken place when Malik Qutbuddin was accountant and later Muqta, according to the *Mirqat*, in the early part of his career, during the life time of Babu Ishaq, *circa* 760-65 H. (1358-63 A.D.). Likewise, Babu Ishaq's visit to Ladnun, accompanied by the saint when they were entertained by the local Headman Malik Alauddin must have taken place *circa* 775 H. (1374 A.D.), if not earlier, for according to an inscription, Malik Alauddin had constructed a mosque there in 780 H. (1378 A.D.)[39] Similarly, an exact date in the career of Malik Shaikhan bin Musa who figures in a number of undated incidents in the *Mirqat*,[40] is furnished by an inscription from Wadhwan in Surendranaga, district of Gujarat, dated 842 H (1439 A.D) in the time of Sultan Ahmed I.[41]

II. Sources

As stated earlier, the author was well-equipped to compile the sayings of the saint and also write a biographical account based on information gathered in his three decade association with the saint. He would be present in the meetings of the saint with his disciples and admirers and would also be granted the privilege of being present at the saint's private and nocturnal vigils. The *Mirqat* contrains, unlike the *Tuhfatul-Majalis*, particulars of the life of the saint from his early childhood, in Rajasthan, when he himself did not have opportunity, it appears, to be associated with the saint; he was evidently too young for that. But his own grandfather Maulana Khurram of Didvana and his son and other kinsmen were known to Babu Ishaq with whom they had more than passing acquaintance. As a matter of fact when after the death of Babu Ishaq, the saint decided to leave Khattu and proceed to visit the Holy cities, Maulana Khurram had beseeched him not to leave Khattu.[42] There were other people who were contemporaries of Babu Ishaq or companions of the saint with whom Maulana Muhammad Qasim must have been acquainted. His own fellow-townsmen and kinsmen also must have known the saint from close quarters. Therefore, the author could gather sufficient information to supplement or to corroborate the account heard by him from the saint's mouth from time to time. Most of these people had migrated to Gujarat like the author himself in the wake of the political upheaval in the Nagor region and were thus available to the author when he was contemplating to accede to the suggestion of fellow-disciples and admirers of the saint and also when he was engaged in writing the work. This opportunity was not available to Shaikh Mahmud Iraji and that is why his *Tuhfatul-Majalis* furnishes practically no information about the pre-Gujarat period life and activities of the saint.

The author claims to have based his book, apart from what the saint had narrated and from what he himself had seen during thirty years of his service, on what he heard from contemporary reliable persons in Rajasthan as well as in Gujarat. In Gujarat, he had migrated in AH. 806H. (1404A.D.) along with his teacher Malik Badh, Sayyid Khizr Khattuwal, etc. He was witness to almost all the events connected with the life of the saint after the latter's arrival in Gujarat in 802H. (1399 A.D.) and more closely after his receiving the "cap of discipleship" from him in 819H. (1416 A.D.). While in Gujarat, he also met people from Rajasthan and elsewhere who were acquaintances of the saint or had come in contact with him in some way. All such persons find mention in the *Mirqat.* Of these, only a few may be mentioned : Sayyid Amir Badh Nagori Mudarris *(teacher)*, Shaikh Mahmud Abul-Fath of Khattu, Shaikhzada Ahmad Kirmani, Qazi Mansur, Qazi Abdur-Razzaq, popularly called Badh son of Qazi Mubarak Walwalji, Miyan Babu son of Qazi Badh Jilani, Qazi Akram of Khattu, Malik Musa Yunus Chandran, a descendant of the celebrated general and *Sahabi* (Companion of the Holy Prophet) Khalid bin Walid, Sayyid Ahmad Arab, an emissary of Shaikh Umar Jili from abroad.[43] Shaikhzada Ahmad Kirmani and Qazi Akram are the foremost sources of the author.

III. Style, language etc.

The *Mirqat* is written, as stated by the celebrated scholar and cataloguer Mr. Wladmir Ivanow, in an unpretentious style.[44] The author was evidently well-versed in Arabic as well as Persian in which latter language he wrote the *Mirqat*. He seems to have preferred to write the book in a simple and direct style, meant as it was for his fellow-disciples and compeers for their benefit and not for showing off his power of expression or laborious style. However, the book is not without stylistic flashes and flourishes. The author uses pithy sentences apt similies and metaphors, play of words, and like devices, but the narration is quite fluent and appealing. Of course in a few places, the usage appears to be archaic and the sense is not clear, but that may be due to scribal errors.

The author is not an exception to other early contemporary and later writers in the use of words from local vernaculars. He uses quite a few of them such as for example, Karehra, Lahsan, Mrudan, Chhajja, Lahlahani Lakhugira, Guru, Odhani, Kath, Bahni, Khat, Tatti, Tuntan, (impudent and insulting mode of address—second person singular), Har, Gunakar-Bhagakar (Multiplication and Division in Arithmetic), Dola, Khep, Karela, Rajputra (Rajput), Phalata, Joda, etc.[45] The author also in a couple of places quotes the local language used by the saint or some one else in the event described.[46] He makes frequent use of words and phrases of Arabic language which was in vogue at the period and which also was in conformity with the specific subject of the work, narrations of discussions on religious and sufistic subjects. At times he uses ingenious similes such as *ghogha tariq-i-gusfandan* "noise like sheep" 47, an equivalent of the English noise like that "in fish-market." His expression is also at times influenced by the local idioms. He so to say uses Persian translations of the local dialect such as,

۔(برس پڑے) برآمدند‘ (بیٹھے سنبھلے) نشستہ‘ (بات میرے دل میں نہیں اتری)۔
۔از دلِ من فرود نمی آید‘ (زبان کھینچ لے گا) زبان بکند‘ (دکھ کے دکھ) بنویس بدار (دغا دیا)
۔دغا داد دیا‘ (رنجیدہ کئے بغیر نہ رہے) نہ ماندی تا نرنجانیدی‘

The *Mirqat*'s contribution to the history of regional languages will be dealt with in the section dealing with the historical importance of the book.

(D) *Mirqat's* Place in Malfuz-Literature with Special Reference to Tuhfatul-Majalis (another malfuz of the saint.)

Hagiographical works written in India furnish comparatively little information about the personal lives of saints in general and those of the Maghribi order to which Shaikh Ahmad Khattu belonged, in particular. Not much could be gleaned about the life of the founder of the order in India, Baba Ishaq Maghribi, from these works. As it is, no biographical work of saints of different orders seems to have been written in India prior to the seventeenth century A.D. No doubt a number of biographical works devoted to a particular saint or a particular group of saintly persons were attempted, but their number does not even add up to half a dozen.[49] These too do not cover main Sufi orders like Suhravardi, Qadiri, Shattari and the like. The earliest of such works, *Siyarut Auliya fi-Mahabbat-il Haq Jalla wa-Ala*, written sometime in the third quarter of the 14th century by Sayyid Muhammad bin Mubarak Kirmani, popularly called Mir Khurd, deals with an account of the Chishti saints of India, upto the time of Hazrat Nizamuddin Auliya of Delhi. A disciple of Haji Taqiuddin, named Haji Rumi, wrote an account of the life of his spiritual guide and his father under the title *Tahrirul-Mutaqid fi Halat-i-Murshid* towards the close of the fourteenth century. Likewise, an account of the life and more specially sayings of the famous saint Amir Sayyid Ali Hamadani Kashmiri entitled *Khulasatul-Manaqib*, was completed by his disciple Nuruddin Jafar Badakhshi at almost the same time. Sayyid Munirul Haqq grandson of the above mentioned Taqiuddin Tatavi, wrote an account of the Sayyids of Bhakkar and various matters relating mainly to sufism in a work entitled *Manbaul-Ansab.* A biography of the celebrated Chishti saint of Deccan Sayyid Muhammad Husain Gesudaraz Bandanawaz a contemporary of Shaikh Ahmad Khattu, called *Siyar-i-Muhammadi,* was writen by Muhammad Ali Samani in 831H. (1427-28 A.D.).

A few historical works writen during the region of Mughal emprors, Akbar, Jahangir and Shah Jahan also contain brief chapters on the saintly personages of their time. Thus the *Ain-i-Akbari* of Shaikh Abul-Fazl devotes a short notice to Shaikh Ahmad Khattu. Later regular hagiographical works like *Akhbarul-Akhyar fi Asraril-Abrar* of Shaikh Abdul-Haqq Muhaddis Dehlavi written in the last decade of the sixteenth century A.D., *Gulzar-i-Abrar* (*circa*, 1612 A.D.), *Majmaul-Auliya* (1633-34 A.D.), *Miratul-Asrar* (c.1650 A.D.), *Bahr-i-Zakhkhar* (1788-89 A.D.), *Khazinatul-Asfiya* (1865 A.D.) etc., by their very nature give scanty details of the life and activities of Babu Ishaq or his spritual successor Shaikh Ahmad Khattu.

On the other hand, from the second half of the thirteenth century A.D., a new type of hagiological literature came into existence in India. The saintly persons having been throughout history important members of Islamic society also, their very presence was a source of strength, inspiration and guidance for men of all walks of life, from prince to pauper. Their sayings and utterances have always served during their life-time and for centuries to come after their death too, as a beacon light for a large number of their followers seeking spiritual uplift and mental peace. As a result, a fairly good number of works containing their utterances (malfuz) also came to be written in India including Gujarat. Among the most authentic malfuz thus written, the first is the *Fawaidul-Fuad* of Hazrat Shaikh Nizamuddin Auliya of Delhi (d. 1325 A.D.) followed by at least three malfuz works of his disciple Shah Burhanuddin Gharib of Daulatabad, *Khairul-Majalis* of Hazrat Nasiruddin Mahmud Chiragh-i-Dehli, about three four malfuz of the fourteenth century Bihar saint Makhdum Sharafuddin Ahmad bin Yahya Maneri and about the same number, the most famous being *Jawamiul-Kilam* of Sayyid Muhammad Husaini popularly known as Banda Nawaz Gesu Daraz of Gulbarga in Deccan, a contemporary of Shaikh Ahmad Khattu, who died at the close of the first quarter of the fifteenth century A.D.[50]

In Gujarat too, this branch of Indo-Persian literature was cultivated, as has been seen in the prologue. In the present state of our knowledge, the *Mirqatul-Wusul Ilallahi war-Rasul*, the work under editing and detailed study and the *Tuhfatul-Majalis* are the earliest of two malfuz or malfuz-like works compiled in Gujarat. While we know of the definite date of the compilation of the *Mirqat*, we are in dark about the date or even approximate time of composition of the other malfuz, *Tuhfatul-Majalis*; a comparative study of both leads us to the conclusion that the *Mirqat* was written first and its compilation made Shaikh Mahmud Iraji, the author of the *Tuhfatul-Majalis,* to compile his work, as will be discussed later on in this section itself.

About this time but slightly later, the malfuz of another eminent saint of Gujarat, Hazrat Sayyid Sirajuddin Muhammad Shah Alam (d.880H.1475A.D.), namely *Kunuz-i-Muhammadi* was compiled by a disciple of the saint Farid Muhammad son of Daulat Shah Jilwani, of which no complete copy is known to exist.[51] From later references to it, it appears to have been a voluminous work. It contained the proceedings of the saint's meetings and his utterances. Its importance as a historical source cannot be determined, but it must have been considerable judging from a perusal of about four out of the seven volumes of another malfuz of Hazrat Shah Alam, compiled, by his direct descendent in the sixth line Hazrat Sayyid Muhammad Maqbul-Alam (d.1045 H./ 1635 A.D.). This latter work, named *Jumaat-i-Shahiya*, is an account of the proceedings of the meetings of the saint after Friday prayers which were open to and attended by all, from high noblemen to ordinary people irrespective of caste and creed; these cover most Friday meetings of the years 861H to 867H. It is almost entirely based on the *Kunuz-i-Muhammadi.*[52] The Jumaat has been described as an encyclopaedic work covering diverse subjects, academic as well as those concerning laymen. It has its share, not exclusive of mention and elucidation of religious matters and still lesser, of fine mystic ideology.[53] But on the whole, it does not furnish as much information on political, social, cultural and like conditions as the *Mirqat*. The later malfuz works too, like *Bahrul-Haqaiq* and *Malfuz-i-Kabir* too, of the famous teacher-saint-author and savant Shah Wajihuddin Alavi (d. 998 H./1590 A.D.), *Khazain-i-Rahmatullah* usually called *Khazain-i-Rahmat*, account-*cum*-malfuz of the saint Shah Rahmatullah (d.887 H. / 1472 A.D.),[54] and the *Miftahul-Qulub* and *Tuhfatul-Qari*,[55] containing the account and sayings of Hazrat Qazi Mahmud Daryayi (d.941 H./1578 A.D.), — the last two dealing more with the supernatural powers of the saint — too, cannot compete with the *Mirqat*'s position as an important source for the early medieval history of Rajasthan and Gujarat, All these malfuz works, including the *Mirqat* and the *Tuhfatul-Majalis*, by their very nature, are not exclusively devoted to sufistic or religious matters, but they cover all topics, in differing degrees, political, social, personal, affecting every member of the society including the saints themselves. The *Mirqat* stands out prominent among these malfuz- works in so much as it is a veritable store-house of information on political, social and like matters as will be seen from the following section.

The other malfuz-work of the saint, *Tuhfatul-Majalis* by Shaikh Mahmud Iraji, also fails to come up to the standard of the *Mirqat* in this respect. The author sought the permission of the saint, in response to the latter's unsolicited offer to him a number of times to ask for fulfillment of any desire or wish, to compile his pearl-seattering utterances which he was hearing from time to time, with a view that the book may remain a memento to him in the world.[56] These he has described as having taken place in seventy-five meetings or assemblies-*majalis*, which unlike Hazrat Shaikh Nizamuddin Auliya's malfuz *Fawaidul-Fuad* by Amir Hasan Sijzi or *Jumaat-i-Shahiya* of Sayyid Muhammad Maqbul Alam, poetically named Jalali, which give day month and the year of each such meeting, does not give any date for these assemblies. This work also more or less covers the same subject as the *Mirqat* but it fails to furnish as much important and new information as the *Mirqat* does. The late-lamented Professor Khaliq Ahmad Nizami, an eminent historian, scholar and chronicler of sufi movements in India, the first to write on a malfuz-work of Gujarat, while correctly considering it to be an inferior malfuz, describes it as the earliest and by far the most important source of information on account of the value of information it contains about the life of the saint.[57] But as has been pointed by Dr. Ziyauddin Desai, Professor Nizami's assessment would have been different if he had before him a copy of the *Mirqat* or its Urdu translation *Sirat-i-Ahmadiya*. He was aware of the Calcutta manuscript copy of the malfuz *Mirqat*, listed under the name *Malfuz-i-Shaikh Ahmad Maghribi*, but he does not seem to have seen it or its Urdu translation. In any case, it is doubtful as stated above, if the *Tuhfatul-Majalis* was written earlier than the *Mirqat* and is therefore the earliest primary source for the account of Shaikh Ahmad's life and achievements. Dr. Desai has expressed his doubt on this score and has strong reasons to believe that the *Tuhfatul-Majalis* is strictly speaking not a purely original work and was compiled later than the *Mirqat*. According to him, it is a hash-up of the information mostly taken from the *Mirqat*, with a little bit of new information of its own. Dr. Desai claims to have based his view on a comparison of the contents of the seventy-five or so assemblies as described by Prof. Nizami in his article with the account detailed in his own lecture-book, but he did not go into details for want of time and in view of the specific nature of his lecture.[58] "A comparison of the *Tuhfatul-Majalis* with *Mirqat* made by me also brings out the validity of Dr. Desai's view. It has been seen and found by comparison, that while Shaikh Mahmud Iraji might have been a regular visitor of the saint's Khanqah at Sarkhej, though the author of the *Mirqat* does not even once mention him as such, it is doubtful if he had enjoyed that nearness with the saint as he vociferously makes it out to be. His very self-presumptive attitude and approach, felt through every folio and page of the book seems to be in contrast with the nature of the saint himself who never liked men with egoistic tendencies as will be seen while describing the saint's nature and character as reflected in the *Mirqat*. Secondly, certain claims made by him are contrary to the fact. For example he claims to have received the *Khilafat* (spiritual-successorship) from the saint;[59] significantly, he does not quote any date while Shaikh Muhammad Qasim gives the day, date, month and year of his being made a disciple (*murid*) only and not a spiritual successor (*Khalifa*) by the saint. As a matter of fact, the *Mirqat* states that the saint had not appointed any one as his successor despite the suggestion of three four names by Sultan Muhammad II, at the saint's death-bed; on his last day, in the presence of Malik Raziul-Mulk, he had Shaikh Salahuddin, his latest ward and attendant, wear the (saint's) turban as a token of his appointment as the keeper of his Khanqah and his spiritual successor.[60]

Similarly, Shaikh Mahmud Iraji relates in more than one majlis, the birth of his children through the blessings of the saint, who according to him used to tell him that he could not tolerate separation from him.[61] Shaikh Muhammad Qasim more or less narrates a similar story related to him by Maulana Muhammad, Khatib of the Jami mosque of Sarkhej who received stipend from the state.[62] The author of the *Mirqat* Maulana Muhammad Qasim's name occurs three four times in the *Tuhfatul-Majalis*. He uses this name himself, while in his narrative the saint is made to address him as "Maulana" which is highly improbable.[63] The saint as is stated by the author of the *Mirqat* himself would address or call him by the epithet Mullan, which is comparatively not as respectful a term as Maulana.

The description of the saint's activities as related by him in the events of Khattu, Didvana, Delhi, Samarqand, etc., as given by Shaikh Mahmud Iraji, can be traced to that of these events in the *Mirqat*. For example, Shaikh Mahmud Iraji's account of Babu Ishaq's journey to north Africa where he became attached to the Maghribi order and was also made to the chagrin of senior disciples and attendants the spiritual successor of Shaikh Muhammad Kimi Maghribi,[64] seems to have been wholly taken from the *Mirqat*.[65] It is just a summary of the account described by Maulana Muhammad,[66] even in his words, omitting interesting and useful details. This only example is sufficient enough to show that Shaikh Mahmud Iraji has borrowed his material from the *Mirqat* and it is not based on the saint's communications to him. It is not necessary to detail all such instances, but a few may be enumerated to further support this view: Babu Ishaq's mention of Shaikh Ahmad's openhandedness; Darya Khan's taking elephants to Gujarat and passing through Khattu; Baba Qiumuddin's account in three *majlis*; Shaikh Ahmad's going to Didvana, with the saint's permission on the eve of the latter's taking ill suddenly and Shaikh Ahmad's hurrying back to Khattu; child Shaikh Ahmad's gladly sacrificing his favourite goat to entertain Babu Ishaq's guest; meeting of Shaikh Ahmad with Sayyed Jalal Bukhari in Delhi; incidents in the course of journeys for pilgrimage and Samarqand; visitor of Pandua in Bengal etc.[67] A comparison between the two respective versions of these two works will amply bear out our view that not only Shaikh Mahmud Iraji's work was compiled later, but it contains material, at times almost verbatim from the *Mirqat*. It would appear that he was not admitted into the near circle of the saint as he claims and presumes. He himself does not give any idea of the length of his being so near the saint, as Maulana Muhammad Qasim does. Since Maulana Muhammad Qasim was in constant attendance of the saint for thirty years, as also a Pesh-Imam of the saint's prayers — which latter fact Shaikh Mahmud Iraji accepts, the claim of the author of the *Tuhfatul-Majalis* would appear hollow. Shaikh Mahmud Iraji, as Maulana Sayyed Abu Zafar noted, was jealous of Maulana Muhammad Qasim and a rival of his. That is why he does not mention him without disparagement in his just four times mention of him.

In one of these, the former states that he recited a poem on voluntary poverty *(faqr)* and the saint praising it said to Maulana Muhammad Qasim, "Maulana! Have you heard this poem on faqr ?" According to Shaikh Mahmud Iraji, the Maulana did not raise his head and kept quiet which the saint did not like.[68] In a second instance, he says that Maulana Qasim (i.e.Maulana Muhammad Qasim) recited a poem in the praise of the saint which after hearing, the saint highly disapproved, saying, "What rubbish is this" and taking the paper from his hands trampled it under his feet. Incidentally, Shaikh Mahmud Iraji once recited a poem which was in a similar strain. But he says that the saint was highly pleased[69] This appears to be highly improbable for the saint to apply two different yardsticks in a similar case. This shows Shaikh Mahmud Iraji's bias against the author of the *Mirqat*.

This is not to suggest that the *Tuhfatul-Majalis* may not be a genuine work or it does not have any historical importance. It contains quite a few pieces of new information. For example, the incident of Shaikh Saddo Merathi (of Meerut), called son-in-law of Sultan Tughluq (evidently Tughlag Shah II) who used to come to see the saint in Delhi on foot, covering a distance of about one kos (3 1/2 kilometres), was advised by the saint to go away towards Jaunpur on account of the impending peril of Timur's invasion;[71] Hazrat Nizamuddin Auliya's gifting away of a substantial amount of money to the Qawwals, having been extremely pleased with their singing a poem which sent the saint into rapture and ecstasy; the saint's meeting with Hazrat Sayyid Raju Bukhari at Uchch (now in Bhawalpur district of Punjab, Pakistan); Maulana Mansur's taking charge of the Khanqah at Sarkhej and arrangement with a local grocer, Shaikh Mahmud Iraji's taking Amir

Bayazid son of Muhammad son of Bihamad[72] to the saint requesting him to make him his disciple; story of the Hormuz merchant's ship being saved from getting wrecked by the saint in absentia and his coming to Sarkhej to offer thanks and gifts; Maulana Hafiz Sodagar, a resident of Sarai Meghchand through whom a Mughal of central Asia sent a horse etc. with a request for prayers for his wife; Shaikh Mahmud Iraji's mention, apropos some occasion, of the exchange of the letters between his maternal great grandfather Khwaja Muinuddin Iraji[73] and Hazrat Shaikh Nizamuddin Auliya quoting the text of the communication; authors' reciting his own verses on a number of occasions in the presence of the saint and the latter acclaiming it; assemblies of Sama, in which saintly persons and savants like Maulana Nizamuddin Surkha, Maulana Muhammad Kaka, Maulana Jani and Maulana Naziruddin Rajgiri;[74]' Qazi Najmuddin Waiz's visit to the saint; author's introducing a poet who had composed a poem in the saint's praise; the saint reciting in a state of meditation and ecstasy his own ghazal in the presence of the author; the saint's interest in the family affairs of the author–getting his wife called from his native place Iraj, making his daughter, blessing them with children, inquiring about the birth of children, asking him to bring them to his presence as he was anxious to see and bless them, etc.; challenge of Shaikh Mithai of Sarkhej to the saint to leave Sarkhej or win a test of entering into fire; construction of a mosque, house and his own tomb by the saint and his desiring the author to go and see those if he had not; *Khwab-nama*, "Letter of Dream" of Shaikh Muhammad Maghribi in which he described his having seen the saint in a dream; incident of Shaikh Kamal Kirmani and the author's being shown respect by him; Sultan (Muhammad II) sending to the saint through a Khwajasara some mangoes out of those sent to him by Rai Gangdas of Champaner, etc.[75]

Of the above information, about more than half pertain to the author himself. As to the rest, at least the incident of Shaikh Mithai recalls to mind the challenge of a Jogi thrown to the saint in a similar manner.[76]

In short, the *Mirqat* is definitely more authentic and gives much more details about the saint's life, travels, activities in Delhi, Rajasthan during pilgrimage journey, during travels to Samarqand, Sarkhej, etc. than the *Tuhfatul-Majalis*. It is also more systematic and gives a far more coherent account than the random assembly talks of Shaikh Mahmud Iraji's work, which by all accounts is inferior to the *Mirqat*.

(E) An Important first hand Source for the Political Social Cultural and Literary History, Particularly of Western India in the Late Forteenth Early Fifteenth Century (circa 1350-1450 A.D.)

The *Mirqatul-Wusul* of Shaikh Muhammad Qasim may perhaps be considered as the most important non-historical source for the various aspects of the history of western India as also to some extent of the imperial Delhi of the second half of the fourteenth century. No other malfuz-work written prior to or after it contains such wealth of historical information on the political and social life of the period it covers as this work does. It is a pity that if has been overlooked by historians of India as well as of Gujarat, by and large. Only recently, an assessment of certain aspects of its historical importance was made in the Khuda Bakhsh Memorial lecture delivered at the Khuda Bakhsh Oriental Public Library, Patna, in 1987, by Dr. Ziyauddin Desai, now retired Director (Epigraphy), Archaeological Survey of India. This lecture running into 63 pages was published in the Journal of the said Library and also in a separate book-form in 1991. This thesis was well under way, when this came to my notice. Having been able to procure a typed copy from Dr. Desai through my teacher the late Prof. Dr. A. N. Quraishi, I have utilized it in this section, and elsewhere, supplementing the matter thereof wherever necessary. I have tried to cover some areas left out by Dr. Desai. I am thankful to both of them.

The *Mirqatul-Wusul illallahi war-Rusul* intended to be a means of attainment of Allah and His messenger, the last of the Prophets, Muhammad by its very nature embodies material on theological, spiritual and ethical precepts and practices that help human spirit cleanse itself of baser instincts and enable it to rise to nobler and high level of being. For describing the saint's teachings and bidding through his utterances the author takes recourse not just to the narration of the precepts in a dry manner but makes it interesting and grappling by describing them through the saint's experiences with his fellow-beings as well as his personal experiences. As a result, the book contains, apart from religious dogmas, theological matters, etc. lot of information that throws new light on the state of life and society of the period particularly in Rajasthan and Gujarat the main field of the saint's activities spanning a little more than a century.

(F) Life-sketch of Hazrat Babu Ishaq

First of all, the *Mirqat* is the only source that supplies material for a biographical sketch of both Hazrat Shaikh Ahmad Khattu and his foster-father Hazrat Babu Ishaq. About the latter, as well as about the history of the Maghribi order which he founded in India, the *Mirqat* is the earliest and perhaps the main work which furnishes particulars of his life and activities – his journey to Islamic lands, getting initiated into the Maghribi order, his return to India and settling down at Khattu in Nagor district of Rajasthan where he passed the last years of his celibate life. The earliest hagiological work to mention him indirectly is Shaikh Abdul-Haqq Muhaddis's *Akhbarul-Akhyar* which does not devote him a separate notice, but speaks of him as the foster-father of Shaikh Ahmad Khattu, in his notice of the Latter. His account of Babu Ishaq just comes down to this that the child (who later on became Shaikh Ahmad Khattu) was lost in a dust-storm at Delhi along with his nurse and ultimately came into the hands of Baba Ishaq Maghribi who was a perfect Darvish and who lived in Khattu which is a village in the province of Ajmer and under whose care and training he was brought up and attained perfection and whose successor he was appointed. His spiritual lineage ends in Shaikh Abu Madyan Maghribi; on account of the unusual 150 years of the lives of the Shaikhs of this order the spiritual lineage of Babu Ishaq terminates in five stages to the Holy Prophet.[77] It may be noted here that this brief account is based on the *Tuhafatul-Majalis* of Shaikh Mahmud Iraji, which itself as has been seen above derives his information from the *Mirqat* (44 ff, *supra*).

As a matter of fact, the *Mirqat* devotes a whole chapter (No. Three) to the notice of Babu Ishaq entitled "(An account of) virtues of His Holiness Shaikh Babu Ishaq son of Mahmud Maghribi the spiritual guide and patron of Bandagi Makhdum (Shaikh Ahmad Khattu)" as seen above (34, *supra*), in which a somewhat coherent account of his is detailed.[78] The *Mirqat* is the only source to give the name of his father, namely Shaikh Mahmud and also to say that he was born in Delhi in 660 H.(1261-62 A.D.). This is a new piece of information, as the Babu is only known to students of Indian history of sufism as Babu Ishaq of Khattu. His house in old Delhi (not present old Delhi which dates back to the time of Mughal emperor Shah Jahan, but Delhi of the Mamluk-Khalji period) existed even after his settling down at Khattu. He had taken his adopted-son child Shaikh Ahmad Khattu with him when he made the first visit to his hometown, after Shaikh Ahmad came into his life, to show him his house. It seems he himself had not earlier visited the house after he left Delhi any time during his frequent visits to Delhi. He took his ward to the locality where the house, of which only the ruined site had remained, was situated and asked people there if any of the owners thereof were there and was told that there was none. When he attained the age of description, he renounced the world and became a celibate. He mixed with all groups of men in search of God and became conversant with their precepts, practices and language and terminology and acquired mastery over the tenets of forty four orders of the saints, some by word and some by action. He had committed to memory the geneological trees *(Shajaras)* of the fourteen saintly houses. He always enjoined upon his ward Shaikh Ahmad to learn these from him but the saint says he could not. Babu Ishaq would recite formulaes (*wird*) at the time of prayers in abundance and he had Persian and Hindi verses by heart which he would often quote. He used to put on a *tanura* (dress put on by dervishes from the middle) and a cap; the dress was stitched. He was clean-shaven, but in later years, he had grown beard etc. and had become devout and deeply religious and was observing all religious rites and injuctions. He was very handsome.

In Khattu, everyday he twice visited the graves of local saints and whenever he went to Delhi, he paid visit to the tombs of the saints of that place. He spent most of his time in meditation and crying, kept night vigils and engaged himself in prayer and meditation when people were sleep. He would not receive anything from any body except when in need. He had a silver tray (*rakabi*) which he would mortgage with the grocer and obtain daily requisites on credit and redeem it when he received some *Futuh*-money; he had named it mortgaged *(giravi)*. He would decline voluntary offerings (*Futuh*) if he was not satisfied with the donor, usually a high official or nobleman. But he would not be loathe to accept even a petty sum if offered in good faith by a sincere admirer or devotee. For example, once he accepted in the presence of Shaikh Ahmad, then a boy, six *fadyas* (paisa-like coin of small denomination), from Malik Umar, a high official. Shaikh Ahmad was perplexed and spoke to the Babu who told him that might be Malik Umar who was a sincere devotee could not afford anything more at that time. Babu Ishaq would at time lose his temper when some one did not behave properly, particularly with his ward Shaikh Ahmad. The latter would tell him he was getting provoked very easily.

For example, due to his getting angry with Malik Ahmad Kath, a fairly high official, for misbehaving with Shaikh Ahmad, the Malik had to suffer loss of some goods due to fire, usually he was quite considerate and tolerant towards people. Once a Qalandar came to him and pestered him to give him six *jital* for *bhang*. The Babu asked Shaikh Ahmad to give him six *jitals* whereupon he remonstrated saying, how was it proper to give money for such a purpose. The Babu said in reply, "We shall be asked about giving and not about his drinking (*bhang*); give him six *jitals*, he may change his mind and eat something else". Due to his benevolent nature, the Babu commanded respect of all from high officials to laymen. He was also respected by non-Muslims including Brahmins.

Before settling down at Khattu, Babu Ishaq had travelled all over the Islamic world. When and why he undertook such a long journey is not stated by the author. He must have done so in order to have further knowledge and experience in spiritual matters. Nor does the *Mirqat* give a systematic account of the travels; perhaps Shaikh Ahmad himself did not furnish him with these details or talked about it, as this had happened long before he had come to the saint at an age of four. Of course, he does relate without usually specifying the time and place, incidents like the Babu's encounter with a Jogi who challenged him if he could eat *halwa-i-dud* (lit. sweet-meat of smoke—in terminology of Jogis "walking on fire"), or incident of the Muqta whose wife entertained him. In the course of these travels, he came to Maghrib (North Africa). There in the city of Kim, he met Hazrat Shaikh Muhammad Hajjaj, a highly respected saint, and requested him to initiate him as his disciple. The Shaikh accorded him a warm welcome and admitted him to his favour and nearness and asked his chief disciples Shaikh Umar Khalifa and Shaikh Muhammad Baizavi, who were men of learning and spiritual station to place absolute faith in the Babu and obey him implicity. On his death at an age of 120 or 150, Shaikh Muhammad Hajjaj Maghribi appointed him as his spiritual successor to the resentment and chagrin of his senior disciples. Babu stayed for sometime in the Khanqah. Then, one day, the above-mentioned two disciples-attendants of the Khanqah came to him saying there was no money left for running the Khanqah. Babu Ishaq for two three days managed to receive the exact daily amount of expenditure from the deceased saint's grave and then ultimately decided to leave Kim.

After leaving Kim, Babu Ishaq travelled through countries and ultimately returned to India in the time of Sultan Muhammad bin

Tughluq Shah (1325-52 A.D.). On his way he halted at a place near the capital, the Muqta of which was Malik Muzaffar Kalal, Due to misbehaviour on the part of other dervishes and jogis who were then halting in that place, Malik Muzaffar took them to the Sultan. When Babu Ishaq's turn came, the Prime Minister Khan Jahan told the Sultan that he was an eminent saint through whose blessings he had risen to the post of prime ministership. The Sultan was highly pleased with the encounter. He asked the saint. "Where do you live" to which Babu replied, " In your kingdom". When asked why did he not pay visit to him, Babu said, "Of what worth are we to think of paying a visit to the Sultan". He gave him money which at first Babu declined to accept saying what would he do with that or of what use it was to him, and came out. The Sultan's servants came after him with money out of which he took one *fadya* and distributed the rest among the people.

Then he went to Ajmer to pay a visit to the tomb of the famous Chishti saint Khwaja Muinuddin Ajmeri . While in Ajmer, he was repeatedly told in dreams by the saint to go to Khattu which was now going to be his place of mission to guide people. When from Ajmer, he came to Koleva, three *kroh* from Khattu, a mad man came there from Khattu side. Coincidently, from the invisible (*ghaib*), a mule laden with laddus (sweet meat balls) came. The Babu sent it to him. The mad man said, "*Laddu Kaddhu*" from where (this) : Laddu ? "The saint said, *Uddhu* (From there - i.e. above, from God)." Then he came and settled down in Khattu and stayed there until his death.

Babu must have been fairly well-advanced in age by the time he came to Khattu. He seems to have first adopted Baba Qiyamuddin who used to attend upon him before Shaikh Ahmad came. He was a high statured person and the inhabitants of Khattu used to call him "Karehra" meaning a faithful lion. Babu Ishaq in the course of his travels had halted in a mosque. A person staying in an adjacent house whose male child fell ill came to the Babu requesting him to pray for his recovery. The Babu consented to pray provided he give away the boy to him. After initial hesitation, when the condition of the boy deteriorated, the man and his wife relented and the boy recovered. Babu named him Qiyamuddin and brought him to Khattu and tried to instruct him in religious and spiritual matters. But he died in the prime of his youth. Baba Ishaq loved him very much and was very disconsolate. Even after he adopted Shaikh Ahmad, he would often cry remembering Baba Qiyamuddin. He had put some hair of his in a slit in the wall of the house from where he would take it out and cry and then again put it back. Once when Shaikh Ahmad was looking up the papers of Qiyamuddin, he found among them a few books of vocabulary and primary texts (*mabadi*). He said to Babu, "Did Shaikh Qiyamuddin possess only this much of knowledge?" The Babu was greatly displeased and replied, "Do not speak of him in disparaging terms. He has gone out of my sight and then only I have directed my love and affection to you".

Babu was 81 when Shaikh Ahmad came to him. The latter was taken out by his nurse for an evening stroll when there arose a terrible dust-storm. The nurse and the child were lost and when the storm subsided joined a caravan of salt-merchants who were going to Didvana. There a childless carder named Najib took him from the merchants and adopted him as a child. In the meantime, after Qiyamuddin's death, Babu Ishaq had a sort of inspiration that a lad with such and such an appearance would come to him. The Babu had asked his friends, disciples and admirers to be on the look out for a lad with these features and bring him to him at any cost. Maulana Sadruddin found him at Didvana and with great difficulty prevailed upon the carder Najib to part with the lad. Babu Ishaq then tried to educate and instruct him with love and affection and took every care to see that he always had good clothes, foot-wear, headgear, etc. He also spared no pains to educate and instruct him in conventional sciences and spiritual matters. He also took special care in imparting training to him in mainly sports like archery, wrestling, etc. and arranged for best arrows for him. He would take him to Delhi, Nagor, Didvana, Ladnun and wherever he went. Shaikh Ahmad would also be usually with him when Babu Ishaq met great divines and savants.

Babu Ishaq was greatly respected by Firuz Shah Tughluq and his officials. He knew the lingo of the jogis and would enter into discussions with them. He loved to host eating parties to learned men and in such parties, after meals, verses on sufistic subjects would be recited and heard with rapt interest. After eating, *Fatiha* would be recited for the merit of saints and prophets.

The end of Babu Ishaq came rather unexpectedly. One day, Shaikh Ahmad had gone to Didvana with some friends, when Babu developed. Some fever and sent some one to fetch him. On return, he found him seriously ill. Next day, he gave some money to Shaikh Ahmad to fetch stone-masons for preparing his grave. He got his grave dug before his own eyes, Momentarily displeased with the suggestion of Fakhruddin, Qazi (religious judge) of Khattu, to have the empty grave filled with grain and give it away in alms, as was the custom among the elite of the society, Babu Ishaq immediately regained his composure and made peace with the Qazi. When Shaikh Ahmad on whose knees the head of the saint rested made a sign that his resentment was not advisable, Babu said, "Come O Qazi, we are pleased with you and you also be pleased with us". After that, one night he had much vomiting; whatever water he drank come out. Babu called Shaikh Ahmad who was sleeping inside and asked him to recite every time some formulae on the water he was to drink. This helped and vomiting stopped. On the fourth day, on Wednesday, night of seventeenth of Shaban, he asked for the grave to be made ready for internment and made the saint seat behind him. Then he sat up reclining against the saint and uttering *Ya Hayyu, Ya Qayyum*. (O Ever Living), (O Eternal), he closed his eyes and breathed his last. To God we belong and to Him we return.[79]

Notes

28. Text, 2.
29. *Irshadat-i-Ahmadiya*, *op. cit*. 3b, 4a, The author of this unique copy does not mention his name, but states that he wrote the book at the instance of Miyan Alauddin son of Shaikh Salahuddin, the spiritual successor of the saint. This would make him flourish in the middle of the third quarter of the fifteenth century.
30. Ali Muhammad Khan, *op. cit*. (Bombay), 22. The Baroda edition of this work (1930 A.D.) omits the word Malfuz from the text, *Malfuz-i-Kabir*, as seen above (f.n.11, *supra*).
31. Text, 1. A somewhat free translation.
32. *Ibid*, 2.
33. *Sirat-i-Ahmadiya*, loc;cit., p. 8
34. Text, 33-34.
35. 26, *supra*
36. Modern historians and writer pronounce his name as Mufarrah or Mufarrih but the correct pronunciation is perhaps. Mufrih, as adopted by the famous Arabicist, E. Denison Ross (Hajji Dabir, *Zafarul-Walih bi-Muzaffar wa-Alih* Vol. III, London 1928, Index).
37. For his life and works, see M. Ayyub Qadiri, *Makhdum Jahaniyan Jahangasht* (Urdu), Karachi, 1963.
38. The *Tarikh-i-Mubarak Shahi,* ed. H. Beveridge, Delhi Reprint 1986, 128,133,138,139,143-146,159, etc.
39. For these inscriptions and other details, see *EIAPS* 1972, 33-36, hl IVa, 23-34, hl.IIIa.
40. Text, 33, 38, 103, etc.
41. *EIAPS*, 1953 and 1954, p.

42. Text, 69.
43. *Ibid.*, 62,102,110,113,114,115,151,154,166,167, etc.
44. W. Ivanow, *A Descriptive Catalogue of the Persian Manuscripts in the collection of the Asiatic Society of Bengal,* Calcutta, Reprint 1985, p. 91.
45. Text, en passant.
46. These will be mentioned later in the concerned section.
47. Text, 203.
48. *Ibid.*, 3, 9, 17, 28, 88, 107, 173.
49. For details, see C.A. Storey, *Persian Literature A Brio-Bibliographical Survey* (London, 1953), 941-52.
50. For an account of these works, see Sayyid Sabahuddin Abdur-Rahman, *Bazm-i-Sufiya* (Azamgargh, 1989) Some malfuz works of the early Chishti saints of the 13th century are also in vogue but their authenticity has been disputed.
51. It is reliably learnt that a defective and damaged copy comprising a few *juz* of this large work exists in the *Khanqah-i-Chishitya Library*, Shahi Bagh, Ahmadabad.
52. For an account of the *Jumaat-i-Shahiya*, see *Diwan-i-Jalali*, ed. by Prof. M.G. Bombaywala and published by the Dargah Hazrat Pir Muhammad Shah Trust, Ahmadabad, in 1995, pp.30-34.
53. *Ibid.*, Introduction, 33.
54. For this work, see Dr. Shaikh Farid, *Shah Bahauddin Bajan*, *Hayat our Gujari Kalam*, Published by the Dargah Hazrat Pir Muhmmad Shah Trust, Ahmadabad, 1993.
55. Of these two, the *Tuhfatul-Qari*, ed. by Prof. Mahmud Saikh and Prof. M.A, Abbasi has also been published by the above mentioned Trust. in 1996.
56. *TM,* 2a; *TMU* 27.
57. Malfuz Literature, et. al. 17. Maulana Sayyid Abu Zafar Nadvi also seems to hold the view that the *Tuhfatul-Majalis* was written earlier than the *Mirqat* (*SA,* 7).
58. *Ibid.*, 16.
59. *TMU*, 64 (wrong by printed as 24).
60. Text, 35.
61. *TM*, 516, *TMU*, 67.
62. Text, 162.
63. *TM*, 42b,46b,67a,98b,99a,; *TMU*, 55, 60, 86, 129, At one of these places(46b), his name is given as Maulana Qasim, which unless a scribal mistake, would make the author's authenticity suspect.
64. *TM*, 37a, *TMU*, 47.
65. *TM*, 37; *TMU*, 47 ff.
66. Text, 51-54.
67. *TM*, 24a, *TMU*, 51, Text, *TM*, 86b, *TMU*, 116, Text; *TM*, 91 ff, *TMU*, 18 ff, Text, *TM*, 9 b, *TMU*, 17, Text ; *TM*, 3a, *TMU*, 4, Text ; *TM*, 11 b, *TMU*, 14, Text ; *TM*, 28b, *TMU*, 36, Text; *TM*, 58 b, *TMU*, 76, Text,; etc..
68. *TM*, 47; *TMU*, 61.
69. *TM*, 54, *TMU*, 66.

70. Maulan Abu Zafar Nadvi (*TMU*,66) has aptly commented on this, "This qasida (praise-poem) in the praise of Shaikh Ahmad and seeking his blessing is in the same strain as the qasida of Maulana Qasim which has been mentioned in Majilis 35. But here, Shaikh Ahmad is stated to be highly pleased. This also shows that there was a little rivalry between Maulana Qasim and Shaikh Mahmud Iraji."
71. *TM*,4b, *TMU*, 6.
72. Maulana Nadvi (*TMU*, 28), has Bahauddin, while the *TM* (22b); has correctly Amir Bayzid Bihamad Tarun.
73. *Ibid.*, 34, confuses him with the celebrated Ajmer saint Hazrat Khwaja Muinuddin Chishti.
74. Maulana Nadvi (SA, 40) as *Chiragh-i-Dehli*, while *TM* 32a, has correctly Rajgiri.
75. *TM*, f 4a, *TMU*, 6; *TM*, f 35a, *TMU*, 45; *TM*, f. 19b, *TMU*, 24; *TM*, f 21a, *TMU*, 26; *TM*, f 22 b, *TMU*, 28; *TM*, f 24a, *TMU*, 30; *TM*, f 25 b, *TMU*, 32; *TM*, f 27a, *TMU*, 34; *TM*, f 28a, *TMU*, 35; *TM*, ff 45a, 46a, 50 b, 51a, *TMU*, 61, 63, 64, 67, 68, 69; *TM*, f 32 b, *TMU*, 40; *TM*, f 34a, *TMU*, 43; *TM*, f 36a *TMU*, *TM*, f. 53 ff, *TMU*, 61-74; *TM*, f 66 b, *TMU*, 86; *TM*, f 70a, *TMU*, 90; *TM*, 72b, *TMU*, 93; *TM*, f 74 b, *TMU*, 96; *TM*, f 82 b, *TMU*, 105; etc.
76. Text 5a,90.
77. Shaikh Abdul-Haqq Muhaddis Dehlavi, *op-cit*, 157. He also quotes profusely from the *Tuhfatul-Majalis* in which also reference to Babu Ishaq is found. In any case, this does not amount to much.
78. It may be pointed out that the account of Hazrat Babu Ishaq's early life before he adopted Shaikh Ahmad Khattu, was related by the latter to our author from time to time in the Babu's own words. However, the author claims to have confirmed certain facts from the Sarkhej saint's contemporaries (Text, 48).
79. Text (in order of the matter described) : 47, 71, 48-50, 72, 61, 62, 68, 49-53, 55-60, 24, 57, 4-8, 54-64, 79, 66-67.

3

LIFE SKETCH OF HAZRAT KHATTU SHAIKH AHMAD

Likewise, the *Mirqat* furnishers the earliest contemporary eye-witness account of the life and achievements of Shaikh Ahmad Khattu himself. As stated above, hagiographical works do not give a detailed account of his life and career. Both the *Akhbarul-Akhyar* and *Mirat-i-Ahmadi* supplement, which gives some account of the saint have mostly utilized the *Tuhafatul Majalis*, which as seen above, does not give a coherent account of the saint's life as the *Mirqat* does as well as be seen from the following detailed notice gleaned from the *Mirqat*.

Shaikh Ahmad whose original name was Nasiruddin, was born in a princely noble family of Delhi in 737H./1336-37 A.D.[80] during the reign of Muhammad bin Tughluq Shah. Haji Dabir on the authority of the *Sharh-i-Risala-i-Maghribiya*, a commentary on the *Risala-i-Maghribiya* of the saint, states that he was born in Khattu in the district of Nagor.[81] However, the statement of Maulana Muhammad Qasim who later on recounts the story of the meeting of the saint's elder brother in Jor-Bagh in Delhi in the course of one of his visits to Delhi with Babu Ishaq when he was (i.e. in 750 H./1349-50 A.D.) his narration of the saint's getting lost in the tempest, showing his house, birth-marks (*lahsan*) on the saint's, his own and their falter's shoulders etc., [82] makes it more probable that he was born in Delhi only.

While yet a child, he got separated from his family in unusual but not wholly improbable circumstances. A furious tempestuous dust–storm overtook the locality when one evening he had been taken out for his usual stroll in the garden near his house by his nurse who got lost and strayed into a lane. Both the nurse and the lad Nasiruddin, apparently after the storm had subsided, in the night found themselves in the midst of a caravan of merchants from Gangetic plain who had camped at Delhi on their way to Didvana in Rajasthan to purchase salt. The lost duo found refuge with one of the merchants and accompanied him, when the caravan left Delhi next morning for Didvana, in Nagor district. At Didvana, Nasiruddin was adopted by a childless weaver, Najib by name. Babu Ishaq who had settled down at Khattu in the same district, as stated earlier, having been told of the boy in a spiritual communion and being in need of a boy-disciple after the untimely death of his young disciple Shaikh Qiyamuddin, had asked one of his disciples and a leading citizen of Khattu, Maulana Sadruddin, a grandson of Maulana Shihabuddin Hamadani, who was going to Didvana for some work, to be on the look out for the boy with particular features and looks. The Maulana, who was informed about such a boy being with a local resident, Najib, prevailed upon him to grudgingly part with the boy and took him to Khattu.[83]

When Babu Ishaq was informed about Maulana's return to Khattu with the child, he went out to receive him and found him to confórm to the description given to him in the dream-stance. He took him into his bosom and brought him home and named him Ahmad and always addressed him as Baba Ahmad. He was four years old at this time and Babu Ishaq was eightyone.

Babu Ishaq brought him up with maternal care and great love and affection. At night he would put him on his chest and sing a lullaby to make him sleep. At times he would spoil his clothes. Babu would get up, wash them and again place him on his bosom. He reared him up, the saint in his later days would fondly say, in the same way and manner as a Malik and a Khan would bring up his son, such as might be the case with very few. He would first see that the boy Ahmad ate . Once no meals was left for the boy. He went early morning to visit the tombs of saints of Khattu as was his wont. People took him to his house and offered him delicious dishes. He would not eat, he said, as he had left his son sleeping in the house. He declined to eat even when the host said he would send food for his son. Ultimately a person carrying food and one pot of butter, one pot of milk and one pot of curds went along with the Babu to his house. Babu did not spare any effort to see that young Ahmad had always dainties and good dishes for his meals . He would see that he wore always good clothes, and best foot-wear. Once he saw him putting on some worn out pair of shoes. He immediately scolded him for wearing it and got a new pair.

In his very early days, it seems, Baba Ahmad did not show much inclination towards academic pursuits, but took more interest in mastering mainly arts and games like horsemanship, archery, wrestling, stick-and-ball, etc,. Babu Ishaq also imparted him trainning in oratory, dispensation of Justice, equity and strength at courage. He gained fame as skilled archer and wrestler and later on used to narrate his expertise in these arts. Once an expert archer, Sayyid Ali Qairwani having heard in Didvana of Babu Ishaq and Baba Ahmad prepared a pair of clay-dumb-bell like instrument (*nalha-i-gilin*)[84] and brought it to Babu saying that if his son were to lift and wield it, he would be powerful and gain strength and will be a good archer. As a result, he became an expert in archery and his shot never missed. His skill in archery was tested successfully when Malik Nasir son of Ahmad, the Muqta of Khattu, held an archery competition and he, his kinsmen, friends, ręsidents of Khattu and the Sherani and other tribes tested their skill, but failed to hit a target set up by the Muqta despite several attempts. When young Baba Ahmad went, all the groups claimed him to be a member of their group. A jealous person gave him a broken (loose) bow and broken thumbstall but he hit the target in the first attempt. Later on, this skill in archery proved useful when once he was travelling with others in a cart from Khattu to Nagor and they were waylaid by robbers. Babu Ahmad going ahead shot a flying partridge with a single shot which overawed and intimidated the bandits, the chief of whom said that this man of such deadly aim had quite a few arrows in his bower and would kill all of them if they tried to confront him and his companions.

The author of the *Mirqat* has noted that for a pretty long time, the saint, who was well past his sixties, used to have the archer's outfit in Sarkhej. The saint was also given training in wrestling by Babu Ishaq. Once a wrestler had come to Khattu when the saint was fifteen years old. Babu Ishaq told him to teach his son young Shaikh Ahmad some fine points of the art of wrestling. But by that time the latter had acquired mastery over the art and impressed the wrestler with his expertise therein by defeating him. On hearing of this incident, a local Hindu cobbler boy, by whose shoe-shop, young Baba Ahmad used to pass every day, and who was also a wrestler, would repeatedly ask him for a wrestling bout. Considering him unequal to himself in the art, Baba Ahmad used to ignore his persistent challenge. One day, taking off his clothes, he intercepted Baba Ahmad and said he would not allow him to leave unless he fought with him. Baba Ahmad asked his fellow workers to dissuade him lest he was injured in the wrestling bout and then he would be blamed for that. They thought Baba Ahmad was not upto the skill and strength of their companion; so they gave an undertaking that if anything happened to him, Baba Ahmad would not be held responsible. In that well-contested bout, ultimately Shaikh Ahmad fell him and he sustained some waist injury. His father complain to Babu Ishaq who went to his locality and made inquiries. Everyone said that Shaikh Ahmad was not to blame.

The saint was physically very strong. He once overpowered an evil-wisher who attacked him in the dead of night while he was passing through his locality. Likewise, once he saved a women of Khattu who had gone to the village-well to fetch water, from being molested by a petty official (muharrir i.e. an accounts clerk), on horse back by virtue of his superior strength. Incidentally, that very man advised Shaikh Ahmad to cultivate his mental faculty and when being told he had no book, he brought him a copy of *Mabadi*, transcribed by himself. The saint was very courageous even in his youth. Number of instances showing his strength, dauntless courage and boldness are related in the *Mirqat*.

However Babu Ishaq also wanted him to take to studies in all seriousness. Baba Ahmad in his early youth seems to have felt inclined to indulge in small trade, as is indicated by a few instances related by him to the author of *Mirqat*. When these came to the notice of Babu Ishaq, he would disapprove of this tendency of his and advise him to acquire learning in various branches of religious knowledge. Babu Ishaq had once taken him to the Madarsa of Qazi Hamiduddin at Nagor and asked the teachers there as also the learned men of the town who had come to meet him, to impart instruction to him in current sciences and branches of learning. The primary books for the beginner's course like *Mizan, Hazar-Alfaz, Masadir, Panj-Ganj,* etc., were procured. Thereafter Baba Ahmad also seems to have seriously turned his attention to acquisition of knowledge, religious as well as secular. He once out of his pocket money, got a copy of *Tafsir-i-Imam Zahidi* made for him by Qazi Imamshah Jalal, who charged the cost of paper only. Once a learned man came to Khattu. Babu Ishaq asked him to impart learning to "this youngster" i.e. Baba Ahmad. The learned man said he was too young, whereupon Babu asked him to take to the mosque and test his memory, grasp, etc. That man was highly impressed by young Baba Ahmad's intelligence and perspicacity and he stayed on to give lessons to him. He taught the whole of the *Aqida-i-Hafiziya* to him.[85]

In the early stages, the saint once told Maulana Muhammad Qasim, he was a voracious reader. He would make a perfect study of one *juz* (eight folios) of the text of *Bazdavi* every night, and then tally his own knowledge thus acquired with its commentary. He also claims to have learned the language and terminology of the Jogis from Babu Ishaq. He also seems to have acquired proficiency in Arabic, Persian and Hindi accountancy (*Hisab*). In Khattu, once, he happened to pass by a gathering of the accountants of Khattu who could not calculate the number of the pearls and rubies threaded in between in a number of strings of a necklace. Shaikh Ahmad who had acquired mastery in multiplication (*Gunakar*) and division (*Bhagakar*) took a slate and made the calculations arriving at the correct number.

But the time Babu Ishaq died in about 781 H. (1379 A.D.) at an age of 120 years,[86] Shaikh Ahmad had acquired a fairly good knowledge in Jurisprudence, Tafsir, Scholasticism, etc. and even took part in discussions, which Babu had with his visitors. After the latter's death, he felt that the yearning for learning and knowledge overpowered him. He tried to raise his resources by claiming money owed to him by some persons who flatly denied having anything due to him. Ultimately, passing through some villages like Banathari, in possession of Chaudhary Daud of Didvana and getting lift in travellers' carts on the way, he reached Didvana where he halted in the mosque of Chaudhry Daud. There, the author's maternal uncle Maulana Khurram visited him and beseached him not to leave Khattu which had been a place of saints like first, Shaikh Shihab, then, Shaikh Maulana Qattal, then Shaikh Bayabani and last Shaikh Babu Ishaq, and he was their successor. Travelling a little away from Didvana, Shaikh Ahmad who was accompanied by an attendant named Salih was joined by an official travelling with a contingent who insisted on his joining them. On his declining the offer, he sent some money and one *laddu* to him. He gave these away to the people. A Dervish who was with Shaikh Ahmad carried the tale to the Malik who advised the saint to part company with him. In the meantime, someone sent a present of a *Kashkul* (Beggar's Bowl) which that Dervish asked for and received from him. On the way, he came to another village whose lease-holder (*Wajahdar*) was a Muslim. Shaikh Ahmad sent Salih to fetch water for ablution. The landlady asked him to first fetch a back-load of fire-wood before she gave water. Shaikh Ahmad called back Salih but the lady who had seen the saint from the reed-curtain (*tatti*) recognised him as a saintly person and called him to her house. She called her own Pir who came to meet the saint with *ijabat-nama* of Sayyid Jalaluddin Bukhari. He was illiterate and retreated after only having a few words with the saint who he had thought was an ignorant person, fearing lest he stood exposed before the lady. After the lady fed them with chicken, he left and ultimately came to Hisar-i-Firuza.[87]

The Muqta of Hisar, Malik Kamaluddin son of Babu Ishaq's sincere disciple Malik Umar the Ariz-i-Bandagan of Firuz Tughluq, welcoming the saint put him up in good lodgings and appointed a young maid-servant, Shakh-i- zar (lit. Branch of gold) by name, to attend to his needs like serving meals, fetching water for ablution, etc. Shaikh Ahmad stayed there for a few months (*chand mah*) and studied *Misbah, Shashi, Husami* and Bazdavi under Maulana Shamsuddin, a learned man, the Allama of his time. After this, Shaikh Ahmad developed an ardent desire to study Hadis (Science of Tradition). He was told that in the Kushi-Nuzul [88] in the Hazar-Sutun (Thousand-Pillar Hall), Maulana Majduddin Muhaddis imparted lessons in Hadis. Shaikh Ahmad thereupon decided to go to Delhi, where he put up in the Muluk-khana (king's gallery) of the Masjid-i-Khan Jahan in the Jajnagar locality of the Firozabad city, modern Firozshah Kotla outside the Delhi gate of the modern old Delhi or Shahjahanabad. During day, he attended lectures on Hadis of Maulana Majduddin and at night, he studied *Bazdavi* without its gloss and attained proficiency therein. Shaikh Ahmad, he himself one told the author of the *Mirqat*, had committed to memory twenty-two out of thirty parts of the Holy Quran. In short , it was after the death of Babu Ishaq in 781 H. (1379 A.D.) that the saint, then forty-two years of age, most ardently devoted himself to the study of religious sciences, going from place to place in pursuit of knowledge. [89] It was this brilliant performance which stood him in good stead in the academic gatherings of Samarqand, Herat, etc. in later years.

Apart from Quran and Hadis, he had acquired mastery over such authentic and standard works as *Zakhira*, *Hidaya*, *Tawali*, *Masabih* and its gloss *Zau*, *Bazdavi*, *Kanz*, *al-Muttafaq*, etc. He had almost committed *Bazdavi* by heart and could quote missing text from a defective manuscript. For example, once Shaikh Ahmad while listening to a portion of the introduction of *Bazdavi*, pointed out that the text there was faulty at that place in quite a few copies. Some agreed and some disagreed. One of those days, a good copy of *Bazdavi* came from Khurasan and he was proved correct. He had acquired mastery over Arabic and used to converse mostly in Arabic in the Arabian lands and Central Asia during his travels there.

As a matter of fact, the only desire of his spiritual guide and foster-father was to make him a Pir, as is illustrated by an incident related by him. He had gone to Didvana with a few friends and had hurriedly come back on a summon from the Babu who was seized with his illness. Thinking that Babu was displeased with him on account of his delay in coming, he did not come forward to face Babu, but went and stood behind his bed as was his wont when Babu Ishaq would be displeased with him.[90] Babu asked him to come nearer. On his dithering a little, Malik Kamal Gakkar, Muqta of Khattu who was present, said, "Mir Ahmad, come a little nearer". Thereupon Babu said, "O Malik, we want to make him Pir (spiritual guide), while you want him to become a Mir (nobleman)." It was then that Babu Ishaq removed the turban from Shaikh Ahmad's head and threw it at Maulana Yusuf Sadr and taking off his own cap from his head, held it in both hands and after reciting something over it, he placed it on Shaikh Ahmad's head with his own hands, as a token of his appointing him as his spiritual successor. [91]

Shaikh Ahmad, particularly after the death of Babu Ishaq, fasted almost continuously and led the life of an ascetic, eating little. He would purposely miss two three meals at a time and thereafter too take meagre meals. [92] For example, once a person brought to him the *sag* of *sarsun* (mustard); he said to Sayyid Akram that it would suffice for his meal. Sayyid Akram who had permission to join Shaikh Ahmad at meals, once learnt that he had not eaten on Friday. He went home and told this to his wife Bibi Nusrat who prepared some meals and sent it through her son with her respects. Shaikh Ahmad did not accept the food and told the boy that his father had no business to interfere in the affair of dervishes. Sayyid Akram found a way out, sending on third day, the local grocer Popa Baqqal who offered to send daily meals to him; when Shaikh Ahmad declined, Popa said he was let off from the state exactions due to Babu Ishaq's intercession and would again, if an occasion arose through him also. But he still refused. Ultimately, at the suggestion of Sayyid Akram who by that time had arrived there, Shaikh Ahmad agreed to receive rations from Popa's shop on credit, comprising two and half a seer of *mung* and one seer of *til* oil, for cooking purpose, as also for lighting the lamp. One day, his son who was managing the shop in the absence of his father when he had gone out of Khattu, refused rations to the saint's man. When an oil-seller came to know of it, he would bring a piece of oil cake to the saint for breaking the fast. His wife on inquiry came to know that Shaikh Ahmad was practicing such asceticism. That day, she mixed powdered sugar with it to make it palatable and tasty. The moment Shaikh Ahmad put a piece in his mouth, he found it mixed with sugar and spat it out and gave up taking that also. When Popa on return came to know of his son's refusal to give rations on credit, he came running to the saint with two seers of walnut-kernel, which the saint refused but through persistent pleadings of Sayyid Akram, agreed to receive *mung* as before.

Shaikh Ahmad also decided to perform a solitary forty day's vigil (*arbain* or *chilla*). He fed his inner self with whatever he deserved for a few days so that it would not bother him during the vigil. He had however not fed it *Kanji* (rice broth) for which he felt a craving during the vigil which he completed by taking with him some forty date-pieces he had. Sayyid Akram who knew Shaikh Ahmad ate well brought hot milk for him and wanted to force the door open, but was prevented by others. On the conclusion of the vigil, on the day of Idul-Fitr, he came out of the *Hujra,* weak and emaciated and was taken to the Idgah on a *dola* (*palki*) covered with curtains. The author of the *Mirqat* says that according to some, his master had performed more than one *chilla*, but he knew of one only. The author also mentions an instance of physical rigorous exercise adopted by Shaikh Ahmad in the manner of Qalandars. Maulana Muhammad Qasim says that he had knowledge not of one out of hundred *Mujahada* (asceticism and rigorous exercises) of the saint. He quotes Sayyid Akram that by his persistent rigorous exercises, in Khattu, Shaikh Ahmad had become very lean and weak. In short, he had tamed his carnal soul by such exercises and had gained full control over it.

After this period of penance and asceticism, Shaikh Ahmad decided to undertake pilgrimage to the holy cities. He perhaps thought of it on hearing a chance remark made by his companion Sayyid Akram who was informal with him. He once told him that one could not attain God by sitting at home, he has to travel widely. On Shaikh Ahmad's asking him the basis for this statement, he said that he had head it from Maulana Raziuddin Abul-Faraj of Didvana, an old acquaintance of the saint also. The saint told the Maulana's grandson Burhan who had come one of those days to Khattu for some work, that his grandfather had no business to interfere in the affairs of dervishes. The Maulana being told of the saint's resentment sent him a letter of denial; quoting a true story of a Hindu lady attaining spiritual uplift, he said how could he say such a thing about him, who had already attained sainthood from his young age and when the people of Khattu, Didvana and Nagor were already aware of it.

In any case, according to the saint's own account, after the death of Babu Ishaq, he passed most of his time in devotion and meditation on the Khattu hillock. Once when he was there, he felt that it was height of lack of aspiration not to pay a visit to the Holy Prophet. There and then, he decided to start on the tenth day. Ultimately, getting a signal of approval in a dream from Babu Ishaq, he gave away the silver-inkpot he had to Sayyid Akram and was bidden by the Muqta and the Sadat, the Sheranis, the Shahis, the learned, the Qazis and the like of the town. His first halt was at Tarnav, a village about twelve *kroh* from Khattu, where its Headman *Har-Ram* accord a warm welcome. He departed from there early morning and came to Nagor and put up at Sarai Chopan where other intending pilgrims from Delhi like Maulana Kamaluddin the Imam of Khan Jahan (mosque), Maulana Shaikh sahib-sajjada of Khizr of Hauz Khas, Maulana Ahmad attendant of Hazrat Shaikh Nasiruddin Mahmud Chiragh-i-Dehli and Maulana Shamsuddin a leading citizen of Delhi, were also staying. Malik Qutbuddin Najm, Muqta of Nagor, a son-in-law of Malik Raziul-Mulk, who was a great admirer of Babu Ishaq and whom Shaikh Ahmad had previously met also, came to know from these people that he was also in town on way to the Holy places. The Malik tried to dissuade him from undertaking the arduous journey as he had become very weak, but he left Nagor and reached the village Mahaba alias Talwara; Rai Malik, the Headman of that village also entertained him and presented him a few blankets and journey-expenses. Next stop was at Ladruva where he lodged himself in the house of a poor old lady which was on the bank of a river. After saving the village by his miraculous power from the sudden flood, and forging truce between Karan, the Headman of the village and his brother Sohad, he left that place and came to Nahrwala (modern Patan) in Gujarat. Malik Fathul-Mulk father of Rasti Khan who was there welcomed him and wrote letter of recommendation to his son who was in Khambhat to afford all help and facility, to Shaikh Ahmad. But when he arrived there, all the ships for Arabia had left except that of Khwaja Muhammad Murad. The ship-owner demanded an exorbitant fare and said, when he was told that the passenger was a great Shaikh (saint), "If he is a Shaikh, I am a disciple of money (*agar ishan shaikh and, man murid-i-malam*).[93]

From Khambhat, he came to Mahaim (modern Mahim in Bombay city) only to find that there also the ships had left. He purchased a small ship for 500 tankas which Rasti Khan had offered as *futuh* and reached Aden. The port superintendent did not charge any landing tax from the luggage of the saint which comprised one bundle of blankets and clothes as also from that of the above mentioned four pious and learned men of saintly establishments who had also just arrived there. The port official behaved nicely with them and offered meals and other facilities. The saint sold his ship there and hired a boat to take him to Jeddah and paid some silver coins in advance. The owner did not turn up at the fixed time next day, and when located, denied having entered into any such bargain. The saint however proved his case, got back his money and luggage which he had given to him for safe keeping and boarded a ship. On way, while trying to take bath, he tell into the ocean and was about to get drowned thinking that his end had come, when he was inspired to recite the great names of God: *Ya Hafiz Ya Hafiz Ya Raqib Ya Wakil Ya Allah Ya Allah Ya Allah* (O Preserver ! O Saver ! O Guardian ! O Protector ! O Allah ! O Allah ! O Allah). While doing so, he found some support beneath his feet and in the meantime, the boatmen lifted him up. From that day, whenever any body wanted an amulet (taviz) from the saint, he would write these great names. After landing at Jeddah, they went to Makka on camels.

About the saint's encounter with two Egyptian princesses, reference has already been made in the preceding lines (26, *supra*). In Makka, a person had presented a pair of fine shoes to the saint. An Indian approached the saint and borrowed the shoes for a while. He never shown his face thereafter. Maulana Shaikh of Delhi when he came to know of the incident, felt very sorry. Next day, he saw that Indian in the bazar, he took the shoes from him despite the saint's forbidding him, as next day they were to proceed to Madinah, which he could not do barefooted. This Maulana Shaikh had also taken few Masudi coins from the saint's attendant Jamal for which also, the saint had told him not to ask for its repayment. Next day, they started for Madinah on foot. At night he reached the camp with great difficulty and when next morning the caravan was on the move, there was no strength left in the saint's feet. He asked Maulana Shaikh to proceed saying he would follow later, but the Maulana wanted to arrange a camel ride for him despite the saint's protesting that he did not have fare to pay nor was Babu Ishaq alive to pay it. He firmly declined and found that he was able to walk. Maulana Shaikh offered him a meal which he declined but the former gave the money he had taken from the saint's attendant Jamal. They sent the money to the baker for preparing a loaf for them which at first he refused to make as it was late, but when he came to know that it was for Shaikh Ahmad, he immediately complied with their need. Then again, his feet started giving way, when a person with five camels came and said in Arabic, "O Shaikh, get on the camel". He demanded money from two Shaikhzadas of that land who were riding his camels. The Shaikhzadas asked him why he was not asking the saint for it. They said, "How can we demand money from him when two days have passed and he has not eaten anything nor has he had the need to perform ablution?" When they halted at a place, the Shaikhzadas insisted that they host him a meal but he stoutly refused. After resuming the journey, as soon as the dome of the Prophet's tomb came in view, he jumped down from the camel's back and started walking towards it with great yearning and desire, saying loudly, "O Prophet of God, O Messenger of Allah, O Chief of both the worlds" and reciting other words in praise of the Holy Prophet, so much so that his mouth started to froth. Earlier, Maulana Shaikh had requested the saint to be his guest in Madinah for a meal. But he had declined it saying be would he the guest of the Holy Prophet. When he neared the tomb, he said. "Salutations and peace be upon you, O Prophet of God". Even in that great throng in front of the tomb, the chief of the Mujawirs shouted at him and threw at him a small bundle of dates saying, "This is the treat for you from the Prophet of God".

After this, he returned.[94] He came to Aden. The port superintendent with whom the saint had kept some of his things for safe keep, refused to hand it over to his man unless he himself came to claim it. When the saint went, he entertained him. At Aden, two Sayyids from Nagor paid him a visit bringing him presents. They also took him to meet the local traders who were anxious to see him. They treated the saint with oven-roasted fish and presented him with a bagful of provisions, one jar of honey and some money. In Aden, he also met one of the holy men of the city, Shaikh Abdul-Latif. From Aden he travelled to Thatta in Sind by ship and from there he came to Tarnav where he informed Dev Raj the headman about his arrival, but he could not entertain him properly as there was drought and scarcity. Without anything to eat, the saint left the place early that night and reached Khattu before midnight. Bibi Mubarak, wife of Amir Shihabuddin Dumka, the Muqta of the place chanced to see him passing through the lane and asked her servant Bahadur to look for him at Babu Ishaq's grave. The latter unwilling to believe that the saint had come went but could not spot Shaikh Ahmad who had lain flat on the ground by Babu's grave. She sent another person who could see him when Shaikh Ahmad heaved a deep cold sigh and moved a little. The Muqta and his neighbours came and met him. The whole town was happy to have him lack in their midst.

The time of this journey of the Shaikh is difficult to fix or specify. The Calcutta manuscript of the *Mirqat* gives 803 H./1400-01 A.D. as the year of his arrival in Makka, which is definitely not correct as he had performed the pilgrimage before Timur's invasion. The saint had accompanied Timur after his sack of Delhi in January 1399 or so and had left Samarqand on 12 Jumada I 802/10 January 1400 A.D. and returned to India via Balkh-Herat-Qandahar-Uch-Malik Wahan-Jaisalmer. It would have been impossible for him to again leave and reach Makka via Gujarat, Aden, in 803 H. Also, Rasti Khan during whose regime Shaikh Ahmad had passed through Khambhat on way to the Holy places was killed in 794 H./1395 A.D.[95] Moreover, Shaikh Ahmad had arrived in Gujarat again, from Khattu, to finally settle down at Sarkhej, towards the close of 802 H. or July 1400 A.D. Maulana Abu Zafar Nadvi is nearest to the truth to place the saint's pilgrimage in the beginning of 779H; during the governorship of Rasti Khan of Gujarat.[96]

Shaikh Ahmad was on one of his visits to Delhi from Khattu when Timur invaded India in 801 H. (1398 A.D.). According to the *Tuhfatul-Majalis*, he had premonition of this catastrophe and had advised one of his disciples, Shaikh Sadruddin,[97] popularly called Shaikh Saddo, of Meerut, to leave and migrate towards Jaunpur.[98] When the latter told him also to migrate, the saint said he would like to be with the people of Delhi in their calamity. According to the *Mirqat*, Timur's men swept on Delhi, plundered it, dug up houses for hidden silver and gold money and took people captive.[99] Shaikh Ahmad came out of Khan Jahan's mosque and wanted to go to Timur and enjoin upon him the Quranic injunction of "Do good" (*Amr bil-Maruf*). Khwaja Kamaluddin son of Sayyid Rasuldar came and wanted to hand over to him his purse containing jewels for safe-keeping, but he declined, saying Dervishes did not keep such things with them. Evidently, on the saint's suggestion, he hid it in the water drain of the mosque. So did Miskin, the saint's servant, who put fifty fadyas he had with him under the staircase of the mosque. Then he went to the place where Timur was and asked for "that accursed tyrant". Some one there restrained him saying that Timur will reply his querry with sword. In the meantime ministers of Timur, Alauddin Simnani, Abdul-Malik and others calmed him down and respectfully asked him to take a seat and sent some one inside to inform Timur. He returned saying that the Mughal king was sleeping. These people made the saint wait in a separate tent. Taking advantage of this opportunity, Khwaja Kamaluddin who had accompanied the saint, got escort from them to take out their belongings. It was also suggested to the saint that he should also accompany them so that no one else could raise any objection. Shaikh Ahmad also agreed, as he wanted to get Delhi prisoners freed. By the time they returned after recovering the things and money from Khan Jahan's mosque, Timur had left. The saint was instrumental in the recovery of the looted property of Delhi residents and release of men made prisoners by them. They released whomever Shaikh Ahmad pointed out and returned his belongings. The saint was lodged by a Mughal, Amir Husain by name, as his guest, in his tent, throughout his journey to Samarqand to get other prisoners released.[100] He thus got released Maulana Muhammad Thanesari in Samarqand, whom he described to his Mughal captor as a more learned man than himself. The saint was highly respected by prince Sultan Muhammad and other Mughal amirs like Ilyas Khwaja the minister, Malik Saiful Muk also a minister, Malik Ainak, etc., who were helpful to him in some way or the other in his successful mission in Samarqand and his return journey.

The *Mirqat* devotes considerable space to the activities of Shaikh Ahmad in Samarqand where he met a number of learned men and holy persons including Khwaja Abdul-Awwal, grandson of the author of the well-known book on Jurisprudence, *Hidaya,* who was an authority on Fatva (religious decrees), his nephew Malikul-Ulama (prince of learned men) Shaikh Husamud-Din and Maulana Abu Said and had discussions with them and other learned men of Samarqand from time to time in meetings or dinner parties hosted by Amir Husain, Amir Ainak and others. He was, in his turn, highly impressed by the eloquent Friday sermon recited in a highly pleasing voice by the Khatib of the Jami mosque of Samarqand.

The saint had highly impressed the princes and the public as well as learned men and holy men of Samarqand with his piety, learning, memory, acumen and intellect. The *Mirqat* records a number of such meetings including one in which Timur's grandson prince Sultan Muhammad had invited, around a round table, all leading learned men of Samarqand for discussion with Shaikh Ahmad. After the discussions, Shaikh Abdul Avval stated that it was a malter of regret that all the learned men of Samarqand were helpless before a Dehlavi. The saint's discussions and encounters with them had become a talk of the town and students and other academic circles echoed with their deliberations. He would get invited to lunch and dinner parties in one of which the famous author and scholar Sayyid Sharif Jurjani is also stated to have been present and there was discussion on a statement made in the famous book *Mirsadul-Ibad* of Khwaja Najmuddin Daya. Such parties some times ended with musical programme like rebeck-playing and were also marked by flashes of wit and humour on the part of Shaikh Ahmad.

Surprisingly, the *Mirqat* is rather some what reticent in describing the very purpose for which the saint had gone to Samarqand, namely to enjoin *Amr bil-Maruf* upon Timur. He dismisses the saint's meeting with the Mughal despot, abruptly ending it after just mentioning their preliminary handshaking and embracing by simply stating that Timur had to leave the meeting suddenly to march to Tabriz straight away from the meeting place, on being informed of Malik Yusuf Qara having seized the province of Tabriz after killing its governor.[101] Saint wanted to follow Timur but was dissuaded by Shaikh Abdul-Avval who pleaded that the time was not opportune. However, the saint seems to have been airing his views publicity about Timur's invasion not having the sanction of religion. This was reported to prince Sultan Muhammad who convened a Mahzar-meeting of the savants of Samarqand and Shaikh Ahmad. Many people including Ilyas Khwaja were apprehensive lest some harm might accrue to Shaikh Ahmad, whom he requested to be restrained and keep quiet. However, at the meeting, after some preliminaries, one of them asked the saint to put forth his views. The latter posed a question to him saying, "Whatever Timur did to the people of Delhi, was it lawful or unlawful" and put him in a quandary. For, if he said unlawful, that would land him in trouble with Timur and if he said lawful, he would undergo risk of being an infidel for supporting an action not allowed by religious law (*Shara*) (of attacking a Muslim king). Malikul-Ulama, the chief spokesman of the local savants asked that man to leave. Then a Baqqal (Hindu Grocer) of Delhi who had got converted to Islam was produced in order that he might bear witness to the fact that in Delhi the sale of wine and committing adultery were rampant and openly done. The saint told him in Hindi, "Have you come here to put to disgrace the place of your forefathers ? That is not loyalty to one's salt". That person left without attesting anything.

In the meantime, prince Sultan Muhammad himself came. He was briefed by Malikul-Ulama and Ilyas Khwaja. Shaikh Ahmad then said something to Shaikh Bakr whom the prince greatly respected. The prince asked as to what did he say. Shaikh Ahmad turned to him and expressed his desire to leave for Hijaz. The prince said it was the snowing season. On consulting an alamanac, it was found that there was about too weeks time for snowfall to start. The prince having acceeded to his request, gave a written permit for the journey of which the *Mirqat* quotes the text. According to the local custom, *futuhs* and gifts were showered upon the saint on the eve of his departure from Samarqand for India (where he decided to return and not to Hijaz). In Samarqand, Shaikh Ahmad had lodged with a pious and devout lady, whose daughter, Murad-bar-avar by name, who attended to his needs, was reprimanded by her mother for asking the saint as to why the people of India were of dark complexion.

Finally, Shaikh Ahmad left Samarqand on 12 Jumada I 802 H. (10 January 1400 A.D.) and had an eventful journey through Balkh, Herat and Qandahar and many villages in between. The landowner of Balkh defying the prince's permit order did not allow the saint to cross the river. There was a dispute between the landowner and the local people about the irrigation of fields from the pond of the former. Shaikh Ahmad being asked to act as an arbitrator gave verdict against him which made him all the more angry. Ultimately, the saint crossed the river from another place outside his jurisdiction. After crossing the river, he came to a village where not finding any place to stay, he passed the night under a wall. Proceeding further, he came to a village where there was a dervish following the creed of Changiz Khan. Then he came to the village where he met Khwaja Mahmud Chishti, from whom his son-in-law was estranged. Shaikh Ahmad brought about truce between them. From there he came to Herat where he met the saintly Shaikh Shihabuddin Jilwani and passed some time in his company. In Herat, Malik Agha wife of Timur's son Shah Rukh, coming to know of his arrival, came and met the saint. She related to him the accounts of forty-four saintly families (*Khanwada*) of Mashaikh (saints). Malik Agha suggested to him that if he decided to stay on, she would build a Madrasa and hospice for him. On his decision to leave Herat, she gave him money which he distributed among people. She then sent some amount by way of journey expense money. In Herat, he had paid visit, at the suggestion of Malik Agha, to the tomb of Imam Fakhruddin Razi.

From Herat, he came to Qandahar. Amir Saiful, Muqta of Qandahar, wanted to present him with a garden, 1000 by 1000 yards situated at the hamlet named Balandi nearby but he declined of the offer. From Qandahar he came to Uchch, where he put up in the Burj-i-mamun. Next day, at forenoon Sayyidus-Sadat Sayyid Raju Bukhari brother and spiritual successor of Makhdum Jahaniyan Sayyid Jalal came to pay a visit and presented him eighteen tankas as "fodder money". From Uchch he came to Malikwahan village where he was put up in the house of a musician. The saint had some misgiving about staying there ,but found it to be a fine spacious place where an old lady was the care-taker. She looked after him very well. He was too tired and slept early after performing short Isha prayers.

From Malikwahan, he got the company of a camel-driver who was bound for Jaisalmer. However, in the course of the travel, the saint's horse being tired, he would lag behind and the camel driver would wait for him. But as he was short of time, he excused himself and told the saint that Jaisalmer was only a day's journey from that place. After passing through a village which had little water due to drought, he ultimately reached Jaisalmer, the Headman of which, Rai Kehar (Kesar), who had been already informed by the camel-driver lodged the saint with him and invited Brahmins to meet him. The Brahmins asked him to put them questions on any subject. Shaikh Ahmad modestly replied that he was not so well-versed in their religious lore except their belief in re-incarnation and heaven and hell. The Brahmins were highly impressed by the saint's talk and arguments and went to three *kroh* to bid him farewell when he left Jaisalmer.

The narrative abruptly ends here, immediately followed by a new chapter on the saint's arrival to Gujarat from Central Asia, which also starts abruptly with his arrival at Nahrwala. It is difficult to ascertain if the saint came directly from Jaisalmer to Gujarat without going to Khattu. But looking to the short period between his departure from Samarqand and arrival in Gujarat — a period of about six months as seen above, it is almost certain that even if he went to Khattu to visit the tomb of Babu Ishaq, he did not stay there and left for Gujarat, en route to Deccan, as we are told a little later.

During this entire journey, Shaikh Ahmad had discussions with learned men, saints, Jogis, Brahmins etc. on a variety of subjects. On way to and at Samarqand, the topics which figured frequently in these meetings were Quran, Tafsir, Hadis, Ruh, Ruyat, Destiny and Providence, problems of jurisprudence, logic, admissibility or otherwise of certain postures or actions, social problems, dress (about saint's putting on black turban in Samarqand), etc. In course of these discussions, standard books like *Bazdavi*, *Tawali*, *Risala-*

i-Rahiq, *at-Tarif*, *Kanz*, *Masabih*, *Mirsadul-Ibad*, *Zhakhira*, *Husami*, etc. were profusely quoted and consulted.

(A) Saints's Arrival in Gujarat

In Rajab 802 H. (27 February - 27 March 1400 A.D.), the saint arrived at Burli (or Parli) in the vicinity of Nahrwala (Patan) during the time of Zafar Khan later on Muzaffar Shah I of Gujarat.[102] Then he came to Nahrwala. Ayyub Qawwal who met him, went to Sayyid Muhammad Gesudaraz's lodging and told Maulana Khanu Muhtasib about his arrival. The latter informed the Sayyid who asked if the information was authentic and was told it was. Next day, he left for Khambhat.[103] Shaikh Ahmad stayed for a couple of days at Patan in the house of a Muslim who later on used to visit him every year after he settled down at Sarkhej and received favours from him. Then he decided to go to Deccan. The reason for his preference for Deccan to Gujarat is not known. He came to Dholka where he fixed up a cart to take him to Khambhat. When he was about to leave, the cartman said he was going to Asawal and not to Khambhat. At that very time, there came another cartman bound for Khambhat and he got on it. Qazi Muin son of Qazi Fakhruddin of Khattu was also travelling by the same cart; his cousins were employed in government service there. They probably did not invite the saint to stay with them, but another compatriot, Sayyid Karamullah son of Rahmatullah of Nagor provided him with lodging. After a day or so, Qazi Nizamuddin uncle of Qazi Muin, with his sons paid a visit and complained about his not having put up with them. The saint felt embarrassed. On Friday, the Qazi came with his kinsmen and relatives to escort the saint to the Jami mosque as they did not want him to go alone when other saints like Sayyid Muhammad Gesudaraz and Shaikh Ruknuddin Chishti would go there with pomp and grandeur, accompanied by their disciples and admirers. He had also brought a good mount for him.

From Khambhat, he went to a place on the Narmada — a ferry — to cross over to the Deccan. Zafar Khan was then engaged in suppressing the disturbances caused by the headman of Nadot. The boatmen declined to carry him telling him that Zafar Khan having come to know of the saint's desire to go to Deccan had prohibited them to let him pass. At the same time, Zafar Khan despatched Malik Burhanul-Mulk Tatarkhani to him to escort him to his army-camp at Ratanpur,[104] and bless him for success in his expedition. He sent a message saying, "Had I not been tied up here for setting right this disorder, I would have personally come to pay my respects to you". The saint making allowances for the acquaintance with Zafar Khan who used to visit Babu and him at Delhi, complied with his request and was lodged in a red tent set up near that of Zafar Khan. The latter's son Muhammad Tatar Khan (later on Muhammad Shah I) sent a word expressing his desire to come and pay his respect, but the saint politely turned it down asking him to come along with his father.

When Zafar Khan met him, the saint asked him why he did not pay heed to the Delhi Sultan's request for help, at the time of Timur's invasion despite his having so many elephants? Zafar Khan explained his helplessness in the matter at some length. Then he arranged for necessary perquisites and rich food to be supplied to him every day. Then he sent through Muhammad Tatar Khan and his brothers a *buqcha* of clothes, one made of wool and scarlet and another of *bhiram* and *salu* (types of fine coloured cloth). Also at the suggestion of Muhammad Tatar Khan, Zafar Khan granted the village Uteliya (in Dholka Taluka) with fertile land, good yield and less tax for the kitchen-expenses of the saint. This village was in the lease-hold (*wajh*) of one lady Bubu Badi for 2,000 tankas. She was given another village in lieu thereof. Then Zafar Khan wrote to his son-in-law and deputy-in-absence Malik Badr Ala to arrange for a good house at a place wherever the saint wanted to settle down. The latter preferred a place in Sarkhej on the bank of the river. Malik Badr Ala handed over to the saint a big and spacious house belonging to one Bada Bohra. The latter's wife came to the saint and said, "Why should you who are *mashaikh* (saintly men) occupy the house of the poor people ?" The saint however convinced her that it was in her interest and also a temporary arrangement, as he would arrange for another house. Afterwards, he constructed another house adjacent to it after paying for the land to its owners.

The village yield was very good in the first year, as its entire land was not without a good wheat-crop. Next year, the contract was given to the village Headman named Satsal. Adhran Tak, Muqta of Dholka, informed Zafar Khan about it. But Satsal defaulted in payment even though the yield was much. The Khan ordered Adhran to pay the village revenue from the treasury and take possession of the village. In the third here Adhran effected a cut of 600 tankas in the saint's share. The saint sent Khwaja Badh, headman of Sarkhej village, to Zafar Khan, who just asked him if the saint was well but did not ask him the reason for his coming. After waiting for quite some time in the camp, the headman returned without accomplishing his mission. The saint purchased two horses. Some one reported to Zafar Khan that the saint had purchased two horses with the intention of going away to Deccan. He asked Adhran about the situation in respect of the village. When he was told about the cut, the Khan took him to task for displeasing the saint and sent his Chamberlain Khwaja Khassa to take 500 tankas from the treasury and beseach the saint not to leave him as long as he was alive. Khwaja Khassa came and told the saint that he should give an account of 100,000 tankas which he might have received from the Khan before he left. The saint said he would render account of 200,000 tankas but he would not stay. Thereupon Khwaja Khassa conveyed the request of Zafar Khan not to leave him as long as he was alive. This calmed down the saint. Khwaja Khassa delivered 500 tankas and also had a parvana of 3,000 tankas as the revenue of the village made and delivered.

Within a short time after this, Tatar Khan getting an opportunity apprehended his father and set him to Broach. After ascending the throne, he came to visit the saint. The latter who was not happy with this development, asked him as to what did he do to "that Shaikh of strangers" i.e. Zafar Khan. He replied that he was in Broach. The saint dismissed him soon. When Zafar Khan assumed kingship under the royal name Muzaffar Shah, there was disturbance raised by the accursed ones, that is to say, the petty Hindu chiefs compelling the people from Asawal, Sarkhej and other places to migrate to coastal towns.[105] The saint also first sent away his servants and attendants to Mahaim (Mahim) and then himself went there and returned after a day. Muzaffar Shah I would not believe of the saint's going to Mahaim when told by his own servant Shaikh Shamsuddin but an official Malik Usman Sarkheji said that he had met the saint there. Then Muzaffar Shah learnt from a Malik who came from Asawal that he had returned and that he himself had met him at Sarkhej.

When Muzaffar Shah returned from his expedition, he came and paid his respects to the saint at Sarkhej. When he was to return he lingered a little and stood at the doorstep of the saint's abode, where Qazi Mansur, Shaikh Tajuddin and Shaikhzada Ahmad Kirmani were also present. The king sent his Chamberlain to the saint saying that thitherto, it was the practice of the saint to recommend the cases of deserving people and dervishes but this time, he did not do it and wondered why that was so. The saint recommended some people who were present there for some help.

A person was granted twenty tankas in cash and twenty bighas of land in the village Choramli. After three four days, the king again paid a visit. The said asked him the reason for such an unusual early visit. He said that he had come to that side for recreation and thought he should have the honour of paying respect to him.

(B) Death of the saint

On 1st Shawwal 849 H (31 December 1445 A.D.) when, after offering Id prayers, he returned from the Idgah, he vomited, along with food, betel-like (red) liquid. This made him worried and he abandoned food. Visitors were also turned back from without after giving them *tabarruk* present. He completely gave up food and talked little. The attendants were asked to stay at the doorstep during the night. A particular disciple who used to boast of *shaghl* (spiritual-occupation) and *tark* (renunciation) and at the time of imparting spiritual guidance, was directed to do this and to do that and had received a riding-coat (*barani*) was illusioned to believe that he had received authority from the saint to act as his successor. He spread news to that effect among the public. Some noblemen heard of it and were anxious to know the fact from the saint. The latter was highly displeased and said that he was still alive, thus repudiating the claim of that particular disciple. Malik Nizam Chhajju in the meantime came and narrated the conversation that took place in the king's presence on this point. The saint uttered the words "God forbid, God forbid", which Maulana Muhammad Qasim who was present throughout interpreted as repudiation of the claim. He also narrated to the saint a story he had read in the *Khairul-Majalis* pertaining to a similar case, as has been stated earlier (26, *supra*). In short till then, he had not named any one as his successor.

The author enumerates the persons who were personal attendants of the saint — Qazi Niku (son of) Alam[106] in Khattu; Qazi Hakim in Khan Jahan mosque in Delhi, Arif in Khurasan; at Sarkhej, Sayyid Husamuddin and Amir Haji in the beginning and thereafter Qazi Abdul-Hayy son of Qazi Mansur for twenty years who was fully familiar with the saint's temperament and highly liked by the saint, then his elder brother Qazi Abdul-Aziz for a year or two, then Baramad, who was a favourite slave, and lastly Shaikh Salahuddin who, though younger in years, performed highly commendable service, understood the saint's temperament fully well and was very loyal and faithful.[107] The saint also, in his last years, depended only on Shaikh Salahuddin so much so that if any one volunteered to help him serve the saint, he would not approve of it.

When his illness started causing worry and Sultan Muhammad son of Sultan Ahmad I came to know of it, he came to Sarkhej. The saint descended from the cot out of respect for the king and lying on a mattress on the ground talked a little. The Sultan went away crying and sent 1,000 gold tankas which the saint asked Shaikh Salahuddin to accept saying that it would come handy to him later. Those present took this as indicating the decision of the saint to appoint him as the manager of the Khanqah-Tomb of the saint, i.e. his successor. After this, Malik Imadul-Mulk (Malik Shaban) and Khwaja Chhajju paraded Talib, Shaikh Salahuddin, Abdullah Junior and Khizr before the ailing Saint to find out from him if these were to be attendants at the saintly hospice or were to be taken into government service. He made a sign with his hand indicating that Shaikh Salahuddin should be left with (i.e. to attend upon) him, while the others were free to choose their vocation. Sultan Muhammad submitted that as he had by God's grace lived a full life enjoying that of kingship also, he had no desire to live and the saint should take him also with him to heaven. The saint put his fingers on his eyes, a gesture of acceptance. After the Sultan left, Talib produced the saint's written instruction (*parvana*) to the effect that when his appointed time came, Mullan i.e. Maulana Muhammad Qasim, author of the *Mirqat*, should recite the *Kalima* (second creed) without fail.

In the night of 14th Shawwal, he fell into a long swoon. After retaining senses, he got up and again lay down. This happened two or three times. When he was seen to be in swoon for some time, those present asked Maulana Muhammad Qasim to recite the *Kalima* as desired by the master, as they thought the end had come. However, Maulana Muhammad Qasim who had seen the saint in such long trances in deep meditation, did not brace himself up to recite the *Kalima* and kept quiet. Thereupon, another person recited loudly the *Kalima*.[108] The saint opened his eyes and said "Who is this person who has recited the *Kalima*? Send him out."

After morning prayers, Malik-Raziul Mulk arrived. The saint got up, sat for a while and had the turban tied round the head of Shaikh Salahuddin, beckoning him and praying for him. Then he, some boys and Shiraz the slave were initiated as disciples. Then Malik Umdatul-Mulk [109] and Qadir Khan came. There were signalled to be seated. Then he took heavy breaths, his lower lip moved a little and then all was over. *For Allah we are and to Him we return.*

The author of the *Mirqat* says that he bathed the saint's body, with Qazi Badh pouring water. Then the body was carried on a palanquin to the tomb. At that time Sultan Muhammad arrived. Maulana Muhammad Qasim requested him to lead the funeral prayers in accordance with the custom of its being a royal prerogative. The Sultan told him that he had been the leader of his prayers through out his life time (at Sarkhej) and therefore he better led it. Maulana Muhammad Qasim led the prayers and then he and Qazi Badh entered the grave, at the head and foot side respectively and laid him to rest on Thursday 14th Shawwal 849 H. (13 January 1446 A.D.). [110]

Shaikh Mahmud Iraji in his last Majlis precedes this account of the saint's illness and demise with a rather detailed notice of the circumstances under which Shaikh Salahuddin son of Tukajiv was brought to the saint. This is no doubt new information but the account recalls to mind the circumstances under which Shaikh Ahmad himself had come to Babu Ishaq. Therefore while the kernel of the story might be true, the details might be the result of Shaikh Iraji's attempt to make it more romantic. According to him, Shaikh Salahuddin was brought to the saint when he was only one year old and he was twenty-five years old at the time of the saint's death. That would mean that this happened in 824 H. in the time of Sultan Ahmad I and not of Sultan Muhammad II as stated in the *Tuhfatul-Majalis*, as also pointed out by Maulana Sayyid Abu Zafar Nadvi (*TMU*, 125 n.1). This also endorses the view expressed earlier (*supra*, 44ff), while discussing the importances of *Mirqat* and *Tuhfatul Majalis*.

(C) Personality

The saint's personality is very well reflected in the pages of the *Mirqat*. He emerges from its narratives as a man endowed with a kind and compassionate nature and affable manners. He had a catholic outlook and his humanitarian behaviour was extended to all, irrespective of status or position, creed or caste. He was responsive to the need of the poor and the indigent and the entire income of the saintly establishment at Sarkhej comprising the yield of the prosperous village endowed for it and the sizeable *futuh* received by him from a large number of admirers who included kings, princes, maliks, merchants, etc. was spent, besides meeting the maintenance and running expenses, to help the poor and the deserving in various ways. No one who came to him for help returned empty-handed. He had also made it a point to send aid in cash and kind to deserving families of Sayyids, widows, etc. at their homes. Some needy women from noble families would come to the saint's hospice under cover of darkness of night for help, but of such of those who could not come out of their houses, widows and the like, he had asked the Sarkhej village headman to prepare a list; as per this list, he would give to him for handing over to them gold and silver, dresses and *doshalas,* etc., presumably for the marriages of their grown up daughters. Once near Jaisalmer in Rajasthan, on his return journey from Samarqand, he met an old man in dire need of a meal; not having any cash with him, he tore his turban into two and gave one half of it to him to enable him to procure a meal or two by selling it. Once he gave to a blind man who had come to him at Sarkhej four *jitals*; when he left, somebody told the saint that he was blind and he deserved more, whereupon the saint immediately gave more money to the compiler of the *Mirqat* asking him to find him and give it to him without telling him who had sent it or disclosing his own identity. Once the saint had gone out for a stroll outside Khattu. He found a Jogi lying restless in the jungle. Going near him, he found that on account of thread-worm, his leg had swollen and he was unable to speak. He indicated by a motion of hands that he was thirsty and wanted water. The saint had a well located and spun some jute-grass into a rope but there was no bucket. He tied pieces of cloth on that rope and sent it down to the bottom to be drenched and drew it and squeezing it a few times gave him water to drink. Then when the Jogi came to his senses and got some strength, the saint brought him to his house and had him treated. When he recovered, he was much grateful and wanted to teach the saint the art of alchemy and demonstrated it also by using a particular herb. The saint declined, saying why should those who were provided with all bounties by God, take the trouble of resorting to the laborious process of turning metal into gold. Incidentally, on inquiry, the author of the *Mirqat* was told that the saint knew what that herb was. Also, some interested people carried tale to Sultan Ahmad that the saint knew the art of alchemy.

The saint was large-hearted and very generous. The *Mirqat* narrates quite a few incidents of his magnanimity and liberality. It would suffice to cite only one instance of his generosity of younger days. Once he had gone to Delhi alone in the time of Firuz Tughluq and he along with others had audience with the king. By his examplary manners and replies, the king was much impressed and wanted him to give him money. He declined to receive any money but on being advised by Khan Jahan that his refusal would anger the king, he said there was a tank in Khattu which required desilting and he would like help in this regard. The money, 2,000 tankas, given by the king was spent in getting the tank cleared. The *Mirqat* describes this in details, showing highmindedness and liberality of the saint. Once during the saint's stay in Khan Jahan's mosque, a quarrelsome person started rudely talking to him. In the meantime, a person came and offered some money to the saint who gave it to that man. At the Sarkhej establishment, every or every alternate month, whatever surplus would be there, would be given away to the poor, the needy, the sadat, the jogis, the wayfarers, the neighbours, the kolis and the like. Each one of them received some cash or cloth or like items. The saint, as was wont with others of his fraternity, would as far as possible return the offerings made to him by matching gifts or presents of equal or more value, particularly in the case of such people as officials or maliks who had become rich recently (*qaribul-ahd,* neo-rich in modern parlance).

The saint's compassion was not confined to human beings only; it extended to birds and animals also. The *Mirqat* has it that sparrows used to come and perch on his head or knees and he would not mind it. Like the *Chiriya chirye ki Kahani* in Maulana Azad's renowned work *Ghubar-i-Khatir*, he had given standing instructions to the servants, that they should see that the young ones of the sparrows were not harmed by the crows. He himself would keep a rod in front of him and frighten away the crows with it as and when necessary. Once he saw a kite lying wounded; he brought it home, lodged it under a basket and arranged for providing it with its daily requirement of meat until it was strong enough to fly away. Once a person came to him with a pelican whose feathers he had pulled out. The saint took it from him after paying its price, kept it in guest-room and arranged with a fisherman to supply its daily quota of fish till it grew its wings and then it was released in the jungle. As and when a huntsman would catch some animal, the saint would pay him for its release.

On another occasion, when, a visiting soldier who had come to Sarkhej with his dog, left it behind as it would not go back with the master. That dog would regularly come and set up a watch at the saint's threshold. When the saint came to know about it, he assigned daily ration for it and asked a woman to supply a loaf daily for it. The dog would act as an escort to the daily visitors of the Khanqah like Qazi Mansur and Accountant (*Muhtasib*) Ibrahim, when they returned home after Isha prayer. Subsequently, when the accountant was going to the saint's village Uteliya, he was asked to take it with him there. At the village, it would act as a watch dog for the herd of animals and cows at home as well as in the grazing-ground. It is also related that once an admirer made an offering of a fat cow to the saint in the month of Sacrifice for sacrifice. The saint gave it to one Tajuddin to use it for milk and like requirements. Instead, the latter sold it to a butcher from whose custody it broke loose and came bellowing to the Khanqah. The commotion attracted the saint's attention. In the meantime, that butcher came running after it, to take it away. When he explained the situation to the saint, the latter paid the butcher from his pocket and set it loose in the animal-herd. Once he saw a dove grazing in the courtyard of the Jamaatkhana of the hospice. He told the attendants to put grain there daily. That dove and other doves then would come daily and have their feed. He was so tender-hearted that the *Mirqat* mentions, he would not perform the rite of Sacrifice with his own hands or even see it done, as a result of which he used to discharge this obligatory duty by paying the animal's price in cash, for which he had found legal justification. In the last three four years of his life, the ceremony of Sacrifice was observed through Maulana Muhammad Qasim the compiler of the *Mirqat*.

The saint was a man of great patience, forbearance and humility. He was always courteous to his visitors and restrained in his behaviour even towards those who would be unreasonable in their talk or rude. He would tolerate them and would even reward them. For example, once an obstinate presumptuous learned man entered into wrong arguments with the saint in the Khan Jahan's mosque of Delhi over the phrase (الشیخ یحیٰ و یمیت). "The Shaikh i.e. the spiritual guide brings to life and causes death". In the meantime, a visitor came and offered four 25-kani coins to the saint who gave it to that man. Then another visitor brought a loaf (*kak*) which also the saint asked him to keep aside. That man said "From where this hungry Shaikh has come (that he does not spare the loaf"). At the time of *iftar*, he invited him to join him and asked him to eat slowly. He again repeated his taunt about the hungry Shaikh. When he was leauing, he asked the saint what to do with the four 25-kanis. The saint told him, "What do we know? You do what you know with it. "He repented of his obnoxious behaviour and remarks. The saint had likewise paid some money as tip-safe-keeping of luggage money to the shipman at Aden who had taken both the fare money and the saint's luggage with the promise that he would keep the ship ready for sail in the morning. But that dishonest fellow did not turn up and the saint somehow traced him but he flatly refused about the hiring of the ship. The saint recovered his luggage from his house and money from his body where he had concealed it. The saint paid him a few dirhams saying, "This is for your keeping my luggage in safe custody for the night."

When the headman of the saint's village Uteliya and the Muqta of Dholka were defaulting in payment of the proceeds of the village to the saint and were playing truant, not caring for his men who were sent to collect money, his influential disciples like some amirs told the saint that they would punish the defaulters if the saint just asked them. But he would not consent. Sultan Ahmad coming to know of this ordered Malik Jalalshah to proceed and punish them. The saint coming to know of this immediately sent the author of the *Mirqat* to Malik Jalalshah with a message to desist from avoidable bloodshed."

He was responsible to good advice and did not take offence if he was told of some lapse on his part. He would be introspective whenever he tendered advice to anybody. He would address his soul on such occasions and recite a Hindi hemistich, the text of which cannot be correctly deciphered, but which meant to this effect that " you are doing the same thing but are advising others not to do it."

Despite his greatness as a Saint and the respect he commanded of as many as seven Tughluq and Gujarat kings, Shaikh Ahmad was humility itself. Nowhere in his memoirs he appears to lose his temper even in unfavourable circumstances and adverse conditions. Once a grandson of Maulana Kamaluddin Samani who was serving in the army of Sultan Muhammad bin Firuz Tughluq, came to see him and was discussing academic matters. When he was somewhat cornered, he told the saint that he was grandson of Maulana Kamaluddin Samani, whereupon the saint told him "O man of God ! Why did you not tell this to me before ? There is no use my arguing with you, who are an ocean of learning and your family is the mine of knowledge". On another occasion, when at Samarqand he came across Maulana Mahmud Thanesari, who was taken captive by Timur's soldiers, he not only got him released as he had many more, but when at that time a bowl of broth was offered to him by a servant of Amir Pir Muhammad, the saint asked him to give it to the Maulana saying, " He deserves it more, since in learning he is far above me". Despite the influence which he wielded with Sultan Muzzaffar I of Gujarat, the saint not only felt unoffended but gracefully listened to the advice, the king once gave him. When the latter came to pay his usual visit, the saint interceded on behalf of an official who was ordered to be imprisoned by the sultan. The sultan explained the case and spoke of the person's treachery but he promised the saint that he would release him on his return to the capital in deference to his wish. But he told the saint that he would also like him to listen to a piece of his advice, namely that a man should not be left unpunished and one should not be complacent about him, for, a man is a man of moods. The saint used to recall this advice whenever somebody did something that he did not like.

The saint's narrative also reveals one more facet of his character and that is his tact, circumspection and practical approach. Once Alp Khan the ruler of Malwa, sent by way of offering 40 gold and 49 silver tankas with a merchant named Buhlul, but the saint declined the offer on the ground made known to the emissary, that its acceptance might annoy the Gujarat's king Sultan Ahmad which he would loathe to do, as he was residing in his dominions. Likewise, on another occasion, the Jam of Thatta sent through Sayyid Abu to the saint a certain amount of gold coins in fulfillment of a vow made for the recovery of his wife from illness and also requested discipleship for his two sons. The saint prayed for his wife and sons but declined to accept the money saying that since he was living in the dominions of Sultan Ahmad from three generations, with whom he had very cordial relations it would not behove him to do anything against his wish. Similarly, once when prince Tatar Khan later on Muhammad Shah I of Gujarat sent a word to the saint seeking his permission to pay a visit to him, the saint's reply was that he could come in the company of his father Zafar Khan later on Muzaffar Shah I. There were situations as for example when a Mughal in Samarqand started talking nonsense about Indians being such and such etc., when the saint, by his tact turned the tables on him. He turned the difficult situation to his advantage by asking him mildly, "O dear one ! Have you learnt only this or anything else ? If you have acquired some learning, we may talk."

Apart from these, the *Mirqat* depicts how cautious and circumspect he was in his dealings with a man in authority, particularly at the lower level like officials and headmen of the village Utiliya, endowed for his Khanqah or of those of Sarkhej where he had settled down. He would always maintain that one should be tolerant and forbearing towards petty district or village officials, even if their behaviour was not proper towards his servants or even himself, as it was not worth the consequences thereof. He once quoted the instance of Maulana Ibrahim Kaithali, a learned man and favourite of Sultan Muhammad bin Firuz Tughluq who ultimately lost his own life in addition to those of his two sons and had his holdings plundered in consequence of the cudgels he took up on behalf of his nurse's son who had picked up a quarrel with the local Muqta's servant on the question of the boundary of tilled fields. On his part, the saint always overlooked the harassment caused every now and then to his men by the local officials. He always restrained his men, and would not allow even some of the king's noblemen and maliks whc were his disciples, and coming to know of the matter, would like to take to task the concerned official, as seen above.

The saint as stated above had a sharp memory and was endowed with great intellect and perspicacity. He was learned and was also a practicing sufi. At the same time, he was human and his assemblies were not merely sessions of dry discussions or exchange of words on serious religious and sufistic topics. As a matter of fact, as the *Mirqat* shows, his meetings were marked with interesting discussions even on serious subjects and occasional flashes of wit and humour made them lively and enjoyable. He was endowed with presence of mind with which he could turn even an embarrassing situation into a pleasant one. Once a disciple had presented to the saint a fine carpet. He was thinking as to whom he should give it away. He had spread it over the old one and was sitting thereon when a learned man came. He posed a question saying what was the purpose of having one carpet above another and one prayermat over another. The saint got up, had the new carpet rolled up and gave it to him saying, "This was the purpose. "The saint's repartee to Pir Muhammad in Samarqand is another instance. In answer to a query about his age by him at a dinner, as to how old he was, the saint counter-questioned him, "How old are you?" Pir Muhammad said he did not remember whereupon the saint said, "When you do not remember your age, how can we who are caught up in such a calamity remember our age?" In Balkh when the official did not honour the permit the saint had to cross the river, the saint in order to persuade him through Amir Sulaiman the manufacturer of coats of mail for Timur, followed him to his place. When the latter asked, "Who brought you here", the saint replied, "You". In one of the assemblies with learned man in Samarqand, there was a discussion on a Hadis. All began to talk at the same time and there was great din of noise. The saint said, "Why all this commotion? Let one of you discuss it with me". A learned man said, "Abu Said Akhawi (my brother) will speak". The saint said, "Whether Ahawi or Laghavi (nonsense-talker), let him speak". When the saint put forth his view, a man who was sitting a little away said, "Listen", the saint retorted, "Speak, speak".

The author of the *Mirqat* says that such repartees took place even at the dinners where he would be joined by visitors and favourite disciples like the author. In Samarqand, when at the suggestion of his attendant Arif, the saint went to see a holy man, he found him with his fellowmen taking meals round a big deep dish. The saint and Arif joined them, but the former did not eat. They were taking big morsels. At this the saint recited this Hadis: "The justice of one movement is better than the prayers of sixty years." One of them said, "This Hadis is not relevant." They again took a big morsel. The saint said, "O brother, (do proper justice)." The holy man laughed and praised the saint for his repartee. When on resuming their meals, they found Arif taking big morsels and commented on that, the saint said, "In one morsel, he eats his own share as also his master's share." All enjoyed this repartee also.

Shaikh Ahmad possessed a poetic bent of mind like Babu. He had a large number of Persian and Hindi verses at heart, which he would frequently recite or quote on appropriate occasions, in the assemblies and would illustrate and make his point quoting Arabic and Persian verses. Some verses and rubais he repeated very often in private, in particular those dealing with *Tauhid* (oneness of God). In Chapter 8 of the *Mirqat*, many such verses are quoted. His assemblies were attended by poets who recited poems in his praise which he generally discouraged. He himself used to compose verses in Arabic, Persian as well as Hindi, though he did not like himself to be called a poet. The *Mirqat* quotes quite a few Hindi dohas and Persian verses recited by him from time to time. It also quotes a few Arabic and Persian verses and Hindi dohas composed by him.[111] An incident of the royal assembly, narrated by the saint, apart from giving a glimpse, into the literary pursuits of Sultan Muhammad son of Firuz Tughluq himself, indicates the saint's poetical acumen and insight. Once, the sultan had composed a Persian verse, which he gave to the court-poets to compose ghazals by way of *Tazmin*. None of the poems submitted by them could come up to the Sultan's liking. Somebody brought to the saint's notice the couplet in question as well as the poems of the poets incorporating the couplet. A perusal of these made it clear to him that the poets were unable to incorporate the couplet befittingly, as they had given preference and priority to the Sultan's couplet in their poems, while in fact the couplet should have been relegated to the end in a befitting context. The saint himself composed a ghazal on this line which was duly appreciated by the king. Likewise, the saint was a good connoisseur of poetic compositions, Once, Sayyid Muhammad son of Rukn Dehlavi, the teacher of the compiler the *Mirqat* and grandson of Sayyid Kamaluddin Rasuldar, recited the following quatrain :

گر جفا کار از جفا بدراندم از ستیغش پوست   من نه با او آن کنم کین فعل من و آن فعل اوست
من مکافات جفا با او کنم چندان وفا   کو خجل گردد بگوید کاین نکو کردن نکوست

The saint liked the poem. Then after thinking over it for a while, he said that the height of toleration is only perfectly illustrated if the word *khijil* is not used, Sayyid Mahmud immediately changed the hemistich to کو بجان و دل بگوید کاین نکو کردن نکوست The saint praised him. The Sayyid said, he had recited that quatrain in the assemblies of poets and learned men, but none had pointed this out.

Shaikh Ahmad was fond of music from his very childhood. He liked to hear melodious songs and music and himself possessed a melodious voice. Once in his young days on a summer afternoon, he was sitting enjoying the coolness on the bank of a step-well when a woman who came to fetch water sang the *sohaila.*[112] He was so enthralled and carried away by the song that falling in a trance, he fell into water. He was pulled out by that woman. Likewise, whenever at Khattu, he heard any one singing a song or a ghazal at the door of Babu Ishaq, he would come out and listen. Once Babu had taken him with him to Didvana where he had put up in the Burhani mosque. He was enthralled by the melodious voice of a person singing outside the mosque. When he praised the singer for his fine voice, the saint told the author of the *Mirqat*, Babu mildly reprimanded him for his exaggerated love for music. Sama musical assemblies were a popular pastime. The saint also refers to the music sessions held at dinner parties. Musicians occasionally attended his assemblies. Minstrels accompanied by instrument (*mazamir*) performed at the gate of his Sarkhej hospice, which was, as the saint relates in one of his discourses, one of the two points, about the permissibility of which a learned and pious man Malik Ibrahim Kaith- ali, a candidate for the saint's discipleship wanted to be satisfied before enrollment. However, he had given up listening to music in his last years.

Notes

80. Abul-Fazl, *op. cit*; give the date of his birth as 738 A.H. 1337-38 A.D.
81. Hajji Dabir, *Zafarul–Walih-bi-Muzaffer wa-Alih*, ed. E. Denison Ross, Vol. I (London 1910), 1.
82. Text, 6.
83. Prof. Nizami *op.cit* who has based his account on the *Tuhfatul–Majalis* (which also mentions his getting lost in the dust-storm and reaching Didvana) states that Babu Ishaq found him in a village and took him under his protection. This is not correct.
84. Dr. Desai, *op. cit.*, p.18 translates this as "pair of clay-shoe-mould" which does not appear to be correct. F.Sterigass, *Persian–English Dictionary*, gives the above meaning of *nal*.
85. Prof. Nizami's surmise that Shaikh Ahmad seems to have received his education at the feet of eminent teachers of Delhi at a time which were the days of Muhammad bin Tughluq (*op. cit.*, 240-41) is far from correct. Shaikh Ahmad's prolonged stay in Delhi was after the death of the Babu in 781H. / 1379 A.D. He had visited Delhi in that monarch's time only a couple of times at the most for a few days only.
86. Maulana Sayyid Abu Zafar Nadvi (*SA*, 25) and Prof. Nizami (*op.cit.*, 242) give the year 776H (1375 A.D.) as Babu Ishaq's date of death. This is not correct, as Babu who was born in 660 H. had died at an age of 120 years. The saint in his *Risala-i-Ahmadiya* (unnumbered modern copy Hazrat Pir Muhammad Shah Library and Research Centre, 46) gives H.781 as the year of Babu's death.
87. Maulana Sayyid Abu Zafar Nadvi takes this place-name literally to mean the "citadel of Firuz Shah" in Delhi (*SA*, 114, n.1), which is inaccurate. This Hisar-i-Firuza is about 150 kilometers west north–west of Delhi. It was founded by Firuz Tughluq and was so called to distinguish it from Hisar-i-Shadman in Transoxiana.
88. This word is also found written in other works like *Akhbarul-Akhya*r in another context as *Kushk-i-narwar*, which also is meaningless. The correct word as suggested by Dr. Z. A. Desai *op. cit* may be *Kushk-i-Firuz* (verbal information).
89. Prof. Nizami's article does not cover this aspect of Shaikh Ahmad's life because his main source of information, the *Tuhfatul-Majalis,* contains pretty little information in this regard. He was misled by stray reference or two in that work to think that Shaikh Ahmad studied and performed many rigorous practices under the instruction of his spiritual master in the Masjid-i-Khan Jahan (*op. cit.*, 241). As a matter of fact, as stated above, this happened after the death of the Babu. Also, the rigorous practices referred to by Prof. Nizami took place in Khattu immediately after Babu Ishaq's death and not in Delhi.
90. Text, 57, 153, etc.

91. Text, 66.
92. Prof. Nizami, misled again by the scanty random information of Shaikh Mahmud Iraji, states that "after the death of Babu Ishaq, Shaikh Ahmad starved for many days" and "the inmates of the Khanqah who did not want him to stay there neglected him against all expectations" (*op. cit.*, 243). This is to say the least misleading, As a matter of fact, there were many persons in Khattu including Sadat and learned men, Babu Ishaq's disciples and admirers, who had, according to *Mirqat*, repeatedly offered and even sent, unsolicited by him, meals to him, which he mostly declined as will be clear from the following lines. Secondly, there was no Khanqah as such in Babu Ishaq's time. Shaikh Ahmad maintained a Khanqah only after he settled down in Gujarat at Sarkhej.
93. Here there is a subtle pun on words *murid* (nomination case) and *mal* having a philological connection with *Murad* (objective case) (his name) and *malam* also meaning a head ship-man.
94. The *Mirqat* skips all details about Hajj rites, etc. Obviously the saint had not considered it necessary to narrate these to Maulana Muhammad Qasim.
95. Sikandar, *Mirat-i-Sikandari* (Baroda, 1961), 15.
96. *SA*, 26.
97. Nizami, *op. cit.*, 246. The *Mirqat* does not mention this- According to Shaikh Mahmud Iraji, he was a son-in-law of Tughluq Shah whom Prof. Nizami takes to be Ghiyasuddin Tughluq Shah (d.1325 A.D.). Could he be Tughluq Shah II (d.1389 A.D.)?
98. Evidently this Shaikh Saddo is the one after whom a mosque is called in Amroha near Meerut *(Annual Report on Indian Epigraphy*, 1962-63, D,290-95).
99. Accounting to *TM*, 4b, *TMU*, 6, the saint was also taken captive.
100. Shaikh Mahmud Iraji gives some information not to be found in the *Mirqat*, about the saint's being taken captive along with other Delhi residents and his miracious power whereby he fed forty captives of his group by providing them with loaves from the Unseen while the other such groups starved. For details, see Nizami, *(op. cit.*, 247).
101. Shaikh Mahmud Iraji, on the other hand describes at length his meetings with Timur, for which see Nizami, *op. cit.*, 247-50. It is, however, seen that quite a good deal of the account of the *Tuhfatul-Majalis* is to be found in different incidents and events narrated in the separate section on the saint's journey to and sojourn in Samarqand, as is the case with some other accounts to which reference has been made in the preceding lines (44 ff, *supra*). For example, Shaikh Mahmud Iraji's account of Timur's meeting with the saint, on a rostrum, in which Shaikh Abdul-Awwal was present is more or less the same as that of the *Mirqat*'s description of the saint's meeting with prince Sultan Muhammad.

102. According to Abul Fazl, *op. cit.*, III, 413, he came to Gujarat in the time of Sultan Ahmad I, which is not correct as also pointed out by Prof. Nizami (*op. cit*,, 244).
103. The *Mirqat* does not make any comment on Sayyid Muhammad Gesudaraz's leaving Nahrwala without meeting Shaikh Ahmad; the same thing happened later at Khambhat.
104. Maulana Sayyid Abu Zafar Nadvi (*SA*, 251) has Rander (new part of) which is not correct. The name is not clear in the hand copy used by him.
105 Maulana Nadvi's translation here (*SA*,256) reads : "The accursed had invaded the coast and people rushed to coastal area." This is self-contradictory.
106. *TMU*, 124, has Nikbakht Sahib-i-Ilm Qazi (fortunate learned Qazi).
107. Shaikh Mahmud Iraji, whose account of the death of the saint more or less agrees with and is apparently taken from the *Mirqat*, omits a name or two and adds one name of Qazi Abdul Baqi son of Qazi Abdul Aziz.
108. *Mirqat* does not mention his name, as in the case of the claimant of the successorship of the saint, but he might be referring to Shaikh Mahmud Iraji.
109. Thus in the text. Very probably, it is a scribal error for Imadul Mulk. The title Umdatul Mulk is not met with in the historical works of Gujarat.
110. The account of Shaikh Mahmud Iraji, the illness and passing away of the saint more or less reads like that of the *Mirqat*, with very few minor changes, except that he says, it was he who was asked to recite the *Kalima* at the appointed hour and he kept quiet and that he and Maulana Muhammad Qasim bathed the saint's body and he only lowered the body it into the grave.
111. *TM*, 41a, b, *TMU*, 53, quotes a complete ghazal of the saint.
112. *Sohaila* was a song in proto Urdu which was in vogue in Gujarat during the time of the saint. *Sohaila* songs are mentioned in the *Jumaat–i–Shahi*, proceedings of the Friday Assemblies of the famous saint Hazrat Shah Alam of Ahmadabad. It was also sung in north India, by people at work, like those drawing water from a well by Persian wheel system, by producing their bullocks. One such instance is mentioned by Hazrat Nizamuddin Auliya (*Fawaidul–Fuad*, Delhi 1990,).

4

MIRQATUL-WUSUL---A PRIMARY SOURCE FOR HISTORY (RAJASTHAN & GUJARAT)

The *Mirqat*ul-*Wusul---a basic source for history of two states (circa, 1330-1445 A.D.),* is in fact the earliest and most important work, among the sources enumerated by Prof. Khaliq Ahmad Nizami,[113] as stated earlier, to furnish a fairly detailed and first-hand account of the pioneer of the Maghribi Sufi order in India, Hazrat Babu Ishaq and his successor the Sarkhej saint Hazrat Shaikh Ahmad Khattu Ganjgir Ganjbakhsh. As has been pointed out above, the *Tuhfatul-Majalis* of Shaikh Mahmud Iraji, used by Shaikh Abdul-Haqq Muhaddis Dehlavi in his *Akhbarul-Akhyar* is neither the earliest nor the most important source of information for the life of the Shaikh. That the *Tuhfatul-Majalis* is not an account of the saint's meetings with him — incidentally in very few of these meetings other people are reported to be present — is clear from a comparison attempted above of both the works. Shaikh Mahamud Iraji's work even wrongly quotes the year of the death of Hazrat Babu Ishaq as AH.776 instead of the correct AH. 781 given by the saint in his Risala referred to above (63, 90 *supra*).

(A) Political History

But the historical importance of the *Mirqat* is not confined to this only. It is a pity that a highly scholarly well-read scholar and great historian of medieval India, who had made a deep study of hagiological and malfuz works, could not consult the *Mirqat*, before pronouncing his verdict — only from a perusal of W.Ivanow's list of contents of the Asiatic Society Calcutta copy of the *Mirqat* — that its contents are more or less the same as covered in the *Tuhfatul-Majalis*.[114] Prof. Nizami would have changed his opinion in this regard, he had an opportunity to glance through the pages of the *Mirqat*. He probably did not think if worthwhile having been misled by Ivanow's emphasis on the *Mirqat*'s considerable interest as containing many allusions to the state of India at the time of Timur's campaign and the interesting story of the saint's journey from India to the court of Timur at

Samarqand and his return to Gujarat.[115] Since the *Tuhfatul-Majalis* did touch these topics, Prof. Nizami did not think it necessary to look up the *Mirqat*, even though as seen above, it contains much more detailed and correct information about this phase of the saint's life; the information given in the *Tuhfatul-Majalis* is scanty as compared to the *Mirqat*.

However, the *Mirqat* does not stand out merely as a primary useful source for such varied and new information about the life and entire career of Babu Ishaq as well as of Shaikh Ahmad from his very childhood, education, spiritual training, ascetic exercises, travels on various counts, pilgrimage, journey to Samarqand, role in the cessation of the Delhi plunder and release of prisoners and his active life in Gujarat. But it also throws considerable light on the life and society of western India — Rajasthan and Gujarat—which these saints had preferred as the centre of their spiritual activities at Khattu in Rajasthan and Sarkhej in Gujarat. It throws a flood of light on the political, social, cultural, literary and like aspects of more than one hundred years (circa 730 H./1330 A.D. to 850 H./1845 A.D.). The *Mirqat* is a veritable store-house of information on various matters ranging from political history to everyday minor affairs and day-to-day routine of contemporary life in medieval Rajasthan and Gujarat towns and villages, as also of those, albeit to a leser extent, in the lands he visited like Arabia and Central Asia including Afghanistan—Khurasan of the *Mirqat*. In perhaps very few, if in none, such hagiographical or malfuz works, such information is available as it is in this single work. Even in spite of having such contemporary and near contemporary historical works as two *Tarikh-i-Firuz Shahis* of Ziyauddin Barani and Shamas Siraj Afif, *Tarikh-i-Mubarak Shahi* of Yahya Sarhindi (histories of Delhi Sultanate), *Tarikh-i-Mahmud Shahi* and *Tabaqat-i-Mahmud Shahi* of Abdul-Husain Tuni and Abdul-Karim Nimdihi general histories written in Gujarat), etc., the information contained on political history in the *Mirqat* is quite considerable.

The *Mirqat* in particular supplies considerable information on some details of political history of the outlying parts under the late Tughluqs and the Gujarat Sultanate. It mentions the atrocities committed by Rao Chonda during his siege of Nagor, and the migration as a result thereof, of the population of that region to Gujarat;[116] siege of Mandor, the old capital or Rathod rulers (Jodhpur),[117] by the Gujarat Sultan; the rebellion of the Chiefs of Nadot and Idar and the Gujarat Sultan's campaigns to deal with them; two invasions of Malwa Sultan and the battles fought, not very far form Ahmadabad; Sultan Ahmad's Deccan engagement; imprisonment at Bharuch—and not at Asawal as is generally believed—of Zafar Khan later on Muzaffar I of Gujarat by his son Muhammad Tatar Khan and the sudden death of the latter and Zafar Khan's release and assuming kingship; Sultan Muhammad I's appointment of a descendant of Hazrat Bahauddin Zakariya of Multan as Shaikhul-Islam of Asawal, his *de facto* capital, a new piece of information; insurgency of the local chief of a *thana* (the name of which is not clear from the book, but which reads like Chadh or Chara); the menace of the accursed ones (*malain*) by which evidently are meant the petty Bhil-Koli chiefs of Mewas in the vicinity of Asawal,[118] when Muzaffar I was away suppressing the insurgence of the Nadot headman as a result of which the general public fled to coastal region as far as Mahim, now part of Bombay and the saint's also having sent his servants and going himself for a day; Muzaffar Shah I 's despatch of Sikandar Khan to Dhandhuka on expedition, evidently to suppress the insurgence of Kathis and Grasias in that region — not mentioned again, in any source; Zafar Khan's expedition to Nadot in 802 H (1400 A.D.) or so when the saint arrived in Gujarat en route to Deccan—a new piece of information; the saint's querry to Zafar Khan as to why with so many elephants (i.e. a big army) at his command, he did not go to the help of the Delhi Sultan at the time of Timur's invasion and his detailed reply—how his army was engaged in defending Nagor against Rao Chonda and if he also went out of Gujarat, how Gujarat would be lost—this also, a new piece of information; Ahmad Shah I's Nagor and Deccan expeditions; the saint seating Sultan Muhammad II on the throne—not mentioned in any source; Malwa Sultan's designs and invasions of Gujarat; Malik Shaikhan bin Yunus (Musa?), a descendant of Hazrat Khalid bin Valid's trouble with the headman of his *thana* and his leading an army against the Malwa Sultan in the time of Sultan Muhammad II and playing a leading role against the same Sultan in the reign of Sultan Ahmad I — historical works do not mention this Malik at all; etc.

But it is in the field of local history of a town, a pargana, a district, that the *Mirqat* furnishes valuable new information not found in historical works. That this new information is authentic is proved in quite a few cases through epigraphical evidence, thus establishing the authenticity and credibility of the saint's discourses as recorded in the *Mirqat*. As is well known, chroniclers of the central as well as provincial kingdoms furnish scanty information about local officials of *shiqs*, *parganas* and villages. Even about high officials like governors, the information supplied by them is meagre. While epigraphical material fills up this lacunae in the local history of Gujarat and Rajasthan as of other provinces of India, the information contained in the *Mirqat* in this regard is much more than that to be found in inscriptions, in concerned cases. Among the local officials of Rajasthan and adjoining areas in the second half of the fourteenth century, the names of officials ignored by chroniclers but occurring in the *Mirqat* are:Malik Qutbuddin Najm, Muqta of Nagor, Malik Ahmad Kath, Malik Kamal Khurram, Malik Kamal Gakkhar, Malik Nasir son of Ahmad, Malik Bughra, all Muqtas of Khattu at various times, Malik Umar, the official-in-charge for presenting petitions and parading petitioners before the king, and his son Malik Kamaluddin, Muqta of Hisar-i-Firoza, Malik Mughis, Hajib of Darya Khan (Zafar Khan II, governor of Gujarat), Sayyid Razi, Hajib, Malik Ikram, *Jamdar* (officer-in-charge of State Wardrobe Department), Maulana Fariduddin, Pardadar, Malik Zain Wala, governor of Didvana. Malik Gunan or Konan (sic, this name is so written in the manuscripts), governor of Nagor, Malik Bughra, Qutb Khwajagi, Shahna-i-Imarat (in charge of the maintenance of Khan Jahan's mosque in Delhi), etc. Among the lesser officials whom the *Mirqat* mentions in some connection or the other are : Shihabuddin Dumak (sic) headman of Khattu, Malik Alauddin son of Mubarak Muqaddam of Ladnun, Dev Raj, headman of Tarnav village near Khattu, Karan Headman of Ladruva, Rai Mandlik, headman of Talwara, Bhupat, Karkun; etc. It may be noted that the local Qazi,was officially designated as Hakim, a shortened form of *Hakimush-Shar* (judge of religious code, i.e. the judge deciding on social matters in accordance with Islamic religious code). The *Mirqat* names a number of such Hakims such as Qazi Fakhruddin, Hakim of Khattu, his son Qazi Khassa Abdul-Malik, of the same town, Qazi Turk, Hakim of Ladnun etc.[119]

Among the above, there are at least three who are known also from epigraphical sources. For example Malik Kamal Khurram is mentioned in a bilingual record from Sambhar, near Didvana, dated 765 H. (1363A.D.) in which he finds mention as the governor of the region only. His full name given there is Malikush-Sharq Malik Kamaluddin Ahmad (son of) Khurram.[120] The *Mirqat*'s reference to him is in connection with one of his routine visits to Khattu which took place well before this date, even before the saint was brought to Khattu in about 741 H. (1340 A.D.). Likewise, another official of high position mentioned is Amir Chopan. The *Mirqat* mentions him more than once as also the sarai built by and known after him, where Shaikh Ahmad Khattu had once stayed. This Amir Chopan is totally unknown to students of medieval Indian history except through the *Mirqat*, which also omits to mention his title and designation. These are known fortunately, from an inscription from Ladnun in Nagor district. According to this epigraph, he was a high official with the covetous title Malikush-Sharq and his middle title was Ikhtiyaruddin and he was governor of the region at least in 780H. (1378 A.D.), when a mosque was constructed there. The saint, who was a frequent visitor to Nagor, Didvana and Ladnun with Babu Ishaq, during his sojourn in Rajasthan, had met him at Nagor during the life-time of Babu Ishaq i.e. before 781 H. (1378 A.D.). Recounting his visit as narrated by the saint, the *Mirqat* states that Malik Chopan had obtained considerable booty in one of his expeditions—a new piece of information on political history[121] out of which he gave a share comprising four select cows to Shaikh Ahmad who sold them to Malik Gonan or Konan for 20 (silver) tankas each. This may be reasonably taken to mean that Malik Chopan had his headquarters at Nagor. He had also constructed there a sarai known as Sara-i-Malik Chopan, where the saint had stayed some time about 789 H. (1387 A.D.) when he passed through Nagor on his way to the two holy cities for pilgrimage (*hajj*), via Gujarat.

But far more historically important case of furnishing authentic and correct information, by the *Mirqat,* regarding an official of note, not mentioned in Persian historical works is of Malik Alauddin son of Mubarak of Ladnun. It was he who constructed the mosque at Ladnun, referred to above in 1378 A.D. during the time of Malik Ikhtiyaruddin Chopan. This official finds mention, besides the inscription, in bardic accounts of Rajasthan which, though containing a core of truth, are full of exaggerated facts, anachronism, etc. The core of truth relates to his having embraced Islam but the circumstances of his having defeated the Delhi king who married his daughter to him and the time factor are highly improbable and incorrect. The inscription, while giving a specific and correct date in his career, is also a little enigmatic and confusing. It mentions him as Alauddin Mubarak *urf* (alias) Jai Singh bin Bhoja Mohel. The mention of Hindu and Muslim names of the father and son was intriguing and it could only be solved, according to Dr. Ziyauddin Desai who published the inscription,[122] by tracing a reference to him in the *Mirqat* copy of the Asiatic Society Calcutta he had a chance to consult. The bardic accounts mentioned one Jai Singh as being the first among the descendants of Mohel Chohan to embrace Islam. But this traditional account did not give his Islamic name nor that of his father. Moreover, this account placed his conversion to about the middle of the fifteenth century, almost three quarters of a century after the date of the inscription mentioning Alauddin (Jaisingh) son of Mubarak (Bhoja) Mohel. This confusion was cleared by the incident related by the saint and recorded in the *Mirqat*. In his visit to Ladnun made in the company of Babu Ishaq, he and Babu were reverently received by Malik Alauddin, a Nau-Muslim (new-muslim convert), the Muqaddam of the town and a disciple of Makhdum Jahaniyan Sayyid Jalaluddin Bukhari of Uchch. He was then the headman of the town. He made an offering to Babu who got prepared a *malida* (wheet flour fried in *ghee* with sugar added to it) and partook of it with local people. The mystery of the names was thus solved. Alauddin was the name given to Jaisingh Mohel after his becoming a Muslim, very probably at the hands of Makhdum Jahaniyan, whom he might have met when the Suhrawardi saint might have passed through the region *en route* to Delhi from Uchch. This also helped to clear the mist surrounding the period of the conversion of Mohel community of the Ladnun region called Mohelwati. It must have taken place a few years before Babu Ishaq's death in 1378 A.D. and not in the middle of the fifteeth century as alleged by the bardic accounts, given credit by leading authorities on Rajasthan's history like the late Dr. Dashrath Sharma and others.[123]

One more high Tughluqian official who finds mention in the *Mirqat* is Malik Qutbuddin Najm, who is also totally ignored by contemporary or later chroniclers or other literary sources. As in the case of the other three officials just mentioned, the historicity of the *Mirqat*, which gives some more details of his career, is proved beyond any doubt by his epitaph discovered a few years back at Nagor, according to which "this magnificent malik, the mine of generosity and magnanimity, master of sword and pen, Malik Qutbuddin Najm, deputy in the *shiq* of Nagor and Jalor, attained martrydom in the army of the Muslims in 791 H. (1389 A.D.).[124] The martyr Malik Qutbuddin Najm could be easily identified though he is not mentioned in historical works of the Tughluq or Sayyid period. The *Mirqat* not only helped identify him through Shaikh Ahmad's mention of him more than once, but it gave some more information about him and his family background. Piecing together the account in different narrations of the saint reveals the information that Malik Qutb Najm was the son-in-law of Malik Raziul-Mulk, a trusted Vizier (*wazir-i-mutabar*) of Sultan Muhammad bin Tughluq.[125] He was acting as the deputy of Malik Haji, his brother-in-law, at Didvana during the life-time of Babu Ishaq. An incident of Babu Ishaq's taking to task the Malik and calling him "son of a betel-nut seller' (*bachcha-i-supari-furush*) — which perhaps may be taken to allude to his ancestral profession of trading — for having paid no attention to the recommendation of Shaikh Ahmad about helping a dervish, was related by the saint. The Babu refused to shake hands with him after Friday prayers. This incident might have taken place in the beginning of Fiuz Shah's reign, *circa* 755 H. (1355 A.D.). After some time, Shaikh Ahmad had gone to Didvana on some errand. Babu Ishaq requiring his presence urgently sent word to Malik Qutb of Didvana to locate the saint and send him immediately to Khattu. Once when the saint had gone to Didvana and visited a local savant Maulana Abul-Faraj Raziuddin, Malik Qutb also happened to come there. It being an year of drought and scarcity, the Malik was distributing ten to twenty measures of grain to every one who was present, but when his turn came the saint left. The Malik then compelled a local resident Sayyid Abu Talib with whom the saint had put up, to bring the saint to his presence. The Malik showed great respect to him and said that he had kept one cart load of grain for Babu Ishaq. The saint declined to carry it whereupon some one present said in Hindawi (i.e. Rajasthani), "Lahrache Jakhan he"[126] and offered it to take it to Babu. The Malik seems to have owed the saint four hundred tankas. After a long time, he was reminded about it in a dream and he sent it to the saint through a draft by a messenger. As a matter of fact, after Babu's death, Sayyid Akram had suggested to the saint to ask the Malik for payment, and the saint ignored his suggestion saying "Now that we have renounced the world, what is the use of asking ?" Malik Qutb Najm who was a devoted admirer of Babu was in Nagor when the saint arrived there on way to the holy cities for Hajj in 789 H. (1378 A.D.) and he had tried to contact him when he came to know from the other Hajj pilgrims from Delhi who had also stayed in Sara-i-Malik Chopan that Shaikh Ahmad had also arrived there that day with the same purpose. But the saint avoided meeting him lest he thought he might try to dissuade him from proceeding for Hajj. For, the Malik had told those pilgrims from Delhi — all respected learned and holy men — that Shaikh Ahmad had become quite weak and would not be able to withstand the arduous journey. The saint always spoke highly of the Maik's generosity and liberality.

Even in respect of Gujarat, which has the distinction of having half a dozen historical and other hagiographical and malfuz works written to depict its history, the *Mirqat* furnishes valuable material for local history. It also supplies names of quite a few new officials, either not mentioned or cursoruly treated in historical works. To mention some, these are:Khwaja Khassa Hajib (Chamberlain) of Muzaffar Shah I; Badr son of Ala, son-in-law and Naib-i-Ghaibat (deputy-in-absence) of also Muzaffar I; Rai Nusrat of Mahaim (modern Mahim, then an island); Yaqub Sikandar Khan; Malik Burhanuddin Tatar Khani; Malik Mubarak Butahari[127] of Khambhat; Malik Usman Sarjkheji; Malik Jalalshah and his secretary (*Dabir*) Khwaja Babu; Malik Shaikh son of Malik Fakhr; Malik Imadul-Mulk; Malik Umdatul-Mulk; Malik Dilawar Khan; Malik Nizam son of Chhajju; Khwajagi Qutb; Malik Shaikhan son of Musa, a descendant of the famous general and Sihabi Hazrat Khalid bin Valid; Qadr Khan; and the like. The officers of lesser rank whose names are found and some details of their career given are : Maulana Khanu, *Muhtasib* of Nahrwala (Patan); Adharan Tak Desai and Karkun of the town of Dholka; Khwaja Badh headman of Sarkhej; Padariya headman of Uteliya; Satsal also headman of Uteliya; Qazi Tujuddin Abbasi *Hakimush-Shar* (Qazi) of Khambhat; etc.

Of these, Malik Badr son of Ala is mentioned by the author of the *Mirat-i-Sikandari* as having joined two uncles of Sultan Ahmad I after his accession to the throne and having been killed at Modasa in 814 H. (1411 A.D.)[128] This again vouchsafes for the authenticity of the account of the *Mirqat* which provides a new piece of important information about him, namely that he was the son-in-law and Naib-i-Ghaibat of Muzaffar Shah I,[129] a fact not taken note of by any modern writer on the history of Gujarat like Dr. Misra. This fact should also provide the motive behind his joining his brother-in-laws w.f. Firuz Khan and Haibat Khan sons of Muzaffar Shah I in the rebellion. The other nobleman is Khwaja Khassa the Hajib (chamber lain) of Muzaffar Shah I, who had sent him to dissuade the saint from leaving Gujarat, the latter having been peeved at the king's having cold-shouldered his emissary Malik Badh, headman of Sarkhej, who was despatched to bring to his notice the prevarications of the concerned petty officials of Dholka and Uteliya in the payment of the revenue of the village to the saint. Khwaja Khassa is first said to have asked the saint to give an account of one lac tankas he had received from time to time from Muzaffar Shah I before leaving. To this, the saint gave a retorting reply that he would give account for not one but two lacs of tankas but would not stay in Gujarat.[130] In this case too, an epigraph has been found at Patan-Nahrwala, the capital of Delhi governors and of the first Gujarat Sultan Muzaffar Shah I which mentions Khwaja Khassa, the Hajib as having constructed a blessed building in 813 H. (1410-11 A.D.). In this epigraph, Khwaja Khassa, "chief of the great grandless and the chamberlain (*Hajib*) " is called Khwaja Khassa bin Wajih; that is to say, he was the son of Wajih a brother of Muzaffar Shah I.[131] Likewise, Malik Shaikhan, who is totally ignored by Persian historians is known from an inscription found at Wadhwan in Surendranagar district of Gujarat. He had constructed a mosque there in 842 H. (1439 A.D.) during the reign of Sultan Ahmad I, which in view of the original findspot of the inscription being the mosque in the Darbargadh — ruling chiefs' residence — shows that he was the governor of the Jhalawar region.[132] The *Mirqat* gives more details about his career, as has been shown in the preceding lines (97, *supra*). From this inscription, it seems that the *thana*, the name of which cannot be correctly determined was somewhere in this region, which was always a source of trouble during the early period of the Sultanate. One more example of the authenticity of the *Mirqat*'s information is concerning Malik Shaikh (son of Malik Fakhr) mentioned therein. While he is not known from any other source, an epigraph from Ahmadabad mentions his daughter Bibi Daulat who had constructed a mosque there in 883 H. (1478 A.D.); she was married to Malik Adil Khan.[133]

The *Mirqat* also contains bits of information about political and social history of Central Asia under Timur. It devotes a full chapter to the saint's own account of his role during and after Timur's invasion as also of his travel to and back from and sojourn in Samarqand. It gives an idea of the impact which his piety and religiosity had made on men from all stations of life — Timur himself, princes, noblemen, holy and learned men, common men, etc., as has been referred to in brief above. (70 ff, *supra*).

Apart from political affairs and officials, the *Mirqat* contains some valuable material for a study of academic and spiritual history of the period in north and west India. It mentions a fairly good number of learned and holy men, many of them not traceable from any other source. These are: Maulana Ziyauddin Sunnami, the teacher of Sultan

Muhammad bin Ṭughluq Shah, Maulana Shamsuddin of Hisar (now in Haryana State), from whom the saint took lessons in *Mufassal, Shashi, Husami, Bazdavi*, etc., Maulana Majduddin of Delhi, a very learned man (*Allama*) and *Muhaddis* from whom also, the saint took lessons in *Hadis*, Maulana Kaddu Dehlavi Ustad and Teacher, Maulana Kamaluddin Muhaqqiq Imam of Khan Jahan mosque, Maulana Sufyan Multani, who used to impart lessons on *Kanz* and its glosses, and had at the tip of his tongue all the variants and symbols of its different manuscripts, Maulana Sayyid Mahmud son of Rukn (Delhi), Maulana Nizamuddin Surkha, Maulana Kamaluddin Samana, Maulana Ahmad attendant of Hazrat Shaikh Nasiruddin Mahmud Chiragh-i-Dehli, etc. Among the saints, we find mention of Sayyid Jalal Bukhari (Makhdum Jahaniyan), Maulana Shaikh Sajjada-Nashin of Shaikh Khizr of Hauz Khas (Delhi), and his disciple Shaikh Bahri of Naraina, Shaikh Nizamuddin Chishti Sahib Sajjada (Delhi), a brother of Khwaja Ruknuddin Chisti, and the like. The elite of this class from Rajasthan mentioned in the *Mirqat* include Maulana Raziuddin Abul-Farah of Didvana, Maulana Yusuf Sadr Hamadani of Khattu, Maulana Shihabuddin Hamadani, Maulana Badh son of Malik Sher Nagori, Sayyid Amir Badh, Maulana Tajuddin Sambhari who had mastered Bazdavi, and the like. The learned men from Gujarat who find mention are Maulana Ahmad well known as Ustad-i-Gujarat, Maulana Ibrahim Mudarris of Nahrwala Patan, Maulana Hafiz Husain son of Shihab of Nahrwala, Qazi Mansur of Sarkhej, Qazi Abdur-Razzaq Abul-Hayy, the saint's Librarian and Scribe, Maulana Mansur Kazeruni, Maulana Sadruddin and his son Maulana Siraj of the famous Bimbani Abbasi family of savants and ministers, Maulana Qazi Sadr, Maulana Daud Mantiqi, Maulana Saifuddin Muallim, Husamuddin Qunduzi, Hazrat Burhanuddin Qutb-i-Alam of Vatva (now part of Ahmadabad city), Hazrat Ruknuddin Chishti, Qazi Kamaluddin *Hakimush-Shar* of Nahrwala, Khatib Ibrahim Dhariwal, Maulana Muhammad *Khatib* of Sarkhej Jami mosque, Najm Rafi Waiz [134] and his son Manjhu and the like. Among Central Asian learned man and saints, he mentions Khwaja Abdul-Awwal of Samarqand, a grandson of the author of *Hidaya*, his nephew Malikul-Ulama Shaikh Husamuddin, Abu Said, all of Samarqand, Shaikh Shihabuddin Jilwani of Herat, etc.

(B) Administrative History

Then, the *Mirqat* also contains some information which enables us to have a glimpse into the administration of the period, both at the capital and the mofussil towns and villages. Among the administrative divisions mentioned are *shiq, pargane, khitta* (city or region with well-marked boundary), *thana, qasba, mauza* and *deh*. The posts and designations that find mention in the *Mirqat* are: *Diwan* (king), *Naib-i-ghaibat* (king's deputy-in-absence), *Hajib, Sayyidul-Hujjab* (Chief of Hajibs), *Sahib-i-Arz-i-Bandgan, Shahna-i-Imarat, Muqta, Wajahdar, Jamdar, Pardadar, Dabir, Fotedar Muhtasib, Kotwal, Sarkhail, Muqaddam, Khot, Desai, Hakim* (for *Hakim-i-Shar* i.e. Qazi), etc. The *Mirqat* also helps the reader have an idea of the specific duties and function of some posts, like *Sahib-i-Arz-i-Bandagan* (*Ariz*) and *Jamdar*. For example, the duties of the *Jamdar* was not confined to the charge of the department of robes and to see that it was kept fully furnished, but he was also the final authority, on the grant of dresses, robes of honour, etc., to officials and non-officials, distinguished persons like envoys, ambassadors, etc.[135] The *Mirqat* relates that two Sayyids of Didvana went to Delhi for renewal of their regular stipend. Qazi Nasrullah, the *Hakim* of Delhi raising some objections rejected their applications. They approached the saint who happened to be then staying in the Khan Jahan's mosque. The saint called his disciple Malik Ibrahim who was the *Jamdar* and gave their application to him asking him to put them before the king Muhammad bin Firuz Shah who in turn asked him to take them to Qazi Nasrullah, who delayed the matter. Malik Ibrahim also delayed the issue of new dresses which were ordered to be given to the Qazi, who ultimately had to sanction the applications of the Didvana Sayyids.[136]

Likewise, the duties of the *Sahib-i-Arz-i-Bandagan* (generally translated as Pay Master) included physical verification of the recruits and non-regular soldiers with their mounts at camps specially arranged at different places, as is known from the saint's narrative of one such function. A camp of such verification of personnel from the towns of Naraina, Khattu and Nagor was held at Naraina by Malik Umar the Pay Master who was a devoted admirer of the saint. Another administrative practice which is known from the *Mirqat* to be in vogue is the recital of the royal farman from the Pulpit of a mosque on Fridays. A somewhat unusual surrender of a farman of land-grant by the donee to the king under protest is also mentioned in the *Mirqat*, on the authority of the saint who was an eye witness. The saint had once gone in his youth from Khattu to Delhi and was among visitors who were to be presented to Firuz Shah Tughluq. Preceding him was a Shaikhzada from Ajmer who, in response to a querry by the king about the purpose of his visit, took out the farman of the grant of a village for the attendants of the Tomb of Hazrat Khwaja Muinuddin Chishti, and said he wanted to return it as the *shiq* officials were making undue great demands on the village.

From the *Mirqat* it also appears that the personnel like imams (leaders of prayers) of mosques, teachers of madrasas etc., received their salary from the State. For example, Maulana Muhammad *Khatib* of the Sarkhej Jami mosque collected his stipend from the concerned department at the capital Ahmadabad. The village headman (Muqaddam) did not receive a regular salary. He would pay the grantee of the village a certain amount in lieu of the produce of the village. This amount was termed *wajh* and the grantee, *Wajahdar*. This yield-share amount of the saint's village Uteliya is stated to be 2,000 tankas when it was in the possession of the previous grantee Badi Bubu. The grantee was also free to have the land cultivated on his own, but this posed a number of problems.

The saintly and learned men and other visitors were given "Journey money", when they left the king's presence; even if he had to return after having incurred royal displeasure; he would be paid some amount, which was actually handed over to him when he left the city's limit. For example Shaikh Musa Warraq who had incurred Sultan Ahmad I's displeasure by repeatedly slandering the saint, was ordered to return to his native place Nahrwala and escorted upto Kochrab — where he was paid some travel-expense — to ensure that he actually left. The *Mirqat* mentions the custom observed in Central Asia of people sending *futuh* and presents whenever an eminent person, like Shaikh Ahmad left.

Spoils of war or booty were shared with people in particular groups of pious and saintly ones. Mention has already been made of the *Mirqat*'s account of Malik Chopan having given such share to Shaikh Ahmad. The book also supports the case of an official Malik Zaina Muqta of Hisar who was imprisned for non-payment of dues, though later on 80,000 tankas buried by him somewhere were unearthed. That there was corruption in one town or the other practiced by officials and people is also known from the *Mirqat*. In one case, the Gilkars (soil-diggers) who had entered into a labour-contract claimed to have removed soil and sand in more measures than actually done and thus got more tankas than due. In another case, a petty official was nicknamed Lakhugira (Taker of lacs) for illegal gratifications.

(C) Geographical and Like Information

The *Mirqat* also furnishes ample material for political geography, routes, communications, etc., of early medieval Rajasthan, Gujarat and Delhi regions as also topography of towns and villages which were personally visited in almost all cases by the saint during his short and long travels and journeys from chilhood to his settling down finally at Sarkhej, covering a period of more than half a century. His reminiscences recorded by Maulana Muhammad Qasim refer to a number of places in these regions and furnish some idea of the means of travel, halting places, like sarais or mosques, or a monumental building like bastion, etc. The names of places in Rajasthan mentioned in the book are: Ahod (or Ahwad)—given in grant to Sayyids of Didvana in Tughluq period, Banathri (or Vanathri) lying between Khattu and Didvana which was given to Chaudhary Daud of Didvana, Jaisalmer, Kathoti, Khattu, Koleva about one *kos* west of Didvana, Kuchera, Ladnun, Laruva, situated on the bank of a river, Mahoba (or Mahoya), Nagor, Naraina, Rewari (or Devri), Seethla or Sathela, Rahol—famous for very sweet water melons, Tarnav, situated at a distance of about 12 *kos* (50 kilometres) from Khattu etc., The above list includes known as well as unknown names and are important in tracing their antiquity to at least middle of the fourteenth century.

The familiar as well as unfamiliar names of Gujarat villages and towns include Birpur (Virpur),[137] Bharuch, Barli, stated to be near Patan, Chadh (or Chara), Champaner, Choramli, Dhandhuka, Dholka, Godhavi (near Sanand), Kapadwanj, Pandarwada stated to be thirty kos from Kapadwanj, Kochrab (now part of Ahmadabad), Mahim (now part of Mumbai city), Mohrasa (Modasa), Nahrwala (Patan), Navsari, Pahlanpur (Palanpur); Petlad, Ratanpur,[138] Sarkhej, Sorath, Uteliya and Vasna (now part of Ahmadabad city). Here again, the *Mirqat* is helpful in tracing the antiquity of today's insignificant villages like Godhavi. The *Mirqat* also mentions the river Mahi and the jungles of Navsari in south Gujarat.

The material on routes and communications, conveyance etc., contained in the *Mirqat*'s narrative, perhaps for the first time, discloses the fact that the route to Deccan from Delhi and Rajasthan generally and conveniently ran via Gujarat's towns Asawal (near modern Ahmadabad), Dholka, Cambay and from there, Narbada river-fords. The route from Delhi to Gujarat passed through the Didvana town of Rajasthan, from Khattu to holy cities via Gujarat through Rajasthan village Tarnav, Ladnun, Nagor, Mahoba (or Mahoya) alias Talwara, Rajasthan, and Ladruva (or Laudara) and then Nahrwala and onwards. The pilgrims sailed mostly from Khambhat but also from Mahaim. However, some pilgrims (e.g. the saint himself) returned from holy cities, disembarking at Thatta in Sindh and then proceeding to Khattu via Tarnav, but this route appears to have been taken in exceptional cases. From Samarqand, the saint had returned via Herat, Qandahar, Uchch, Malikwahan, Jaisalmer and Khattu. The mode of travel and means of conveyance as reported in the *Mirqat* are horse, camel (in Rajasthan), Palki, Dola (Palanquin), Bullock cart (Gardun) for travel as well as transport of goods like wheat, grain etc., luxury carts called Bahini (Vahini), boats and ships, etc.

(D) Topography of Places

The *Mirqat* also supplies some information about the topography of towns and cities like Delhi, Didvana, Khambhat, Khattu, Nagor, Sarkhej, Uchch etc. The only building of Uchch, now in Bhawalpur district of Punjab in Pakistan, where Makhdum Jahaniyan Sayyid Jalal Bukhari, grandfather of Hazrat Qutb-i-Alam of Vatva lies bured, mentioned in the book is Burj-i-Mamun, where the saint had stayed on his return from Samarqand. The locatities and monuments of Delhi mentioned in the *Mirqat* are: Tomb of Prince Fath Khan (in Nabi Karim locality of Pahadganj), Bhilsa gate (obviously of Firuz's Capital Firuzabad) near the said Tomb, mosque of Khan Jahan,[140] stated to be situated in the Muhalla Jajnagar of Firuzabad — a very important piece of information for fixing the extent of Firuzabad founded by Firuz Shah Tughluq,[141] Kushk-i-Hazar Sutun, where Maulana Majduddin Muhaddis lived and ran a madrasa for teaching Hadis, as stated earlier (64, *supra*), Hauz Khas, which also was then as today a place of tourist interest and Jod-Bagh,[142] also frequented by people then as even now for morning and evening stroll.

Of the buildings of Nagor mentioned in the book are Madrasa of Qazi Hamiduddin Nagori, a celebrated savant and holy man of the thirteenth century A.D.— the site of which cannot be determined now as Nagor had undergone much demolition during the rule of the Rathod rulers of Jodhpur, Sarai of Malik Chopan, also non-extant now and the Tank. Didvana, according to the saint's memoirs, had two tanks, one on the east and the other on the west of the town, a fort, a mosque called Masjid-i-Burhani, mosque of Malik Daud on the western extension of the town, and Sarai Ghani. The only place of note that finds mention in the *Mirqat*, of Khattu, where the saint passed about half of his life, is the tank called Hauz-i-Khan. The *Mirqat* also mentions the Tank of Naraina.[143]

Among the other tanks mentioned are one at Dholka and another at Khambhat, called Nera, as it is now also exactly so called. A location of cultivable land near Sarkhej called Chah-i-Khabadiya. (lit. Khabadiya well)[144] is mentioned in the *Mirqat*. The antiquity of the villages Kochrab and Vasna on the opposite bank of the river Sabarmati running to the west of the walled city can be traced to early fifteenth century at least, on the basis of the statements of the *Mirqat*. These villages now part of the city existed by the same name then and the road to Sarkhej where the saint lived was as it is now also through Kochrab and Vasna at that time. It is suprising that though Maulana Muhammad Qasim had arrived at Ahmadabad from Rajashtan a few years before the foundation of the city of Ahmadabad, he makes no mention at all of the role played by the saint in the coming up of a new city named after him or the Sultan or the Ahmads who are believed to have taken part in the foundation of the new capital as detailed earlier On the other hand, contemporary Shaikh Mahmud Iraji describes the event at some length.

The *Mirqat* does not give any detail of the funerary monuments of any of the places—Khattu, Nagor, Didvana, Delhi, Khambhat, Ahmadabad, etc. Though Babu Ishaq and the saint had made it a regular habit of visiting the tombs of saints (*maqabir-i-buzurgan*), whenever they visited these places or even in Khattu, the *Mirqat* does not mention any tomb or mausoleum by name except for the Hazira-i-Fath Khan at Delhi referred to above. However, the book furnishes a very important piece of information that the saint had laid the foundation of the "New Jami mosque" at Sarkhej and probably also a Tank at Sarkhej.[145]

(E) Coins, Measures, etc.

The *Mirqat* also mentions a few coins of various denominations (in case of Indian coins) current in those days in Delhi, Rajasthan, Gujarat, Central Asia and Arabia, such as Alai gold Tanka (put in use by Alauddin Khalji, d. 1316 A.D.), Jital, Kani, Chaharkani, Panjkani, Shashkani, Dihkani, Bistkani, Bistpanj-Kani, Dokda, Fadya and Fadya- i-Firuz Shahi; Juni or Chuni (latter, perhaps Chuanni—one forth of a silver tanka).[146] The book also mentions the currency Masudi of Arabia.

The measures of weight and length that find mention in the *Mirqat* are *seer* and *man* and *tolcha* and *bigha* respectively. It also refer to the village method of measuring depth by ropes of particular length, etc. For example, the clearance of the Hauz-i-Khan of Khattu was measured as so many chhajja - measures.[147]

(F) Medieval Society of Gujarat and Rajasthan

Lastly, the *Mirqat*'s historical value as depicting the early medieval society may be detailed. From the saint's memoirs as recorded by Maulana Muhammad Qasim, with some of his own, it would appear that the routine life in a medieval society, particularly in the mofussil areas, was not different from that of the present one — at least of until a decade or two back. The globalization era has no doubt changed the character of Indian society, values, character etc., to a certain extent in cities and towns and also in large villages. Neverthless, the reader of the *Mirqat* can easily visualise the state of the then society as the one in remote villages even today. People used to live the same hard, but by and large leisurely and honest, life and their vocations during non-work seasons or leisure hours were not very different. Village houses had, as of now, thorn-hedged backyards and the doors of the houses of at least the Muslims were covered with hanging curtains (*tatti*). Some houses had more than one storey. The main item of furniture was stringed bed as well as stringed chair (*Kursi-i-risman bafta*). Human failings and lapses are also strikingly similar. The butcher whose clientele included the saint's Khanqah at Sarkhej sold the meat of a stolen animal, as a result of which a boy was specially appointed to get the daily ration of meat from Ahmadabad city from a geniune shop. The instance of Shaikh Tajuddin whom the saint had given a fat cow for the milk, curds and butter needs of his family had sold it to a butcher for hard cash.[148] An Indian had borrowed the saint's pair of new shoes pledging to return them shortly, which he never intended. The ship-owner at Khambhat wanted a much higher fare, taking the advantage of all the ships having left in the Hajj season and would not make a concession in the case of a saintly person even when requested. The corruption of officials, high as well as low, has already been refered to (105, *supra*). Sayyid Khassa and Sayyid Ismail of Didvana falsely entered their names in the document as the sons of their decased uncle Sayyid Sadruddin and went to Delhi to have the grant of a village renewed, in the time of Sultan Muhammad bin Firuz Shah. An interesting and amusing case, typical of a facet of

Indian life is that of Maulana Fariduddin whom the saint had appointed as a teacher in a local madrasa at one tanka a day. One day, be came to see the saint and entered into academic discussion with him. Not being able to get an upper hand, he was getting excited; an official who had also come to pay his respects motioned the Maulana by the sign of hand to desist. Then, the Maulana asked for his stipend for one year, totalling 360 tankas. The saint who did not have cash at hand offered him a prayer-carpet and a Mus-haf (Holy Quran), but he wanted cash. At this, an accountant-clerk (*Muharrir*) who had by then come to pay his respects, obtained the saint's permission to settle the matter. He told the Maulana, "You sit in Chilla twice a year i.e., for 80 days you do not teach; you observe Fridays and Tuesdays as holidays, which means no work for say 100 days; this leaves only 180 tankas as your legitimate dues. As against this, in the previous year, you were paid 360 tankas which means you were overpaid 180 tanka. Thus you have already received your 180 tankas of this year as pre-payment. How do you, a religious person, prefer a claim which is not just ?" Being outwitted, Maulana Fariduddin said, "You are depriving me of the prayer-mat and Mus-haf even, which the Makhdum (i.e. Saint Shaikh Ahmad Khattu) was giving". The saint then gave him the Mus-haf.

Some facets of the life in mofussil as refleted in the *Mirqat* relate to village beliefs, superstitions and innocent pastimes and games like strength-lesting, making bets, etc. For example, there was in Khattu a heavy round stone-slab with a hole in the middle like a flour mill grind-stone which the wrestlers and champions of physical strength would lift and wear on their neck and move about to demonstrate their strength. The saint, in his younger days, in response to a challenge, put his head into the hole, lifted it and walked with it around his neck, taking a few rounds. On another occasion, on a pitch dark night—it must be *kalichaudas*, *amavasya*, preceding Divali, when even today in villages such bets are made—the saint successfully accepted a bet to go and tie a turban on a particular tree in the forest. Taking omen and like rituals appears to have been common. The *Mirqat* in one of its discourses refers to the saint's taking omen (*fal*) from the Quran. It also relates a story of the wife of a Muslim village headman, who had entertained the saint when he was passing through the village, to take a few steps in their field before he left, for *barakat* (blessing, for good yield of crop). This lady had also invited her Pir, a Sajjada with a *shajara* to meet the saint whom he tried to impress by asking him to read the *Ijazanama* of Makhdum Jahaniyan, but being himself illiterate soon left lest he got exposed in the presence of his lady disciple. The saint used to give *tawiz* containing the great names of God.

The *Mirqat* has described the saint's account of his visit to a Hammam in Samarqand in which, apart from discussions with learned men, his attendant Arif played an innocent joke with some ladies of noble family who knew him. Arif had a "flower" in one eye. Seeing him, one of the ladies jokingly said, "O blind man ! What is that which you have in your hand ?" Arif who had only a book of Persian verses in his hand, replied, "The Holy Quran". He was asked, "Why the Quran here ?" His reply was, "You who have come here to take a bath will have to declare on oath whether it is a legal bath or otherwise. That is why." The ladies felt embarrassed and said to one another that had he not been taunted as blind, they would not have had to hear that retort.

The local rivalries between individuals and groups of people were also part of the social milieu of the period, as it is now also. The work of desilting of the tank at Khattu proposed to be started by the saint on his receipt of 2,000 tankas from the Delhi Sultan caused the local Hakim (Qazi) to do the same before it could be started by the former, but he had to give it up.[149] With the balance of the amount left after getting the job done, the saint excavated another tank. A local grocer, out of rivalry started another.[150] In the *Mirqat*, reference is also made to petty village fueds as are witnessed even to day, such as dispute between owners of two adjacent fields over the boundaries. In one such quarrel, between Maulana Ibrahim Kaithali's nurse's son and the employees of the Muqta of the place, the Maulana and his two sons got killed. Likewise, friendly contests or game competitions were held on individual or group or class basis as is being done even now. Once the Muqta of Khattu had fixed up a target which was to be hit with an arrow. The official's kinsmen, the Khattu public, the Sheranis,[151] the Shahis and the like took part in the competition but no one could hit the target. The saint who was then in his youth and a skilled archer reached the spot. The public claimed him to be of their group and the official of his. The saint hit the target with the first shot with a none the too good bow given to him by a jealous fellow.

The saint has himself related how in his younger days, he along with his age-mates would go to see an unusual spectable in the town. Once the Gujarat governor Darya Khan was passing through Rajasthan along with his troops which had elephants. The saint and his mates went to Kathoti to see the elephants. As per the usual practice, pupils and students were presented to the passing dignitary, for receiving their stipend. The *Mirqat* relates one such incident in which young Shaikh Ahmad was also asked to line up along with them, as the amount would serve as travel - expenses, but this he declined.

The *Mirqat* also refers to the custom in vogue in certain saintly establishments of reciting *takbir* or *fatiha* after meals for the commencement of a journey. Likewise, it was perhaps customary among the saints also to have their graves prepared in their life-time and fill them with grain every year to be distributed in alms. The *Mirqat* also refers to the custom in Maghrib country — North Africa — under which whenever an affluent person visited a grave, he would place some offering in cash at the grave. Reference is also made to a custom observed in the Hammams (public baths) of Samarqand where academic discussions between learned men took place; according to the custom, the participants would pour water over the head of one who was judged best. After academic discussions, those present would be served with meals and treated with *rubab* (rebeck) music. Holding of musical parties or *sama* at dinners including *Valima* dinner also finds mention more than once in the *Mirqat*. Likewise, the *Mirqat* points to the existence of the customary practice of a visitor taking something by way of present to the person visited or of the offerings made by kings, ministers and officials to saints. The list of such items of present or offering include such things as : *laddu*, sugar-candy, *shir-biranj* (*kheer*), dates, apricots, flour, ghee, mutton, cows and cloth of different varieties, costly dress, fine knife, carpet, candle-stand, lamp, *kashkul* (beggar's bowl), golden hilted dagger, jewel-studded ring, coconut, etc. Clothes, sweets and coconuts were given to spectators who would come to see the launching or completion of some project of public utility. Female workers were given fancy names like Shakh-i-Zar (golden branch).[152] Highly respectable visitors were seen off to the door, when they left. The saint once started without putting on shoes, to see a visitor off, but the latter out of respect put the shoes before him to be put on by him.

Some refreshing evidence of the tenets of universal brotherhood and love preached and practiced by the Sufis in those days is to be found in the pages of the *Mirqat*. The saint who himself had come into contact with Hindu jogis[153] and Hindu families, never speaks of them with a dislike, leave alone contempt. He would allow himself to enter into discussion with jogis or Brahmins on topics proposed by them or answer questions put by them to him. The picture presented by these references is of a society living in peace and harmony. The saint's wrestling bout in his youth with a Hindu cobbler-boy, referred to earlier, shows lack of any feeling of untouchability on his part. Babu Ishaq and the saint did not look to the caste or creed of a person who came to them for help. A Hindu grocer of Khattu, Popa, had, as already seen above, gratefully acknowledged Babu Ishaq's help in getting him released from the custody of officials for non-payment of government dues.

The Hindus also held Muslim saints in great esteem and reverence. The saint was always treated well by the Hindu headmen of villages and other people in the course of his journey and he would enjoy their hospitality for two three days. The Hindu trading community had their normal dealings with their Muslim fellow-townsmen. Once an official set apart a calf for Babu Ishaq and requested him to collect it. When it grew into a fat cow, the latter asked a Hindu banya to collect it. An interesting episode illustrating how a Muslim savant duly recognised the piety and righteous conduct of Hindus is described in the *Mirqat*. After the death of Babu Ishaq, it was reported to Shaikh Ahmad that one of his good acquaintances Maulana Raziuddin Abul-Farah of Didvana had remarked that one could not attain God by merely remaining confined to one place but by undertaking journeys. On being communicated, Shaikh Ahmad's dislike at this remark alleged to be made in regard to him, the Maulana sent a letter describing it at length how he who respected an illiterate, uneducated young Hindu bride for having attained some sort of clairvoyance by just practising piety at home, could think of passing such a remark about a religious-minded righteous Muslim Unitarian like him who had renounced worldly pleasures and undertook perpetual fasts ?

The so-called miracle of walking-on-fire was also claimed and practised those days too. The saint in one of his journeys came to the village of a Hindu Rai who treated him with respect. There, some other Darvishes who were also patronised by him, out of jealousy, challenged the saint to eat *halwa-i-dud* that is to say , walking on fire. The saint accepted the challenge and entered the fire, after reciting God's great name and came out successful in the test.[154]

The migration of people from one region to another, far or near, due to various factors like service-transfer, search of livelihood, better prospects, compulsion due to political and like upheavels, etc., has been more or less heard of in all periods of Indian history and offers a good subject for study to researchers of social history. The presence of Nagori Muslims and Hindus in various parts of Gujarat, and Nagori Muhallas — more than one — and a Nagori Sarai in Ahmadabad and elsewhere is thus explained by a number of direct and indirect references to migration of people from Nagor, Didvana, etc. to Ahmadabad, Bharuch, Cambay, Patan, etc. The *Mirqat* mentions quite a few men such as Sayyid Qasim Nagori, Saiyyad Rahmatullah Nagori, Maulana Khatiruddin of Didvana, Qazi Muinuddin Nagori, the author (of the *Mirqat)* Maulana Muhammad Qasim and his companions and kinsmen like Maulana Abdus-Salam, etc.

From the *Mirqat*, one can also have some idea about the food and dress of the people of Gujarat and Rajasthan. Khichdi including that of millet (*bajra*) and liberal helping of ghee was much in vogue. Wheat loaf and mutton or chicken or fish or vegetable curry was also served to guests in well-to-do circles. Biryani is also mentioned. Breakfast meal seems to comprise of butter, buffalo-milk and curds. *Malida* (a dish made out of lightly roasted crushed loaf, ghee and sugar) and *Kanji* (rice broth) also appear to have been items on the menu. Oil-cake or smashed banana like fruit was also considered a substitute in the time of non-availibility of any regular food item. Among vegetables, the only mention in the book is of bitter-gourd (*Karela*) and mustard-leaf (*Sarson*), *lobiya* (a common dish in Khattu), moong, etc. The *Mirqat* also quotes the saint as mentioning some sect of Dervishes who did not take meat. The dessert items mostly consisted of *laddu*, sugar candy, date and *kheer* (*shir-biranj*). Seasame oil was the medium of cooking as well as of lamp-lighting. Betel-nut (*supari*) was also used.

The fruits that find mention in the *Mirqat* are melons or kharbuzas (of Rajasthan), pomegranates and mangoes (of Gujarat) and berry (*ber*). The Rahol village near Nagor which was held in subsistence grant by Burhanuddin, Qazi and Khatib of Nagor, was famous in the entire region for its very sweet water melons and the Qazi used to host kharbuza-parties in the village to which the presence of the saint was very much desired. Apricots were also available in Khattu. The only item of intoxicating drink mentioned in the book is of Bhang, a favourite drink of some Qalandars.

Among flowers, the *Mirqat* only mentions casually the white Champa of Nagor, which was famous for its sweet scent and beauty in the entire region. Basket-fulls of them used to be offered to prominent personalities like the saint by the local Muqta at the time of their visit.

The most common item of wear of saintly persons and elite, in particular, as gathered from the *Mirqat*, appears to have been cloak — labada or barani or doshala of different material; one with woolen exterior and broad cloth (*saqarlat*) interior was considered to be a luxurious item for present to big personalities like saints. Turbans usually of a length of twenty gaz, and mini turbans and *kulahs* (caps) were the items of head-wear. Small towels (napkins or handkerchiefs) were also used. *Khirqa* and *Taqiya* were normal sufi wear. The saint's own dress in Samarqand was a *Fota*, a *Pishwaz* and a cap or black-coloured turban; the turban-colour had generated a good deal of sensation there, black colour being disliked by the Mughals there. The waist-bands had dagger or like weapon tucked in them. The saint is reported by the author of the *Mirqat* to wear the outfit of an archer for quite some time in Sarkhej. Rings were also worn.

The varieties of dress material mentioned in the *Mirqat* are *Bheram* or *Bherun*, Salu,[155] *Sharbati, Bafti, Kambhal* (?), *Saqarlat, Firangi*, etc. It does not furnish any information about their place of make etc., but at least Firangi must have been imported as the very name tends to suggest.

About the health problems, the information gathered is that in this part of the country, diseases like gripe (belly-ache), scrofula (glandular swelling in the neck-mumps), guinea-worm, thread—worm, *phool* (eye-disease, Persian *gul-dar-chashm*), were rampant. Serpent bite was also not so uncommon. While expert physicians were there, the common man resorted to homely medicines or treatment of quacks. The saint, the *Mirqat* states, had dissuaded a disciple of his from giving quack treatment. The latter was advised and accordingly had procured a human skull-piece to apply its powder to the mumps-affected part of his brother. Before going in for the treatment, he came to pay his respect to the saint who told him that it was not proper to use a dead man's body-part.

In the field of agriculture products, Rajasthan, for most part of the time, a chronic water-scarcity area, the yield of grain etc. was limited in quantity and variety both. From the *Mirqat*, it is gathered that *Lobiya*, a variety of beans, was the main crop of Khattu and hence the staple food of its people. During the crop-season, *Lobiya* was cooked and would be offered with or without ghee; it was served with ghee to guests including saints and high state officials. Moong (pulse) also appears to have been grown. Salt was the main non-agricultural project, which was supplied to other regions. Caravans of merchants from Gangetic plains would visit Didvana to carry bulk-supply of the commodity. The area between Sambhar and Didvana was the major salt-providing site.

Water in this arid land was scarce due to frequent droughts.[156] It was considered a prized commodity. Once in one of his travels, the saint sent his attendant to get some water from the house of a village headman; the lady of the house asked him to fetch a bundle of fuel-sticks before she gave him water. In another incident, in a far-off place he demanded water from an old man who could not provide it as it was not available, that being the drought year. During the drought time, grain was distributed to people on loan or by way of government aid by the State as well as well-to-do individuals. A grocer of Khattu is mentioned in the *Mirqat* of having distributed grain on one such occasion on credit.

Not much information is available on this score from the rich and fertile land of Gujarat. The only piece of information we get is that the saint's village Uteliya was a village of very fertile land, where wheat grew in plenty. Wheat-crop also was yielded in good measure in the land called Khabadiya-well near Sarkhej.

Likewise the information about trade and commerce evidently gathered from the *Mirqat* is not much. Nevertheless, some useful information is found. The salt-trade has already been mentioned. Merchants from outside Gujarat like Malwa, Bengal, etc., evidently for trade purposes are mentioned as visiting Sarkhej to pay their respect but no direct specific mention of their transactions or ware is given. For example, the *Mirqat* mentions that the Malwa Sultan Alp Khan (Ghori) had sent gold and silver tankas to the saint through a trader Buhlul who had come from Dhar, the capital of Malwa, to Sarkhej to pay his respects to the saint. The *Mirqat* gives some more information about piety traders like village grocers, such as Popa who used to supply provisions to the saintly establishment from Babu Ishaq's days. This was usually done on credit basis as has been seen earlier. The *Mirqat* furnishes an interesting piece of information that Babu Ishaq had a silver-tray (*rakabi*) which he would pledge with the grocer against the supply of articles including cloth on credit and redeem it when money was received. From the saint's own memoirs as recorded in the *Mirqat*, it appears that in his younger days, he was inclined to take up trading as profession. Once he deposited one hundred tankas, given to him by Babu Ishaq for safe-keep, with a trusted grocer who had proposed to invest it in trading in moong on behalf of the saint, when the moong-prices fell. However, the profit made in this transaction was distributed by the saint among poor and needy people. Incidentally the price of moong, six *jitals* per 1/6 maund then in vogue and the price of a fat cow quoted as 20 tankas in the *Mirqat*, give some idea of the price structure of those days. The presence of Indian traders from Nagor in Aden is also known from the book. We also know from it of the practice — observed even today by sophisticated men also — of people undertaking a journey carrying with them for sale some Indian goods which might have a market value at the place of their arrival. Even Hajj pilgrims did this, the saint being no exception.[157]

The professional people known from the *Mirqat* are weaver, oil-presser, butcher, mason, betel-nut-seller etc., apart from state officials. Transcript of manuscripts was also practiced as a means of living. For example, Qazi Raja of Dholka was a *Katib* (scribe) by profession, according to the *Mirqat*. Spinning by women as well as men was also practiced.

From the saint's memoirs, Nagor appears to be a major town of Rajasthan after Ajmer in the early medieval period, when Jodhpur, Bikaner, etc. had not come into being. Decades before it became the capital of the independent dynasty of the Khanzadas, it was the marketing centre for the region around, where all types of goods and commodities were available. Babu Ishaq, according to the *Mirqat,* used to specially order fine shoes, cloth, good arrows, etc. from Nagor for his ward Shaikh Ahmad.

Among other miscellaneous items, the *Mirqat* refers to the method practiced in those days in the villages—and is practiced even now in remote villages—of the detection of crime through foot-print experts, the Pagis, as they are now called.[158]

Another very important thing about the book is that it helps fix up the time of the Khambhat saint locally called Pir Parvaz. According to a note encased in glass put up at his tomb—a modern rectangular hall, situated in an extensive old graveyard—which is the repository of more than two dozen epitaphic marble tablets originally belonging to the graves of persons who lived in the thirteenth through fifteenth century A.D., "his name was Ali al Jaulaqi, who flourished in the twelfth century A.D." However, Shaikhzada Ahmad Kirmani told the author that when Pir Parvaz Khambhaiti (i.e. of Khambhat) went back after meeting the saint (in Khambhat), he told his companions that the eyes of Shaikh Ahmad were those of men of spiritual station (*ahl-i-iradat*). To one of them who observed that he did not witness any (miracle or significant) thing from him, Pir Parvaz reported that his eyes were tainted. This shows that Pir Parvaz was a contemporary of the saint. The *Mirqat* also relates an instance of how a Sayyid of Didvana settled in Bharuch came to Sarkhej asking the saint to sign an attestation note — to the effect that he had performed so many prayers and had attained Sayyidhood — which was signed by the Sayyids of his family, but the saint declined quoting a *Hadis* in support of his stand. And also, the *Mirqat* has preserved the names of the Imams (leaders of prayers) like Maulana Imam son of Shaikh, the Imam of Sultan Muhammad II of Gujarat, Maulana Kamaluddin Imam of Khan Jahan etc.

(G) Literary History of Gujarat

Lastly, the *Mirqat*'s importance as a source for literary history of Gujarat may be evaluated. The state of learning and learned men has already been mentioned earlier. Obviously, the saint had no occasion to dwell upon this aspect in his meetings and hence it is not surprising that not much information is available on this score. It may be remembered that other sources are also not very useful in this regard. Anyway, it is known from the *Mirqat* that the languages spoken and studied were Arabic, Persian and Hindi or local language (Rajasthani in Rajasthan and Gujari and Gujarati in Gujarat). Persian was widely understood. The masses including the trading class, particularly Hindu grocers, spoke the local language of their respective regions, which the *Mirqat* simply designates by the general term Hindi or Hindawi and which was also widely known and spoken by the learned. The saint himself was at ease in all the three languages in which he could converse. In Arabian cities of Aden, Makkah, Madina, etc. and in Central Asia at times, he conversed in Arabic, while he mostly spoke Persian in Samarqand, Herat, Qandhar, etc. A few examples of Hindi words and phrases have already been quoted in the section of literary style of the author of the *Mirqat*, which also repeatedly says that Babu Ishaq and the saint conversed with the jogis in their parlance.

A few but important pieces of information about literary activities furnished by the *Mirqat* are that Maulana Ziyauddin Sunnami, the teacher of Sultan Muhammad bin Tughluq had written a commentary on *Al-Muttafaq*. Malikzada Shaikh Shihabuddin Surkhani had sent to the saint a *Risala* written by him on spiritual path and his Persian verses on sufistic subjects. Of these, the saint found that he had gathered the material in the *Risala* from various books but the overall arrangement was not that good. However, he found his Persian verses of a very high order. Unfortunately, none of these verses are quoted, as evidently the saint was relating an event of the past. Similarly Maulana Muhammad Qasim himself was a poet. The *Mirqat* has quoted a Persian Rubai of his teacher Sayyid Mahmud Rukn grandson of Sayyid Rasuldar of Delhi who was a poet; this has already been mentioned in the preceeding lines (84, *supra*).

The *Mirqat* (and also the *Tuhfatul-Majalis*) are the only sources which furnish the information that the saint was a poet and used to compose verses in all the three languages mentioned above. As related to the author of the *Mirqat* by the saint himself, when Babu Ishaq came to know of the young Shaikh Ahmad's interest in trade, he mildly repremainded him, saying, "Give up the idea of business and strive for acquiring knowledge and learning". Then he felt inclined towards poetry. He composed and recited before Babu Ishaq a Persian Rubai, in praise of the latter, who however asked him on oath, not to compose verses in praise of any one, as it also ammounted to a means of asking. It is a pity that the saint did not remember it. The *Mirqat* has quoted the ghazal which the saint composed incorporating therein the hemstitch composed by Sultan Muhammad bin Firuz Shah, which other poets at the court could not succeed in doing. The *Mirqat* has quoted, apart from *dohas*, quite a few Persian and Arabic verses of the saint at the end of the Chapter. The Persian verses include a *ghazal* and a *rubai* also. He had also by heart a large number of verses in Arabic, Persian and Hindi/Gujari which he would recite in his meetings with disciples and visitors on appropriate occasions. He used to compose *dohas* in Hindi also. Quite a few of these verses have been quoted in the *Mirqat*. There being very few specimens of fourteenth-fifteenth century Persian poetry, their importance for the history of contribution of this part of the country to Persian and Hindi/ Gujarati literature cannot be overstressed, all the more since it has been by and large overlooked. Below are given, for the sake of record and reference, the verses composed by the saint:

غزل

شوریدگان خسته و زاریم آه آه
واماندگان صحبت یاریم آه آه

سرگشتگان سوخته با پختگان عام
دلدادگان سینه فگاریم آه آه

مستان ز شب چو می بکشند آن کو بکو
گر در شراب و گه بخماریم آه آه

رندان مفلسیم و حریفان ناقصیم
جز نیستی و حسرم نداریم آه آه

نه در شمار مرد نه اندر شمار زن
معلوم نیست در چه شماریم آه آه

خواند اگر بلطف بیاییم شاد و شاد
راند اگر بقهر برآریم آه آه

The saint prayed for the health Khawaja Bakhtiyar Kaki, thus :

من ای صبا بیاد ده رفتن بکوی دوست ندارم
تو میسر روی بسلامت سلام من برسان

رباعی

در جهان بی وفا گردیم بسی
عاجز تر ز خود ندیدیم بسی
تا زمانه روزگار چشیدیم بسی
از دست دل خویشتن از دست بسی (کسی)

اگر بلطف بخوانی مزید الطاف است
وگر بقهر برانی درون ما صاف است
بیان وصف تو گفتن نه حد امکان است
چراکه وصف تو برون ز حد امکان است

می برد هر کس نصیب خویشتن
درمیان احمد بهانه بیش نیست

Dohas

توجانہ کرتار جی منجھ سائیں بیرہ
سائیں کی ہی ساریا نجر مانہ جو من لبسنہ

توجانہ کرتار جی منجھ سائیں بیرہ
سائیں کی ہی ساریا نجر مانہ جو من لبسنہ

دوکہا کاجل جی کروں تو سوکن دکھ دینہ
نہ پیو دیکھن دینہ مجھ نہ آپ دیکھ سکینہ

دیا بجھری اک پل جالوں برس پچاس
جی کن دیکھی دلیں کی برس انت نہ ماس

ٹٹی بندھی کنزی جو وہن ادجھل ہوئے
مورکھ رکھی نین دو من کہ رکھی کھوئے

In short, the *Mirqatul-Wusul* is a very important first hand source for the study of medieval Indian history and culture in all its aspects. Therefore, it is a pity that it has been overlooked by the modern historians. Even the recently written and published Political and Cultural History of Gujarat in Gujarati in eight volumes by the Seth Bholabhai Jesingbhai Research Institute of Gujarat Vidya Sabha, Ahmadabad, has totally ignored this source.

It is hoped that this critical edition of the *Mirqat* with a detailed notice of its author and the assessment of its varied contents will help research scholars and students in their study of medieval Gujarat and Rajasthan history.

Notes

113. Prof. Nizami has not taken note of the references to the Sarkhej saint in the hagiological works, like *Dah-Hikayat, Chihl-Hikayat, Sad-Hikayat*, *Jamiut-Turuqil-Burhaniya* and the like written by the sajjadas and disciples of the saint's contemporary Hazrat Sirajuddin Muhammad Shah Alam (d. 880 H./1475 A.D.). While the *Mirqat* makes only one mention of the meeting of Shaikh Ahmad with Hazrat Shah Alami's father Hazrat Burhanuddin Qutb-i-Alam, these works by the Shahi Bukhari saint-scholars contain considerable material bring to light the nature of relations

of Shaikh Ahmad with his friend Hazrat Qutb-i-Alam and his son. Shah Alam is reported to have been visiting the tomb of the saint (*Sad Hikayat*, Story No.42 Ms in the Khanqah of Shah Abdul-Halim, Ankleshwar, Dist. Bharuch), Xerox copy in the Dargah Hazrat Pir Muhammad Shah Library,).

114. Nizami, *op. cit.*, 237,238.
115. Ivanow, *op. cit.*, 91-92.
116. Incidentally, the two Nagori Muhallas of Shahpur and Kalupur in Ahmadabad were obviously inhabited by the people of Nagor and its vicinity.
117. Not Mandu as printed in historical works in Persian and accepted by all modern historians writing on the subject.
118. Not mentioned in any historical work. Incidentally, Maulana Sayyid Abu Zafar Nadvi has attributed this menace to the Portuguese, which is not correct see also n.105 above.
119. Text, 100,150,169,etc.
120. *EIAPS*, 1955 and 1956, 57, pl. XVa.
121. It is a pity that the saint's narration omitted the place and time and like details of the expedition.
122. For detial, see *EIPAS*, 1972, 23-31, pl. IIIa.
123. *Ibid*, It is a coincidence that two three conversions of members which later on formed the ruling families of Khanzadas of Nagor, Mohels of Ladnun and Khanzadas of Mewat took place at about the same time in these regions of Rajasthan and neighbouring Mewat.
124. *Ibid.*, 33-36, where a detailed account of Malik Qutb will be found.
125. Barani, *Tarikh-i-Firuz Shahi* (Calcutta, 1862), 454; Yahya Sarhindi, *op. cit.*, 98. According to Shams Siraj Afif, *Tarikh-i-Firuz Shahi* (Calcutta, 1888-91), 299, he held the post of Deputy Ariz-i-Mamalik (Pay-Master of the Kingdom). The *Mirqat* calls him "Firuz Shahi", i.e. he was then a noble under Firuz Shah. See also *EIAPS*, 1972, p.35, n.6 for further references.
126. The text may be corrupt here. The purport seems to be : "The young man is acting foolishly".
127. This is on one hand an important piece of information and on the other, another instance of the authenticity of this memoirs. Regrettably no further details about him are given except that the saint was so much kind to him that when he fell ill, the saint went to Khambhat to see him and the Malik was also very happy, and he recovered from his illness and he and the saint went round the tombs of the holy men of the town. This mention of the Malik (as flourishing in the reign of Sultan Ahmad I) shows that like the Abu Raja family, the Butahari family of Khambhat had preferred to settle down in Gujarat, his first known ancestor being Malik Daulatshah Butahari who had constructed two mosques, one being the Jami mosque, at Bharuch, in the reign of Ghiyasuddin Tughluq (1320-25 A.D.) and the Jami mosque of Khambhat in H. 725 (1325 A.D.) and the Idgah of Bharuch next year, in the reign of Muhammad bin Tughluq Shah (1325-51 A.D.). Malik Mubarak Butahari must be his grandson or great grandson. For details of Malik Fakhruddin Daulatshah son of Muhammad Butahari and his inscriptions, see *EIAPS*, 1957 and 1958, 29-31 and 30, n.20. This Fakhruddin Daulatshah's father Muhammad is mentioned by Ibn Battuta

in his *Rihla* as pointed out by S.C.Misra, *op. cit.*, 96, where however he confuses the son with the father. The Bharuch inscriptions call him Fakhruddin Daulatshah Muhammad Butahari which means Daulat Shah was his name and Muhammad that of his father.

128. Sikandar, *op. cit.*, 30; Misra, *op.cit.*, 171-72.
129. Text, 228; *SA*, 253.
130. Text, 230; *SA*, 256.
131. *EIAPS*, 1963, 12-13, pl. II a. Needless to say, this inscription which has a great bearing on the date of the accession of Sultan Ahmad I has not been taken note of by writers on the history of Gujarat.
132. *Ibid.*, 1953 and 1954, 56-57. Incidentally, modern historians who have noticed this epigraph like Prof. Commissariat, give the name of the Malik as Muhammad son of Musa, which is incorrect (*Ibid.*, 56, note). Dr. Misra overlooks this epigraph first noticed in *Bombay Gazetteer*, VIII, Kathiawar and subsequently quoted by Prof. Commissariat.
133. Dr. M.A. Chaghatai, *Muslim Monuments of Ahmedabad* (Poona, 1942), 63. According to Dr. Chaghtai, Malik Shaikh "was one of the nobles in Gujarat in 778 A.H./1376 A.D.", for which he does not quote any authority.
134. Najm son of Rafi Waiz appears to the identical with Qazi Najm, of the time of Mahmud Begda, who had ordered breaking up of the golden *rubab* (musical instrument) made by a goldsmith for the Sultan. He later on became a disciple of Hazrat Shah Alam. An unique copy of the collection of his sermons (*waz*) in Persian entitled *Lulu-i-Majalis* is to be found in the Goverment Oriental Manuscripts Library Madras and a paper on it by Dr. Ziyauddin Desai was read at the Ahmadabad Session of the All India Persian Teachers Conference in 1982.
135. *Jamdar-i-Khass* was the officer in charge of the Royal Wardrobe or dresses.
136. For details and conversations between the Malik and Qazi, Qazi and King and King and Malik, see Text, 156, *SA*, 194-96.
137. According to *the Tuhfatul-Qari* (written 1119 H./1708 A.D.), Birpur was founded by Hazrat Qazi Shah Hammad father of Hazrat Qazi Mahmud Daryai; it might have been the habitation on the other side of the river on which the tomb of the latter is situated.
138. Not Rander, as stated in *SA*, 251 and in *Malfuz Literature, op.cit.*, 42. In *Ibid.*, Santij is also included in the list of Gujarat villages. But this does not appear to be correct, looking to the context (Text, 218).
139. *Ibid.* reads Tartav or Tartar.
140. The mention of Muluk-Khana of this mosque in the *Mirqat* is very important, as being the earlist mention of this architectural term of India. For details see *bid.*, 46.
141. For details, see *Ibid.*, 43.
142. It is wrongly written as *Bagh-i-jud* in Persian historical works. For the correct name and identification of this garden, which has given the name Jor-bagh to Delhi's famous once posh residentical area, see Dr. Ziyauddin A.Desai's article on Bara Gumbad Mosque Inscription published in K.V.

Soundara Rajan Felicitation volume, New Delhi.

143. This must have been later on built pucca in 1437 A.D. by Mujahid Khan, ruler of Nagor and nephew of Muzaffar Shah I who named it Mustafasar (*Epigraphia Indo- Muslemica*, 1923-24, 16).

144. *Malfuz Literature*, *op. cit.*, 45 has Khabadja.

145. It is not possible to say for certain, if by these are meant the Jami mosque and the Tank in the present Roza complex as is stated in a recently published article in Gujarati (Dr. Zubair Qureshi, *Gujarat ke Mashahir Ulema*, Ahmadabad, 1991). There is a much smaller mosque of the same age not without architectural merit and a low lying area nearby on the outskirt of the Sarkhej village. This could perhaps be meant by Maulana Muhammad Qasim. The Sarkhej Roza tank was constructed in the time of Muzaffar Shah II according to a Gujarati inscription found engraved on the south wall of the Big mosque at the western half of the north side of the tanks (*Studies in Epigraphy*, Epigraphical Society of India Journal, no. 6, 1980).

146. The word is written with *jim-i-arabi*; it could be with *jim-i-farsi*. Maulana Sayyid Abu Zafar Nadvi (*SA*, 76) takes it to be *Juni* and states that it was so designated after prince Juna Khan, later on Sultan Muhammad bin Tughluq Shah. In the fairly well developed study of Indian numismatics, a coin with the name *Juni* is not known.

147. The exact connotation of the vernacular term *chhajja* is not known.

148. The instances of cows given to Brahmins in *dakshina*, going the same way, are not unheard of in these days too.

149. For details of this somewhat lengthy account, see Text, 23 ff, *SA*, 68 ff., and *Malfuz Lit.,* 48.

150. Text, 24-26, *SA*, 69-72, *Malfuz Lit.*, 49.

151. This is perhaps the earliest literary referece of Sheranis inhabiting this part of the country. Even until very recently, there was and may stil be there a settlement near Chhoti Khattu, called Sheraniyon-ki-Dhanchi to which the celebrated Persian and Urdu scholar, critic and literary historian Hafiz Mahmud Khan Sherani (father of the famous Urdu poet Akhtar Sherani) belonged.

152. Such fanciful names do not appear to have been confined to one region only. For example, in Chanderi in Madhya Pradesh too, such names are known. Sabah-i-Khair and Gul-i-Bihisht were names of two slave-girls of a local saint (*EIAPS*, 1964, 76).

153. Some high Muslim officials, like Malik Muzaffar Kalal of the time of Muhammad bin Tughluq Shah also patronised jogis (Text, 54, *SA*, 99, *Malfuz Lit.*, 55.).

154. For details see Text, 50, *SA,* 95, *Malfuz Lit.*, 55. According to the *Tuhfatul-Majalis* (*TM*, 56 b,*TMU,* 86), this very feat was performed at Sarkehj on challenge by a Muslim saint Shaikh Mithai. Such a practice of *alav* in the month of Muharram is in vogue even now in our country.

155. The Salavi community of manufacturers of superfine *Patola* wear of Gujarat owes it's name to this cloth-variety which is stated to be a coloured superfine cloth for ladies wear like Sari, etc. The *patola* sari made by them fetches 75,000 to 1,20,000 rupees, even now.
156. The *Mirqat* as related to its author by the saint, mentions the *Betaala* a famine which must have occured in the forty-second (*baitalis*) year of the 15th century Vikrama Samvat, that is 1442 or 1386 A.D. (Text, 186). The Urdu translation (*SA*, 220) does not mention this word as it was perhaps unfamiliar to its translator. Such terms like Sattasiyo, etc. are common in Gujarat and perhaps elsewhere.
157. Incidentally, the Mughal emperors used to send their aid to the deserving people as well as the Sharif of the Makkah — Arabia was then a poor country — in kind. Material was purchased at Surat and sold in Makkah at 100 per cent profit which doubled of the aid amount.
158. This is now done in cities by specially trained dog squads.

5

EPILOGUE

In the foregoing lines, an attempt has been made to present an exhaustive and intensive study of a totally neglected primary source for the various aspects of the history of life and society of Western Indian states of Rajasthan and Gujarat in the medieval times. This source, the *Mirqatul-Wusul-Ilallahi war-Rasul* is in Persian and is based mainly on the reminiscences narrated by the famous saint Shaikh Ahmad Khattu Maghribi of Sarkhej near Ahmadabad. This work, even otherwise comprising by itself a valuable example of the contribution of Gujarat to Persian literature, is not so well-known to students of Indo-Persian literature or historians of medieval history of India including that of Gujarat.

The work is not totally unknown, as its existence was known through its manuscript copy, then considered unique, of the Asiatic Society of Bengal, Calcutta and was described at length, with its list of contents fully quoted in the Catalogue of manuscripts of the Society as long back as in 1924. Its notice was taken by the late Prof. Khaliq Ahmad Nizami who wrote an article on the Sarkhej saint but he based his account exclusively on another malfuz of the saint, the *Tuhfatul-Majalis*, from its manuscript in the British Museum (now British Library). Prof. Nizami did not think it worthwhile to consult the *Mirqat*, though as it has been shown in the present study, it was far richer and more authentic and correct in its account, than the *Tuhfatul-Majalis.*

Unfortunately the learned Prof. was not aware of the Urdu translation of the *Mirqat* published as long back as in 1945, under the title *Sirat-i-Ahmadiya (Biography of Ahmad)*, by the late Maulana Sayyid Abu Zafar Nadvi, a great scholar and author of many works in Urdu on the history of India including Gujarat. He had also translated in Urdu the *Tuhfatul-Majalis* and published it earlier.

Despite this, no note of the rich material contained in the *Mirqat* was taken by the writers on the history of Gujarat and Rajasthan. In the meantime, a manuscript of the work, prepared from two more manuscripts (which are untraceable now), was got made by the late Maulana Nadvi for the Dargah Hazrat Pir Muhammad Shah Library when he had taken up the translation of the Mirqat from a hand copy of one of the said two copies. While thinking of the topic for the doctoral thesis, my teacher Prof. Dr. A.N. Quraishi, then head of the Department, of Persian, Gujarat University, suggested to me to prepare a critical edition of the *Mirqat* and make a detailed study of its contents. Accordingly, the work was taken up. In the meantime it was learnt that a study of this work as a source for the medieval history of Gujarat and Rajasthan was made by Dr. Z.A. Desai Director (Epigraphy), Archaeological Survey of India.

Consequently, work was started under the guidance of Prof. Dr. B.A. Tirmizi who had by that time succeeded Prof. Dr. A.N. Quraishi. The manuscript copy of the Asiatic Society Calcutta could not be obtained due to many reasons, one of them being the unhappy state of affairs. Later on, a xerox copy could be obtained and the new copy and the hand-copy used by Maulana Nadvi were traced and on the basis of these, a critical edition was prepared and a detailed study of the work was made and presented.

The present thesis thus makes available to the historians as well as students of Indo-Persian literature alike a fifteenth-century Persian source. The importance of this work as a primary source for the political, social, cultural and literary activities of the period was highlighted in the Introduction, where a detailed life-sketch of both the Sarkhej saint, whose malfuz the *Mirqat* is and of his foster father and spiritual mentor Babu Ishaq was presented for the first time. Likewise, the study also attempts a detailed account of the author, his education, his family, his scholarship, etc. It also takes stock, in great details, the wealth of source material the *Mirqat* possesses under various headings and sub-headings. As a matter of fact the Section on the *Mirqtul-Wusul* is a sort of a detailed account of the contents of the book.

Needless to say, the text has been prepared with great care and deliberation and it can be said to be as correct as humanly possible. If the original manuscript from which the hand-copy referred to was made were available, it would have helped determine the correct text in about half a dozen places which have defied attempts.

In short, the present critically edited text and exhaustive introduction will fulfil the purpose for which this doctoral thesis was undertaken and meet with the needs of medieval historians of west India and also those interested in the study of sufistic movements in India as also growth of Indo-Persian literature.

PART TWO

CRITICAL EDITED TEXT OF THE

MIRQATUL-WUSUL ILALLAH-I-WAR- RASUL

1

MANUSCRIPTS USED

As in the case of malfuz and hagiographical works and treatises quite a good number of which were compiled in the fifteenth and subsequent centuries,[1] very few copies of the *Mirqat-Wusul* are available. The main reason for non-availability of those works is the policy of the saintly families not only to part with the manuscripts of malfuz works of their saints, but not to allow them even to be seen, let alone read by others. Therefore with very few exceptions, such works which were available in the ninteenth century are not to be found in liberaries in India or abroad. It is doubtful if these are still available in private collection of Khanqahs and saintly houses, for as gathered from the personal experience of scholars and others who have had occassion to have a glance at them, their condition is far from satisfactory and whatever of the sizeable number of them are with them are likely to be perished or became unservisable.

Of the two copies of the *Mirqat*, known to be exist one is the Asiatic Society of Bengal Calcutta, As to the other, it has not been possible to know for certain, where it is now saintly families of Ahmadabad like Khanqah-i-Chishtiya and the Qazi Sahibs of Ahmadabad might possess a copy thereof. It appears that this other copy of which a transcript copy was made available to the late Maulavi Sayyid Abu Zafar Nadvi, Urdu Translator of the *Mirqat*, by the late Sayyid Manzur Husain Alavi, popularly known as Husaini Pir,[2] must have existed and even now exist in one of the two said families, very probably Qazi Sahib's family. A third incomplete copy of the *Mirqat* was received in the Dargah Hazrat Pir Muhammad Shah Library through the late Qazi Ahmad Miyan Akhtar of Junargadh. In the meantime, the transcript copy of the *Mirqat* of Husaini Pir was also used by Maulavi Abu Zafar Nadvi who completed the defective copy with the help of that transcript and a fresh complete copy was got prepared by Maulavi Abdul-Ghafur a local calligrapher, for the above mentioned Dargah Library.

I have made the Dargah Hazrat Pir Muhammad Shah Library manuscript copy, just mentioned, as the base copy and collated it carefully with Husaini Pir Sahib's hand-copy and the copy of the Asiatic Society Bengal Library. This Calcutta copy which was once in the Library of Tipu Sultan of Mysore is full of scribal errors and omissions. However it has proved useful in determining the correct text of the *Mirqat*, which it is hoped will be found as faithful a copy of the original work as possible. Had the original manuscript of Husaini Pir Sahib's hand-copy been available, it would perhaps have helped to clear up the text at about half a dozen places.

The Description of Used Copies is as Under:

Ms. Dargah Sharif Hazrat Pir Muhammad Shah copy. A modern copy in fine *Nastaliq* made by the late Maulavi Abdul-Ghafur, pages 237, size 130 x 220, 15 lines per page.

Ms. *Ha* (ح) : Husaini Pir Sahib's copy, in running hand in *Nastaliq* characters 130 pages. The original manuscript was transcribed by Muhammad son of Mahmud Khatib son of Ismail Khatib, son of Siddiq Khatib son of Yusuf Khatib son of Mahmud Khatib, Ghaznavi, for Daulat Muhammad Zakir, son of Haji Mahmud Muhammad son of Shaikhji son of Hasan. According to a note, it perusal was completed on 27 Rajjab 1128 Hijri by Hayat Manjhanshahi who describes himself as the most humble devotee of the *astana* of Hazrat Shah Alam or Manjhan Shah (d. 880 A.H.) In all probability this manuscript copy was transcribed not very long before this date.[3]

Ms. *Kaf*, (ك) copy in the Asiatic Society, Calcutta, Library, called in the catalogue *Malfuzat-i-Ahmad-i-Mghribi.* folios 166, size 220 x 120, 160 x 75, lines 15 per page. Ordinary paper. Indian *Nastaliq* condition good. It was first in the Tipu Sultan Library later on taken over by the British and kept in Fort-William College, Calcutta and donated to the Asiatic Society Library.

Notes

1. For example, early nineteenth century *Mukhbirul-Auliya* mentions a fairly good number of such works quoting extensively from most of them. Some of these treatises and works are even unheard of. For example, according to the author of the *Mukhbirul-Auliya* comprising about 900 folios, Hazrat Shaikh Rashiduddin Maudud Lala, he had earlier complied a larger biographical work named *Shamailul-Wasilin* (Ms. Khanqah-i-Chishtiya, f.2b).
2. *SA*, 2.
3. Ivanow *op. cit.*, 93.

PERSIAN TEXT

مِرقاتُ الوصُول

اِلی اللہِ وَالرَّسُولِ

حضرت شیخ گنج احمد مغربی قدس سرّہٗ

جمع کردہ

مولانا محمد قاسم رحمۃ اللہ علیہ

مقالہ برائے پی۔ ایچ۔ ڈی منظور شدہ از گجرات یونیورسٹی

تقابلی اور تنقیدی مطالعہ

پروفیسر نثار احمد انصاری

کتاب بھون

۱۷۸۴۔ کلاں محل، دریا گنج، نئی دہلی ۱۱۰۰۰۲

نام کتاب	:	مرقات الوصول الی اللہ والرسول
تالیف	:	حضرت شیخ گنج احمد مغربی قدس سرّہ
جمع کردہ	:	مولانا محمد قاسم رحمۃ اللہ علیہ
مرتّب	:	پروفیسر نثار احمد انصاری
سنِ اشاعت	:	۲۰۰۴ء
نوبت چاپ	:	چاپ اوّل
شمارہ شابک	:	۸۱-۷۱۵۱-۳۵۱-۴
چاپ	:	نائس پرنٹنگ پریس، خوریجی خاص، نئی دہلی-۱۱۰۰۵۱
ناشر	:	نصرت علی ناصری برائے کتاب بھون
		۱۷۸۴، کلاں محل، دریا گنج، نئی دہلی-۱۱۰۰۰۲

Name of Book	:	Mirqatul Wusul Ilallah-i-war-Rasul
Author	:	Shaikh Ganj Ahmad Maghribi Qudus Sirrahu
Collection	:	Maulana Muhammad Qasim (R.A.)
Edited	:	Prof. Nisar Ahmad Ansari
Language	:	Persian - English
Date of Publication	:	2004, Ist Edition
ISBN	:	81-7151-351-4
Printed at	:	Nice Printing Press, Khureji Khas, New Delhi-110051
Published by	:	Nusrat Ali Nasri for Kitab Bhavan 1784, Kalan Mahal, Daryaganj, New Delhi-110002 (India)

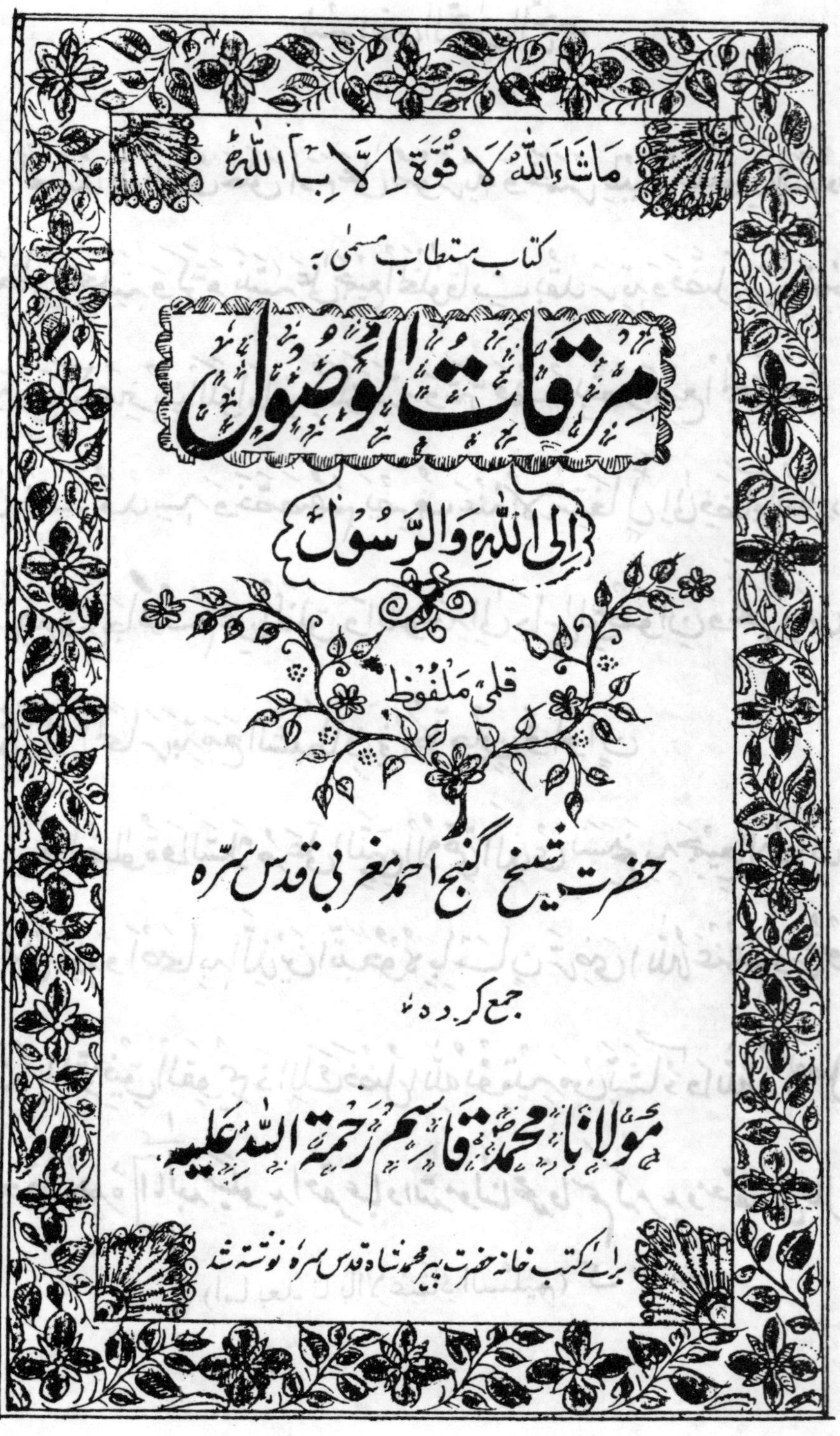
ماشاء اللہ لا قوۃ الا باللہ
کتاب مستطاب مسمّیٰ بہ
مرقات الوصول
الی اللہ والرسول
قلمی ملفوظ
حضرت شیخ گنج احمد مغربی قدس سرہ
جمع کردہ
مولانا محمد قاسم رحمۃ اللہ علیہ
برائے کتب خانہ حضرت پیر محمد شاہ قدس سرہ نوشتہ شد

بسم الله الرحمن الرحیم

اَلْحَمْدُ لِلّٰهِ الَّذِی خَلَقَ اٰدَمَ عَلٰی صُوْرَتِهٖ وَخَمَرَ طِیْنَتَهٗ لِلْفَوْزِ بِالسَّعَادَةِ الْعُظْمٰی بِحِکْمَتِهٖ وَکَرَّمَ نَبِیَّهٗ عَلٰی جَمِیْعِ الْمَخْلُوْقَاتِ بِقُدْرَتِهٖ وَفَضَّلَ مِنْ نَبِیِّهِمُ الْاَوْلِیَاءَ بِمَزِیْدِ الْکَرَامَاتِ بِمَکْرُمَتِهٖ وَنَشَرَ فَهُمْ بِقَصْرِ جَمِیْعِ الْمُهِمَّاتِ اِلٰی جَنَابِ قُدْسِهٖ وَخَصَّصَهُمْ یَصْرِفُ عَنْهُ الْاِشْتِغَالَ اِلٰی فِضَاءِ السُّرُوْرِ وَرَفَعَ دَرَجَاتِهِمْ عَنِ الْخَلْقِ وَالتَّوَجُّهِ اِلٰی دَارِ الرِّضْوَانِ وَتَجَرَّدَ عَنِ الدُّنْیَا وَالْمُحَارَبَةِ مَعَ الشَّیْطَانِ فِیْ کُلِّ حِیْنٍ وَّ اَوَانٍ

وَالصَّلٰوةُ وَالسَّلَامُ عَلَی النَّبِیِّ الْاُمِّیِّ الَّذِیْ نَسَخَ بِهٖ جَمِیْعَ الْاَدْیَانِ وَعَلٰی اٰلِهٖ وَاَصْحَابِهِ الَّذِیْنَ اتَّبَعُوْهُ بِاِحْسَانٍ رَضِیَ اللّٰهُ عَنْهُمْ وَرَضُوْا عَنْهُ بِالتَّوْفِیْقِ الْقَوِیْمِ ذٰلِکَ فَضْلُ اللّٰهِ یُؤْتِیْهِ مَنْ یَّشَاءُ وَاللّٰهُ ذُو الْفَضْلِ الْعَظِیْمِ [اما بعد میگوید احقر عباد الله مولنا محمد قاسم که مرید و معتقد سی سال

۱ (اما بعد تا باالاِعتِقادِ السَّلیم) ک = ندارد

حضور خدمت و امامت کرده بود هر چه از زبان دُربار و گوهر نثار شنیده و خود معائنه کرده در ملفوظ آورده

بسم الله الرحمن الرحیم

اَلْحَمْدُ لِلّٰهِ الْکَرِیْمِ الْوَلِیِّ الْقَدِیْمِ الْعَزِیْزِ الْحَکِیْمِ الرَّؤُفِ الرَّحِیْمِ وَالصَّلٰوةُ عَلٰی رَسُوْلِهِ الْحَکِیْمِ النَّاهِجِ عَلَی الْمَنْهَجِ الْمُسْتَقِیْمِ مُحَمَّدٍ وَّ اٰلِهِ الَّذِیْنَ اتَّبَعُوْهُ بِالْاِعْتِقَادِ السَّلِیْمِ [1] وَبَعْدُ فَقَدْ قَالَ سَمِیُّ نَبِیِّ اللّٰهِ امن کم (ابن کثیر) صَلَّی اللّٰهُ عَلَیْهِ وَاٰلِهِ وَسَلَّمَ وَعُفِیَ عَنْهُمَا وَسَلَّمَ [2] لَمَّا حَتَفَ لِیْ فِیْ جَمٍّ غَفِیْرٍ مِّنَ الْاِخْوَانِ وَالْحَثِّ عَلٰی سم کَثِیْرٍ مِّنَ الْاَقْرَانِ اَنْ اَکْتُبَ لَهُمْ لَهُمْ مَا وَهَبَ [3] اِذْ فِیْ ثَلٰثِیْنَ عَامًا مِّنْ مَّلْفُوْظَاتِ الشَّیْخِ الْاِمَامِ قِدْوَةِ الْاَنَامِ قُطْبِ الزَّمَانِ شَمْسِ [4] سَمَاءِ الْوِلَایَةِ فِی الدَّوَرَانِ مُحِیْطِ مَرَاکِزِ الْعُلُوْمِ الْاَدْیَانِ الْمَخْصُوْصِ بِعِنَایَاتِ اللّٰهِ الْاَحَدِ شَمْسِ الْحَقِّ

١ ک = اما بعد ٢ ح = لما اختلفا
٣ ک = وغمت ٤ ک = شمس الحق

والشرع والدین شیخ احمد مغربی تغمدہ اللہ بلطفہ الابدی وکنت

لیھم کل مرتب اعتذار ان ذالک امر متنضر[1] فرصوا الابواب

لعساکر الکرام بحثہ[2] واصحاب الدفاتر والحکام فصرت

متحیرا و سبب متفکر بس بس، ان کان ولو کان افتان وخیزان

قدام کرد و باشیب وعیب بعدا ز[3] [رحلت شیخ جہاں دامت برکاتہ

دوازدہ سال اہتمام کرد وسعی جمیل وجہد جزیل داشت کہ از الفاظ

دمیان نشان چیزی فرو نگذاشت و مناقب و اخلاق بندگی

شیخ المشائخ ابو اسحاق المغربی قدس اللہ سرہ العزیز و الی بردہ چنانچہ

ز حضرت آن قطب الزمان شیخ جہان دامت برکاتہ، شنیدہ بالصدق والا

لاص والراس باز دید] وچون دیباچہ سادہ ببرکت آن سجادہ تمام شد لختی بر سر دا[4] شت

اگاہ جمال باکمال بندگی قطب الزمان شیخ جہان دامت برکاتہ[5] بین النوم و الیقظۃ

۱ح = متصمز ۲ ک = بعثوا ۳ از (بعد از رحلت تا والراس بازدید)
۴ ک = پہلو بربستر ۵ داست برکاتہ = ک - ندارد

دریافت فرمان شد با یا مقصود بکام رسید غرضه[1] برآمد آری ای ولی سعید دل شاد شد

و درونه برباد شد گفتم الحمد لله عنایت حق تعالی یار است و مدد ایشان در کار است و نام[2]

این ملفوظ [مرقات الوصول الی الله والرسول کرده آمد][3] بر شانزده[16] فصل

قسمة[4] [مرقات الوصول الی الله والرسول و فصله علی ستة عشر من الفصول]

فصل اول در بیان مشایخ و کیفیت رسیدن بخدمت بابو و پرورش ایشان کردن در کار تیر و کمان گوی و چوگان و عمل دلاوری

فصل دوم در ذکر اقبال و قبولیت و عظمت و ایثار و تجرید و علو همت بندگی مخدوم

فصل سوم در مناقب بندگی شیخ ابو اسحاق بن محمود مغربی که پیر و مربی بندگی مخدوم

فصل چهارم در شروع کردن علم[5] بندگی مخدوم در انواع

فصل پنجم در بحثهای علم که با علمای نامدار و خوابهای بندگی حضرت فرموده اند

فصل ششم در ذکر خوابها که بزرگان در باب حضرت مخدوم دیده اند و خود معاینه کرده اند

فصل هفتم در عبادات بندگی حضرت مخدوم و صیام و ذکر با خلاص و دفع وسواس در نماز

فصل هشتم در توحید حضرت مخدوم و ابیاتی که خود فرموده اند و بیان مناسب در ابیات

فصل نهم در نصائح بندگی مخدوم که با مریدان و معتقدان و دوستان فرموده اند

فصل دهم در ذکر قلت طعام حضرت مخدوم و مجاهده و ریاضت و اربعین ایشان[6]

فصل یازدهم در خوارق و کشف و کرامات و عجائبات حضرت[7] جهان و قطب زمان

فصل دوازدهم در سماع بندگی حضرت قطب العالم مخدوم شیخ احمد مغربی

فصل سیزدهم کیفیت روان شدن[8] بندگی حضرت قطب العالم مخدوم شیخ احمد مغربی برای حج گزاردن

فصل چهاردهم در کیفیت روان شدن حضرت مخدوم در سمرقند برای امر معروف بر بادشاه تیمور

فصل پانزدهم بازگشتن حضرت مخدوم از خراسان در عهد مظفر شاه و در گجرات آمدند

فصل شانزدهم در سفر آخرت بندگی حضرت شیخ جهان قطب زمان[9] و الغفران علیه الرحمة

۱ک = غرض ۲ ونام = ک- ندارد ۳ از مرقات تاکرده آمد = ک -ندارد
۴ک =قسمت کرده است ۵ک = علوم ۶ = ک = --- ایشان مخدوم
حضرت شیخ جهان وقطب زمان شیخ احمد مغربی
۷ک =علیه الرحمت والغفران

نامدار با بندگی حضرت مخدوم کردند و جواب ہا کہ بندگی حضرت مخدوم فرمودہ اند **فصل ششم** در ذکر خوابہا کہ بزرگان درباب حضرت مخدوم دیدہ اند و حضرت مخدوم خود معائنہ کردہ اند **فصل ہفتم** در عبادات بندگی حضرت مخدوم و صیام و ذکر با خلاص و دفع وسواس در نماز **فصل ہشتم** در توحید حضرت مخدوم و ابیاتی کہ خود فرمودہ اند و بیان مناسب در ابیات **فصل نہم** در نصائح بندگی مخدوم کہ با مریدان و معتقدان و دوستان فرمودہ اند **فصل دہم** در ذکر و قلت طعام حضرت مخدوم و مجاہدہ ریاضت و اربعین ایشان **فصل یازدہم** در خوارق و کشف و کرامات و عجائبات حضرت جہاں قطب زبان مخدوم شیخ احمد مغربی **فصل دوازدہم** در سماع بندگی حضرت قطب العالم مخدوم شیخ احمد مغربی **فصل سیزدہم** در کیفیت روان شدن حضرت مخدوم برائی حج گذاردن **فصل چہاردہم** در کیفیت روان شدن حضرت مخدوم در سمرقند برائے امر معروف بادشاہ دوران میر تیمور صاحب قران **فصل پانزدہم** در بازگشتن حضرت مخدوم از خراسان و در عہد مظفر شاہ در گجرات آمدن[1] **فصل شانزدہم** در سفر آخرت بندگی حضرت شیخ جہان قطب زبان علیہ الرحمۃ والغفران

فصل اوّل در بیان منشاء شیخ جہان قطب زبان بزبان مبارک فرمودند کہ پیش از خدمات[2] شیخ حضرت بابو اسحاق بابا قوام الدین میکردند مردی دراز قد بود خلق کھٹو او را کر ہر می گفتند یعنی شیر جوان و قصہ او عجب است کہ خدمت حضرت بابو در اثناء سیاحت در مسجدی از مقام فرد آمدہ بودند و در جوار آں مسجد طفلی را ملازت نزد آوردہ بود پدر آں طفل بخدمت حضرت بابو آمدہ

[1] ک: آمدند [2] ک: خدمت

عرض کرد که آن طفل را دعا کنید تا ببرکت دعا آنحضرت نیکو شود بندگی حضرت بابو فرمودند که اگر مرا بدهند دعا کنیم پسر من باشد او برزن خود رفت و کیفیت گفت زن گفت از دل من فرود نمی آید چون ملالت و الم سخت غالب شد بحدی که هلاک موت آغاز شد و الم بالا شدن گرفت[1] زن را چاره نشد شوهر را گفت ببر این طفل را شیخ بده پدر او را بخدمت حضرت بابو آورد بندگی حضرت بابو فرمودند که بعد ازین کسی از جهت آن طفل دعوی نکند با در و پدر هر دو قبول کردند خدمت حضرت بابو دعا فرمودند از کرم الله تعالی و ببرکت دعا ایشان طفل را قرار شد هلاکی موت رفت[2] بندگی حضرت بابو او را شیخ قوام الدین نام کردند و بتعظیم و تربیت کردند و این شیخ قوام الدین با طفلیت[3] در کهٹو در خدمت حضرت بابو بود و از خلق فتوحات در هنگام فصل پیشتر[4] غله لوبیا بود زیرا چه دران قصبه اغلب همان غله می شد چنانچه در مثل است کهٹو چهور لو جیوار روزی شیخ قوام الدین لوبیا پخت بخدمت حضرت بابو آورد و التماس کرد که چیزی نان خورش نیست اگر اشارت شود کٹوری گرو داشته روغن بیارم حضرت بابو فرمودند بابا قوام الدین در چه خیال افتاده قانع شو هر چه پیش می آید هم بآن ساز مبادا از لوبیا محروم گردی شیخ قوام الدین برای روغن ستدن رفت ملک کمال خورم بخدمت حضرت بابو آمد و گفت حضرت بابو برحکم القادم نیز از عمل نگردید[5] من درین مقام نو آمده ام و برای ملاقات من نیامدید خدمت حضرت بابو فرمودند این در باب من نیست و آن لوبیا پخته تمام پیش ملک آوردند ملک لقمه چند خوردند باقی دیگران را دادند و وداع کردند باز گشتند شیخ قوام الدین آمد لوبیا نیافت بندگی حضرت بابو فرمودند هرکه روغن بخواهد از لوبیا محروم گردد بعد در

1. ک: دم 2. ک: ملا کی موت رفت 3. از طفولیّت 4. ک: بیشتر
5. ک: نکردید 6. ازبندگی تا مجال سکونت 5. ک ندارد

محلت جوانی ملول بود شیخ قوام الدین نیز ملالت داشت آن جوان را چون سکرات موت شد جوان
فریاد ها کردن گرفت شیخ قوام الدین گفت ای فلان تو می روی من هم می آیم جوان نقل کرد
شیخ قوام الدین هم نقل کرد بندگی بابو را مونس سخت بود بسیار گریستن گرفت موهای سر
شیخ قوام الدین که بعد محلوق کردن از سر فرود می آمد در شگاف دیواری میداشتند و سنگریزه بران
شگاف داشتند چون شیخ قوام الدین را یاد می کردند نزدیک آن شگاف می رفتند و می نشستند
و از آن موها را سنگریزه دور می کردند و می گریستند[1] و می گفتند بابا قوام الدین چون فارغ شدند
موها در آن شگاف می داشتند باز سنگریزه همان جا می داشتند درین اثنا الهام من الله تعالی شد
و حلیه نمودند که خوردگی بدان حلیه خواهد رسید از آن خاطر جمع خواهد شد بنابر آن حضرت بابو در تفحص
بودند بلا زنان و عزیزان را فرموده بودند که خوردگی بدان صوت و بدان حلیه پیدا شود نگذارید اگر شما
نتوانید مارا علم دهید درین اثنا آن مولانا صدر الدین نبسه مولانا شهاب الدین همدانی از کهتور دنیده و
برای غرض خود می رفت بوداع پیش حضرت بابو آمدند بندگی حضرت بابو فرمودند که اگر خوردگی[2] بدان
صوت و بدان حلیه پیدا شود نگذارید برای خاطر خادمت بابو مولانا صدر الدین در دنیده وا رفتند و
شنیده اند که نجیب نام نساج را خوردگی[3] پرهنجار و نیک دیدار از قافله میان دواب که برای نمک در قصبه
دنیده وانه آمده بود بدست او آمده است مولانا نجیب را گفت که بندگی حضرت بابو اسحاق قدس الله
سره العزیز مرا بجهت این بچه براه کرده اند تسلیم من کن تا بخدمت ایشان ببرم و اهل دنیده وانه سالها

۱ مارا قوام الدین ۲ خردگی ۳ خردگی - پریهنجار

کرامت و خوارق خدمت بابو معائنه کرده بودند کسی را مجال عدول از فرمان ایشان نبود هر چند الحج[1]
کرد و عاجزی بسیار نمود که من لاولدم بمن بگذارید مولانا صدر الدین گفت که اگر این خوردک را
بگذارم نه مرا مجال سکونت در کهتو بماند و نه ترا در دین و دانه و این کیفیت از این قسم نیست که پوشیده
بماند به تحقیق بخدمت حضرت بابو خواهد رسید پس عظمت خدمت حضرت بابو در کار شد نجیب را
چاره نشد که امتناع از تسلیم کند بعده مولانا دران قافله رفت تحقیق کرد که این خوردک به شما از کجا رسید
گفته که در شهر دهلی بادی عظیم با غبار خاسته بود کنیزکی این خوردک را در کنار خود کرده کوچه گذاشته از
دهشت سرگردان شده در قافله ما آمده شخصی آن کنیزک را دلداری داده برخود داشته بود بعد ازان قافله
از آنجا انتقال نموده و کنیزک با او آمده این حکایت تحقیق کرده از آنجا طرف کهتو روان شدند
چون حضرت بابو اسحاق را خبر شد که مولانا صدر الدین بندگی مخدوم را از نجیب ستده می آرند
استقبال کردند و ملاقات نمودند و گفتند[2] که چنانچه صورت و حلیه که در الهام من الله تعالی نموده بودند
همان یافتیم[3] بندگی مخدوم را در کنار گرفته بخانه خود آوردند شیخ احمد نام کردند مولانا چهار ساله بودند
و عمر بابا اسحاق دران زمان هشتاد و یک سال بود و آنچنان پرورش کردند که هیچ ملکی و خانی فرزند
خود را بدان عزت و آب نکند و چنان در مأکل و ملبس پرورش کردند که حضرت شیخ جهان
قطب زمان دامت برکاته نیز بر سبیل مباهات و مفاخرت کرات و مرات[4] فرمودندی که این چنین
پرورش کم کسی را دست دهد در ایام خوردگی[5] که مرا پرورش کردند در کار تیر و کمان و گوی و

۱ الحاج ۲ گفتند ۳ یافتند ۴ ح= ندارد ۵ خردگی

چوگان و بیان و انصاف و عدالت و قوت شجاعت بدان ای عزیز مخلص در وفا خالص که بندگی شیخ جهان قطب الزمان لازالت برکاته منشورة کما کانت مقاماته معمورة از ملک زادگان شهر دهلی بودند زیراچه فرمودند که چون بندگی بابو ما را در دهلی برای زیارت پیران بردند روزی در باغ خبوارفته[1] بعبادت مشغول شدند من موازنه دوازده ساله بودم و در تماشای باغ مذکور می گشتم[2] ناگاه از یک خانه جوانی بیرون آمد با جامهای مهین و تیغی با تهنان ولبنان[3] نقره بر دست و کمر بند ابریشمی مرا گفت ملک نصیرالدین تو برادر منی یک برادر دیگر است و مادر و پدر در صدر[4] حیات اند چند سال است که در جگر مادر و پدر از سوز فراق تو سوراخها افتاده است در خانه ما بیا من او را اگذاشته بخدمت بابو آمدم او هم بخدمت بابو آمد عرض داشت کرد که این بچه برادر من است برین دلیل که در شانه این علامتی سرخ است که آن را در هند لهسن گویند ببینید در شانه بنده هم هست و شانه خود هم مو بهمان علامت بود و گفت در شانه والد ما هم همین است خدمت بابو فرمودند این بچه از شما چه گونه جدا شد او گفت که یکبار در شهر دهلی غباری بادی بعد از عصر برخاسته بود آن چنان که روز روشن همچو دیجور سیاه شد مرد کسی مرد دیگری را نمی دید و این ملک نصیرالدین برادر صغیر بود در کنار دایه خود از غایت تاریکی دایه کوچه فراموش کرده طرفی دیگر برد صباح هر چند تفحص کردیم نیافتیم این زمان در نظر آمد اگر اشارت شما باشد در خانه ببرم خدمت بابو جوان را فرمودند برو والد خود را بیار جوان در خانه رفت والد نیافت دیر شد بندگی بابو در مسائل شرعیه احاطه حواین تمام بمعنی حاوی

---

۱ جور ۲ گشتند ۳ ح= تنهال ولینال ۴ صدد

داشتند و فرمودند احمد چه میکنی بر پدر خود میروی یا نه عرض داشتیم که حضرت بابو پدر من شما
آید[1] دیگر کجا روم خدمت بابو برخاستند روان شدند من فکر کردم که اگر بر سبیل فرض حکایت
برادر راست باشد این عزت و حرمت که بخدمت بابو مراهست هرگز در خانهٔ پدر نباشد خدمت
بابو مرا هزار آرزو و تعهد میکنند و نعمت و نازمی پرورند چنانچه[2] بیان کرده اند و راه دین می آموزند
و دلبستگی بجای شده است که یک ذات گشته ایم اگر می بایم رنجش خدمت بابو مرا از بیخ برکنند و این
صحبت عالیه کجا بینم بر فور برخاستم در رکاب حضرت بابو روان شدم نماز شام در قصبه دیوری
دوازده کروه از دهلی گزاردیم همان جوان باردوم در آنکه مادر مسجد خانجهان بودم رسید بسیار
الحاج[3] کرد و جهد نمود که بر بابیا نرفتیم تا باعی آن کس را شناخت جان را چکنند فرزند
و عیال و خانمان را چکنند دیوانه کنی هر دو جهانش بخشی دیوانهٔ تو هر دو جهان را چکنند و درین
بار بندگی بابو همه مقابر اکابر و حوضها و روضها دهلی مرا نمودند و در روضه فتح خان نبیسه[4] سلطان
فیروز آمدیم خدمت بابو در حجره تکیه داشتند نماز دیگر چند نفر با طاقهای سفید بسیار با جماعت
کثیر در صحن حجره شده درون روضه می رفتند بخدمت بابو من عرض کردم که این طاقها چیست و این
و جماعت کیست فرمودند سید جلال الدین بخاری محل درون نزول کرده اند خلق را مرید می گیرند
خادمان طاقیها[5] برای آن جماعت می برند اگر ترا مطلوب باشد تو هم مرید شو عرض داشتم که من
غیر از حضرت بابو مرید کسی نخواهم شد روز دیگر تفرج در حوض خاص بردند در کنارهٔ حوض گنبدی

۱ک = اید ۲ک = چنانکه ۳ک = الحاج ۴ک = نبیسهٔ ۵ک = طاقها

با تکلف بود دران نزول فرمودند ناگاه سلطان فیروزشاه[1] سواری کرده پیدا شدند در طرف
گنبد نظر کرد خدمت بابو و جماعت درویشان برخاستند و مقابل ایستادند یک درویشی
پشت داده نشسته ماند حاجب را فرمان شد برو تفحص بکن این کیفیت[2] حاجب آمد درویش
بر وضع جواب نداد اما چون حاجب نیک بود باز گشت عرض کرد درویشی ست درد کمر دارد
سلطان اغماض کرد بندگی بابو را شناخت فرمان شد که این لنگر بحواله شیخ اسحاق کنید
حاجب باز رسانید بندگی بابو ناخوش شدند سلطان باز گشت بندگی بابو رکوه[3] گرفتند و فرمودند
هر کرا هوس لنگر باشد او بماند و از آنجا روان شدند در کهتو آمدند اکنون که کیفیت (چهاگل) قافله با کیفیت
جوان که در جور باغ ملاقات شده بود موافق آمد تحقیق شد که حضرت شیخ جهان قطب زمان دامت برکاته
از اکابران شهر دهلی اند این کیفیت در کهتو اظهر من الشمس واشهر من الامس بود منتشر شد همه باور داشتند
بندگی حضرت شیخ جهان قطب زمان دامت برکاته میفرمودند[4] که در ایام صبا اگر من بازی کنان بخدمت
بابو می آمدم بازوهای مبارک فراز کرده مرا در آغوش خود می گرفتند و می گفتند بیا بابا من محمود
من و نام پدر حضرت بابو محمود بود از برای من جامهای شهان بافت و چیرهای[5] مخصوص از ناگور
می رانیدند و کفشهای نازنین و تیرهای مهین مهیا بجهت من داشتند گاهی کفش من باز گون شد
قدری رخنه در نعل افتاده بود در نظر مبارک خدمت بابو افتاد سخت ناخوش شدند و فرمودند بابا احمد
در حیات من تو این چنین کفش چگونه پوشی و بعد بزرگ شدن چون ما از سفر بازگشته بخدمت بابو

١ ح = فیروز سواری ٢ پ و ک = کیفیت ٣ زکوة
٤ ح = میفرمودند. ندارد ٥ ک = بهیرو

می آمدیم پابوس میکردیم بدست مبارک خوی من دور می کردند و چهار کانیها سر کرده ریختنی بر سر ما می کردند و گوی و چوگان بدست مبارک خود بجهت من راست می کردند و بال می نمودند و طعامی بروح میت از جائی می آمدی روانه می داشتند که در حلق من رود تا من از طعام فارغ نمی شدم خود دست نمی انداختند پیش ازین مجرد بودند تعلق کسی بر خود نمی گرفتند اما از جهت صغر من به به ورثش متعلق گشتند شبی برای من نهاری نمانده بود صباح برخاستند به زیارت مقابر کھٹو خود رفتند نظر اکابران کھٹو بر آن افتاد که خدمت بابو زیارت می کنند همه پیش بندگی بابو آمدند باعزاز واکرام در مقام خود بردند و الوان نعمت بخدمت بابو آوردند خدمت بابو فرمودند که شیخ احمد را در بستر خفته گذاشته ام تا او نخورد من نخورم عرض داشتند که شیخ احمد را دیگر می فرستیم شمان تناول فرمائید هم نخوردند ایشان آنچه پیش آورده بودند بر سر شخصی داشتند و یک سبو مسکه روغن و یک سبو شیر و یک سبو جغرات در رکاب خدمت بابو کردند و کل جماعت با خدمت[1] بابو تا مقام بابو آمدند من چون خدمت بابو را دیدم دویده پیش آمدم گویا که جان یافتم خدمت بابو در آغوش کردند و فرمودند احمد ما صاحب نعمت است نشسته[2] نعمتها برای من همچنین برسد

حکایت

چون سید علی قیروانی[3] تیرانداز کیفیت بندگی شیخ جهان قطب زمان دامت برکاته در دینا روانه شنید که این چنین فرزند نیک بخت بخدمت بابو رسیده است نعلها گلین راس کرده بخدمت بابو آورد که اگر شیخ احمد این نعلها بردارند قوی شوند و قوت بیفزاید و تیرانداز شوند خدمت

۱ ک = خدمت تا مقام ۲ ک = شسته ۳ ک = خیروان

با بو بر سید علی بسیار لطف کردند و خوش شدند که بدوستی و رضا ما برای شیخ احمد نعلها آورده
و بندگی شیخ جهان قطب زمان تا سید زنده بود مراعات و مراقبت اولازم داشتند و ایثار نعم میکردند
و بعد سید بر فرزندان سید هم لطف داشتند وفاداری چندان بود که در تحریر راست نیاید می فرمودند که در
کار تیر آنچنان شدیم که خطا نبودی روزی ملک ناصر احمد مقطع کهتو هدفی نصب کرده بود تیر می انداخت
با یاران و تباران خود و سکنه کهتو و شیرانیان و فرقه دیگر[۱] تیر بران هدف می فرستادند تا میانه روز
کسی هدف نزد و چون ما رفتیم سکنه گفتند که شیخ احمد از زمره ما است که ایشان از جمله سکنه اند و
ملک زادگان گفتند از ما ست زیرا که اکابر است کمانی سستی و تیر سوفار شکسته منافقی آورده
داد که شما هم این تیر بفرستید بعنایت الله تعالیٰ[۲] تیر اول بر هدف زدم همه در تعجب شدند بار دیگر
هم از کهتو در ناگور می رفتیم ما با کاروان سوار بودیم و دو نفر برابر بودند یکی خوط موضع ترتا[۲] و دیوراج نام
و دوم برادرم حسام الدین ناگاه سواران گروهی مستعد با اسلحه از راستا پیدا شدند و عنانها بجانب
ما داشتند پیش من از باهنی فرود آمدیم تیر بر کمان وصل کردم[۳] ایشان قریب رسیدند خوط گفت
اگر اشارت شما باشد پیشتر شوم دریابم چه مقصود دارند گفتند ما ایشان را بزنیم و گردون بستانیم
خوط گفت آن وقتی باشد که اول[۴] افتاده باشیم ناگاه دراجی پیش ایشان دوان[۵] می رفت من که تیر فرستادم
سمت تیر بود و لیکن یک[۶] دو قدم ازان دراج پیش نهادیم[۷] تا آنکه تیر آنجا برسد دراج انجا رسید[۸]
تیر خورد خوط گفت این مرد دوازده تیر دارد هر یکی را از شما بیکان یکان تیر خواهد[۹] داشت

۱ ک= دوم ۲ حق تعالیٰ ۲ ک= ترتاء ۳ ح کردم ٤ ح و ک = من ۵ دوان
ک= ندارد ٦ ح = لیکن لریک ۷ پیشتر ۸ ح = برسد ۹ ح و ک = خواهند

چون هراس ایشان را

معلوم شد باز تیر وصل کردم مقابل ایشان پیشتر شدم ایشان خوط را گفتند بازگردان این بزرگ را
معذرت کن ما در راه خود می رویم شما در راه خود بروید خوط آمد منت کرد ما ترک مقابله[1] کردیم بندگی
حضرت شیخ جهان قطب زمان دامت برکاته در سیر کهیج مدتی ترکش می بستند و می فرمودند که ما در
قوت چنان شدیم که پهلوانی در پانزده سالگی پیش بندگی بابو رسیده بود او را فرمودند که فرزند ما را هنر
کشتی بیاموز پهلوان ساق قدم پیش نهاد و گفت بگیر گفتم ما در پای کسی دست نخواهیم زد دست بیار
او دست داد ما در کشتی خواهی[3] داشتیم بعلی از دست بر پشت او رفتیم او را خجالت پیش آمد زیرا که میان
پهلوانان رسمی است که بر پشت رفت برد او راست پهلوان گریستن گرفت که مرا شیخ احمد دغا داد
من قوت نکردیم دانستم مگر چیزی در کشتی نمی داند تا عمر من است کسی بر پشت من نرفته است بندگی
حضرت بابو او را منت و معذرت کردند چیزی دادند بازگردانیدند چون کیفیت پهلوان مشهود شد
پسر یک کفش گیری بود هر بار که ما پیش دوکان او میگذشتیم بدعوی کشتی از ما خواستی و ما از سبب
غیر مناسب با او آویزش نمی کردیم یک روز جامها کشیده پیش ما آمد گفت امروز نگذارم همکاران
او را گفتم که مانع شوید مبادا او را آزاری رسد باید که مواخذه نباشد همکاران همه دانستند که اندازه
شیخ احمد نیست که از و تواند برد همه قبول کردند مواخذه نباشد تا دیری در آویز شدند آخر کار
سخت قوت کردیم بر گرفتیم او را بر زمین زدیم در کمر او آزار رسید پدر او پیش بندگی بابو فریاد آمد بندگی بابو
در محلت ایشان رفتند تحقیق کردند همه گواهی دادند که گناه شیخ احمد نیست بسیار منع کردند که مناسب ما

۱ مقاتله ک = ندارد ۲ گفت ک = ندارد ۳ ک = خواهشی

نیست چون او سخت شوخی و خیرگی کرد شیخ احمد اہل محلت را علم داد که گواه باشید سر کرا آزار رسد بدعوی پیش نیاید بندگی حضرت بابو فرمودند ای روستائی پاره دوز گناه پسر تست فریاد بر چه میکنی بعد بزرگ شدن ہم آن کفش دوز میگفت که ہنوز آزار کمر من باقیست و بار دیگر در ہوا اسرما بمیزه خود را پوشیده و دستها گرد آورده آخر شب به محلت منافقی می رفتم او دید که این تنہا است ویل یافت از پس پشت من رسید و ہر دو دست بازوہا را گرفت تا بیند از دو گفت ای تیسر مرد چه قدرت داری آخر بحیله رستیم و از دستہائی او خود را بقوت کشیدیم و او را فرود انداختیم در کمر او کتاره بود کشیده شد او فریاد کرد که مسلمانان فریاد برید شخصی در مسجد آن محلت تہجد مشغول بود آواز منت تخلیص کرد کیفیت برو گفتیم منافق گفت من زور آزمائی میکردم او بروی عتاب کرد که در آخر شب چه وقت زور آزمائی بود لاجرم جُرم از طرف تست **حکایت** از بعضی مخلصان مسموع است که در قصبه کھتو سنگ گردانی بود پہلوانان سنگی آن را بامتحان در گلوی می انداختند و در خود امتحان میکردند روزی بندگی حضرت شیخ جہان قطب زمان خواستند که آنرا بر دارند دوستی برابر بود عرض کرد که بنده بالمری خواہد داد رخصت ندادند و فرمودند که نخواہم توانست از تو پشتی خواہم خواست او را دور کردند گلوی در سوراخ او در آوردند و تنہا قوت کرده بر آوردند و در گلوی کرد تا دیری می گشتند ہمه یاران متحیر و سر گردان شدند که این چه قوت است که حق تعالی شیخ احمد را عطا کرده است بعده تنہا آن سنگ را از گلوی کشیدند و ہیچ آزاری نرسید و می فرمودند که یک شبی در خانه ابہور

۱- ح = سرمایم زخود، ک = سرمابمیزز

در سر کهیج دروازه غلطیدیم[1] ناگاه دیوی سر تا باسمان رسیده بالای بام پیدا شد هر چند
باز گونه بر زمین زدیم
لاحول گفتیم خنده و مسخرگی میکرد و نمی رفت برخاستیم و چسپیدیم و بر سینهٔ او نشستیم عجز و
الحاح[2] کرد که بگذارید بعد ازین درین محلت نیایم و هیچ کسان شما را نترسانم بعده رها
کردم و در عدل و انصاف بندگی شیخ جهان قطب زمان دامت برکاته در حیات[3] خدمت بابو
مستثنی شده بودند چنانچه یک بار در دیندوانه رفته بودند و در سرای غزنی نزول کردند یکی
نویسنده هم در درون سرای فرود آمده بود عورتی را دید بجهت آب در حوض جهله می رفت میان
راه مزاحم شد عورت مذکور جمیله بود نظر او از دور بر ما افتاد فریاد کرد که شیخ احمد شیخ احمد.
ما رسیدیم او را مانع شدیم او قوت کردن گرفت ما اگر چه تنها بودیم جسپیدم چیزی نمانده بود که
او را از اسپ جدا کردیم[4] و عورت را گذاشته ما ازان قوتی که با او کرده بودیم در وثاق او رفته بودیم
برای عذر خواهی نزد رفته بود و ثاق نبود شنیده که ما در وثاق او رفته بودیم
او در وثاق ما آمده جهد کرد که شما در دیانت و تقوی راسخ هستید چرا علم شروع نمی کنید
گفتم بر ما نسخه نیست او نسخه مبادی تعلم خود نوشته بر ما آورد و گفت تا آنکه من این جا ام
نسخهٔ مذکور ضبط کنید و اگر نه گاه شما پیش خدمت بابو کنم نسخه مبادی یاد[5] و ضبط شد. و
بندگی مخدوم دلاوری بجدی داشتند که میفرمودند در قصبهٔ دیندوانه یک جوال گندم خدمت
بابو بر سید ابو طالب امانت داشته بودند در کهتو مقداری نرخ غلّه بر رفت فرمودند که گردونها
کهتو در دیندوانه میروند گندم مذکور در گردونی انداخته بیار و بر ما اسپی بود کوچک محکم سوار شدیم رفتیم

1. ک و ح = غلطیده بودیم 2. ک و ح = الخاح 3. ح = صدر حیات
4. ح = جدا کنیم 5. ک = باوی

وگرد و نهار گفتیم شما در کھتو کی بازمی گردید گفتند صباح پیش از صباح برخاستیم جوال گندم
بران اسپ نداختیم شخصی از پیش آمد و گفت که گرد و نهار وان شده ما نیها اسپ را روان داشتیم
درکنارهٔ نمک زار شده کوه بهانه کرده رفتیم شب بسیار بود نزدیک دیهه باوی رسیدیم شخصی ستوران
خود را در آخر شب می چرانید او را هیبت زدیم او صوت ما نشناخت گفت شیخ احمد درین وقت کجا
رفته بود یدا اعتماد بروی نکردیم گفتیم نزدیک ما نیائی بر ما تیر و کمان است او گفت من فلانم پسر
فلانم گفتیم بگو راه کجا است او نشان داد صبح هنوز نه دمیده بود که بخانه آمدیم خدمت بابو فرمودند
در گرد ول چپانه انداختی کیفیت مذکور عرض کردیم ناخوش شدند که چرا تنها قصد کردی بار دیگر منع فرمودند
در آنکه از قصبه سرکهیج در قصبه رانیر رفتیم شیخ تاج الدین و اسمٰعیل مقدم بچه برابر بودند
و باهنی ما بیرانند وقت بازگشتن چون لب آب منهدری گذار شدیم تنگهای مطول
رسید و در آن تنگهای بارها راه قطع می شد در نظر ما افتاده که چند پیاده
از پیش راه گرفته نشسته اند و باهنی تیز وقت پیاده گان دانسته که بر ما می آیند برخاستند
چون نزدیک ایشان آمدیم مهار از دست اسمٰعیل گرفتیم و اسپان را تیز کردیم در میان پیاده گان شده
باهنی مرد و ار گذار کردیم سلامت آمدیم و در آنکه از خراسان باز گشتیم شیخ تاج الدین از رانیر قصبه اج[1]
بر ما پیوست با غلامی چند و اسباب در خطه ٹهٹه رسیدیم در مسجد جامع فرود آمدیم شیخ تاج الدین
نا گفته در خانه ضابط ٹهٹه رفته و سوار در دهلیز او در آمد و دران ایام در ٹهٹه خوف مغلان بود مردمان
ٹهٹه دانستند که ما ایلچیانیم از طرف مغلان[2] برای تجسس آمدیم شیخ تاج الدین را از اسپ
فرود آوردند بستند و اسپان او ستدند هر چند گفت برابر شیخ احمد کهتو آمده ام مسلم نداشتند

۱ ک وح = اچ ۲ ح = ایلچیان مغلانیم

ملک خروج کردند و مسجد را گرد گرفتند نا اسلحه پوشیده حمله کردیم همه را تنها بطریق گوسفندان
راندیم یکی از ایشان ما را نشناخت برضابط گفت تحقیق شیخ احمد کھٹو اند ضابط پسر خود را با
خدمتی بر ما فرستاد و در خانهٔ خود برد و ضیافت مطول کرد و اسباب شیخ تاج الدین را تسلیم نمود
دیگر در آنکه موضع اوتیلیه در وجه خرج مطبخ بندگی شیخ فی دم جهان قطب زمان دامت برکاته
تعین شد برای دیدن موضع مذکور روان شدند شب بر حوض دهولقه نزول فرمودند مقدمان قصبه
دهولقه منت کردند که درون قصبه نزول کنید یکی از ایشان اسپ ما را بر سر کرد که بخانهٔ من نزول
کنید خاطر او خواستند که درون قصبه بروند دیگری گفت این جا خوف کفار هم است بندگی مخدوم
فرمودند هر جا که خوف است مسکن ما است همان جا ماندند این حکایت منقول است از شیخ[۱] کرمانی
که برابر بود **حکایت** دیگر شبی با بقال بچه کھٹو در دلاوری مذاکره افتاد او گفت در فلان
جنگل درختی هست اگر بر آن درخت دستارچه بندید و بیائید آنگاه دلاوری شما تحقیق شود و پیش
از آن که آنجا رفته تا می رفت او را آسیب می شد بندگی شیخ جهان قطب زمان فرمودند که ما بندیم
و بیائیم چه گرد بیاری گفت چنین ما قصد کرده رفتیم دستارچه بر آن درخت بستیم باز گشتیم آواز غلغله و غوغا
از خلق در گوش افتاد و هم شد مگر این غوغا همان است که خلق را می ترساند بوی هم بر رخ آن غوغا
آوردیم دیدیم که با آن بقال بچه گفتاری می کنند که تو با شیخ احمد درین کار چرا گردستی ناگاه شیخ احمد
را چیزی آسیب شود بخدمت ما بوجه جواب باشد بقالان را ما آواز دادیم که ما بسلامت آمدیم شما

۱ ک وح = شیخ احمد کرمانی

اوراچیزی نگویند تعلق نیست **فصل دوم** در ذکر اقبال و قبولیت و عظمت بندگی مخدوم شیخ جهانیان قطب زمان دامت برکاته و ایثار و تجرید و علو همت که در اوان صغر که بجناب حضرت بابو مقبول گشتیم حکایت آمیفرمودند و در آنکه چهار ساله یا پنج ساله زیر مبارک[1] بابو رسیدیم شخصی را دیو مسخر شد خلق بدیدن وی میرفت ماهم برابر کسی رفتیم و او را خبر شد که شیخ فرزند بابا اسحاق می آید دیو گفت جائی که ایشان بیایند مارا مجال نباشد که ما بمانیم در حال او خلاص شد دیو رفت **حکایت** چون در کھٹو خبر شد که دریاخان فروامیان کھٹونی شده در گجرات می رود و موضع کھٹونی از قصبهٔ کھٹو دو کروه باشد پیش بندگی بابو التماس کرده شد که پیلان را وقتی ندیده ام خلق بدیدن لشکر و پیلان میرود اگر رخصت خدمت بابو باشد من هم تماشای پیلان و لشکر ببینم بندگی بابو چند نفران برابر دادند و اجازت کردند صباح در موضع کھٹونی رفتیم قاضی فخر الدین حاکم کھٹو و سید اکرم تذکره متعلمان[2] می نبشتند سید قاضی را گفت شیخ احمد هم با چند نفران آمده اند نام ایشان هم بنویسید تا خرچ راه شود قاضی نه نوشت ما قاضی را گفتیم خوب کردید که نام ما نه نبشتید قاضی مرا گفت چون بابو شما را فتوحی می آید مارا گاهی یاد می کنند گفتیم نه برای چه یاد بکنند ناگاه لشکر نمودار شد ما با نفران خود در راه ایستاده نظر می کردیم قاضی و متعلمان استقبال رفتند ملاقات کردند ملک مغیث حاجب را نظر بر ما افتاد اسپ را چوب کرده بر ما آمد جامها و لباس خوب دیده گفت این فرزند کیست یاران گفتند این فرزند شیخ ابو اسحاق مغربی اند و ملک بندگی بابو را نیکو

[1] ک و ح = پای مبارک [2] ح معلمان

میدانستند ما را گفت شما این جا ایستاده بمانید و بر خان رفت و خبر کرد و چون نزدیک رسید عنان اسپ بسوی ما کرد چند قدم پیشتر شدیم مصافحه کردیم خان اشارت طرف سراپرده کرد که این جا بیایند ما همان جا ماندیم رفتیم ملک مغیث شخصی را فرستاد آوازکنان رسید شیخ احمد شیخ احمد گفت ملک میطلبند رفتیم ملک مغیث حاجب چند سلاک زر پیش ما آورد به تعظیم پیش نهاد متعلمان را هم چیزی داد قاضی بر سبیل لاغ گفت آنچه شمان یافتید و آنچه ما یافتیم یک جا کرده قسمت کنیم ما گفتیم قاضی قسمت چرا میکنی حوض کهان بریگ انباشته شده است و چه ما و شما یک جا کرده ریگ بکشائیم خلق را در آب وسعت شود نفع عام باشد قاضی خجل شد گفت تو توانی ما نتوانیم شب همانجا ماندیم زر را مخفی در محلی دفن کردیم چنانچه کسی ندانست تا مبادا کسی بعد خفتن بستاند چون صباح شد گفتیم زر در کمر ما نیست چه شد اثر پایها تتبع کردند در مقامی که خفته بودند اثر پایهائی بعضی معائنه شد یاران غوغا کردند گفتیم ما همان زمان فکر کرده دفن کردیم غوغا بگذارید بروید بیارید در خدمت حضرت بابو بردیم بابو خوش شدند نفس راندند احمد ما مقبل و مقبول است فی المثل اینچنین شدیم که اگر خاک بر دست می گرفتیم زر می شد حکایت یک روز بقالی آشنا بر ما آمد و گفت که شیخ احمد مونگ شش جیتل دانگی در منی شده است و وجهی بر من صد تنگه ازان شما است امانت اگر اشارت شود مونگ بخرم گفتیم مبلغ مذکور بندگی بابو تحقیق مرحمت نکرده است ناگاه یاد کنند تعلق شود بقال گفت اگر بندگی بابو یاد خواهند کرد من از محلی دیگر

تفویض کرده خواهم داد مونگ مرا باشد چون بآخر وجه شماں را بدهند مونگ ازان شما باشد بقال مونگ خرید کرد و یک حاسدی[1] بندگی بابو را خبر کرد که شیخ احمد صد ٹنکه را مونگ خریده است که سودا خواهند کرد بندگی بابو فرمودند احمد وجه مذکور کجا است ما ازان بقال و چه مذکور بر آن قول آوردیم پیش حضرت بابو نهادیم بابو متعلق شدند که حال احمد میاں این حساد بعد ما چه خواهد شد وجه مذکور را بمن دادند من بقال را دادم پیشتر چند روز یک دانگ از نرخ افزود بعد دو ماه شش جیتل در منی افزون شد ما مونگ مذکور بفقرا و ملازمان خود را قسمت کرده دادیم مقصود بیان کیفیت اقبال بود **حکایت** چون ناگور بجهت کاری روان شدیم خدمت بابو فرمودند ملک شیر ملک و قاضی اسحاق را ملاقات کنند[2] بدیدن ملک رفتیم[3] یک سبد گل چنبه سپید بردیم و گلهائی ناگور بغایت خوشبو بود ملک خوش شدند فرمودند ملک خوبان را چه بینید باید که من حاضر باشیم قاضی اسحاق را دیدم بسیار نوازش کردند در نظر قصور گرفته بود فرمودند مگر لحیه خفیف آمده است کسی از ایشان گفت سنبلت[4] هنوز نه رسیده شده است دیگر بقالی ناگوری خلق را مونگ قرض میداد و گفت شیخ احمد شما هم چیزی مونگ بستانید تا مارا ایمن باشد دو بیست من مونگ ازو قرض ستدم و همان بقال را گفتیم در کھٹو بر سال هر چه خرچ راه و کرایه شود آن هم خواهم داد بقال مونگ در کھٹو فرستاد و ملک خوبان در تاختی غنیمت بسیار آورده بود مارا چهار ماده گاو خوب دهانید بیست گان ٹنکه بر دست کونان ملک فروختیم مقدم موضع کوچره میان اکابر

١ ک = حاوی ٢ کنید = ح ٣ ک = بدیدن رفتیم ٤ ک = سبلت

شکسته بود بدین ما برخاست و گفت شیخ احمد چیتو[1] از حوض کہان کہٹو که حوض قدیم

است و بریگ انباشته شده بود ایشان ریگ تمام کشیدند این چنین اقبال و همت

دارند مال مونگ از همان جا دادیم و یک شانه بافتی از کہٹو برای آن بقال فرستادیم مونگ را بخدمت

(و نام ثوب)

بابو عرض کردیم بابو چیزی خرج کردند و چیزی فقیران را دادند و فرمودند احمد تو جهد در علم کن

خیال سودا بگذار بعده هوسی بر نظم شد رباعی در اوصاف خدمت بابو پیش بندگی بابو عرض

افتاد فرمودند احمد زنهار در مدح کسی نظم ننویسی سوگند دادند که این نیز از اسباب سوال است

حکایت — وقتی در رکاب بندگی بابو در قصبهٔ دیند واته بودیم ملک قطب الدین

نجم داماد ملک رضی الملک فیروزشاهی به نیابت ملک حاجی پسر رضی الملک کارکنی در دینده و آنه

میکرد بر درویشی چندیری بهم بر آمد و رنجانید درویش بر بندگی بابو مستغاثی شد روز جمعه بندگی

بابو چون از نماز فارغ شدند ملک قطب الدین برای دست بوسی آمد و ایستاد و بندگی بابو

بر ملک بر آمدند فرمودند ای سپاری فروش بچه تو که باشی که مسکین فقیر غریب را برنجانی ندکری

تذکیر میگفت ملک یاران را گفت این شنیده بیائید آنچه مذکر می گوید آن هم بشنویم ملک

از بابو فسرده رفت تذکیر شنید پیش آن مذکر یک شمع لطیف و چیزی وجه نقد آورد دادند آن

سپید کرد بندگی حضرت بابو فرمود ای پسر کو دندان سپید چه میکنی او گفت یکی را الله تعالی چیزی

داده است این سخن از آن مذکر مارا سخت دشوار نمود بندگی بابو به زیارت متقابر طرف حوض

[1] جیو- این لفظ جیو باشد که کلمه احترام است-

شرقی قصبهٔ مذکور بیرون آمدند ما هم برابر بودیم استخاره کردیم که باری[1] کریم اجازت فرمودند

از آنجا پیش دروازه مسجد جامع قصبهٔ مذکور شده در نظارهٔ لشکر که از دهلی[2] در گجرات می رفت

رفتیم لشکر در حوض غزنی جهله نام فرود آمده بود بوهپت[3] کارکن کالا[4] خواجه در حوض ملاقات شد

با او آشنائی سابق بود او را محلی کار آمده بودیم در وثاق خود برد شیرینی ولڈو پیش آورد در خیمهٔ

او خوردیم او بر خواجه رفت خیلی نیم شب گذشت بازگشت ما را دید تاسف کرد که مرا کیفیت

شما فراموش شد باز رفت بر خواجه گذرانید خواجه ما را طلبید تعظیم نمود از جهت ملاقات خدمت

بابو بسیار عذر خواهی کرد که ما را علم نشد که خدمت بابو این جا اند صباح لشکر کوچ می کنند

خدمتی بابو این وجه ببرند و پابوس من عرض دارند وجه مذکور چهار گانیها بود رئیس قصبهٔ مذکور

اسمهٔ عبدالملک پسر قاضی فخرالدین حاکم کهٹو لباچهها را کنانیده بخواجه آورده بود خواجه لباچهها

قسمت کردن گرفت رئیس گفت وجهٔ مذکور تسلیم من بکنند تا بندگی بابو را برسانیم شیخ احمد درمیان

راه خرج خواهند کرد خواجه از فراست دانست که رئیس بعناد میگوید و رئیس را با ما نیفتادی

بعدهٔ خواجه گفت شیخ احمد این چنین لباچها مناسب شما نیست بهای لباچها ما را نقد داد

شب بسیار گذشته بود بیگاه از و بازگشتیم بندگی بابو فرمودند شیخ احمد کجا رفت متعلق بودند

درویشی بابو را خبر کرد که شیخ احمد بخواجه کالا اند خواجه تعظیم ایشان خیلی کرد بندگی بابو منتظر ما نشسته

بودند که ما رسیدیم وجهٔ مذکور عرض میکردیم آن مذکر در سرای غزنی[5] فرود آمده بود حاضر شد گفت

۱ک وح= باز گردیم ۲ک وح= دہلی
۳ح= بوہت اسم صحیح بھوپت است ۴ک=کلا ۵ غزنه، غزنین

آں وجہ از کجا گفتیم آں نیز خدائے تعالیٰ یکی وادہ گفتہ ہماں مذکر تکرار کردیم بندگی بابو را این سخن هم پسندیده آمد خوش شدند مذکر از آن سخن نادم و محزون بود در کھٹونز دیک بابو التماس ارادت کرد یک جمد هر طلی خدمتی ما کرده و خدمتی بابو با تکلف آورد حق سبحانهٗ و تعالیٰ مارا این چنین مقبول کرده بود هر کجا که رفتیم و قدم زدیم نعمتهای فراوان دست می داد و حُسّاد در تشویش می بودند الحمد للہ علیٰ ذالک قبولیت و اقبال از مواهب الٰهی است چنانچه در حدیث صحیح است که چون حق تعالیٰ بنده را دوست دارد بفرماید جبرائیل علیه السلام را که فلان بنده رامن دوست میدارم تو هم دوست دار پس جبرائیل علیه السلام او را دوست دارد پس فرمان شود جبرائیل را ندا کند بر اهل آسمان که خدائے تعالیٰ فلان بنده را دوست میدارد فرمان بشود شما هم دوست دارید اهل آسمان همه او را دوست دارند بعده آں بنده قبولیت نهاده شود در زمین او را دوست دارند تا بحدی که ماهیان در آب هم او را دوست دارند و این معنیٰ عین معائنه در ذات بندگی حضرت شیخ جهان قطب زماں دامت برکاته موجود بود و قتی تشخصی اوصاف قبولیت و اقبال و نیک بختی بندگی مخدوم در حضرت بندگی بابو بسیار کرد بندگی حضرت بابو فرمودند پس دعا مارا مگر اثری نگیرد بندگی مخدوم عرض داشتند که همه قبولیت و اقبال مارا ببرکت تاثیر دعا و نظر بندگی بابو است و همه بنام بندگی بابو خواهان[۱] می شوند آں دو بیتی لیاقت دارد رباعی زاں روی که بندهٔ تو بدانند مرا؛ بر مردمک دیده

۱ح= خواهان ما

نشانند مرا، لطف و کرامت عنایتی فرمود[۱] ورنه چه کسم[۲] من که بدانند مرا، حکایت
روزی بندگی مخدوم بخدمت بابو عرض داشتند که اگر اشارت شود بجهت جامهای خریدن
بروم اشارت شد چندین ٹنگه در فلان مقام است بیرون بعده در آخر شب مرا بیدار کردند فرمودند
احمد تا دشمنان بیدار شده سوار شو چون سوار شدیم بیرون آمدیم در خاطر خدمت بابو تعلق شد
که مبادا اطرف دیگر برود برخاستند بر در آمدند آواز دادند در گوش من آواز مبارک رسید
مرا گریه کشاد در خاطر بابو آگاه شد که در محلی دیگر میرود اسپ را در کوچهٔ دیگر راندیم صباح
یاران را پرسیدند که احمد بر شمان محلی رفتن را گاهی چیزی میگفت یا نه گفتند یکبار می فرمودند
ما خدمت بابو را گران شده ایم طرفی خواهم رفت خدمت بابو را تعلق زیادت تر شد بگمان آنکه در
دینه وانه رفته باشد شخصی را الملک قطب نجم فرستادند وجهه نبشتند که اگر احمد ما آنجا آمده باشد
طعام و آب آنگاه بخورند که بر ما فرستند مرا از جهت او تشویش بسیار است بلکه هر طرفی[۳] نفران
برای تفحص ما فرستادند ما دینه وانه را راست گذاشته نماز شام در دیهی رسیدیم خانهٔ یک عورتی
ماندیم آن عورت را بر ما مهر شد بسبب آنکه او را پسری بود در گذشته صورت او مانند بصورت بابو
او را گفتیم ما هم سبب خدمت بابو محزونیم او شفقت کرد طعام خورانید بستر داد وقت خفتن
شوهر او آمد گفت بعضی دهقانیان اندیشه می کنند که این مسلمان را تلف کنند و اسپ و جامه را
بستانند زن و شوهر هم در اول شب خار نشیت خانه خود از بس پاره کردند و ما را سوار کرده کشیدند

[۱] ح = فرموده است [۲] ح = کیم چه دانند، ک = فرمود [۳] ک = طرف

گفتیم مرا سمت دهلی بنمائید ایشان ستاره نمودند من بران ستاره اسپ راندیم صباح را چند
مسلمانان پیاده از پس رسیدند کیفیت خود بر ایشان باز نمودیم ایشان را هم بر من شفقت
شد گفتند برما رخت ملکی است که ما را بشتاب در دهلی فرستاده است اگر اسپ شما با ما توانند
رسید برانید بعد ظهر اسپ کاهلی کردن گرفت پیاده شدیم یکی گفت موزه ها مرا بسپار دوم[1] تعجیه
برگرفت دیگر زین اسپ بر سر خود کرده چهارم[2] اسپ را می راند نماز شام بمقامی رسیدیم همه را
مهمان گرفتیم مالیده کنانیده یکی از ایشان آب گرم کرده ما را مردن داد وجود شستیم و یکی غمخوارگی
اسپ می کرد قائضه کرده و گیاه و دلیده خورانید ایشان بجهت ما بستر صوف و سقلاط
که در رخت بود به نیت محافظت فراز کردند صبح را برخاستیم و بقافله رسیدیم شخصی ستور لاغر می
فروخت آن را خریدیم آن پیادگان با ما وداع کردند که ما را شتاب باید رفت و با این قافله
شما سه روز در دهلی خواهید آمد در میان راه تفقد ستور مذکور شد در دهلی به چهار[3] جیتل فروختیم
ملک زیادت و به محمد حاجی و دریا خان و دلاور خان ملاقات کردیم ایشان سید الحجاب
را گفتند که در تذکره آیندگان برای ملاقات سلطان فیروز نام شیخ را بنویس سید الحجاب
نام شیخی از موالی شیخ معین الدین که از اجمیر آمده بود مقدم ننوشت هر چند که خواهیم مذکور جهد
کردند که نام شیخ احمد مقدم دار قبول نکرد اما اول همو را پیش برد فرمان شد بچه مصلحت
آمده اند او فرمان کشید که این حجت آن دیه است که برای ملازمان روضه شیخ معین الدین

۱ح و ک = دویمین ۲ح و ک = چهارمین ۳ک = چند

داده اند در دیوان گرد آرند که کارکنان شق فرمایشها در دیهه مذکور بسیار میکنند سلطان
از بازداد[1] فرمان سخت بی ذوق شد فرمان شد مثال را در دیوان تسلیم کنند و پنجاه ٹنگه
خرچ بدهند تا ایشان بحج روند بعده سید الحجاب نام ما را خواند فرمان شد که ایشان بسنه[2]
خوردند چگونه آمده اند گفتیم مناقب حضرت سلطنت از خدمت بابو که بسیار شنیدیم اشتیاق
ملاقات غالب شد این زمان مشرف شدیم فرمان شد سید الحجاب به بین حسن ادب این خوردک
و بی ادبی آن اجمیری فرمان شد شیخ زاده را بپرسند چه مقصود دارند گفتیم جز ملاقات بادشاه
دیگر نبود در اثنا آن شخصی فریاد ملک احمد نام مقطع کھٹوکرد فرمان شد شیخ زاده را بپرسید
گفتیم ما میدانم فرمان شد شما ان بزرگ آن مقام باشید چگونه ندانید گفتیم آری آن عزیز سخنی بی
وضع بر ملک احمد آمده گفت ملک بی ذوق شد تفتی کرد فرمان شد که رعایت شیخ زاده بکنید
و در دیوان ببرند به پرسند بعده برخوانین فرمان شد که بر سید الحجاب نخوانید[3] گفت شماں برویده
تفهیم بکنید ایشان گفتند مصلحت آن است که چیزی التماس بکنید گفتیم که من بدین نیامده ایم
چه گوئیم ملک محمد حاجی گفت با شما صورت لطف است مبادا طریق اجمیری وضعی دیگر شود
چاره نیست که چیزی التماس بکنید گفتیم در کھٹو حوضی است نام کہان دار دبر یک انبا نشته شده
است چیزی مرحمت شود که آن ریگ را بکشند بر خانجهان فرمان شد چه باید داد عرض کرد
پانصد ٹنگه فرمان شد باز بگوئید گفت هشت صد[4] ٹنگه فرمان شد باز بگوئید گفت هزار ٹنگه

[1] ک=ندارد [2] ک وح = هر دو "بسنه" دارد تصحیح قیاسی بسن
[3] نخواهند [4] ک=هیصد که آن هم صحیح است۔

فرمان شد دو ہزار تنگہ بدہند فرمان مرتب کنانیدہ بر پرگنہ کھٹو وجہ مذکور آوردیم بندگی بابو را گذرانیدم فرمودند احمد ما را در بیت المال نصیب بسیار باشد برکات انفاس متبرکہ ایشان تا غایت اثر آن نفس بعد پس پردہ ہم ظاہر می شود و درین حکایت مقصود آنست کہ بندگی بابو فرمان مذکور در روز جمعہ بر دست قاضی فخر الدین حاکم کھٹو دادند و قاضی بر ممبر برآمد فرمان مذکور خواندن گرفت خدمت بابو برای تعظیم فرمان ایستادہ شدند عرض داشتیم کہ حضرت بابو این ایستادن را چہ معنی است فرمودند بابا نمی دانی آخر ما را ہمان مقام اشارت بمقام سلطان محمد تغلق کردند بضرورت ماہم برخاستیم خدمت بابو را رعایت ادب بادشاہان چندین بود و آن اجمیری را از یک بی ادبی دیدیم کہ چہ پیش آمد حکایت چون بندگی حضرت شیخ جہان قطب زمان دامت برکاتہ را در خدمت بابو اتفاق شد کہ ریگ حوض کہان بکشانید باہمہ اکابر قصبہ بر حوض رفتند قاضی فخر الدین مذکور با پسران خود در محلی رفت دو انگشت ریگ را دور کردند و گفت ریگ اندک است اگر ما بکشائیم نام تو و پسران قبول کردند بعدہ خلق را قاضی گفت کہ ریگ مذکور ما می کشائیم بندگی مخدوم چون این سخن شنیدند باز گشتند سید اکرم قاضی را گفت کہ اندازہ شمان نخواہد بود کہ تمام ریگ بکشایید شیخ احمد توانند کہ بکشایند اگر شیخ احمد سعی بکنند خدمت بابو سعی کنند و چون خدمت بابو سعی کنند مقطع ہم سعی کند و چون مقطع سعی کند ہمہ خلق سعی کنند قاضی اندازہ شمان دو سہ نفر آن نیست و قدرت آن ہم ندارید کہ با تمام رسانید

قاضی دم درکشید و ساکت شد سیدا کرم بندگی مخدوم را فرمودند که لله فی الله برای رضاء خدای
تعالی باز گردید و شروع در کشانیدن ریگ بکنید همه خلق دویدند پایها بندگی مخدوم گرفتند
و باز گردانیدند در حال بندگی مخدوم فرمودند قصابان را بطلبند و ماده گاؤ بیارند و ذبح بکنند
بقالان فرمودند که بیست من آرد بیارند و خلق را فرمودند که هر یکی از خانه کلند و زاغ نوک
سبد بیارند ماده گاؤ ذبح کردند سیخ و کبابها و بریان شد در قصبه کهتو صلاء عام را دادند
خُرد و بزرگ آمدند در گاویدن مشغول شدند و سیخ و کبابها و گوشت و نان تنگ می خوردند و
کار می کردند چنانکه در روز اول دو چهچه درست از میان ریگ بیرون آوردند چند روز متواتر
هم برین نهج بیرون آوردند ناگاه گل کاران[1] رسیدند بندگی شیخ جهان قطب زمان حوض بدکور
بحواله گل کاران بکردند چنانکه ریگ و گل کشیدند و همه چهچها کهان بیرون آوردند شخصی از گل کاران
پیش بندگی مخدوم آمد عرض داشت کرد که گل کاران بدکور با شما چندین تنگه را دغا کردند گافتن[2]
نیم گز بود[3] ریسمان بربلندیها داشته موازنه صد و چهل تنگه را حرکت دادند بندگی مخدوم مساحان
دیگر را آوردند[4] و از سر بیهودگی کردند و دغا بدکور ثابت شد آنکه بر دغا راه نمونی[5] کرده او را جامه داده
آن صد و چهل تنگه را بیک نو کشیدند و حوضی دیگر نوازان: خود خاصه شروع کردند و یک بقالی
دیگر حوض آزان خود خاصه شروع کرد چنانکه در سر چند روز هر دو حوض مرتب شد باران بارید بقال
ساختگی کرد که برای تماشا کنان حوض را جامه و خیرتی و نار یلها بدهند بندگی مخدوم را تعلق شد

۱ ح = کلالان بجای گل کاران در نسخهٔ ح کلالان است ۲ ح = کاشتن
۳ ح = بود کافتن ۴ ح = آرامیده ۵ ح = راهنموئی، ک = راه نمودنی

که بقال چندین ساختگی کرده است خلق همه در تماشا حوض او خواهند رفت در خانه آمده غلطیدند
خدمت بابو فرمود بابا احمد کجا است یاران گفتند درین حزن افتاده اند بعد ازان خدمت بابو
فرمودند بابا تعلق مکن در حوض تو آب خواهد آمد و خلق هم در حوض تو خواهند آمد باران بارید شخصی
آمد خبر کرد که شیخ احمد هر دو حوضها پر شدند نفس بندگی بابو در کار شد آخر شب شخصی دیگر آمد گفت
حوض بقال پاره پاره شد آب تمام رفت و حوض بندگی مخدوم سلامت است صباح بندگی بابو
چون بر سر حوض رفتند همه خلق پیش بندگی بابو آمدند آن نفس ثابت شد که در حوض تو ما خواهیم آمد
الغرض حکایت ها اقبال و قبولیت بندگی حضرت شیخ جهان قطب زمان دامت برکاته
اگر بنویسند مجلدات شود در ولایت تمام آوازه شد که بندگی شیخ احمد حوض کهان را از سر کاویدند
و حوض دیگر خاصه خود بنا کردند میان مقدمان آن ولایت و سران او این کیفیت منتشر شد خدمت
بابو فرمودند که چندگاه ازین جا انتقال بیاید[1] کرد تا بابا احمد را سلامتی باشد مبادا احساد ملتفت
کنند خدمت بابو در قصبه دیندوانه رفتند در مسجد برهانی فرود آمدند در یک کناره مسجد شخصی
نوا سامری نواخت ما بی تعلق خالی ذهن به بابو عرض کردیم که این نواخت مگر سامری است بندگی
بابو بر ما مزاج گرم[2] کردند که این چه خیالست[3] ما خانمان گذاشته می رویم و شما در خیال آواز نواختن هستید
خدمت بابو صباح روان شدند در حصار رفتند مقطع حصار ملک زینا و الا[4] بود دوا و اعتقاد بر
خدمت بابو بسیار داشت سبب آن ما سبقت نمودیم بر ملک رفتیم ملاقات کردیم ملک گفت

۱ بباید ۲ ک=ندارد ۳ خیالست ٤ ک=ولا

شیخ احمد نماندی تا بابو را رنجانیدی ما ازین سخن سخت رنجیدیم ما تحمل کردیم ملک تذکره بجهت خدمت
بابو نبشت نقد چندین ماده گاو چندین و آرد و روغن چندین و غیر ذالک هم دران ساعت نظر ما
بر بوهپت[1] افتاد دیدم در بند ملک گرفتار است ملک را گفتیم که بوهپت را بگذارید ملک از غایت
عظمت خدمت بابو ما را جواب بمسامحت داد اگرچه سخن سنت ما خوش نیامد گفت این لکهوگیرا[2]
کار است چه طور توان گذاشت بوهپت را علم شد که بر ملک بجهت رها کردن او جهد کردیم ملک
نه شنید چون از ملک باز گشتیم با بوهپت ملاقات شد گفت او نفس قسمان رد کرده است
خواهد دید بروی چه کنم ما بر بابو تذکره خدمتی او گذرانیدیم و کیفیت گفتار او عرض داشتیم حضرت
بابو خدمتی او را قبول نه کردند و فرمودند او را چه مجال باشد که سخن تو رد کند چون اکابر حصار
بعد نماز جمعه بمصافحه خدمت بابو مشرف شدند بندگی بابو دست ملک زینا ولا رد کردند
فرمودند تو نفس احمد ما را چگونه رد کنی بعده سلطان[3] آمد ملک پیش سلطان رفت کیفیت بوهپت[4]
عرض کردیم که بروی چند بقایا است بوهپت بقایا قبول کرد و گفت ملک محلی هفتاد هزار
تنگه دفن کرده است نفران دیوان بیایند عین نقد بیارم[5] در حال نفران یافت رفتند وجه مذکور
نقد در خزانه آمد خدمت بابو در مسجد نزول کرده بودند زن ملک هم بخدمت بابو اعتقاد بسیار
داشت سو خیلی را بخدمت بابو فرستاد که شما در فرد خانه ما بیایند و نزول فرمایند بسبب رعایت
و حرمت آن عورت خدمت بابو در فرد خانه ایشان آمدند عورت مذکور هر روز الوان طعام و میوه

۱ کذا در هر دو نسخه این اسم خاص بهوپت است ۲ ح = لکهو گهرا
۳ ک = ملک را غلطان ح = ملک را طلب سلطان ۴ یعنی بهوپت ۵ ک = بیایم

با تکلف بندگی بابو را می فرستاد و ما را یقین شد که این طعام با ذن ملک خواهد بود چون خبر آمد
که ملک را سلطان بند کرد بندگی بابو هم در دہلی رفتند ما برای ملاقات ملک در بندی خانہ رفتیم ملک
بالحاح پیش آمد که بندگی بابو را بگوئید که دعا کنند تا مر اخلاص شود ما بخدمت بابو گذرانیدم بندگی
بابو دعا کردند پنجم یا ششم روز خلاص یافت در محلی که وجہ مذکور دفن کردہ بود رفت چون دید
که وجہ مذکور بر وند زہرہ ملک ترقید جان بحق تسلیم کرد مقصود ازین حکایت آن است که ملک
بحضور این درویش سخن بی وضع گفت که بہ شیخ احمد نماندی تا خدمت بابو را رنجانیدی
و سبب رہائش بوہیبت منت کردیم نشنید دل ما را خستہ کرد و آزرد چون تقدیر او ہمچنین رفتہ
بود فر و اقبال ما[1] از نظر او سلب کردند لاجرم او را این روز پیش آمد قول مشائخ است از کوہ افتادہ
بہ نہ از دل درویش و نفس بابو برای درویش ہمچنین است و نیز فرمودند که ہر که با شیخ احمد
بر آید بحیل[2] افتد که ہرگز بر نخیزد (ن) حکایت روزی بندگی بابو بالائی دروازہ نشستہ
بودند نمی دانم که از ما چہ خطا زاد که خدمت بابو مزاج گرم کردند[3] و چہار پائی خرد یعنی کرسی پیش
بود طرف ما انداختند تا گاہ پائی مبارک بابو دران غصہ بلغزید از بام افتادند من ہم خود را افگندم
در پائی خدمت بابو دیدم که قدری آزار شد من سلامت ماندم خدمت بابو فرمودند تو چگونہ
افتادی عرض داشتیم[4] که چون خدمت بابو را دیدم که افتادند مرا طاقت نماند خود را انداختیم خدمت
بابو فرمودند ہر آئینہ یک جان در دو قالب است و نفس مبارک راندند ہر که با شیخ احمد بر آید

ن- بیت: ہر آن کہتر از مہتر ستیزد- چنان افتد که گاہی بر نخیزد=ک
۱ ک=ندارد (ما) ۲ ک و ح= چنان ۳ ک=کردن ۴ ک=داشتم

همچنین افتد که اسحاق افتاد شیخ احمد ما شیخ است و ما ابداً الیم بندگی حضرت شیخ جهان قطب زمان ع[1] می فرمودند اگر بدست بزرگی برای خدمت با بو چیزی فرستادی ناخوش شدند تا حمل بران نیفتد که شیخ احمد سوال میکند و بر بابومی برد تا روزی در دینه وانه برای ملاقات مولانا رضی الدین ابوالفرح که یکی از اکابر علماء و مصاحب مشائخ بود رفتند ناگاه ملک قطب نجم بر مولانا رسید سال گران بود آن قدر مسلمان که در مجلس بودند دیگان هیبت کان سیر غله هر یکی را دادن گرفت چون نزدیک ما آمد برخاستیم باز گشتیم ملک ناخوش شد پرسید کجا فرود آمدند گفتند در خانه سید ابوطالب ملک سید را گفتند اگر خیریت میخواهی شیخ احمد را من بیاری سید ابوطالب در خانه ما آمده بر ما گفت اگر شما قدم رنجه نمی کنید ملک از مار وی میگردانداز کرده ع[2] ما مرحمت بر کند بیائید بضرورت رفته شد ملک تواضع کرد و برخاست گفت یک گردون گندم برای بندگی بابو داشته ام ببرید گفتم من نخواهم بر د فلان لیلهانی برخاست بزبان هندوی گفت لهراچه جهکنجی یعنی بیهوده میگوید مرا بدهید تا برسانم ملک بردست او فرستاد در علو همت و ایثار و تجرید بندگی حضرت مخدوم میان عالم ممتاز و مستثنیٰ بوده اند و یکی از عادات لازمه ایشان این بود که در ایام مسغبه بیشتر خود گرسنه می ماندند حصه خود هم از پیش بفقراء میدادند چنانچه در سال آهسته و سحالوه ثانی معائنه افتاده است بارها میگفتند که حظ دو یشان آنست که کسی را چیزی بخوراند در کهٹو هم در ایام مجاهده و ریاضت چون از غیب چیزی می رسید همت آن بود که حضار

[1] ک = دامت برکاته [2] گروه

چیزی بخورند و خود نمی خوردند و در هر ماهی و دو ماهی هرچه در سرکهیج جمع می شد صلاء عام می دادند
فقرا شهر و سادات و علما و نوائت و جوگیان را و همسایه گان را و کولیان و هرکه دست فراز
می کرد همه را می رسانیدند اصناف و اجناس خلق در خانه جمع میکردند چهارگان و نیجگا بهدیه
میدادند کسی محروم باز نگشتی بقیه هرچه ماندی خدام و ملازمان را و خدمت گاران را قسمت
می کردند و الیشان را نود هر روز نعمتهای می رسانیدند و عورات مستوره بعد عشا هر شبی
در آستانه عالیه می رسیدند کسی را غله کسی را جامه و کسی را نقد می رسانیدند و چند بار در ماهی ملازمان
را وجه تسلیم کرده در هر محلتی می فرستادند تا هر فقیری و شکسته که پیش آید بدهند گاهی
مردی نابینا رسیده بود میان هجوم بر دست او چند جیتلی داد او باز گشت کسی گفت که این
نابینا مستحق است بندگی مخدوم بنده مؤلف یعنی مولانا محمد قاسم را دو جونی[1] دادند که دنبال او
برو و برسان و نگوئی که این فلان فرستاده است و من فلانم بنده دنبال شد قریب خانهٔ
قاضی منصور رسید چنان بر دست او داد که او نه دانست که کدام کس فرستاده است
و که داده است مقدمان سرکهیج را تنگهای زر و نقره و پهتیها و بهیرونها و قبابها و دوشاب[2]
هر سالی مرحمت می کردند و مقدمان را می فرمودند تا تذکرهٔ عورات بیوه گوشه نشینان هر یکی
بکنند بیارند ایشان نوشته می آوردند مال تسلیم ایشان می شد این کیفیت همه تجربه و معائنه
کاتب مؤلف شده است هیچ کسی از ساکنان سرکهیج ازین در آنگاه[3] نیست و علو همت ایشان[4]

۱ ح و ک = جونی ۲ ک و ح = دوشاب تصحیح قیاسی دوشاله
۳ آگاه ٤ صفت

درخراسان ومکه مدینه ودهلی وناگور وگجرات وهندوستان اظهر من الشمس واطلع من الامس منتشر است علماء آفاق وملوک خراسان وعرب وهند همه مشتاق ملاقات ومصافحه بوده اند هر که یک بار روی مبارک ایشان دیده باشد طاقت صبر از ایشان او را نباشد بیت

دیده که ترا نه دیده باشد، آن دیده بگو چه دیده باشد، و هر که حاضر می شد همین میگفت که محبتی ولطفی واخلاصی که برمن است باغیری نیست وچون چیزی در مصرف میدادند بغایت منشرح می شدند ابیات فارسی وهندی ملائم ومناسب آن در زبان میخواندند دوهه

هبه مکهاه بلده چون تهوره تهوره آه، اکین هانها نبانیان لبسام اگواه، وچون فقیر را از ایثار شادی دیدند زیادت می کردند زیراکه در حدیث صحیح است که یکی از علامات قبول صدقه انشراح دل فقیر است وکسی که کافر نعمت بودی از و متنفر بودند و هر کس که فتوحی می آورد هم دران مجلس یکی بیک ونیم یا بد وپیش او می آوردند که اگر موازنه او موجود بودی به مجالس متفرقه در آویز می کردند واز ملوکی که دولت ایشان جدید العهد بودی یا نظر بر مال داشتند فتوح ایشان ستدن کم بودی میفرمودند ملک عثمان سرکهیجی روزی انگشتری با نگینه قیمتی آورد موازنه آن درحال پیش آوردند دیگر بار لباسچه قیمتی آورد وچهار تنگه زر بدست قاضی منصور برائی ملک فرستادند ملک قاضی را گفت چه باشد ما باعتقاد درست چیزی پیش می آریم که قبول شود بندگی مخدوم دو جهان باز عنایت می کنند قاضی برآمده گفت ملک همچنین میگفت

۱ بسیاهر کوا

گفتیم ما تا بتوانیم شرمنده کسی نشویم و ملک شیخن موسی و خواجه قطب خواجگی هم چون چیزی می
آوردند هم دران ساعت باز گردانیده هم بدست ایشان مرحمت می کردند و می فرمودند نه می
ستانیم مگر آنکه عرض می داشتند که نذر است یا بروح حضرت با بواست و هرکه و هرکه انذر می
کرد در حال می ستدند و هم دران وقت یا مجلس دیگر مکافات می کردند صفت علو همت
بندگی حضرت شیخ جهان قطب زبان دامت برکاته در کتاب نگنجد حکایت درآنکه خواجه
رکن الدین چشتی را از دیهه بیرپور سکندر خان یعقوب در مهراسه باز گردانیده آورده داشته
بودند اقارب سکندر خان اوصاف همت خواجه بیان کردند که روزی چندین فقرا را چندین
تنگه میدهند نیاز مولانا محمد قاسم اسمه عبدالسلام خورم بران ملوک گفت که شیخ احمد ما [انداز انکه مشائخ]
سلطان المشائخ دیگر[۱] زائر که می آید آن مشائخ طرف دست آن زائر نظر می کند که چه آورده
است و شیخ ما طرف دست خود نظر می کند که بر دست چیست و این زائر چه می باید داد
همه تحسین کردند که راست میگوید کاتب مولانا محمد این حکایت پیش بندگی حضرت
مخدوم قطب زبان گذرانید فرمودند مولانا عبدالسلام شهید و تسکری بود سلطان مظفر چون
ایشان را در دریا فرستاد ایشان از موضع سانند و گو دهای قاضی داود خاله زاد خود را
با دو سطر کاغذ نبشته بر ما فرستاد که دران طرف می فرستند معلوم نیست که چیست درویشان
بلنند که مولانا چه کرده است بنده او را بعرض سانید فرمودند که اگر این درویش بدانستی

۱ انداز انکه مشائخ دیگره = ک و ح

که از مولانا این گناه صادر شده است سبب آن مولانا را دردریا می فرستند و در پای خود جامه
بستی بر سلطان و ویدی اما چیزی که مقدر است بیقین ظاهر می شود اندازه کیست که بگرداند
حکایت روزی در دیندوانه مولانا عبدالسلام با قاضی ناراینه بحث
میکردند این درویش طرف قاضی سخنی گفت مولانا آغاز کرد که بندگی مخدوم من بندهٔ
خدمت گار شما ام و ما هم شهر یا نیم شما طرف قاضی چگونه شوید[1] مولانا این چنین شیرین و نرم گو
بود حکایت وقتی سکندر خان یعقوب لباچه اعلی[2] ایک طرف صوف دوم طرف
سقلات بر دست مولانا برای این درویش فرستادند از مولانا ادب خلق و شیرین
زبانی آنچنان بود که لباچه با انشراح هم مولانا را پوشانیدند مولانا گفت اگر خان بشنود مراد شوار
شود گفتیم برو داده درویشان چه توانند گفت حکایت چون سکندر خان
در لشکر سلطان مظفر در قصبهٔ دهندوکه میرفت بملاقات درویشان آمده بازگشت
بر دست مولانا دو خوان پهیه پهاپر کرده فرستاده درویشان هم به مولانا دادند اما[3] در حیات
خدمت بابو طاب ثراه یک بار شیخی[4] بر درویشان از مولانا رسیده بود قدری تفرقه شد
درویشان در دهلی بوده اند قاضی محمد خطیب ~~او ور زاده~~ شیخ زاده انصار را درویشی
گفت که شیخ اسحاق در لکهنو نقل کرد مولانا از و شنید و مولانا با ملک حاجی همراه در
دهلی بود هر کسی گفت او برما خبر آورده داد درویشان کاری داشتند آن کار گذاشته در لکهنو

١ ک= کنید ٢ ک= علی ٣ اما= ح= ندارد
٤ ک= سخنی پردروبشان، ح=شیخی

آمدند بندگی بابورا در صدر حیات یافتند شکرانهٔ حق تعالی بجا آوردند از مولانا نیاتو خوش بودند
چون مولانا از دہلی آمد گفتند این معنی از شما غریب نمود گفت چه کنم قاضی محمد ہم چنین گفت
بنده ہم متعلق شد که چون این چنین حکایت افتاد می فرمود اگر از درویشی وردی یا وظیفه فوت میشود
آوازهٔ موت او در عالم منتشر میگردد حکایت چون خلق ناگورو ونیدوانه برای غرض در
دہلی آمدند بیشتر آشنایان برای دیدن درویش در مسجد خانجہان آمدند مگر دو کس یکی سید
رحمة الله و دوم مولانا ناگور سید گفت شیخ ولایت ما گذاشته در شہر آمدند بکنایت آنکه در شہر
فتوحات بسیار برسد بر شیخ چه رویم آخر سید ہم رسیده و سید یکی از دوستان و معتقدان
بود مولانا را دیر شد نیامد یک روز میانه وقت بود که نبات مصری در دست کرده پیدا شد درویشان
گفتند ما را با شما سخن کردن نمی شاید مولانا گفت یا الله امروز روزینه خرچ راتب ملک حاجی را
ہم چون تدبیر کرده رسانیدیم آن گاه مخلص شد دل و جان بنده زیر پای بندگی مخدوم است برادر
مولانا مذکور اسمه عبد الرحمن برای ما کتاب ضوء شرح مصباح بقلم خود نبشته آورده بود ہر
روز از دہلی در فیروز آباد پنج گروه بر پا می آمد میان ما و ایشان محبت قدیم بوده است
و حکایت مولانا خورم ہر بار تکرار می کردند که مولانا خورم گفت شما کھونگذارید حکایت
مروی است از سید مکرم اکرم که روزی بندگی حضرت شیخ جہان قطب زمان دامت برکاته
نشسته بودند و در خلوت حکایتہای ولایت خود میکردند سید عرض داشت که بجا شما چند

ا ک = عرض ۲ ح = رسانیده ام

بچسپیم بندگی مخدوم فرمودند چگونه چه میگویند سید گفت میگویند که غنی را عطا بسیار میدهند
وفقیران را اندک فرمودند دیگر چه میگویند سید گفت که عورات که بزیارت می آیند پیش خود آمدن
رها میدارند فرمودند دیگر چه میگویند سید عرض داشت که کیمیا دارند واگرنه چندین از کجا می دهند
جواب[1] فرمودند روزی پیغامبر صلی الله علیه وسلم با بی بی فاطمه رضی الله عنها طعام میخوردند درویش
بر در آمد سوال کرد حضرت صلی الله علیه وسلم یک لقمه طعام فرستاد بعده[2] اعرابی بر در آمد حضرت[3] تمام صحنک
بدست مبارک خود پیش[4] او بردند بعده بی بی فاطمه عرض نمود که یا رسول الله درویش را یک لقمه فرستادید
و اعرابی غنی را تمام بدست مبارک خود دهند که درین چه سر است پیغامبر صلی الله علیه وسلم
فرمودند هوای فاطمه درویش بیک لقمه خوش می شود و غنی به لقمه خوش نمی شود ملکسم بر نجد
و آینده را خوش باید کرد و نه رنجیده و بر بنده مولف جوابی دیگر فرمودند و آن آنست که فقیر را چون
حق سبحانه تعالی رزق فراخ نگردانیده است اگر او را بسیار دهند مبادا قهر در کار شود که ای بنده
تو چگونه فراخ کنی رزق[8] کسی را که ما تنگ کرده ایم و دیگر میفرمودند مقدار هر که برائی می آید در دل
القامی شود همان مقدار ش میدهند شعر[9] می برد هر کس نصیبی[10] خویشتن ؛ در میان احمد
بهانه بیش نیست " از جهت کیمیا جواب فرمودند که نظر دولت ان کیمیا است یعنی ما منظور
نظر آن واصل حقیم که هر کرا که ایشان نظر کنند او را نعمتها دینی و دنیاوی از غیب برسد چنانکه[11]
حکایت از شیخ ابوسعید ابوالخیر رحمة الله علیه مرویست که در صغر از مکتب

۱ جواب = ک ـ ندارد ۲ بعده' ۳ بر در آمد حضرت ـ ک ندارد
۴ پیش او تا خودند هند ـ ک ندارد ۸ رزق = ح ـ ندارد ۹ ک = بیت
۱۰ ک = نصیب، ح = نصیبی ۱۱ ک = چانچه

بازگشته در خانه می رفت درویشی را دید که در گرمای آفتاب نشسته بود خرقهٔ خود می دوخت عرق عرق وار شده بود شیخ ابوسعید به تختهٔ خود او را سایه کرد چون باد بروی رسید سر برآورد و دید شیخ ابوسعید به تختهٔ خود سایه کرده است وفا شیخت در کار شد آن درویش بزبان راند ابوسعید این دو سوزن از بخیهٔ بنام تست یک برای دین و دوم برای دنیا نظر و نفس آن درویش چنان کارکرد که طنابهای آفرشیمی و میخهای زرین در سرای رده شیخ ابوسعید بودی و از نعمتها دنیاوی هر جنسی بی اندازه آنچنان داشت که درویشی را در بازار او و مویشی او چون گذر افتاد غبطه در روی غالب آمد کفنی خود کشید طرف آسمان بر تاب کرد و گفت این هم ابوسعید را بده کفنی در هوا شد بر شیخ ابوسعید رفت و افتاد خادم را فرمودند که در بازار فقیری آمده است بیار خادم او را بر شیخ برد شیخ آن فقیر را فرمود ای عزیز چندین نعمتها که دیدی حساب آن بر ما نباشد ما را ازین پیراهن که پوشیده ایم بپرسند نظر دوبستان ازین جهت اکسیر و کیمیا گفته اند جواب آمدن عورت همچنین فرمودند که برغبت رضا من پیش می آیند اما بعجز و الحاح ایشان تشفیع می شود که تو بادی شهوتی و آرزوئی و نظر بدنداری فانی شده چرا آزار خاطر ایشان روا میداری برین صورت رخصت کرده می شود اگرچه حق آن است که عورات را نشاید که بزیارت درویش روند و درویش را نه شاید که ایشان را رخصت بآمدن زیارت بر خود کند

حکایت

می آوردند که شخصی پیش شاه عرض نمود که درویشی است که چهل سال برآمده است که مقام خود درون چاه ساخته اند

١ک=حکایت ٢ک=آمد ٣ برغیب=ک
٤ک وح=من پیش ٥ الحاح ٦ک=بادشاه می آرند

که تا از مزاحمت خلق ایمن باشد پادشاه بزیارت او رفت بدلو نشست درون چاه درآمد بزیارت او مشرف شده بازگشت و قصه آن درویش بر زن خود گفت زن او رخصت خواست که اگر اجازت شما باشد تا من هم بزیارت مشرف شوم پادشاه اذنش داد عورت زرینها پوشیده و عطریات بسیار بر خود مالیده رفت شیخ بروی دست[1] دراز کرد اشارت بدست کرد که بنشین زن از شرم خود گرد[2] آورد شیخ فرمود تو خواهر منی باید که بعد ازین تاریخ هوس بزیارت همچو منی نکنی که خود را در چاه مقام کرده است و ریاضت و عبادت می کند عورت را رخصت کرد **حکایت** خراسانی دانشمند روزی بملاقات بندگی حضرت شیخ جهان قطب زمان در سرکهیج رسید بحث ها خوب کرد بغایت مستعد بود بندگی مخدوم چند تنگهازر و نقره او را مرحمت کردند روز عاشوره بود خراسانی مذکور بر سلطان احمد گفت در گجرات یک مرد قدر آینده میداند و آن شیخ احمد اند که مارا چندین وجه نواخت و از رومال خود آن تنگها زر و نقره که بندگی مخدوم داده بودند کشیده نمود و بازگشت سلطان احمد ملک شیخن موسی و خواجه قطب خواجگی را گفت شما می گفتید که شیخ احمد را سخت تنگی است خراسانی را چندین مال دادند شیخ احمد کیمیا دانند ایشان بر بندگی مخدوم آمدند و کیفیت مذکور عرض داشتند بندگی حضرت مخدوم فرمودند کیمیا سهل است نظر درویشان کیمیا است **دیگر** خدمت سید السادات سید برهان محمود بن سید جلال الدین بخاری رحمة الله علیه هر سالی برای ملاقات بندگی حضرت مخدوم دو بار از احمد آباد می آمدند و هر باری دو تنگه زر بندگی حضرت مخدوم به سید می دادند یک بار التماس نمودند که بنده

[1] ک = درازی کرد زن [2] خود را گرد آورد

از بسیار مشائخان مجاز است اگر بندگی حضرت مخدوم اجازت دهند از خانوادهٔ مغربی هم مجاز گردد
بندگی حضرت مخدوم نهالچه که دران نماز ظهر کردند به سید برهان الدین داوندٔ و اجازت کردند و طشت
و افتابه که بندگی حضرت مخدوم بدان وضو ساخته بودند در نظر رسید افتاد آن را هم التماس کردند آن را
هم به سید دادند و خدمت شیخ بده پسر شیخ رکن الدین چشتی هم پیش بندگی حضرت مخدوم نیز بسیار
می آمدند و بندگی مخدوم من فرموده‌اند یک بار مارا کناک زور آورده بود تجلد کردیم کمر بند بر کمر بسته
شیخ بده را درون محل طلبیدیم شیخ بده با عتقاد تمام عادت داشت که دیری سر بر آستانه
می نهاد و بعده پرسید[۱] آنچه داد ندازان بکسی از ما علم نشد و شیخ دو قطعه چهر تلی بهر دو دست گرفته
آورده بود[۲] **حکایت** پدر شیخ تاج الدین و شیخ بدر الدین در آنکه از شیخ رکن الدین شفاعت نامه
آوردند مضمون آنکه شیخ عیسیٰ مردی ستعه است چنانچه معائنه خواهد شد میخواهد با پسران زیر
پای شما سکونت گیرد و اعانت او بر ذمه کرم خود گیرند و در حاشیه بدست خود نبشته بودند آرزوی
ملاقات بسیار است **دیگر** چون ملالت وجود ملک مبارک پوتهاری در کهنبایت معلوم شد
بندگی حضرت شیخ جهان قطب زمان دامت برکاته را با ملک بسیار لطف بود برای اعادت
در کهنبایت رفتند ملک را برکت قدوم بندگی حضرت مخدوم شفا شد و در زیارت مقابر کهنبایت
سوار شدند و ملک را با شیخ رکن الدین هم بسیار محبت بود و بر شیخ رکن الدین گفته فرستادند
که من شیخ احمد را در حوض نیره در گذر لشکر خواهم آورد و اگر مقصود ملاقات باشد بکنید[۳] بندگی حضرت
نام تالاب

۱ ک = برسید ۲ ک = آمده بود ۳ ح = بکنید

مخدوم را در زیارت کردن میانه روز شد ملک عرض داشت کرد اسپان تشنه اند در گند آب باید داد بندگی حضرت مخدوم خالی ذهن در آب دادن اسپان مشغول شدند ملک بر شیخ رکن الدین نفر فرستاد شیخ در قیلوله بودند کسی بیدار نکرد بندگی مخدوم بعد آب دادن اسپان در وثاق خود آمدند شیخ چون از قیلوله برخاستند علم شد ملک مبارک نفر فرستاده بود بدان میعاد که ملاقات با حضرت شیخ احمد کهتّو شود از قیلوله شما را بیدار نه کردند شیخ رکن الدین دست بر زانو افسوس زد که بی سعادتان مرا چرا بیدار نه کردید و تاسف بسیار کرد و برادر شیخ رکن الدین مذکور اسمه شیخ مظهر الدین که در دهلی صاحب سجاده بود بر بندگی حضرت مخدوم در مسجد خانجهان بسید رسیدی و بملاقات مشرف شدی دیگر شیخ بحری درویشی بود از مریدان شیخ خضر بر حوض خاص در قصبه نارائنه علم از درویشی بر آورده بود خلق ولایت ناگور را بروی توجه و رجوع بسیار بود و از زائر پرسیدی که نماز پنج وقت می گذاری و اهل بیت را به نماز تحریض میکنی در هر که قصور دیدی بروی تفت شدی ملامت کردی و از پیش خود راندی خدمت بابو راحق تربیت بروی بسیار بود وقتی بخدمت بابو آمده بود تا جای بندگی حضرت شیخ جهان قطب زمان را ملاقات شد گفتند الحمد لله شما را پیش نظر خدمت بابو فتح شد مرا از نعمتهای خود محروم نکنید و یاد آرید روزی بندگی حضرت شیخ جهان قطب زمان از زیارت مقابر حظیره فتح خان در دروازه بهکیسه[۱] میان دهلی در می آمدند ناگاه پالکی خدمت سید جلال الدین

۱. ک = بهبکسه

بخاری با ہجوم بسیار پیش آمد بندگی حضرت مخدوم در گوشۂ دیواری رفته ایستادند چون پالکی
نزدیک رسید حاملان را سید فرمودند که پالکی بدارید ایشان پالکی داشتند خدمت از طرف
بندگی مخدوم نظر کردند بندگی حضرت مخدوم بخدمت سیّد رفتند خدمت سید از پالکی بیرون
آمدند و بندگی مخدوم را در کنار گرفتند و گفتند ای جوان ما را فراموش نکنی بدین عبارت و بنشانی
این حکایت ہیری دہلوی پیش بندگی حضرت مخدوم در سرکہیج آمده بود و گفت که من دران وقت
حاضر بوده ام **دیگر** بندگی حضرت شیخ جہان قطب زمان دامت برکاته فرمودند یک شبی
با سیّد شرف الدین مشہدی ہم تمام شب گذشت وقت فجر برای نماز فرائض برخاستیم
سید گفت شمال چہار اندام تازه کنید گفتیم بچه سبب گفت آن که از بینی شمان آواز بر آمد
گفتیم آن از نواقض وضو نیست ما را عجب آمد که ما را یاد نیست واگر واقع بوده باشد سید از
نواقض چرا گفت مگر این مسئله نه می دانست **حکایت** وقتی علی خان[۱] از دہار بر دست
سوداگری اسمه بہلول چہل تنگه زر و چہل تنگه نقره فرستادند بہلول ندکور پیش بندگی
حضرت شیخ جہان قطب زمان آورده عرض کرد بندگی حضرت مخدوم فرمودند سلطان احمد
باز پرس ما دارد اگر ما این وجه قبول کنیم بیدل شود از ما برنجد چون در ولایت او باشیم چگونه
برنجانیم ہر چند بہلول سوگند خورد که من کسی را خبر نکنم بندگی حضرت مخدوم قبول نکردند باز گردانیدند
باردوم بہلول برائی وداع رسید که در کھنبایت می روم چون بندگی حضرت مخدوم

۱۔ الپ خان تصحیح قیاسی ۲۔ علی خان=ح الی خان=ک

برای او بجهت طعام در محل درون رفتند بهلول وجه مذکور در خریطه کرده زیر بالشت بندگی حضرت
مخدوم مخفی داشت و طعام خورد و وداع کرد و چون بندگی مخدوم برای استراحت بر پلنگ
رفتند بالش بلند نمود تتبع کردند خریطهٔ مذکور یافتند خواهرزادهٔ بهلول را از احمدآباد آرانیدند
وجه مذکور تسلیم او کردند و بنده مؤلف را فرمودند در کهنبایت بر عبدالعزیز پسر قاضی منصور
برو یک جا شده بهلول را بگوئید که با درویشان دغا کردن زیان پیش آرد بنده و کهنبایت
رفت با عبدالعزیز به بهلول رفتیم و گفتیم وجه مذکور بندگی حضرت مخدوم تسلیم خواهرزاده
تو کرده اند مخصوص از سرکهیج مارا برای علم دادن تو فرستاده اند و فرمودند این چنین دغا با درویشان
کردن زیان دارد و بهلول گفت غلط افتاد توبه کردم بنده بازگشت در سرکهیج آمد کیفیت
بحضرت شیخ جهان عرض نمود و دوم روز ملک جلال شه به بندگی حضرت مخدوم رسید کیفیت
مذکور بندگی حضرت مخدوم به ملک جلال شه گفتند ملک گفت هرآئینه ذات پاکی بندگی
حضرت مخدوم همین اقتضا کند سلطان احمد و سلطان محمد و سلطان مظفر دوستان همان
اند و مخلصان قدیم اند بازگشت و کیفیت مذکور بر سلطان احمد عرض نمود سلطان را گمان شد
که مال ستاده باشند بر بهانه می گشد سوار شد بحضرت مخدوم آمد ملاقات کرد و بندگی
حضرت مخدوم بر عادت قدیم طعام آرانیدن گرفتند سلطان عذر کرد که طعام خوش نمی آید
بندگی حضرت مخدوم گفتند ای بار خدایا تو عالم سر و خفیاتی سلطان را وداع کردند ملک جلال شه

شه را

گفتند سالها باشد که همچو فرزند خود را کنار کرده می پروریم وفا این کردند درویش را استوار نمی دارند و فرمودند که هیچ دوستی از دوستان خدا تعالی هرگز دروغ نگوید ملک رفت بر سلطان عرض کرد سلطان پشیمان شد باز دران هفته بخدمت بندگی شیخ جهان قطب زمان دامت برکاته آمد و عذرخواهی بسیار کرد و طعام معتاد خورد و بازگشت **حکایت** ضابط (حاکم) ٹھٹھہ (نام شهر) نیز خیند سنگهار بدست سید ابو فرستاده بود تا بندگی حضرت شیخ جهان قطب زمان را بگذرانند حلیله (زن) او ملالت داشت نذر[1] کرده بود که اگر صحت شود این خدمتی در سرکهیج به بندگی حضرت مخدوم بفرستد والتماس کلاه برای دو پسران خود کرده سید وجه مذکور بدست خواهرزاده خود در سید جلال الدین حسین فرستاد بعد ادای ظهر ایشان پابوسی کردند عرض داشت ضابط مذکور خواندند او را و زن او را و پسران او را دعا خیریت ایشان کردند و فرمودند که ما در بلاد و ممالکت سلطان احمد می باشیم بر مزاج ایشان[2] باید بود ناگاه که بر مزاج نباشد فائده نکند ما را سیوم کرسی ست بایشان موافقت و مودت است وجه مذکور نیز باز گردانیدند سید ابو کیفیت مذکور پیش سلطان احمد گذرانید فرمان شد شیخ احمد عقل و فراست بسیار دارند **حکایت** چون بر سلطان احمد شاهزاده از شاهزادگان التماس کلاه بندگی حضرت مخدوم می کردند از خزانه فتوح بحضرت شیخ جهان قطب زمان دامت برکاته بآن شهزاده می فرستادند و درخواست کلاه می کردند و گفتند که او را از مریدان کنند آن شهزاده را مرید میکردند بعده سلطان محمد را هم اشتیاق غالب شد بحضرت شیخ جهان

۱ ح و ک = نظر تصحیح قیاسی ۲ (ایشان تا مزاج) = ک۔ ندارد

قطب زمان ارادت آرد جدهٔ مادرین خود را بر بندگی حضرت مخدوم فرستاد و التماس کلاه
نمود که مارا پیوند دهند بندگی حضرت مخدوم فرمودند که کیفیت مذکور در سمع همایون باید رسانید
جدهٔ مذکور بر سلطان احمد گذرانید فرمان شد بر ایشان کرا مجال است که امر کنند اگر در نبیرهٔ شمان
صلاحیت کلاه خواهند[۱] دید کلاه عطا خواهند کرد چون سلطان احمد برحمت حق پیوست سلطان محمد را
بندگی حضرت مخدوم بر تخت بدست مبارک نشاندند و بعد چند روز در سرکهیج آمده مرید شد
کلاه یافت **دیگر** چون سلطان احمد را در ابتدا پادشاهی ملالت شد ارکان دولت همه اتفاق کردند که
بندگی حضرت مخدوم اگر قدم رنجه فرمایند دوگانهٔ شفا بر بالین سلطان بگذارند امید است
که شفا شود مشورت کردند و گفتند که ملک عثمان سرکهیجی بروند شاید که بیایند و سلطان را
آماس ورم عورت غلیظه شد که بیهوش افتاده بود ملک عثمان در آستانهٔ مبارک آمد
و تضرع بسیار نمود بندگی حضرت مخدوم را برد بر بالین سلطان بندگی حضرت مخدوم بنماز
مشغول شدند و دعا کردند و دست سلطان گرفتند ای جان جهانیان برخیز بعنایت الله تعالی
همان زمان شفا شد سلطان را هوش بازگشت با عز و اکرام تمام بازگشتند یک شب مانده بود
و در آنکه مرض رحلت سلطان احمد را شد در عیادت رفته بودند سلطان سخت ملول افتاده بود
دست سلطان گرفته فرمودند که حق سبحانه و تعالی توبهٔ شمان قبول کند در سلطان چیزی نمانده بود
سخت محزون بود چون دعا قبول توبه در سمع رسید سلطان بغایت منشرح شده برخاست

۱ح = خواهید

ونشست با بندگی مخدوم وداع کرد باز گردانید وتمام حرم از کوشک طرف باهنی مخدوم چشم
داشته بودند تاکه باهنی از کوچرب گذشت عظمت واقبال وقبولیت بندگی حضرت شیخ
جهان قطب زمان این چنین بود که هشت پادشاه درهند معتقد بودند وپادشاهان عرب و
خراسان منقاد شدند ونفس بندگی بابو درکار بود که خاطر جمع دار پادشاهان محتاج سخن تو
باشند ودر شفقت ونرمی بر همه احام ممتاز بوده اند آزار هیچ مخلوقی را روا نمی داشتند چنانچه
گنجشک گان بر سر وزانو مبارک می آمدند ومی نشستند وبچه گان گنجشک را محافظت
می فرمودند وخدمت گاران را مالی میدادند تا زاغان را از تعرض رسانیدن دفع کنند وعصاد
مبارک پیش می داشتند تا زاغان را بترسانند روزی نظر مبارک بر علیوازی کا خشا که بازوی
او مجروح[۱] است پریدن نمی توانست درآستانه مبارک آوردند وزیر سبد کرده میداشتند
وهر روز گوشت برائی او تعیین کردند چون بازو فراهم آمد پرید ورفت شخصی حواصیلی (نام جانور) را بخدمت شیخ
جهان وقطب زمان آورده بود وپرهائی او را کشیده بود او را وجه داده ستدند ودر زفرخانه
داشتند وملهی ماهیگیران را فرمودند که روزینه آن قدر ماهی که بخورد رسانند منقار او بزرگ
بود گربه را متعرض او شدن مجال نبود بعد مدتی پرها آمد نفران را دادند که این را در جنگل
ببرید بگذارید چون ببرد باز گردید ایشان بروند او پرید ودر هوا رفت بعده باز گشتند و
صیادان چون شکار زنده می آوردند مال داده شکار ایشان رها میکنانیدند ذبح چیزی تحمل

۱ح=جراحت شده است

نداشتند و در قربانی وجه نقد می دادند چنانچه در روایت آمده است اگر قربانی دست
ندهد بهاء او بدهد و پیش از رحلت دو سه سال برای احیاء سنت رسول الله صلی الله علیه وسلم
بندهٔ مولف را اشارت شد از جهت تو ذبح کن دو گوسپند بنده در فرد خانه ذبح کرده
و در محل درون میفرستادند و احتیاط در ماکل و مشارب بسیار میکردند وقتی معلوم شد
که قصابان ماده گاوی[1] دزدیده ذبح کردند از خوردن گوشت احتراض نمودند بندهٔ مولف
عرض داشت که کودک را اشارت شود تا از احمدآباد بیارد و جیونان را شش کان چیتل
روزینه ورای موظف او تعین شد هر روز وجه گوشت نقد می ستد و گوشت نو از احمدآباد
می آورد و گاهی سگی برابر لشکری آمده بود آن لشکری چون بازگشت هر چند کوشش کرد آن سگ
باوی نرفت سگ را گذاشت و گفت بر محل مانده است آن سگ در آستانه ملازمت
کردن گرفت بندگی حضرت شیخ جهان قطب زمان را خبر شد و سیر غله علوفه تعین فرمودند
عورتی را اشارت شد هر روز می پخته آن سگ را می خورانید چون قاضی منصور ناگوری بعد از نماز
خفتن باز می گشت او را هم تا خانه می رساند بعده ابراهیم محاسب موضع او تلیه باز میگشت
دنبال او تا خانه می رسانید بعده ابراهیم را اشارت شد که این سگ را در دیهه[2] ببری[3] و علوفه موظف
بدهی تا مواشی را محافظت کند آخر شب چون مزارعان زراعت خاص مواشی را در چراگاه
می بردند آن سگ برابر رفتی هر ستوری که راستا یا چپا می شد آن را حائل شدی جدا شدن نمی داد

[1] ک=نادگاوی [2] دیهه=ک-ندارد [3] ببر=ح

ع۱ وقتی ماده گاوی فربه مهیب در ایام قربانی بندگی حضرت شیخ جهان قطب زمان دامت
برکاته را معتقدی آورده قربانی مذکور شیخ تاج الدین را عطا شد بشرط آنکه در خانه بدارد و دوشانیده
شود شیخ تاج الدین آن را به قصابی بها کرده داد ازان قصاب زور کرده جدا شد در آستانهٔ مبارک
آمد بانگ کرد اشارت شد این ماده گاو کدام است عرضداشت می کنند مگر بقصاب داد که فریاد آمده
است قصاب رسید و جدا (او) از آستانهٔ مبارک داوند و فرمودند که ما دانستیم ع۲ که فریاد آمده است
ماده گاو را میان مویشی گذاشتند این چنین مهر و معرفت و فراست داشتند روزی فاخته در نظر
مبارک افتاد که در صحن جماعت خانه می چرید اشارت شد هر روز دران مقام دانه ها می داشتند آن
فاخته و همتا او می آمدند و می چریدند عجب تحفهٔ روزگار بوده اند و مکارم اخلاق ایشان در عد حصر
نیاید ما را شکر حق سبحانه و تعالی هر دم باید کرد که این چنین بزرگی کامگار را از قرن بخدمت مشرف
شدیم

فصل سویم در مناقب بندگی حضرت شیخ بابو اسحاق ابن محمود مغربی رح

مربی و پیر بندگی حضرت شیخ جهان و قطب زمان مخدوم شیخ احمد قدس الله سرهما العزیز بندگی حضرت
شیخ جهان قطب زمان می فرمودند که شیخ ابو اسحاق مغربی فرزند دهلی بودند و تولد بندگی حضرت بابو ع۳
اسحاق سنه ستین وست مائة (۶۶۰) بود زیرا چه بار اول که مرا در دهلی بردند فرمودند خان ها مارا در دهلی
ع۴ کهٹ بود بیا تا ترا بنمائیم دران محلت بردند همسایه گان را پرسیدند از صاحبان آن مقام کس هست
گفتند کسی نیست زمینی خراب افتاده بود و فرمودند پدر مرا شیخ محمود نام بود و فرمودند بعد بلوغ

۱ ک=وقتی که ۲ ح=تادانستیم ۳ ک=بابو ۴ ح=کیٹھ

در قسم ترک و تجرید اقتدا دیم و از اقربا علیحده گشته بطلب حق در هر زمره مصاحبت نمود و قواعد رسوم و اصطلاح هر
قومی دانسته و چهل چهار طبقات مشائخ که [بر سوی زمین اند][1] بعضی بعمل و بعضی بصحبت ضبط کرده شجره ها چهارده خانواده
یاد داشتند میفرمودند بابا این همه را از ما بیاموز و در صحبت ما ملازمت کن و تمامی مرا ملازمت میسر نشد و ورد ها نماز از کثرت
خواندن خدمت بابو مرا ضبط نشده بود و مناسب هر مقامی بیتی مثل پارسی و هندی از زبان مبارک ایشان یاد بود
و سکه تنوره پوشان و کلاه داشتند و دوخته خود می پوشیدند و کاتب از مولانا یوسف صدر و هم سنان بندگی حضرت مخدوم تحقیق کرد
که بندگی بابو پاک تر ازش بوده اند و این مجرد آن پاک و تارکان سر پاک[2] است که از لوث دنیا و آلایش فارغ گشته و نعل
باژگونه زده از صحبت مخلوق ممتاز شده بدرگاه بی نیاز پیوسته چنانکه شاعر گفته است شعر زنهار درین راه ببازی
نیائی[3] تا رسم قلندری نسازی نیائی این جا بیکی مهره دو صد سر می بازند زنهار درین راه ببازی نیائی
و سخت جمیل بوده اند چنانکه فی المثل اگر کسی پیش جبهه لامع ایشان میگذشت عکس او در جبین مبارک پیدا
می آمد و بندگی حضرت شیخ جهان قطب زمان می فرمودند وقتی سید اکرم بی سرفه زبان در محفل[4] نشسته می گفت
شیخ بابو[5] اسحاق ریش نداشتند شب در خواب دید که بندگی حضرت بابو سید را بفتی میفرمایند بیا سید
ریش ببین سید متحیر از خواب برخاست بر ما آمد پشیمان شد که غلط کردم قاضی عبدالرزاق و توالجی که موثوق
حضرت بود و عهده کتابت و کتاب خانه دانست و محافظت کلید ها انبار ها غله و خرج آن بحواله او بود او را قاضی
بده میگفتند از بندگی حضرت شیخ جهان قطب زمان مخدوم روایت میکنند که بارها میفرمودند که بندگی حضرت
بابو در آخر عمر ملتجی بودند و نیک متشرع بوده اند و عورت را مجال نبود که نظر ایشان بگذرد[6] و اگر اتفاقاً

١ برسوی زمین = ک - ندارد ٢ ح = برپای ٣ ک = نیائی
٤ ک = محل ٥ ک = ابو ٦ ک = بگذارد

درنظر آمدی طرف او نحوی میکردند و در کھٹو زیر دیواری خانه سنگی بود بران نشسته می بودند و مردان را مجال نبود که بوجود ایشان دران محلت بگذرند مگر صاحب حاجتی یا سائلی و خدام را پیش خود نمی داشتند و دور شده می بودند و در وقت بزیارت مقابری رفتند و در مقام فکر علو شان بودند و بکا بسیاری کردند چنانچه در ایام صغر بندگی حضرت مخدوم روزی عرض داشتند که حضرت بابو جیو چنین چه سبب میگریند فرمودند بابا احمد خواهی دانست و شب بیداری و مشغولی این چنین داشتند که وقتی که خلق در خواب گاه خود آسوده می شدند آن وقت بیداری و مسواک و وضو ایشان بودی و در صحن خانه تخته سنگی بود بران مشغول می شدند و راستا و چپا یکان سنگ دیگر متکا داشته بودند تا صبح مشغول می گشتند در میان رقص پهلوی نبودی بندگی حضرت شیخ جهان قطب زمان گرات فرمودند مارا آن شب بیداری و مشغولی که بندگی حضرت بابو داشتند میسر نمی شود و چیزی از کسی قبول نمی کردند مگر وقت ضرورت مقدار حاجت می گرفتند و باقی باز می گردانیدند و یک ٹنگه نقره رکابی بود آن را گروی نام نهاده بودند وقت حاجت او را گرو میداشتند از فتوح اول آن را رها میکنانیدند ملوک را تعظیم بر موازنه می داشتند وقتی ملک نورم باکرو فر در کھٹو بزیارت خدمت بابو آمد و خدمت بابو نشسته بکاری مشغول بودند برنخاستند و برای مصافحه یک دست دراز کردند ملک گفت سی صد و شصت ٹنگه در روزی یک ٹنگه برای بندگی حضرت بابو تعین میکنم اگر اشارت نشود محلی حواله

۱ح=وپهلو ۲سی=ح و ک-ندارد

کنم قبول نه کردند و فرمودند ملک تعین لعین[۱] است سید اکرم حاضر بود ناخوش شد گفت
بندگی بابو چرا قبول نمی فرمایند فقراء و مساکین از دولت شما بیاسانید فرمودند سید
تعین لعین است چون ملک بازگشت فقرا[۲] و مساکین بر ملک رفتند یکی گفت مستحق آن سی صد
و شصت سید است ملک گفت مستحق آن منم و پیش آمدن در کهٹو بیشتر سیر در عالم داشتند
بندگی حضرت مخدوم از بندگی حضرت بابو حکایت می کردند وقتی در زمین رای کافری
رسیدند رای مذکور تعظیم و نوازش بسیار کرد و مقامی طریف[۳] بجهت تکیه داده بملاقات
حاضر می شد براهین و کرامات بسیار دید شیفته شد و[۴] برای جماعت درویشان دیگر
پیش از خدمت بابو آمده بودند ایشان را وظیفه کرده دانسته بود درویشان را رشکی در کار شد
چند گردون هیزم خرید ند و خرمن آتش کردند انگشت کرد بخدمت بابو مقدم ایشان
آمد گفت شیخ شما را حلوای دود می توانید خورد فرمودند آری توانیم خورد خدمت حضرت
بابو اصطلاح میدانست که حلوای دود خرمن انگستان را گویند که بعضی درویشان درآیند
از برکات اسماء اعظم که از پیران خود یافته باشد خرمن آتش پائمال کنند آتش مذکور خاکستر
گردد و در پائها هیچ آفتی نرسد ایک[۶] بسم الله گفت در حال با چند تنی که برابر بودند برخاستند
و بران خرمن آمدند الله الله می گفتند و در ان خرمن دور میکردند میان یک ساعتی پائمال کردند آتش
مذکور خاکستر شد و در پائها هیچ آزار نرسید این کیفیت بسمع رای مذکور رسید از ان درویش قدیم

---

۱ لعین = ک ـ ندارد ۲ ک = فقیر ۳ ظریف = ح ـ ندارد
۴ ح = برای ۶ بسم الله الرحمٰن الرحیم گفته سیرود = ح

رنجید و وداع داد که این چنین بزرگوار را برین طریق امتحان چرا کنند بار دیگر در شهری[۱] مسجدی بود
دران نزول فرمودند در جوار آن مسجد خانه مقطع بود زن مقطع شنید که بزرگواری درین مسجد فرود آمده
است برای خدمت بابو ضیافت نیکو کرد اجناس طعام فرستاد مقطع شنید که بزرگواری
اندر بر عورت مزاج گرم[۲] کرد که برمن چرا نیامدند ملاقات نکردند حکم خدای عز و جل رسید درمیان شب
مقطع را درد شکم برخاست که حیران شد عورت را گفت که بر شیخ برو و مدد خواه پیش بندگی
بابو رسید الحاج[۳] بسیار کرد و بندگی حضرت بابو فرمودند اکنون سود ندارد عورت عرض کرد پس
انتقال ازین مسجد مصلحت است اقارب ملک مبادا مزاحمت دهند خدمت بابو فرمودند جرمی
خطائی از ما قولاً و فعلاً نشده است ما را تعلقی نیست عورت بازگشت ملک را دید که جان بحق
سپرده است و از برکات خدمت بابو از اقاربان کسی دم نزد و در اثنا سیر به زمین مغرب رفتند شهر
کیم بندگی حضرت شیخ[۴] محمد حجاج را ملاقات کردند شیخی کامگار[۵] مجتهدی نامداری یافتند
در مجلس ایشان علما کبار و فقها پرکار بتلمیذی[۶] حاضر می شدند از شیخ التماس پیوند کردند شیخ محمد
بصفاء باطن دریافتند که عاشقی صادقی و واصلی[۷] مشتاقی است فرمودند بابا اسحاق ما منتظر شما
بودیم با استعداد تمام آمده آید در مجلس اول فی الحال بشرف خلافت مشرف کردند و کلاه مبارک
از سر مبارک خود کشیدند و مرا پوشانیدند و من ارادت بخدمت ایشان آورده ام[۸] و بخدمت
کلاه و سجاده نواختند و بندگی شیخ محمد چهل حج کرده بودند و بمذاهب اهل سنت

۱ ک = شهر ۲ گرم = ک = ندارد ۳ الحاج ۴ ک = شیخی ۵ ح = کامگاری مجتهدی
۶ ک = بتکمیذی ۷ ک = واصلی ۸ ک = آوردم آورده ام

وسند اکابر مشائخ آراسته و صد و بیست سال عمر داشتند و به روایتی صد و پنجاه دو سال عمر بود و خانقاهی روان آسا و روضهٔ گلستان صفا ساخته بودند و لنگر برنج جاری بود و دو خادم داشتند یکی شیخ عمر خلفی و دوم شیخ محمد بیضاوی و این بزرگوار دانشمندان کارگذار و واصلان نامدار بودند بندگی حضرت شیخ محمد حجاج مذکور خادمان مذکور را نصیحت کردند باید که مراعات شیخ ابواسحاق را و مراقبت تعظیم او را بر خود لازم دانید و چنانچه بر من ملازمت می کنید بر شیخ ابواسحاق ملازمت کنید[1] و او را بجای من شمرید و خلق آن بامید خلافت سجاده سالها خدمت ایشان کردند و چون وفات ایشان قریب شد خلافت و سجاده این درویش را دادند و هم دران ایام بندگی حضرت شیخ محمد حجاج کیمی دعوت حق را لبیک گویان اجابت کردند و سفر آخرت گزیدند[2] بندگی حضرت بابو چنانچه اشارت بندگی شیخ محمد بود چند گاهی در خانقاه بندگی شیخ محمد ماندند روزی خادمان مذکور گفتند امروز بجهت کندوری و خرج خانقاه چیزی نیست راتب کندوی لنگر بدهند که شما بر سجاده ایشان نشسته اید و این درویش مسافر بود در گره چیزی نداشت و خلق آن مقام در خاطر کرده بودند که این مسافر راتب از کجا خواهد داد ضرورت یکی از ایشان بر سجاده خواهد نشست و این درویش بزیارت خود شیخ محمد حجاج مغربی کیمی مشغول شد و استمداد بروحانیت ایشان کرد وقت صبح یک گره و سیم بسته نزدیک قبر متبرکه یافته شد بنور باطن دریافتند که این گره سیم

۱ (برشیخ تاکنید) = ک - ندارد ۲ ح = کردند

بستہ نزدیک قبر متبرکہ بجہت نوازش ما است درحال ستدند و در مقام ایشان آمدہ بر سجادہ

نشستند چون خادمان برایشان آمدند و راتب کندوری برنج و لنگر طلبیدند گرہ سیم بستہ خادمان

را سپردند تا کندوری برنج و راتب لنگر کہ جاری میکردند بکنند چون خادمان گرہ کشادند شمار کردند

راتبی کہ در حیات بندگی حضرت شیخ تعین بود سیم ہمان مقدار است نہ یک چیتل[۱] زیادت و نہ نقصان

خادمان و خلق آن مقام متحیر ماندند و در خاطر خود اندیشہ کردند کہ این مسافر مال از کجا یافت و در آن

روز طعام بختند و در خانقاہ خرچ کردند و بندہ مؤلف از از بندگی بابو[۲] شنیدہ است کہ در ایام

ماضیہ رسم این بود کہ چون اکابر بہ زیارت قبر کسی میرفت فتوح پیش قبر داشت و دوم شب ہم

نزدیک قبر متبرکہ پیر خود مشغول شدم وقت صبح گرہ سیم بستہ نزدیک قبر متبرکہ یافتم بامداد خادم

خانقاہ را دادم چون ایشان گرہ کشادند دیدند کہ ہمان مقدار راتب است کہ نہ یک چیتل زیادت

و نہ نقصان طعام بختند و در خانقاہ خرچ کردند بعدہ خادم و خواتین خانقاہ را در سینہ

کینہ زیادہ تر شد کہ[۳] با وجود چندین اکابر علماء[۴] مخول فضلا شیخ را چہ مصلحت افتاد کہ غریبی

بی دیار و اجنبی را نگسار ساختند، ؎ خلاف رائی عزیزان چہ مصلحت دیدی ٭ کہ دوستان

وفادار خود بیش ببریدی ٭ و بعطایا[۵] غیب و جوائز لاریب مدد می نمایند ہم دران شب خدام در واقعہ

دیدند کہ سہام غیب و طعن غیب برایشان گذارمیکرد کہ ای مریدان طریقت مشائخ وای مالان

از سبیل رواسخ ہمیں زمان سیف حسد باحیف بعد از غمد ضمائر و غلاف سرائر صریح

۱ ک = چیتل ۲ بابو = ک ۔ ندارد ۳ ک = ندارد
۴ ح = مخول علما واصول ۵ بعطیا ۔ ک = ندارد

کشیده وزخم خیانت برخود گردید سحر را بر نور چشم باطن خدمت بابو چشم ظلمت سینه
پرکینه ایشان نظر افتاد و عزم انتقال مصمم کردند سیوم شب این درویش نزدیک قبر پرنور خود
رفت و گذرانید که در هر شبی این درویش بیاید و بسبب راتب خانقاه مزاحمت بد بی ادبی
تمام است برحمت وداع کنند روحانیت ایشان وداع کردند و در عالم سیر شدند بعد مدتی[1]
مدید و عهدی بعید در وقت سلطان محمد تغلق در مقامی رسیدند که بتصرف ملک
مظفر ذاته کلال بود قحط بود مظفر شنید که دو جماعت درویشان در مسجد نزول کردند یکی
جماعت خدمت بابو و دوم جماعتی سیاحی دیگر بعد نماز خفتن مظفر یکسر بریانی پاکیزه و چند
نان تنگ[2] و شیر چند پیش جوشیده فرستاد و پیش خدمت بابو آوردند خدمت بابو قسمت
کردند درویشی از جماعت دوم سرفه زبان نداشت بدگوئی مظفر کرد کسی از آرندگان طعام این
کیفیت در سمع مظفر رسانید مظفر همان زمان این کیفیت بر سلطان محمد[3] تغلق
نوشت هم دران شب کسی درویشان را علم داد که کیفیت شما بر سلطان در قلم آوردند
شاید که شما همه را علی الصباح بگیرد تا توانید انتقال ازین شهر بکنید درویشان بخدمت بابو
متوجه شدند که چه باید کرد بندگی حضرت بابو فرمودند افتراق غنیمت دانید همه متفرق شدند
و خدمت بابو ماندند صباح کسان مظفر آمدند جز ذات خدمت حضرت بابو کسی را نیافتند بندگی
بابو را بردند در مسجد داشتند و مظفر مذکور معتقد جوگیان بود جماعتی از جوگیان بسیار که در قسم جوگ

۱ ک=مدت ۲ ک=تنکه ۳ محمد=ک-ندارد

نامدار بودند بر مظفر می ماندند چون ایشان بر مظفر بدعاء صباحی آمدند مظفر قصهٔ دوش بر ایشان گفت وطعن طعنه ایشان بر بندگی بابو نهاد جوگیان گفتند او کجا است و جماعت کجا است تا خود جگر هاء ایشان و پاره پاره کنیم بعده شنیدند که جماعت متفرقه شد یک نفر صاحب سکه مانده است ایشان بر بندگی حضرت بابو آمدند و خدمت بابو بر اصطلاح و زبان ایشان حاوی بودند با ایشان بوضعی برخاستند که اطفاء نائرهٔ غضب ایشان شد ساعتی نشستند. بندگی حضرت بابو واقعه شب بیداری آن یک نفر ندکور و متفرق شدن ایشان و ماندن خود گفت ایشان را عبارت و فصاحت بندگی حضرت بابو و اطلاع بر اصطلاح ایشان اسیر گرد چون ایشان دیدند که بندگی حضرت بابو یکی از رؤسا و صلحاء این طائفه است گفتند ما را مشکلی است اگر اشارت شود استفسار کنیم[۱] خدمت بابو فرمودند چیست ایشان پرسیدند در آسمان کجا است بندگی حضرت بابو فرمودند من جواب این میدانم اما شما را سوگند گرو یعنی پیر شما است که چنانچه از گرو شنیده اید اگر موافق باشد عدول نکنند گفتند نکنیم بندگی حضرت بابو فرمودند در آسمان خبر و است چون آفتاب بر آید در کشاده شود چون فرو دررود در بسته گردد ایشان همه گله بر زمین آوردند و بمقتدائی قبول کردند مظفر را گفتند شیخ را بگذار از شیخ خطائی نیست شیخ مقتدایان ما است مظفر گفت کار بر دست من نمانده است هم در اثناء آن فرمان آمد که آن جماعت را در حضرت بفرستند بندگی حضرت بابو را میان جماعت درویشان کرده پیش سلطان محمد تغلق بردند

۱ـ ک = کنم

اول شیخی بود می گفت کہ بر سر من پیغامبر صلی اللہ علیہ وسلم در خواب دست فرود آوردہ اند و پنجہ
مبارک در نارک من بر آمدہ است تفحص کردند پنجہ دیدند گذاشتند دوم شیخ فلان سبزی خوار
بود فرمان شد از نعمتہا محروم است اورا گذاشتند سیوم سید محمود بہارنگی[1] بود فرمان شد سید است
بگذارند چہارم یاد نماندہ است پنجم خدمت بابو اسحاق بودند خانجہان سلام کرد و عرض
داشت کہ این درویشی است کہ مارا در صغر گفتہ بود کہ این وزیر خواہد شد آنچنان پادشاہی را کہ[2] پیش
ازین نبود و نخواہد شد فرمان شد شیخ کجامی باشند بابو گفتند در ملک شما فرمان شد در ملک باشد
مارا چرا ملاقات نکنند بندگی بابو گفتند ما در چہ خوایم[3] کہ ملاقات کنیم فرمان شد دو طشت پر تنکہ زر
آوردند قبول فرمایند بندگی بابو دست بر خرقہ پشمین نمود بردہ اشارت کردند ما این راچہ کنیم
و مارا چہ کار آید بندگی بابو را گذاشتند و باز گردانیدند چون از دردوم بیرون آمدند دوبدرہا
پھدیہا[4] از دنبال فرستادند کہ سلطان این شمارا دادہ است فرمودند پارہ کنند بندگی بابو
یک پھدیہ بستدند و باقی خلق را قسمت کردہ دادند و بیرون آمدند بعد چند گاہ در اجمیر زیارت
خواجہ معین الدین رسیدند شیخ را در واقعہ خواب دیدند میفرمودند کہ شیخ اسحاق شما در کھٹو
بروید از خواب بیدار شدند یاران را فرمودند کھٹو کجا است یاران گفتند کھٹو ازین سوی ناگور
است طرف جنوب فرمودند شیخ معین الدین مارا کھٹو فرستادند شب بسیار[5] بود خفتیم پیش
کردند شیخ باز واقعہ دیدند کہ میفرمودند شیخ شمان در کھٹو بروید بیدار شدند تکیہ بستن گرفتند۔

۱۔ ک=بہاری ۲۔ کہ=ک۔ ندارد ۳۔ درخوایم=ک
۴۔ فیروزی=ک ندارد ۵۔ باز=ک۔ ندارد

یاران گفتند کفار این مقام[1] صله ها می گیرند تا صبح فرصت بدهند شب بسیار است باز چشم پیش کردند باز شیخ معین الدین را در واقعه دیدند بعفونت میفرمودند که شیخ شما در کهٹو چرا می روید بندگی بابو برخاستند و تکیه بستند و از کوه فرود آمدند یاران[1] را چاره نشد در رکاب شدند چون در موضع کوہیوه من اعمال کهٹو سه کروه از دیندوانه رخ مغرب رسیدند از طرف کهٹو دیوانه آمد مصافحه کرد و گفت بیا مقطع حال و موازنه یک آماج تیر زیر درختی رفت و نشست قضا[2] همان زمان از غیب ستوری پر جوال از لڈوها بزرگ بخدمت بندگی بابو رسید صاحب ستور جوال مذکور بالڈوها پیش آورد خدمت بندگی بابو او را نگفتند که کیستی و که فرستاده است دلڈو برای دیوانه گفت لڈو کده هو یعنی از کجا خدمت بابو فرمودند داهو یعنی از آن درگاه است[3] از کوہیوه در کهٹو آمدند ساکن شدند خلق بسیار تعظیم و اطاعت نمودند خانه مسقف عرض کردند خدمت بابو دران ایام پرورش شیخ قوام الدین می کردند خلق کهٹو او را کرهره[4] می گفتند یعنی شتر جوان که ذکر آن بالا کرده شده است روزی کاغذهای شیخ قوام الدین را این درویش مطالعه میکرد نسخه چند از لغات و مبادی بود پیش بندگی حضرت بابو[5] عرض داشت که شیخ قوام الدین را همین مقدار علم بود خدمت بابو ناخوش شدند و فرمودند کلام[6] اهانت بروی مگو او از نظر من رفته است آنگاه مهر او بر تواند اخته ام

حکایت روزی که بندگی حضرت بابو در دهلی رسیدند در مسجد نمازگاه دهلی رفتند بر سر منبر بر آمدند فرمودند که بابا احمد احمد خان را خبر کن یعنی احمد کاتبه را خبر کن تا برای ملاقات بیاید

١ک=بازانرا ٢ک=قضاء ٣ح=درکارهست
٤ک=کوهره ٥بابو=ک-ندارد ٦سخن=ک-ندارد

یک دو نفر برابر داوند خانه احمد خان مذکور آمدند حاجب را علم دادند تا بر خان بگذارند خان گفت بگو چون سلطان فیروز بیایند و فلان وزیر و فلان خان بیایند من هم بیایم باز گشتند و کیفیت به بندگی حضرت بابو عرض کردند بندگی حضرت بابو بغصه فرمودند برو و بگو می آئی یا بیارانیم خان هنوز براهی در سرای رفتن سوار نشده بود که بر حاجب گفتند بگو بند که بندگی بابو[1] همچنین گفته فرستادند حاجب گفت مرا مجال نیست که این چنین سخن گفتن توانم خان چون بیرون آمدند بندگی حضرت مخدوم فرمودند که خدمت بابو فرموده اند که می آئی یا[2] بیارانیم خان را این سخن در دل زد و چابک بر بندگی مخدوم زد کرد پایه خندق درمیان بود زیانه چابک تا بمخدوم برسید در تمام مجلس هیهو پس خان که بود بیک زبان گفتند هی هی هی چنانکه غوغا برخاست بندگی حضرت مخدوم میرزی او دهنی که پوشیده بودند میخ آهنی در تخته در برآمده بود میرزا ازان آزار رسیده پاره شد بندگی حضرت مخدوم ازین هر دو معامله شکسته خاطر شدند پر غصه پیش بندگی حضرت بابو آمدند بندگی حضرت بابو بر منبر نمازگاه نشسته بودند و تکیه عصا بر زنخ کرده چون نظر بندگی حضرت بابو بر بندگی حضرت مخدوم افتاد بندگی حضرت مخدوم را منغض دیدند فرمودند خراب یا آباد بندگی مخدوم هیچ جواب نگفتند در گوشه رفتند نشستند و خدمت بابو همانجا ماندند خیلی وقت گذشت ناگاه آتش پرنهیب در شهر برخاست بندگی حضرت بابو فرمودند شیخ احمد خانهٔ احمد خان کدام سوی است بندگی حضرت مخدوم عرض داشتند خانهٔ[3] او طرف دیگر است بندگی حضرت بابو فرمودند این آتش هم در خانه اوست مصاحبانی که در رکاب بندگی حضرت مخدوم

۱ بابو=ک-ندارد ۲ ک=که ما ۳ خانه=ح-ندارد

رفته بودند ایشان هم عرض داشتند خانه او مقداری راستا یا چپا است باز بندگی حضرت بابو فرمودند
این آتش هم در خانهٔ اوست خان در دیوان بود باز گشته در خانه می آمد کیفیت مذکور شنید در خاطر
کرد که این آتش از بندگی حضرت بابو است خان باز گشت که بر سلطان بگویم که فلان درویش[1] ساحر
آتش هم چنین انداخته است پیشوایان گفتند که خان مصلحت نیست که بر سلطان بگوید کسی که در خانهٔ
شما آتش انداخته است او تواند که در خانهٔ سلطان هم اندازد چاره نیست پیش بندگی بابو اسحاق
بروید بعده خان حاجب را گفتند که یک طشت خرما بستان و پیش بندگی بابو برو و عذرخواهی
کن حاجب پیش بندگی حضرت بابو رسید گفت خان خدمت رسانیده است و عرض داشته است
که بلطف عفو فرمایند سبب حادثه این آتش تقصیر شد و اگر نه درین زمان می آید از آن حاجب
پرسیدند که این آتش از کجا برخاست و چه سوخت حاجب عرض داشت که آتش از درون حجره
زرادخانه برخاست اسباب زرادخانه زره و کارول (رکاول) و زین و لگام و کنعل[2] بسوخت بعد ساعتی
بانواع خدمتی آمد مقابل بندگی حضرت بابو دست بسته ایستاده بندگی حضرت بابو روی مبارک
از او گردانید طرف دیگر کردند خان توجه به بندگی حضرت مخدوم کرد که برای رضای خدا تعالی پیش شوید
بندگی بابو را شفاعت کنید بندگی حضرت مخدوم دران طرف رفتند و ایستاده شدند بندگی حضرت بابو
فرمودند مرا چه می گوئی او را بگو که در پای تو بیفتد در حال در پای بندگی حضرت مخدوم افتاد بندگی
حضرت بابو فرمودند خان کاته بوده اما نرم[3] کردیم[4] بحکم باری تعالی مقصود ازین حکایت همان بود که

١ ک=دروبساحر ٢ ح=کنفل ٣ ح=ماترانرم ٤ ح=کردم

چندیں بلا از شامیت آں بود که چابک به بندگی مخدوم بر گرد می زد بندگی مخدوم پاره شد[۱]

و بندگی حضرت بابو ازان اشارت کرد که مرا چه میگوئی برو بگو که در پای تو بیفد بعده بندگی بابو خود منی

او قبول نه کردند باز گردانیدند چوں سخت مزاحم[۲] شد بندگی حضرت مخدوم را بندگی حضرت بابو

فرمودند که شیخ احمد چیزی ازین بستان بندگی حضرت مخدوم دو لڈو بزرگ ستدند و چه طاقه

کهنبل گرفتند فحسب **حکایت** فرمودند که در مسافرت زناداران موحدان با ایں درویش

بحث می کردند و در توحید ایشان رانیک رسانیت بود و این درویش گفت که اوتار در دین

شماں میگوید چیست ایشان گفتند شخصی نقل کرد روح آن شخص در رحم عورتی که فرزند جدید

در آن است در قالب او روح در می آرند اوتار این است و ایں درویش بزبان هندوی بر

[۳] که شما سرگ و نرک میگوئید ایشان گفتند آری ما میگوئیم این درویش گفت

ایشان گفتند روح یکی و قالب دو میگوئید[۴] مگر بکنید که سرگ و نرک یک قالب را باشد

دوم قالب چه شود ضائع رود ایں سخن شنیدند فی الحال اسلام آوردند و در پای ایں درویش

افتادند و گفتند دین شماں برحق است و دین خود را باطل دانستند بندگی قطب العالم فرمودند

کرم حضرت بے نیاز درباب[۵] ایں درویش چنداں[۶] است که شکرانه آں کی تواند بجا آورد

حکایت چوں احمد خان را پرگنه کهٹو در وجه شد و در کهٹو آمد هوا و باران بود جامها و اسباب

تر شد در قصبه در نیامد بیرون دروازه تخته سنگی بزرگ بود که موازنه دو بیست مردمی نشستند بر آن

قرار گرفت سید اکرم ملازم مخدوم احمد خان را ملاقات کرد خان پرسید که بابو توی هندست هست

۱ شد= ک-ندارد ۲ ک=مزحم ۳ که شماتا گفت= ک-ندارد
۴ ک=که ۵ ک=را ۶ ک=چندان رحم

سید گفت نیکو اند خان را خنده قهقهه بسیار کنا و سید را باز گردانید سید بخدمت بابو آمد و کیفیت خنده گفت قدری بابو نا خوش شدند چون میانه روز شد خان یک طشت خرما بر دست خواص[۱] خود فرستاد و گفت شیخ احمد را بگوئی که ما تر شده ایم بجهت خشک کردن جامه و رخت بر دروازه مانده ایم بخدمت بندگی بابو عرض دارند خواص مذکور بخدمت بندگی حضرت شیخ جهان قطب زمان دامت برکاته آمد و کیفیت مذکور گفت و باز گشت بندگی مخدوم بخدمت بابو عرض داشتند که شمان یکایک بگفتار کسی مزاج گرم نکنید خان عذر خواهی کرده طشت خرما فرستاده است بابو فرمودند تو چه گفتی گفتیم که حالیا خدمت بابو در استراحت قیلوله اند چون برخیزند بگذرانم بعد نماز ظهر خان رسید پابوس خدمت بابو کرد باز خان رید اشارت خدمت بندگی بابو شد که چه می خندیدی[۲] خان عرض داشت که در عمر خود دو عجوبه دیدم از آن می خندم یکی آنکه در زراد خانه[۳] کسی نبود و حجره با مقفل بود آتش از کجا خیزد و درون خانه که برد این عجب از خاطر من نمی رود دوم آنکه روزی در بغل من دستارچه کشیده خوب بود من سوار در دیوان می رفتم دیوانه آمد گفت ای خان آن دستارچه که در بغل تست بمن ده از تو خواهد رفت گفتیم که من بر طریق احتیاط خواهم داشت رفتن چه باشد دیوانه گفت چنانچه دانی بداری بر تو نخواهد ماند مرا بده هر چند که او جهد کرد دستارچه ندادم بمحافظت در بغل داشتم چون از دیوان در خانه آمدم دستارچه در بغل نیافتم حیران و متحیر ماندم و هنوز در تعجب هستم[۴] حکایت در صحبت روزی بندگی قطب زمان شیخ جهان

۱ خواص=ک-ندارد ۲ ح= خندیدی ۳ ک=درزادخانه ٤ ک=هستم

دامت برکاتہ از دروازہ کھٹو بیروں میرفتند می فرمودند از پس ما خماری آمد و بندگی بابو از پیش پیدا شدند چوں نظر بندگی بابو بر خمار افتاد مرا فرمودند احمد این کیست کہ دنبال تو می آید گفتم فلان را نمی دانم کہ کی رسید و مرا علم نیست کہ او با من می آید از آن روز باز متنبہ شدم صحبت اراذل و اسافل گذاشتم **حکایت** روزی با بقالی در کھٹو مرا کاری بود در خانۂ او رفتم دیدم عورتی حیشش میکوفت بوی آن در دماغ من رسید درد سر شد در خانہ آمدم بیخود شدم بابو را خبر شد کہ شیخ احمد تکلم نمی کند بی تاب افتادہ است خدمت بابو آمدند آواز دادند بہوش آمدم کیفیت دماغ گفتم فرمودند احمد ما بوئی مست است ؎ ہر بوئی مست و ساقی پر دہد پیمانہ را چہ من از آن روز دون[1] (باز درون) خانہ کسی نرفتم **حکایت** روزی قلندری بخدمت بابو رسید مزاحمت می نمود میگفت ششش چینیل (جینیل) برائی بھنگ بدہ خدمت بابو فرمودند احمد این را ششش چنیل بدہ ہان بندگی قطب ربانی شیخ جہان دامت برکاتہ را تسوار نمود گفتند این چنین کسی را برائی این معنی چیزی دہانیدن کجا روا باشد بابو ساکت شدند و بعضی روایت کردہ اند کہ خدمت بابو ہمچنین گفتند کہ ما را از دادن نخواہند پرسید نہ از خوردن او و او را ششش چنیل بدہ تا باید چیزی دیگر نخورد اما این مولف از شیخ این روایت یاد ندارد بعدہ سید امیر بدہ ناگوری مدرس بخدمت بابو رسید خدمت قضیہ قلندر مذکور گفتند و اعتراض ما بر سید مذکور فرمودند و گفتند یا امیر بدہ روبہ[2] سی سالہ و روبہ بچہ سی و پنج سالہ سید انگشت نمود و تعجب در دہان کرد چوں سید بازگشت من برای وداع بر بر رفتم

[1] ک = دون [2] ک = روبہ

سید فرمود شیخ احمد شمان را محل اعتراض با خدمت بابو نیست بابو عالی مرتبه اند با من قول کن

بعد ازین بر بابو اعتراض نکنی **حکایت** روزی دیگر قلندری رسید بر خدمت بابو شیخ کشیده

قادر شد خدمت بابو فرمودند هلا ای نامرد شخصی او را از خدمت بابو از بیرون شناخت و دوید[۱] گردن

قلندر را از پس گرفت کشید بابو قلندر مذکور را چیزی دهانیدند و آنکه او را کشید او را هم چیزی مرحمت کردند

حکایت[۳] چون خدمت بابو از کهتو بزیارت شیخ معین الدین سنجری[۲] طرف اجمیر قصد کردند

ملک جهینگل بعز ابرابر بود از قصبهٔ نارائنه شیخ بحری هم برابر شدند و شیخ بحری اگر چه مرید شیخ

خضر حو ضحاض بود اما بسیار تربیت از خدمت بابو داشت چون نزدیک[۴] تیهلا رسیدند و این درویش

صغیر بود با نفران جهینگل شده از پس می آمدیم خدمت بابو هر بار از جهت این درویش درنگ می کردند

یک بار درنگی بسیار شد خدمت بابو متعلق شدند چون دیر شد بر ملک بغرا آمدند که نفران تو

پسر مرا گم کردند ملک عرض داشت که اگر شیخ احمد نیاید جهینگل را بخدمت شمان خدمتی کنم خدمت

بابو فرمودند قربان کرده صد جهینگل بر تار موی بابا احمد هم چنان بودند که این درویش رسید خدمت بابو

را قرار شده شیخ بحری را فرمودند در سر احمد پخته گی شده است موی سر او فرود آر چنانچه[۵] آزار

نرسد شیخ بحری موی سر ما فرود می آوردند و ما را گریه گشت خدمت بابو بر شیخ بحری تفت

شدند فرمودند برمن بیارید دست مبارک خود بمقراض موی سر ما فرود آوردند و ما را بهمان جا

واشتند خود بخدمت دراجمیر رفتند چون صباح شد ما بابو را ندیدیم در گریه شدیم ملک بغرا ما را در کند

۱ ک=دویدن ۲ کذا-درح وک ۳ حکایت=ک-ندارد
۴ نزدیک=ک-ندارد ۵ ح=چنج

کرد و بر سر راه آورد داشت و می گفت اینک خدمت بابو می آیند بعد ساعتی خدمت بابو
آمدند ما را قرار شد دیگر خدمت بابو در ناگور رفته بودند و این درویش هم برابر بودم ناگاه شیخ
خضر مذکور با جماعت خود آمد گفت شخصی برای ما اسباب ضیافتی داده است بیایید در حوض
پنشین برویم چون بر پل حوض مذکور رفتند نشستند مطربان آمدند سرود آغاز کردند شیخ خضر گفت
چیزی گوشت دارد و روغن ایشان را بدهند باز گردانند خدمت بابو گفتند مبادا اندری
باشند خوب نباشد چند چیتل نقد و پان دادند باز گردانیدند شب درون شهر کردند ستوبادی ستورهای
ستوران را درون دروازه بیار - خدمت بابو از سخن شیخ خضر سخت کاره
شدند و فرمودند که خدایتعالی از کسی حق او نستاند و بدیگری ندهد -
ایشان بیرون دروازه بسته بودند شیخ خضر گفت ای بحری ستور کجاست شیخ بحری گفت
پیش از دروازه بسته ام بخدای سپردم شیخ خضر گفت جوان مرد است از یکی بستاند بدیگری بدهد
شیخ را سرقه سخن نیست این صحبت باید گذاشت با شیخ خضر نماند بر قاضی برهان الدین خطیب
ناگور رفتند او سخت معتقد حضرت بابو بود عرض داشت کرد که ما را دیهی است رهول نام خربزه ها
خوب در و شده است آنجا تفرج[1] باید کرد قاضی خدمت بابو را در دیهه مذکور برد و بسیار خربزه ها
آرانید خربزه ها در رهول سخت شیرین و نامدار در آن دیار اند قاضی بدست خود پوست
خربزه ها فرو می آورد و پیش خدمت بابو شگاف کرده می داشت و خدمت بابو و ما تناول
می کردیم و قاضی را الحان خوب این چنین بود که آدمی سخت دل را هم نرم کردی قاضی توحیدات
را بخدمت بابو خواندن گرفت که چنانچه[2] خدمت بابو را لهجه قاضی و نعمه او سخت گرفت تا دیری

۱ ک = تفرح ۲ ح = چنج

در وقت[١] بودند و زاری می‌گریستند یک شب بابو را قاضی بر خود داشت صباح کرد بعد و دستور
از دیهه آوردند و خر پر ها بار کردند سوی کهٹو باز گشتند چون در موضع آهوا در رسیدند[٢] و این آهواد
برای سادات دینیدوانه از سلطان فیروز انعام بود سادات مذکور خود را پیدا نه کردند و ملاقات
نه کردند خدمت بابو[٣] هم بگردون رهول در کهٹو آمد آن خر پر ها قسمت کردند کیفیت آخرت بندگی
شیخ ابو اسحاق تغمده الله بالرحمة و الرضوان بندگی شیخ جهان قطب زمان دامت
برکاته می فرمودند که قصبهٔ دینیدوانه رفته بودیم که بندگی بابو را تپ آغاز شده بعد چند[٤] روز
شخصی را بر ما فرستادند[٥] او آمد و بر ما نگفت شاید از بهر آنکه چند روز نعمتهای بخورد در روزی
دل ما سوی خدمت بابو سخت کشان شد یاران را گفتیم آرزوی لقای[٦] خدمت بابو بر ما غالب
شده است در کهٹو برویم آن آینده گفت که مرا بندگی بابو بطلب شمان فرستاده اند
و در وجود مبارک بابو تپ است گفتیم ای بی انصاف ما را چرا نگفتی عذرهای تقیم کرد چون بحضرت
بابو رسیدیم فرمودند بابا احمد چه خواهی کرد این دنیای فانی را بابو تو رحلت میکند[٧] گمان که
مگر خدمت بابو در مکث کردن مارنجیده اند پس پشت مبارک ایستاده شدیم و معتاد[٨]
پیش از آن هم برین منوال بود که چون گرم مزاج می شدند مقابل نمی ماندیم خدمت بابو تکلم نمی کردند
ملک کمال ککهر منقطع کهٹو پیش خدمت بابو بود خواست که در تکلم آرد[٩] ما را گفت که در کدام راه آمدید
خدمت بابو فرمودند این جا بیا ما را] تو هم مکث شد ملک کمال که تشنه بود بر زبان او رفت

١ـ ک=وقت ٢ـ ک=رسید ٣ـ بابو=ح ـ ندارد ٤ـ چند=ک ـ ندارد
٥ـ ک=فرستاد ٦ـ ک=آغاز ٧ـ شد=ک ـ ندارد ٨ـ ک=معتداد
٩ـ (ار ـ ـ ـ مارا تا بیام)=ح ندارد

میر احمد نزدیک بیا سید خدمت بابو بروی چشم باکشیده فرمودند بگذر می خواهم
که پیر بکنیم این میرمی گوید دستار را ز سر من گرفتند بمولانا یوسف صدر بر تاب کردند طاقیه
مبارک خود از سر فرود آوردند زه طاقیه بهر دو دست گرفته چیزی می خواندند بعده بر سر من بدست
مبارک خود نهادند من و گریه شدم عرض داشتم که در تحمل این مقام مرا یاری و رهبری[1] نیست فرمودند تعلق
پادشاهان محتاج سخن تو باشند خلق لکهنو هم برای عیادت آمده بودند بایشان وداع[2] کردند
روز دوم دو تنگه نقره مرا دادند که برای سنگ تراشان بده تا قبر راست کنند بعده حفاران را طلبیدند
پیش خود قبر کاویدند قاضی فخر الدین حاکم لکهنو آمد و گفت که بزرگان را رسمی است که قبر می کنند و گندم
در قبر می اندازند و هر سالی آن گندم صدقه می دهند خدمت بابو را این سخن خوش نیامد فرمودند
پس تو بار استوار می داری سر مبارک بر زانو من بود بدست اشارت کردم که مصلحت نیست
دست قاضی گرفتند و فرمودند بیا قاضی ما تو خوشنود یم تو هم از ما خوشنود باشی و باز گردانیدند
و آن روز روز شنبه بود بعده یک شب استفراغ بسیار شد آبی که می نوشیدند آن هم باز[3] می گشت
من درون غلطیده بودم فرمودند احمد برین آب چیزی بخوان بده من خواندم دادم قدری
فرق شده بعده[4] هر بار که آب می خوردند می فرمودند که بخوان و بده من در خواب مستغرق بودم فرمودند
کلیت احمد این جا بیا ربعنایت حق تعالی تشنگی کم شد استفراغ بکلی ماند چون چهار شنبه شد
هفدهم ماه شعبان فرمودند گور ساخته کنید و مرا پس پشت[6] مبارک نشاندند اطاعت کردم

۱ ح=زهره ۲ وداع=ک- ندارد ۳ باز=ک-ندارد، ک=زهیری
۴ ک=بعده ۵ ک= آغاز ٦ شت ک ندارد

بمن تکیه کردند نشستند و بلا[١] زبان مبارک آوردند یا حیُّ یا قیوم یا حیُّ یا قیوم و چشم بستند جان بحق تسلیم نمودند اِنّا للّٰه وَ اِنّا اِلَیهِ رَاجِعُون **فصل چهارم** در شروع کردن بندگی قطب زمان شیخ جهان دامت برکاته در علم می فرمودند در ایام صغر بندگی بابو طاب ثراه ما را در ناگور بردند در مدرسه قاضی حمید الدین ناگوری رحمة الله علیه نزول [٢] خطبا ناگوری علما حاضر شدند خدمت بابو فرمودند که این خوردک را علم بیاموزند همه عرض داشتند که هنوز خورد هستند خدمت بابو فرمودند کتاب های مبادی جمع کنید هر کسی نسخه آورد مولانا تاج الدین امام مسجد جامع نسخه میزان راست کرده بالتکلف آورد و کسی هزار الفاظ آورد دیگری ادوات[٣] یکی پنج گنج و مصادر و غیر ذالک آوردند قاضی امام نسه جلال هم حاضر بودند مذاکره تفسیر امام زاهد افتاد که تفسیری معتبری و معتمد است مرا اشتیاق غالب شد گفتی بر دست من بود قاضی امام را دادم که تفسیر مذکور برای من بخرید خدمت بابو فرمودند که قاضی امام تم چه خواهی کرد قاضی گفت کاغذ خرید خواهم کرد و خواهم نبشت بعد مدتی در لکهنو دانشمندی بزیارت بندگی بابو رسید خدمت بابو فرمودند که این[٤] خوردک را علم بیاموزید او گفت که هنوز خورد است خدمت بابو فرمودند در ناحیه مسجد برید یک مسئله زبانی تقریر کنید طبع این بیازمائید آن دانشمند مسئله از علم کلام برمن تقریر کرد و گفت من آنچه گفتم شما برمن تقریر کنید هرچه آن دانشمند گفته بود بترتیب تقریر کردم دانشمند خوش شد بخدمت بابو گذرانید کم را نیت بود که بعد ملاقات خدمت بابو بسرعت باز خواهم گشت اما ذکا این خوردک مرا باعث شده است

١. ک=بزبان ٢. خطباء تا فرمودند=ک- ندارد
٣. ک=اوادت ٤. این=ک ندارد

که نسخهٔ عقیدهٔ حافظیه دوگان سگان مسئله هر روز تلقین کنم همچنان کرد تا تمام کردم آن بزرگوار
وقف کرد چون خدمت بابو دعوت حق اجابت بلبیک مقرون کرد هوس علم غالب شد
چیزی برابر تنها معین یافته داشتیم طلب کردیم تا خرچ راه شود معین مذکور گفت کدام
وجه گفتیم وجه آن ستور که فلان کوتوال نذر کرده بخدمت بابو عرض داشت که در آنکه گو[١] ساله بود
به نیت خدمت پرورش کردم درین وقت بزرگ شده است کسی بفرستید تا تسلیم کنم
خدمت بابو فرمودند احمد کسی را بفرست ستور مذکور بیاورد شخصی بزنار دار فرستادیم او ستور
مذکور تسلیم نمود چون نزدیک قصبه رسید ستور مذکور قوت کرد از دست او رها شد گریخت
ما چند نفر بر راه میکردیم تا بگیرند و بیارند شمان آمدید و گفتید که ستور مذکور بر دست
من[٢] نفر و شید وجه ستور مذکور بشمان من خواهم رسانید ستور مذکور گرفته در خانه خود آورد دید
مال ما هنوز نداده اید معین[٣] گفت آن مال هم دران روز ها رسانیده ام اگر نه رسیده است
[٤] ما دیدیم مجادله
یک دلاسا بدهید ملحم اولا با راه درویشی نیست ترک دادیم بر دیگران هم چیزی
یافتم داشتیم کسی چیزی نداد توکل بر خدای تعالی کردیم مولانا یوسف صدر برابر بود
گفتیم مولانا شمان باز گردید مرد گم شده جائی میرود چون در جوار موضع بنا تهری دیهه داؤد
چودهری قصبه دیندوانه گذشتیم صالح درویش در رکاب بود دور شده در ماه صیام
کنار خوزان می آمد او را آواز دادیم سید اکرم میان دیهه بود آواز شناخت بیرون آمد ملاقات کرد

١ ک = کوه ساله ٢ من = ک - ندارد
٣ کذا در هر نسخه ٤ ک = دید مجاد که دلاسا

در گریه شد گفت همچنین کردید گفتم سید ابا زگردید گفت التماس دارم کفشها خود پیش نهاد که این کفشها بپوشید گفتیم برهنگی پای اختیاری ست نه اضطراری و این حدیث خوانده‌ایم وامشوا حفاة عراة ترون الله جهرة ای آشکار سید بازگشت چون نماز شام گذاردیم صلح گفت مخدوم شما را دینه روز هم روزه طی بود اگر قدری وقفه کنید من کنار کوفته[۱] پیش شما بیارم قبول نکردیم شخصی از دیهه بیرون آمد ما را شناخت از نجاست گفت گردونها دینه دوانه اینک می روند چون بگردونها رسیدم ما را ایشان نشناختند بر گردون سابق نشاندند وقت افطار ستوران کشادند هر یکی توشه خود پیش ما آورد نهاد شخصی گلیمی بزرگ که بساط گردون می باشد از گردون خود فرود آورد فراز کرد ما را در صدر نشاندند گفتیم یاران شما هر روز هم بدین صورت روزه می کشاید گفتند خیر مخدوم هر کسی تنها بر گردون روزه افطار می کرد امروز جهت تعظیم شما گردونها داشتیم تا شما را ملاوت و در افطار باشد نفس را گفتیم چرا محزون می باشی حق تعالی می خواهد ترا تبعظیم دارد چون دینه دوانه رسیدم درون قصبه نرفتیم در مسجد داود مذکور که جانب غرب از قصبه است فرود آمدیم صباح خلق دینه دوانه هجوم کرد مولانا خرم جد ما درین این مولف رسید عرض داشت کرد که شیخ احمد شما را کهتومگذارید اول در کهتو شیخ شهاب بود بعده شیخ محمود قتال بود بعده شیخ بیابانی بود بعده شیخ ابواسحاق بود و این زمان شمائید شما کهتو مگذارید چون از دینه دوانه دور رفت[۲] ملکی با لشکر از پس بما پیوست بر ما اعتقاد بسیار کرد

۱. ک = گرفته ۲. ک = رفت، رفتند = ح تصحیح قیاسی

هرچند که خواست که با ما افطار کند جواب ندادیم وقت فرود آمدن در منزل هر روز بیست و پنج جیتل نقد و یک لڈو و شیرینی[1] برای ما می فرستاد بخلق الله می دادیم درویشی مصاحب ما بود بر سبیل سعایت بر ملک گفت بیست پنجگانی لڈو که شما بر شیخ می فرستید اصلا نمی خورد بدیگران می دهد ملک گفت این درویش بد خواه شما است داشتن او بر خود چه مصلحت است بعده یک کرة کولی خوب بر ما رسید همین درویش مسالت نمود که کرة کول[2] من بیابم گفتیم برو ببر

حکایت در یک دیهی رسیدم صالح را بجهت آب وضو درون دیهه فرستادم از خانه وجهدار مسلمان آب طلبید زن او گفت بشتواره بیدرم بیار آنگاه آب بخواه گفتار او در سمع ما رسید صالح را گفتیم آب خانه ایشان محفوظ کمتر باشد باز گرد عورت را از میان ستی نظر بر ما افتاد دریافت که مردی عارف است گفت مخدوم ما مسلمان زاده ایم وجهدار این دیهه زوج او است پیری مستعدی صاحب سجاده و شجره داریم پیر را خبر کرد پیر اجابت نامه سید السادات سید جلال الدین بخاری آورد ما را دید جوانی مخطط گفت چیزی بخوان گفتیم چه بخوانیم گفت الف ب بخوان اجازت نامه ما از دست او ستدیم و خواندیم دریافت و خود خواندن نه می دانست ترسید که مبادا چیزی بپرسد بحضور عورت خجالت پیش آید کاغذ از ما گرفت و باز گشت عورت مذکور بجهت ما مرغ ذبح کرد بالمزاج[3] گفتیم این جا ذبح کردن کسی داند عورت گفت پسران و داما دان ما با خبر اند و دختر کی داشت تعرض کرد گفتیم ما همه چیز ترک کرده ایم گفت اهل قدوم

1 ح = شیرینی 2 کذا در هر دو نسخه اغلب این لفظ کجکول باشد ک = وشیرین
3 ک = بالمزاج

مبارک خود در کشت من بپندازند تا دران کشت برکات شود **حکایت** در حصار
فیروزه رسیدم مقطع ملک کمال الدین پسر ملک عمر عرض[1] بندگان بود فرد خانه خوبی داشت
مارا فرود آورد و شاخ زر نام کنیزکی جمیله داشت برای ما پیش آورد کنیزک مذکوره وضوی کنانید
و طعام می آورد مولانا شمس الدین دانشمند علامه روزگار آنجا بود پیش اوشان مفصل و شاشی و حسامی
و بزدوی هم خواندیم چند ماه گذشت یک روز شاخ زر آب بجهت وضو می آورد و مقابل آمد عورتی
ظریفه با اجناس زرینه پوشیده گفتم کیستی کجا می آئی از پیش من دور شو او چون مار انفت دید
بازگشت نماز شام عورتی زال چراغ آورد گفتم کیستی گفت دادا فلانه خدمت گار قدیم ملک مذکور
گفتم شاخ زر چرا نیامد گفت امروز بندگی مخدوم برو مزاج کردند بعده مرا فرستادند گفتم درو بیان
تا غایت او را احساس نکرده بودند امروز چون متقابل آمده دانستند مگر عورتی بیگانه است از ان
بازگردانیدند ایشان عجب آمد که مردی بجوانی را چند ماه شد که عورتی آراسته داده بودند[2]
زهی بزرگوار که وقتی طرف او نظر نکرد تحقیق نادر روزگار است و تشیعی کامگار ملک را
علم شد معتقدتر شد و پدر ایشان ملک عمر معتقد خدمت بابو بود بندگی بابو را در دهلی یک بار
در خانه خود مهمان برد بعد طعام خورانیدن ششش بهدیه بر دست پسر بخدمت بابو فرستاد خدمت
بابو بهدیه بوسیدند قبول کردند ما سخت بیدل شدیم که ششش بهدیه چه لائق بابو است
بعده پسر را فرستاد که بندگی بابو را بر و باد کن و دست خود پسر را نمود که من خدمت بابو را چندان

۱ کذا در هر نسخه لعل لفظ عارض باشد بمعنی عرض کننده ۲ ک = بود

یاد کرده‌ام که در کف دست من هنوز نشّی از کثرت یاد باقی است، بندگی بابو فرمودند احمد ببین یعنی ملک عمر این چنین مخلص است شش بهدیه ببین شاید دیگر تدبیر شده باشد دیگر چون ملک عمر برای عرض ستدن از سکنه ناگور در کهٹو وزرانه از دهلی بر حکم فرمان آمد تمام حشم را درنارانه طلبید ند برادر حسام الدین که یکی از سکنهٔ کهٹو بود، با ما محبت داشت، در خدمت بندگی بابو بسیار ملازمت کردی پیش بندگی بابو عرض داشت که من چکنم اسپ ندارم که عرض بکند رام [۱]بر عمر بگوکه من ملازمت آنجا دارم او

بندگی بابو فرمودند برو نام ما بر ملک عمر درنارانه رفت، [۲]چنانچه اشارت خدمت بابو شده داشت

بود عرض ملک فرمود تو برو [۳]جای نماند دوم روز ملک فرمود برو عرض تو صحیح شد خدمت ما به بندگی بابو برسانی بعده بندگی قطب زمان شیخ جهان دامت برکاته می فرمودند ما را هوس بر علم حدیث شد شنیدم در کوشک نزول میان هزارستون مولانا مجد الدین محدث علم حدیث را سبق می گویند از ملک کمال عمر اجازتی خواستم ملک سوار شد ند چند کروه رکاب آمدند گفتند چیزی در فرد خانه مانده است چکنیم گفتیم که چه رخت است گفت گلیم ها این چنین چندین جامها چنین و کذا و کذا گفتیم آن رخت صاحب خانه است ما را بدان ملکی نمانده است ملک را وداع کردیم در دهلی آمدیم زیارت مقابر چنانچه سنت خدمت بابو کردیم قریب مسجد خانجهان در محلت جاجنگر در فیروز آباد میان بازار عبد الرحمن مولی اسلام که در کهٹو بر ما می بود دیدیم با او ملاقات شد گفتیم الحمد لله که برای اقتدای دوم نفر شد وقت عصر شده بود عبد الرحمن

---

[۱] بر عمر تا او = ک ـ ندارد [۲] ح = چنج ، ک ـ ندارد
[۳] جائی تا برو = ک ندارد

عذری کرد رفت مادر مسجد مذکور در آمدیم ملک اسمٰعیل قرابت خواجه قطب خواجگی برهر فرابالش[1]
مسجد مذکور بود ملاقات شد گفت مقام شما در ملوک خانه است مادر ملوک خانه یک ساعت
نشستیم تا جماعتی بیاید وقت ضیق شدن گرفت کسی نیامد برخاستیم بیرون آمدیم ملک اسمٰعیل
گفت کجا می روید گفتم برای جماعت کسی نیست گفت من اقتدا خواهم کرد نماز گذاردیم همانجا ماندیم

هر روز در درس مولانا شیخ مجد الدین در سماع علم حدیث حاضر می شدیم و شب را بزودی[2] مطالعه
می کردیم متن را چنان تحقیق می کردیم که هیچ خفائی نماندی بعده در حواشی میدیدیم همان می بود که ما[3]
اول دانسته بودیم[4] دیگر[5] در ابحاث علمیه که علما استفسار از بندگی مخدوم کرده اند قاضی
کمال الدین حاکم شهر نهرواله روزی عرض داشت که اطلاق[6] شیئ بر حق سبحانه و تعالیٰ توان کرد یا نه
فرمودند آری قاضی گفت پس قوله تعالیٰ اِنَّ اللّٰهَ عَلٰی کُلِّ شَیْءٍ قَدِیْرٌ تقاضا آن کند که
حق سبحانه و تعالیٰ قادر باشد بر آخرین[7] (آفریدگا) همچو خود جواب فرمودند متکلم در تحت خطاب داخل
نیست بنده را این سخن در خاطر جای نگرفت زیرا که ظاهر این آیت از خطاب خالی است
مدتی رفت بعد رحلت شیخ از روح شیخ استمداد نموده آمد بعنایت الله تعالیٰ فتح شد
که در سیاق این آیت آمده است اَیْنَمَا تَکُوْنُوْا یَاْتِ بِکُمُ اللّٰهُ جَمِیْعًا اِنَّ اللّٰهَ عَلٰی کُلِّ
شَیْءٍ قَدِیْرٌ دیگر آنکه از[8] (در آیة) شیئ مقدور مراد است بدلالت علیٰ و ذات خدای تعالیٰ مقدور نیست
مثلی هم[9] مقدور نباشد پس مراد از متکلم ذات پاک حق سبحانه و تعالیٰ باشد و مراد از خطاب

۱ کذا در هر دو نسخه فراشی (؟) ۲ ک = بزودی ۳ ح = من ۴ ح = بودیم
۵ دیگر = ک و ح ـ ندارد ۶ اطلاق = ک ـ ندارد ۷ در هر دو نسخه تصحیح قیاسی
۸ ک = آیات ۹ هم = ک ـ ندارد

دیگر

لفظ تیبی بود دانشمندی خراسانی در مسجد خانجهان رسید سید کمال الدین بنده سید رسول دار در مجلس بندگی مخدوم نشسته بود و شیخ درون محل رفته بود ند خراسانی گفت شیخ احمد کجا است سید فرمود مقصود چیست خراسانی گفت بحثی مشکلی دارم سید گفت کدام بحث است بفرمایند مارا بندگی مخدوم همه بحث ها فرموده اند خراسانی گفت عزم من بر شیخ است هم در میان [۱] آن شیخ رسیدند خراسانی بحثی عرضداشت شیخ جواب او فرمودند خراسانی باز گشت سید گفتاری چند که با خراسانی کرده بود عرضداشت بندگی مخدوم فرمودند سید تمارا چه گفته اند سید عرضداشت چه نگفته اند [۲] فرموده اند که از هزار یکی نگفته اند [۳] [سید عرضداشت از آن هزار که یکی نگفته اند] یکی بفرمایند بندگی شیخ قدس الله سره العزیز فرمودند که مسئله است مشهور و مختلف میان ما و معتزله در خلق افعال معتزله بر آنند که خالق افعال بنده است اگر همچنین نباشد ما مامور بشرایع چگونه شویم تا فعلی از ما در وجود نیاید از ذمه ما مامور به ساقط کی شود پس ثابت شد که خالق فعل خود بنده است سید متحیر شد وجواب این آنست که سنت الهی جاری برین است چون بنده عزم فعلی میکند حق سبحانه و تعالی خلق آن فعل در وجود بنده می کند بدین معنی آن فعل را باریتعالی امیگویند و کسب بنده

دیگر

روزی در حمام سمرقند رفتیم عارف نام خادم هم برابر بود و چند عورات هم در حمام می آمدند و عارف را شناختند و بر دست عارف سفینه ابیات بود و عارف بیک چشم گل داشت عورات گفتند که ای کورک بر دست چه داری گفت مصحف

۱ آن = ک - ندارد ۲ ح = فرمودند ۳ سید عرض تا نگفته اند = ک - ندارد

گفتند برای چه گفت: برای آنکه حالی غسلی که خواهید کرد سوگند نخورید که از حلال است یا[1] از محلی دیگر نه مسنده شده ندکه بحضور این بزرگوار اگر او را کور نه می گفتیم چرا مارا این سخن گوید چون وجود می شستم در یک گوشه حمام علما از شاگردان سید شریف بحث می کردند که در رسالۀ حقیق از تصنیف شیخ شهاب الدین سهروردی قدس الله تعالی سره العزیز آورده است که لاحجاب الا وجودک استاد تقریر کرد نیست حجاب از حق مگر وجود تو از انجا آن استاد را هیبت زدیم که وجود را حجاب مگو تقرب بوجود است توصل بوجود است حضور بوجود است مشاهده بوجود است مکاشفه بوجود است استاد درین ملزم شد و در حمام رسمی است چون کسی بحث می برد هر کسی کاسهای آب بر سر اوج می ریزد اہل حمام کاسهای آب بر سر این درویش ریختند بحث شد کور پیش سید شریف بردند سید شریف فرمودند هر دو جانب بحث بر ثواب است یعنی بندگی شیخ جهت ذات گرفتند و شمان جهت کون وصفات که مراد مصنف است گرفتید و موجود مشترک است بین الذات والکون **حکایت** دانشمندی در سمرقند در درسی سبق میگفت این درویش حاضر شد آن سبق را داشتند گفتیم مولانا چرا سبق نه می فرمائید گفت مخدوم مدتی است مشقت می کنم درین وقت می خواهند غیر را درین محل بنشانند گفتیم چون ما و شیخ عبدالاول یک جا شویم شما حاضر شوید او همچنان کرد شیخ را گفتیم ابن مسکین مدتی است مشقت می برند چرا محروم می کنید گفت گفت مخدوم این عزیز مسئله وضو هم تحقیق نه می کند گفتیم تحقیق صعب کار است ادراکه درین محل

---

1. یا از = ک - ندارد

می خواہید کہ بشنا نید بر سید کہ لفظ اٰمَنُوْا در قولہ تعالیٰ یَا اَیُّھَا الَّذِیْنَ اٰمَنُوْا اِذَا قُمْتُمْ چہ معنی دارد ظاہر آنست کہ مخاطب کسانی باشند کہ پیش از خطاب ایمان آوردہ باشند او حاضر بود گفت این جا ہر سہ معنی دارد کسانیکہ ایمان آوردہ اند و می آرند و خواہند آورد مارا این سخن دشوار نمود گفتیم از کجا می گوئی از کسی شنیدہ یا جائی دیدہ یا عندیات است شیخ را این سخن گرفت فرمود جواب این بندگی مخدوم فرمایند گفتیم توان گفت ہر کہ ایمان آورد ایمان او ماضی شد در تحت اٰمَنُوْا درآمد شیخ اسکات نمود مدرس قدیم را فرمود ہم شما ملازمت کنید دیگر در متن ہدایہ آمدہ است والاصل قولہ تعالیٰ یا ایہا الذین آمنوا اذا قمتم سوال داد دلیل را بر مسئلہ چرا مقدم داشت جواب شارحان گفتہ اند کہ برای تیمن وتبرک بندگی مخدوم ایراد کردہ اند باید کہ در ہر مسئلہ رعایت تیمن وتبرک باشد وہمچنین نیست علما ہمہ گفتنداا کہ جواب این ایراد ہم مخدوم فرمایند مخدوم فرمودند کہ این ایتی است کہ عین مسئلہ درین آیت مذکور است برای آن مقدم کرد روزی سید کمال الدین نبسہ سید رسولدار کہ در مسجد خانجہان ملازمت بندگی مخدوم می نمود از انجاست بزدوی[۲] طریق امتحان باز نمودن[۳] گرفت فرمودند یک جز از آغاز بر ما بیارند سیدان را آورد در دور بر سید گفتند لفظ خالق النسم[۴] را ہمہ شارحان برین قرار دادہ اند کہ درین براعت استہلال است توان گفت براعت استہلال را لفظ خاص باید و نسم[۵] اطلاق بر غیر نشر ہم می کنند پس براعت استہلال نباشد بمسئلہ در سطری

۱گفتند- ک- ندارد ۲ ک=بزودی ۳ ک=نمودند
۴ح- السم ۵ح=السم

یکگان دوگان ایراد نوشتند و سید را دادند سید متحیر شد با علما و مشائخ دهلی بحث ها می کرد

ع[1] بزودی
بعده
دانست که مخدوم بزودی نیکو می دانند مشائخ دهلی بعد نماز خفتن بالای

ع[2]
بام مسجد مذکور ملازمت کردن گرفتند چندگاه بحث در تعریف فقر بود یکی گفت الفقر

ع[3]
سواد الوجه فی الدارین گفتیم این تعریف نیست بیان استغنا است دیگری گفت اذا تم
الفقر فهو الله گفتیم این هم تعریف فقر نیست . هر شبی هر کسی چیزی میگفت

رومی کردیم بعده ایشان بندگی مخدوم را گفتند شما را اگر تعریفی جامع و مانع یاد باشد بفرمائید

ع[4] یکبار
در حال گفتیم الفقر فقد الشیء مع الطلب همه منصف شدند قبول کردند بنسه مولانا

کمال الدین سامانه که بر سلطان فیروز ملازمت داشت برین در دلش آمد یکبا پوشیده بلباس

ع[5]
نرگس بن ران بحثی آغاز کرد جواب او گفتیم باز ایراد کردیم گفت این مسئله قضا و قدر است

ع[6] گفتیم همچنین
گفتیم مولانا مسئله قضا و قدر مگر داخل مسائل نیست که برین وضع میفرمائید گفت همچنین آنچه

لفظ است گفت بندگی مخدوم مگر بنده را نمی شناسد گفتیم خیر گفت من بنده بنسه مولانا

ع[7]
کمال الدین ام گفتیم بنده خدا تو ما را این قدر اول چرا نگفتی ما را با شما چه جای بحث است

شما بحر علوم و خانه شما کان علم است بعده گفت مولانا عبد السلام

مرا در سرای ملاقات شده بود پرسیدم از کهتو شیخی کی آمده است چگونه کسی ست مولانا عبد السلام مناقب شما

در راه طریقت و ریاضت بمبالغت تقریر کرد و گفت در علم نمی گوئی بی انصاف

روزی
نگفت که مجتهد در علوم شده است دیگر ملک زاده شیخ شهاب الدین سر ع[8]

خانی رساله در علوم سلوک و اشعار خوب از انشا خود برین درویش فرستاد

۱ک= بزودی ۲ک= گرفت ۳ح= حکمی ۴ح- دیگر
۵ک= گفتم ۶ک= قدرت ۷ح= خدای ۸ح= سیر خوانی

رساله چون مطالعه شد دانستم که التقاط از محلها مختلف کرده است اما پیوند خوب نیامده است و لیکن اشعار بغایت بلیغ و ظریف و عاشقانه افتاده است چنانچه بود جواب گفتیم فرستادیم ناگاه خود برین درویش آمد حضار مجلس از مریدان او چنانچه مولانا فریدالدین پردهٔ دار[۱] و امیر کمال الدین همه گفتند این از اکابر چشتیان است مقداری تعظیم باید نمود گفتیم اشعار شمان سینه ها سوخته گان را شربت خوشگوار است مولانا فرید تحمل کردن نتوانست گفت چه حکمت بود که مهتر موسیٰ را بر خواجه خضر فرستادند سید کمال الدین گفت تا از علم و علمناه من لدنا علما خبر دهد درویش گفت که ای میر مولانا را باید شناخت که موسیٰ کیست و خضر کیست ملک زاده انگشت شهادت زیر دندان کرد و سر جنبانید مولانا فریدالدین را زجر کرد گفتیم پنج تنگه را نبات مصری برای ملک زاده بیارند تا شربت بخورند ملک زاده گفت مخدوم این پنج تنگه نقد مرحمت شود و سنده بر سر داشته بازگشت و این درویش فرید ندکور را مدرس دران مسجد ساخته بود یکان تنگه روزینه تعین کرده و بعد ازان غصه بر بازو آورده گفت امسال را چیزے نه رسیده است سی صد و شصت تنگه مرحمت کنید گفتیم موجود مصلا و مصحف داریم حالیا همان بستانید باقی هم خواهم رسانید گفت درخیر تاخیر روا نیست سید جلال بخاری

۱- ح و ک= پرده دار تصحیح قیاسی

در جواب مرا امشب گفته است که حسنهٔ مقبول نبود چرا ضایع می کنی هم درین گفتار بودیم که محررے نیک بخت دانا و پرکار رسید گفت اشارت شود تا بنده مولانا را تفهیم کند گفتیم زهی[۱] دولت نویسنده گفت شما را یکان ٹنگه روزینه از جهت سبق گفتن است و شما در چهله اعتکاف می نشینید هشتاد ٹنگه آن رفت و شما متدین هستید روز جمعه و سه شنبه روز تعطیل در درس نمی آید دوگان ٹنگه هر هفته این وضع شود صد ٹنگه آن وضع کرده باقی صد هشتاد بماند سالها گذشته را هم در هر سالی وضع باید کرد دو سال گذشته را تمام حاصل شده است برین حساب شما را سال حال را چیزے نباشد شما اهل دیانت هستید وعید[۲] (از وعده) زیادت ستدن در قیامت وبال باشد فرید مذکور ملزم شد گفت مخدوم مرا مصلا و مصحف میدادند شما مطلق پابوس میکنید محرر گفت انصاف همچنین است با این هم[۳] مخدوم حائل را به مولانا دادند و بیشتر[۴] (بیشتر) احوال آن محرر را تحسین یاد می کردند **دیگر** دانشمندے[۵] به خدمت بابو رسیده بود و کسے طعام برائے خدمت بابو فرستاده بود آن دانشمند را خورانیدند بعد فراغ خدمت بابو فرمودند بارواح اولیاء انبیاء فاتحه بخوانند دانشمند مذکور گفت اولیا را بر انبیا چگونه تقدم دارند خدمت بابو مجیب نشدند باز او تکرار کردیم جواب نه دادند مارا دشوار نمود گفتیم مولانا سوال بچه گان بر بزرگان کردن نمی شاید اگر رضاء خدمت بابو شد حالیا جواب تو گویم طرف خدمت بابو دیدم تبسم میکردند بران دانشمند گفتیم این تخصیص بر تعمیم است چنانچه در والعاقبة للمتقین والصلوٰة علی رسوله متقیان را مقدم بر رسول کرده اند زیرا که در متقیان رسول صلعم داخل بود بس در اولیا هم ذکر انبیا داخل باشد بعده ذکر انبیا مکرر شد

۱ زہی = ک- ندارد ۲ ح = وعید ۳ ک = بہم
۴ ح و ک = پیشتر ۵ ک = دانشمند

از برائے تعظیم ایشاں دیگر[1] فرمودند وَالعَاقِبَۃُ لِلْمُتَّقِیْن دعاست وہر دعائے[2] کہ مبدا او
اَلحَمْدُ لِلّٰہ باشد ومختم او درود بر پیغامبر بود موجب اجابت باشد درود از جہت آں تکرار کرد
بچوں ایں جواب گفتیم آں دانشمند برخاست دست در پاے ما انداخت وگفت شاگرد کسے کہ ایں استعداد
دارد استاد از وے ہرآئینہ فائق تر باشد بانواع بعدہ ہر بار کہ ما در جمع او می آمدیم قیام می آورد خدمت بابو فرمودند
شما بآمدن آں خرد ک چندیں تکلف مفرمائید دانشمند گفت تعظیم ایشاں بر ما واجب است زیرا کہ اہل اند **یک روز**
در مسجد خانجہاں قطب زماں شیخ جہاں دامت برکاتہ مولانا سفیان قاضی قصبہ ملتان علامہ زمان رسید بطریق تعظیم بخدمت[3]
بندگی مخدوم را گفت کہ قول امام اعظم رضی اللہ عنہ است[4] اُحِبُّ الصَّالِحِیْن وَلَسْتُ مِنْھُمْ میفرمودند کہ میگویند[5]
در دہلی میان علما کسے را اشکال شدے و یاد روایتی نمی یافتند بر مولانا سفیان می نشستند (می نشنید) از و تحقیق
می شدے و کتاب کنز را بغیر حواشی سبق گفتی وہمہ اختلافات و علامات یاد داشت گفتیم[6] امام اعظم در
صدق ممتاز و در عشق راست باز بود چگونہ گوید وَلَسْتُ مِنْھُمْ مولانا گفت برائے کسر نفس گفتیم[7] امام مقتدا
عالم و پیشوای اعظم دستور حق و حجۃ الخلق بود در باب ایشاں ایں جواب نمی تواں شنید بعدہ گفت از[8] ایں صالحان
انبیا مراد داریم گفتیم[9] مصراع دوم ایں تاویل را مانع است کہ لَعَلَّ اللّٰہُ یَرْزُقُنِیْ صَلَاحًا [10] غیر نبی را روا نیست کہ تمنائے
نبوت کند چوں بازگشت نعمہ بنت کہ اگر دوستان خداتعالے از خدا بخواہند کہ قیامت قائم نشود نشود اما چوں وعدہ و
ارادت خداتعالی بر قیام قیامت نیست ایشاں نخواہند بلطف از حق تعالی بخواہند کہ فرزند[11]
عبد الحی رافع زندان از بنین و بنات روزی نشود[12] **دیگر**[13] بندگی

۱ـ دیگر=ک ـ ندارد ۲ـ ک=دعاء ۳ـ بخدمت=ح ـ ندارد ٤ـ است=ک ـ ندارد
٥ـ ح=میفرمودند ٦ـ ک=گفتم ۷ـ ک=گفتم ۸ـ ح=این ۹ـ ک=است
۱۰ـ ک=گفتم ۱۱ـ ک=فرزندم ۱۲ـ ک=شوند ۱۳ـ دیگر=ک ندارد

قطب زمان شیخ جهان دامت برکاته، بین الصلوتین ساختگی وضو میکردند پسر ملک تسر ملک
دانشمند خطهٔ ناگور اسمه ملک بڈہ رسید بحث در قرأت بلند و آهسته افتاد که بیشتر علما
بران اند که جهر آنست که همسایه بشنود و آنچه همسایه نشنود و خود بشنود سر است ملک بده گفت
بروایت دوم آمده است که جهر آنست که هم خود بشنود فقط پس سر کرا گویند ما در تأمل شدیم
امام در تحریمهٔ عصر شروع کرد ما را در تحریمه همیشه مقارنت مقصود می بود یاد آمد ملک زاده را گفتیم
که سر بتصحیح حروف باشد ملک زاده گفت که اکنون این جواب نتوان شنید جواب مذکور از
توجه مخدوم است شما را در توجه فتح اسرار الٰهی است درین وقت از شما بحث که تواند برد ما را دیگر
حصیری خوبی باریک صادقی آورده بود در فکر بودیم کراین حصیر کرا بدهیم آن حصیر را بر بساط قدیم
فراز کرده نشسته بودیم ناگاه عالمی رسید بران حصیر نشستم او در حال ایراد کرد که این چیست
یعنی مصلی بر مصلی یا حصیر بالای حصیر چیست برخاستیم آن حصیر به پیچاندیم[۱] و آن عالم را دادیم
و گفتیم دوم برای این است **حکایت**[۲] روزی دانشمندی آمد و بر ما پیراهنی بود نو پوشیده
دیگر چیزی موجود نداشتیم درون محل رفتیم پیراهن کشیدیم ته کردیم و مصلائی بود بر وجود در پیچیدیم
پیراهن مران دانشمند را پیش آوردیم او گفت پس معنی و لاتبسطها کل البسط چه باشد گفتیم
این آیت برای تعلیم کسانی است که بدرجه کمال یقین نرسیده اند امیر المومنین ابوبکر صدیق رضی الله
تعالی عنه چون بدرجه کمال رسید کل داد پس بدرجه کمال یقین قبض منظور نهانند[۳] بحث های

۱ح = پیچدم ۲ک و ح = دیگر ۳دیگر = ک۔ ندارد

خوب موجه با علماء سمرقند که شده است و در کیفیت رسیدن او[1] امر معروف کردن بر سلطان محمد بهادر پور امیر پادشاه خراسان و بر وزراء ایشان مندرج[2] است روزی بندگی قطب زمان شیخ جهان دامت برکاته چاشت میگذارند بنده مؤلف بر در حاضر بود خادم ماتاک بر در حاضر بود گذرانید که مولانا محمد قاسم آمده است اشارت شد که بیاید بنده درون رفت و خدمت مخدوم در صلوٰة بودند بنده ایستاده مانده بعد سلام اشارت شد بنشین بنده خدمت کرد[3] نشست بپالشت تکیه کرده زانو های مبارک ایستانیده ند و روی مبارک طرف قبله کرده سبب غلبهٔ شیب هم بر جای صلوٰة غلطیده تسبیح بر دست کرده مشغول شدند چون چند بار تسبیح مذکور گردانیدند اشارت شد سیا اکرم کتاب المتفق در دین دوانه بر مولانا کدو دهلوی چند بار خواند عرض آمد دو بار و بیش ازان آن کیفیت بنده در حضرت بندگی قطب زمان شیخ جهان دامت برکاته عرض داشته بود برای تحقیق می پرسیدند بعده اشارت شد مولانا ضیاء الدین شامی شارح متفق استاد[4] سلطان محمد تغلق را بعضی اجتهاد[5] خام[6] افتاده است چنانکه اجتهاد بر پالکی[7] نشستن و او قیاس کرده است بر کتف کردن یعنی امیر المومنین عمر رضی الله عنه نا دان[8] را از بام فرود آورده بودند بعد زحمت میزاب مذکور خلق را بعده بعضی از صحابه بر امیر المومنین عمر رضی الله عنه خبر کردند[9] که شما را ازکجا شاید که فرود آرید میزابی را که حضرت رسالت صلی الله علیه وسلم نصب کرده باشند بعده

۱ مغلان = ک ندارد ۲ مندرج = ک ۳ کرد = ک - ندارد ۴ استاد = ک - ندارد
۵ ح = اجتهادہا ۶ ک = خادم ۷ ک = پالکھی ۸ ک = ناردان ۹ ح = کرد

امیر المومنین عمر رضی الله عنه شخصی را بر کتف خود سوار کردند و فرمودند تا آن ناودان را بجانب نصب کنند پس برین قیاس روا باشد که کسی را بر کتف سوار کنند بنده برای تائید سخن بندگی قطب زبان شیخ جهان دامت برکاته عرض داشت که امیر المومنین که بر کتف خود سوار کرده بود برای کسر و زجر نفس را کرده و آن علت در پالکی[ع1] نیست پس قیاس مع الفارق باشد بر سخن بنده هم اعتراض نکردند و خود هم وجه خاص اجتهاد مولانا را بیانی نه کردند و دیگر هر بحثی که کاتب با زان را بندگی مخدوم کردی حضرت خوندکار برای رعایت زائر خود مجیب می شدند علی الخصوص چون کاتب را با مولانا خطیر الدین ناگوری خالو بحث می افتاد مگر یک بار بحث چون در رویت شد کاتب گفت رویت بمعنی علم آمده است مولانا قبول نکردند بندگی قطب زبان شیخ جهان دامت برکاته فرمودند آری رویت بمعنی علم آمده است چنانکه حدیث بمین

حکایت

مولانا قاضی صدر الدین بنماتی[ع2] طاب ثراه بر مخدوم قطب زبان شیخ جهان دامت برکاته ایراد کرد که لون سواد را بالقطع سواد میگوئید و در روی تجدد امثال قائلید و بدین صورت قطعیت نه می ماند بر بدیهه جواب فرمودند مولانا چنانچه در سواد تجدد میگوئیم[ع3] در حانیه بصر هم تجدد می گوئیم پس یکی بر یکی قطعی باشد

دیگر

مولانا سراج بنهانی[ع5] بخدمت بندگی مخدوم چون آمدی بحثی نکردی یک روز بندگی شیخ فرمودند[ع4] لمن عرف الله صغر فی عینه کل شیء ای عم مولانا سراج عرض داشت میان صغر و عدم چه مناسب است که او را بدین

١ ک = پالکهی ٢ ک = بنماتی ٣ ک = میگویم ٤ ح = فرمود

تفسیر کنند بندگی قطب زمان شیخ جهان دامت برکاته بر بدیهه جواب فرمودند که صغر صیغهٔ مبالغه [است چنانکه کبر مقتا عند الله و از مبالغه] صغر عدم لازم آید مولانا سراج مذکور حیران ماند و گفت زهی محقق

دیگر در آنکه از بندگی مخدوم قطب زمان شیخ جهان دامت برکاته از خراسان باز گشته و در کنهایت رسید بد متعلمی از معتقدان خدمت سید جلال الدین بخاری رحمة الله علیه ایراد کرد که خدمت سید جلال بخاری بجای ولمن توالد ولمن والد منخواندند مخدوم جوابش فرمودند که این دعا ماثور است و تصرف در ماثور عمل مشائخان نیست پس از سید چگونه

دیگر در آنکه در مسجد جامع قصبه سرکهیج بنا خاص بندگی مخدوم قطب زمان شیخ جهان دامت برکاته اقامت جمعه شد سلطان احمد طاب ثراه مخصوص حاضر شد خطیب در خطبه خواند العلیم الذی یحیط علمه بما لا ینناهی عده و احصاده سلطان مخدوم را ایراد کرد که احاطه ما لا یتناهی چگونه معقول باشد بندگی مخدوم فرمودند عدد انفاس بهشتیان را مخلوق می دانید یا نه گفتند مخلوق مخدوم فرمودند چون مخلوق گفتید تحقیق شد که معدود و محصور باشد قاضی خانون محتسب گفت پس فنا بهشت و اهل بهشت او لازم آید و آن قول مردود است که مخالف کلام ربانی است سلطان احمد منصف شد گفت شما جواب شیخ فهم نکرده اید شیخ تردید کرده اند در جواب فرمودند که مخلوق میگوئید یا نه چون بمخلوقیت قایل شوید قطعا معلوم و محصور الزامی گردد

۱ است تا مبالغه = ک - ندارد

زی استعداد سلطان که سخن مخدوم چگونه فهم کرد و دانشمندان فهم نه کردند و شارحان طوالع
جوابی دیگر گفته اند مطولست و بندگی مخدوم هم بر تقریر مقدمات سوال جواب مختصر فرمودند
روزی خواجه قطب خواجگی را مولانا داود منطقی سوالی تلقین کرده فرستاد که درمیان عقیده حافظیه
افتاده است که الاراده صفة توجب تخصیص المفعولات بوجه دون وجه و وقت دون وقت
پس سموات را نیز وقتی باید که سموات نیز از جمله مفعولات اند و وقت نتیجه سموات است
بندگی قطب زبان شیخ جهان دامت برکاته درحال مقدمه که او گفت که مخصص سموات نیز باید
باشد که وقت[۱] انکار کردند و فرمودند که این لازم نیست چند سال درین جواب ایشان غوض کردند
درنیافتند مراد بندگی مخدوم آن است که تخصص مفعولات بوقت هم لازم نیست زیراچه یجعل الله
است و حق سبحانه و تعالی قادر است تواند که تخصیص بچیزی دیگر کند چنانچه صاحب عقیده
هم لفظ وجه دون وجه زیادت کرده است و شارحان جواب دیگر گفته اند که مخصص سموات
بوقت تقدیری است چنانچه[۲] درکلام مجید آمده است خلق السموات والارض فی ستة ایام
ای فی قدر ستة ایام و هم[۳] در بحث ارادت و عقاید افتاده است که مخصص مفعولات[۴] قدرت نه تواند بود
زیراچه قدرت عام است شامل[۵] بر موجودات و ممکنات معدومه و موجوده را و علم هم مخصص نمی
تواند بود زیراچه علم تابع معلوم است بندگی قطب زبان شیخ جهان دامت برکاته فرمودند که
اطلاق لفظ تابع بر صفات خداتعالی چگونه روا باشد و ایشان ارادت را تابع مراد گفته

۱ ح=انک ۲ ح=چنچ ۳ ک=دیگرهم
۴ مفعولات=ک-ندارد ۵ شامل=ک- ندارد

اند پس لازم آمد که ارادت هم مخصص نباشد و هذا خلف روزی بحث می شد [دیگر]

که اسباب علم چند است بندگی قطب زبان شیخ جہان دامت برکاتہ فرمودند سه است

مولانا ابراہیم مدرس ملک جلال نموده گفت خیر مخدوم بسیار است سه چرا می فرمائید

ہر چند تفہیم کردند فہم نکرده دوم روز پشیمان شده آمد گفت چنانچه[1] بندگی مخدوم می فرمایند

ہمان سه است حکایت در متن بزدوی[2] در اتمام دیباچه در بعضی نسخ افتاده است که و ہذا الکتاب

لبیان النصوص لمعانیها[3] و تعریف الاصول بفروعها[4] علی شرط الایجاز والاختصار ان شاء اللہ

تعالیٰ بندگی قطب زبان شیخ جہان دامت برکاتہ فرمودند که این محل ان شاء اللہ تعالیٰ نیست

بعضا علما معترف شدند و بعضی نشدند ناگاه نسخه از خراسان رسید در ان ہم نبود دیگر

قاضی منصور شسته بود متعلمی نسخه مصلیح آورد محلی سقم داشت بندگی قطب زبان شیخ جہان

دامت برکاتہ فرمودند این جا دو سطر بدین عبارت ترک است قاضی قبول نکرد مخدوم

نسخه خود دیدند چنانچه[5] فرموده بودند بدان عبارت بیرون آمد قاضی شرمنده شد حکایت

دانشمندی در مسجد خانجہان بحضرت بندگی قطب زبان شیخ جہان دامت برکاتہ

سوال کرد قوله تعالیٰ وَمَا تَشَاءُونَ اِلَّا اَنْ يَّشَاءَ اللّٰهُ این اقتضا می کند که در مشیت

است وچون مشیت باریتعالیٰ مقرون[6]

بنده مشیت باریتعالیٰ مقرون باشد باید که وجود مشی لازم بود کما قال اللہ تعالیٰ انما امره

اذا اراد شیئا ان یقول له کن فیکون پس لازم آید که ہرچه بنده بخواهد باید که موجود

۱ح=چنچ ۲ح=پژودی ۳ک=بمعانیها
۴ک=بفروغها ۵ح=چنچ ۶است تا مقرون=ک-ندارد

نشود و در واقع همچنین نیست جواب فرمودند در ارادت بنده وجود مراد لازم نیست زیرا چه
ارادت باریتعالی لازم فعل نیست والله یفعل مایشاء و ارادت بنده لازم فعل نیست
لان العبد رب شیئ یشاء و لا یوجد ذالک[١] پس بنده را یسار[٢] فعلیها باشد که با ارادت بنده موجود نشود
دیگر[٣]
و ارادت حق سبحانه و تعالی در ان فعل ارادت محض است نه ارادت وقوع ان فعل
بحث در میان وجه شبه افتاد که الملاقات مقسومة کما قسمت الارزاق (رزاق) وجه شبه چیست مولانا
منصور گازرونی در مجلس بندگی مخدوم نشسته بود گفت وجه خطست بعده متعلی دیگر گفت
تخصیص رزاق چیست بندگی قطب زبان شیخ جهان دامت برکاته فرمودند تشبیه به اشهر باید
و رزق اشهر است دیگر[٤] بحث در این افتاد که من زار حیاً و لم یرزق منه شیئاً فکانما زار میتاً
بندگی قطب زبان شیخ جهان دامت برکاته فرمودند مراد ازین ذوق رزق و طعامی فقط نیست بلکه هر چیز
دران حظ و نفع باشد مراد است - روزی بندگی سلطان احمد را بحث در تناسخ افتاد
تناسخ[٥] آن است که روح یکی در بدن دیگری در آرند و بمذهب مسلمانان این باطل است
سلطان گفت حدیث ان ارواح المومنین لفی طیر خضر صریح افتاده است باطل چگونه باشد
چون این بحث به بندگی قطب زبان شیخ جهان دامت برکاته رسید فرمودند بدن جدید را قائل اند
و طیر خضر بدن جدید نیست احتمال دارد که بدن سابق باشد و شرط دیگر آن است که روح
موثر باشد در بدن جدید و در طیر خضر روح مومن موثر نیست دیگر بندگی قطب زبان شیخ جهان
دامت برکاته مفسر مودند در آنکه در مسجد خانجهان می ماندیم شخصی ملازمت کردن گرفت بعده
بریکی از قراباتیان خود گفت که این چنین بزرگی در مسجد خانجهان آمده است او بدیدن ما آمد و گفت

١- ح = ذاک ٢- ح و ک = یسا ٣- دیگر = ک - نداراد
٤- دیگر = ک - ندارد ٥- تناسخ = ک - ندارد

از کجائی و مرید کیستی و پیر تو چه نام دارد بی ادب وار تکلم کردن گرفت و گفت الشیخ یحیی و یمیت گفته اند در کسی که این قوت باشد که مرده را زنده کند او خود را شیخ بگویانند گفتیم معنی الشیخ یحیی و یمیت همچنین نیست که تو میگوئی گفت شیخ شیوخ همچنین گفته است و در فلان کتاب هم همچنین مذکور است گفتیم که همچنین نیست بلکه معنی آنست که یحیی القلب المیت بتعریف معرفت الله وصفاته و یمیت نفسا کانت حیاتها بالقوی الشهوانیة والغضبیة ونحوهما بعده زائری رسید چهار بیست پنجگانی (پیش) داشت آن بجات را گفتیم بردار او برگرفت دیگری یک کاگی آورد همو را گفتیم[1] که این کاگ را نیکو نگاه دار آغاز کرد (این) شیخ گرسنه از کجا پیدا شد و ما را صوم بود چون وقت افطار شد گفتیم آن کاگ را بیار در میان داشتیم گفتیم تو هم بخور اما اندک بخوری باز او کاهش کردن گرفت که این شیخ گرسنه از کجا آمد بعد افطار وقت باز گشت چهار (ببیست) پنجگانی مذکور پیش آورد که این را چه کنم[2] گفتیم ما چه دانیم چنانچه[3] تو دانی بکن گفت پس شما مرا دعا داده اید گفتیم دعا تو کرده[4] ما دانسته بودیم که صادقی بزیارت آمده است با ادب تکلم خواهد کرد تو آمده باتون تان[5] گفتی از کجائی مرید کیستی بحضور دیشان بر وضعی[6] تکلم کردی پشیمان شد دوباره که آمد با اعتقاد با ادب تکلم کرد و گفت مخدوم بنده از دست صنمی در مانده است پسرے[7] دارد که بارکشتی من میکند اما صنمه[8] هر بار بر لقمه سنگ دار بر سر می زند بیش ازین کتابت کردن می توانست درین وقت نمی تواند و نمیداند که از دهن چه بیرون می آید.

۱ک = گفتم ۲ح = کنیم ۳چنچ = ح ۴ح = کردی
۵باتون نان = ح و ک تصحیح قیاسی - تون تان کلمۀ گجراتی است بمعنی بزبان بی ادبی ۶ک = سنه ۷ک = پسر ۸ح = صنمه

مغی غلبه[1] شده است گفتیم تعلق مکن همدران ایام اسلام خان بر ما آمد گفتیم از سلطان چه عهده وارید
گفت کار همه بندگان سلطان از سلطان بحواله بنده است مشاهره ایشان وتتبع حاضر
وغایب بنده میکند گفتیم می توانی که یک مشاهره ما دهی گفت بسر و دیده گفتیم شش ماهیه
بیارد درحال دو ثنگه زر پیش آورد گفتیم این منت از جهت خواجه یعقوب کرده ام اسلام خان
خوش شد عرضه داشت مخدوم از کرامت فرمودند مرا هم از جهت او تعلق بود شاید چیزے
وسیلت هم خواجه مذکور را با اسلام خان بود هر دو ثنگه زر تسلیم اسلام خان کردیم تا او را بدست
خود بدهد و بشارت مشاهره هم بگوید **دیگر** ملک عثمان سرکھیجی بحضرت بندگی قطب زمان
شیخ جهان دامت برکاته ایراد کرد ما التنفس بندگی قطب زمان شیخ جهان دامت برکاته
فرمودند هر تن[2] ملک را[3] قابل نیست او گفت در کلمات قدسی افتاده است[4] که بهتر داود
پیغامبر علیه السلام را فرمان اعدی[5] عدوک نفسک[6] التی بین جنبیک چگونه راست
آید بندگی مخدوم فرمودند این برائے محل ظهور اوست بندگی قطب زمان شیخ جهان دامت برکاته
فرمودند در اول مطالعه علم بسیار بود یک جز تن بزودی هر شبے تحقیق میکردند بعده در
حواشی نگاه میکردند میدانستند که چنانچه[7] ما متن را تحقیق کرده ایم هم بهمان است دمی
فرمودند که کتاب ذخیره تمام مطالعه شده است وقتی مولانا احمد خواجه استاد گجرات در سرکھیج برائے دیدن[8]
بندگی قطب زمان شیخ جهان دامت برکاته آمد بندگی مخدوم فرمودند وجود را علت رویت گفته اند

۱ ک=علیه ۲ ح=بهی ۳ را=ک=ندارد ٤ که=ح-ندارد
۵ ک-اعدا ٦ ک=نفس که ۷ ح=چنچ ۸ دیدن=ح-ندارد

یعنی هرچه موجود باشد باید که ببینند سید محمود رکن استاد این مؤلف در حال عرضه داشت

وما لا یری ع[۱] من الاشیاء فلیعد ع[۲] مراجراء سنة الله تعالی بر رویت مولانا احمد گفت بحث در

کلی است جواب این هم از بندگی مخدوم باید شنید بندگی مخدوم فرمودند آں رویت ایجادیست

فردا قیامت باصره را آں قوت دهند که بینند مولانا پسندیده گفت جواب این است روزے بندگی

قطب زماں شیخ جہاں دامت برکاته شنیدند که درویشے است در دہلی که او را نوتنی مرد میگویند

صاحب وقت است برائے ملاقات او عزم گردید در اثنا راه درویشے لنگردار ملاقات شد ع[۳] سوال کرد

که ملائکه ع[۴] اتجعل فیها من یفسد فیها ویسفك الدماء از کجا دانستند بندگی مخدوم جواب فرمودند

ملائکه قیاس کردند برآنکه سابق ازایشاں تصرف در دنیا جنیاں را بود وایشاں در دنیا فساد و

خون کرده بودند چوں ازیشاں ملک دنیا را کشیدند و بملائکه دادند و ملائکه اہل عدل و تسبیح

تہلیل اند باز ہمیں که فرمان شد انی جاعل فی الارض خلیفه قیاس کردند که باز مگر نوبت اہل فساد

شد جواب دوم آنکه ملائکه را اطلاع بر لوح محفوظ بود وایشاں در لوح محفوظ نبشته ع[۵] دیده

بودند که بعضے آدمیاں ظلم و فساد خواہند کرد ازاں گفتند که اتجعل فیها من یفسد فیها لنگردار مذکور

عرضه داشت که در وقت گرما کجا قصد کرده بیروں آمدند بندگی قطب زماں شیخ جہاں دامت برکاته فرمودند

شنیدیم درویشے است نوتنی ع[۶] مرد میگویند بجہت ملاقات او گفت او بدیں منت با نیت که برو

شما بروید خانی ع[۷] بجہت کاک ستدن خواہد آمد بخدمت شما خواہم فرستاد رومال خود کشید گرد خاک ع[۸]

۱ ک=تری ۲ ح و ک = فلعدم ۳ ک=کرد ۴ ک=ملائکه گفتند
۵ ک= نوشته ۶ ک= خوش ۷ ح= خانی ۸ اضافهٔ قیاسی

از کفشہائی مخدوم واز پاہای مبارک افشانند و گفت شما واصحل حقیقہ او بدین موازنہ نیست **دیگر** مولانا منہاج الدین صدر بنبانی بحضرت بندگی قطب زمان شیخ جہان دامت برکاتہ آمدہ بود وافرمودند فردا در جنت کہ رویت شود تا بکدام قرینہ بدنیم کہ مولارا دیدیم مولانا ہیچ جواب نہ گفت و بندگی مخدوم بیش ازاں ہم بحضور بندہ مؤلف دانشمندے دیگر راہم پرسیدہ بودند او ہم جواب نگفتہ[۱] بندہ مؤلف را در خاطر میگذشت کہ تواں گفت کہ از صفات سلبیہ بداند عزیزے[۲] دیگر بدیں[۳] عبارت میگفت چنانچہ در دار دنیا معلوم شدہ است ہمچناں بیند پس معلومست قرینہ باشد و بریں ہر دو عبارت ہنوز بحث باقی است وآں آنست کہ لازم آید کہ دیدار طائفہ مخصوصہ[۴] را باشد مگر آنکہ گویم کہ فردا ہمہ با استعداد[۵] بر انگزیند **دیگر** صاحب کشاف در[۶] ملک بر انس دلیل می آرد کہ در آیت لَنْ یَّسْتَنْکِفَ الْمَسِیْحُ اَنْ یَّکُوْنَ عَبْدَ اللّٰهِ وَلَا الْمَلٰٓئِکَةُ الْمُقَرَّبُوْنَ[۷] ترقی از ادنی بسوئے اعلی است ودر عرب ایں صفت ہمیشہ مرعی است پس ملک را فضل باشد بر انس جواب او[۸] بندگی قطب زمان شیخ جہاں دامت برکاتہ فرمودہ اند آں قاعدہ در عرب اگر ہمیشہ مرعی بودے در آیت شَهِدَ اللّٰهُ اَنَّهٗ لَآ اِلٰهَ اِلَّا هُوَ وَالْمَلٰٓئِکَةُ نقص لازم آیدے زیرا کہ حق سبحانہ وتعالیٰ اعلیٰ است وملک ادنی از حق است ونقص دیگر ہم بر قول او نیز لازم می آید در وَالْمَلٰٓئِکَةُ وَاُولُوا الْعِلْمِ زیرا کہ ترقی از ادنی بسوئے اعلیٰ اگر مرعی کنیم پس فضل انس لازم آید بر ملک پس ایں صفت

۱ ک = گفتہ ۲ ک = عزیز ۳ ک = بدان ۴ ک = مخصوص
۵ ک = استعداد نام ۶ ک = در فصل ۷ ک = المقربین ۸ او = ک۔ ندارد

برائے حجیت نمی تواند بود **دیگر**[1] دانشمندے گفت که الہام حجت نیست بندگی قطب زماں
شیخ جہاں دامت برکاتہ فرمودند مولانا بگو که الہام حجیت را نمی شاید این بگو که حجت
نیست زیرا چه در حق ملہم حجت باشد **دیگر** مولانا حسین شہاب حافظ دانشمند
که از شہر نہرواله در دیار رفته بود باشتیاق روضۂ شیخ خود بندگی قطب زماں شیخ جہاں
دامت برکاتہ استقامت ترک داده در سرکھیج باز آمد روایت میکرد که خطیب ابراہیم
ساکن شہر مذکور برائے ارادت ہرجا که می رفت چوں حکایت دنیا از دمی[2] شنید فاتحه میخواند
باز میگشت بعده بر حضرت رسالت صلی الله علیه وسلم ہر روز چند ہزار بار درود میفرستاد
ملازمت میکرد و می گفت من مرید حضرت رسالتم شبے از شبہا حضرت را صلی الله علیه وسلم
در خواب دید که میفرمودند مولانا فتح کار تو از شیخ احمد کھٹو است برو مرید او بشو[3] خطیب مذکور
بحضرت قطب زماں شیخ جہاں دامت برکاتہ آمد عرضه داشت که من فرستادۂ حضرت رسالت
صلی الله علیه وسلم بجہت ارادت آمده ام دو سخن در خاطر دارم اگر جواب آں بفرمایند طاقیه[4]
بستانم یکے آنکه مطرباں بر در بندگی مخدوم می آیند و مزامیر می نوازند ایشاں را چیزے
میدہایند این چگونه است حضرت مخدوم فرمودند بابا ہر که پیش درویش می آید او معروف
حال خود می شود و یاد می دہاند بضرورت چیزے می فرستند اگر نفرستند در غیبت می افتد
وسبب غیبت[5] گفتن او این درویش شود خطیب مذکور این سخن قبول کرد دوم[6] آنکه ملک زادگان

۱ دیگر = ک۔ ندارد ۲ ح=بازوایدی ۳ ک=شو
٤ ح=طایفه ٥ ح=غیب ٦ ک=حکایت

دستها بسته برائے سبق خواندن برین ضعیف می آید چون این ضعیف در نماز تحریمه می بندد
حال[1] ایشان مشوش میشود پیش حضرت مخدوم که چندین امرا و ملوک هر روز می آیند حال بندگی مخدوم
چیست جواب فرمودند با با شما نظر[2] هم برایشان میکنید درویش نظر بران حضرت دارد که می[3]
فرستد با با این خلق همان خلق است که انبیا را بنا حق کشته اند وَیَقْتُلُونَ النَّبِیّٖنَ بِغَیْرِ حَقٍّ برین
درویش گماشته اند درویش در حیرت است خطیب مذکور قبول کرده و در سلک مریدان باعتقاد
تمام منسلک شد و بطاقیه مشرف گشت و بر قاضی بده مبارک[4] والوالحی گفت تا غایت من چشم
نداشتیم از طفیل بندگی قطب زمان شیخ جهان دامت برکاته مراد و چشم شد و بنده مؤلف را
یاد است که چون خطیب مذکور بحضرت مخدوم پیوست چنانچه وضع مریدان و معتقدان است
تواضع نمیکرد هر کسے در خیال او[5] شد که شیخ را بر وضع تواضع نمیکند سر کشیده می آید چون
اشکال ایشان او را بندگی مخدوم حل کردند انکسار و تعظیم را مایه ساخت و فقاهت خشک را
گذاشت و در وے حالی پیش آمد که خلق شهر معتقد او شدند و بندگی قطب زمان شیخ جهان
دامت برکاته در قسم حساب عربی و فارسی و هندوی وقوف داشتند چنانکه روزے در
مجلس محاسبان قصبه کهتو گذر افتاد ایشان هاری را[6] فرض کرده بودند که در وے چندین
رست از مروارید بود در هر رستی چندین دانه لعل و در هر لعلے چندین مروارید
محاسبان مذکور چند روز در استخراج حساب این هار مشغول بوده اند حساب کسے راست نمی آمد و

۱ ح=حال ایشا ۲ ح=نظر هم ۳ می=ک-ندارد
۴ ح=وابوالحی ۵ او=ک-ندارد ۶ را=ک-ندارد

بندگی مخدوم درکنار کار یعنی در ضرب و در بهکاهر یعنی تقسیم وطرح بسیار حوایت[۱] داشتند مرآں محاسباں را فرمودند اگر ما این حساب را راست آریم چه گر د بیا رید گفتند چندین درحال تختۂ خاک را طلبیدند و بحضور ایشاں ضرب وقسمت کردند حساب مرتب کرده گرد ندکور بردند وایشان همه اقرار کردند که درقصبۂ کھٹو درحساب دیگرے این چنین نیست

فصل ششم

درخواب ها بندگی قطب زماں شیخ جهاں دامت برکاته که خود دیده اند[۲] و دیگران درباب ایشان دیده اند

نهم ماه جمادی الاولی سنه ۸۴۹ھ تسع اربعین وثمان مائة آخر شب دوشنبه ششش طاس مانده بود قاضی کمال الدین دانشمند حاکم شهر نهرواله بربندگی قطب زماں شیخ جهان دامت برکاته میگفت درخواب دیدم صحرائے است درمیان آں مسجدے است از سنگ سفید دو در دارد بیک در بندگی شیخ احمد نشسته اند ودوم در بندگی شیخ عبدالله یافعی من بر شیخ عبدالله یافعی گفتم مرا بحضرت سیدالمرسلین علیه الصلوٰة والسلام بگذرانید شیخ عبدالله فرمودند من درباهم حجابت بندگی شیخ احمد میکنند بحضرت شیخ احمد رفتیم شیخ احمد دست من گرفته درون مسجد بحضرت سیدالمرسلین بردند و سیدالمرسلین علیه السلام بالائے ممبر نشسته بودند ودو نفر بر بر دو بازوئے سیدالمرسلین ایستاده بودند هر چند[۳] احاس کردم درنیافتم[۴] که کیانند بندگی شیخ احمد در[۵] حضرت سیدالمرسلین علیه الصلوٰة والسلام گذرانیدند که کمال قوام حاضر شده است حضرت سیدالمرسلین علیه السلام فرمودند تائب شده است شیخ احمد فرمودند

---

۱ ک=درایت ۲ ودیگران تا اند=ح-ندارد ۳ هر چند تا احمد=ک-ندارد
۴ ح=درنیا فتند ۵ خدمت=ح-ندارد، بخدمت=ک

بیش ازین تائب است حضرت سید المرسلین فرمودند تائب بکنانید **دیگر** بندگی

قطب زمان شیخ جهان دامت برکاته، بیش از چند سال از رحلت خود در خواب دیدند

که بزرگے آمده[1] است دستارے بر دست کرده درویشان[2][3] اورا گفت تمامے بستید آں

بزرگ گفت من عبد القادر گیلانی ام یکطرف دستار ایں درویش را داد[4]

گفت[5] ببندید و طرف دوم خود گرفته بود[6] درویش[7] تمام دستار بر سر خود بست[8]

بیدار شدند و ایں خواب در رساله مغربیان که تالیف مخدوم است نبشته آمده است

بندگی شیخ بعد ایں خواب بیشتر اوقات منشرح بوده اند بندگی قطب زمان شیخ جهان

دامت برکاته در مسجد خانجهان که در فیروزآباد است میان ملوک خانه در قیلوله[9]

در خواب دیدند گویا که شخصے بحلیه مخصوص

پیش در ملوک خانه محلی که ما نماز میگزاریم، نماز میگذارد از خواب که برخواستیم در کتاب دیدیم

معائنه کردیم[10] هم بداں حلیه و هم دراں جائے شخصے نماز می گذارد تعجب کردیم که زهے خواب راست

دیگر در آنکه در مسجد مذکور نزول کردیم دوم روز جوانی رسید و در طاق ملوک خانه

خواب کرد پاے بهای او جانب ما بود ما را ازاں علم نه چوں جوان مذکور دهشت خورده از خواب

بر جست گریخت بعد دو سه ساعت مادر و پدر او را آوردند و بر پاے ما ایں درویش

انداختند و گفتند مخدوم ایں گناه بنخشید گفتیم چیست گفتند ایں پسر ما دریں طاق

۱ک=آمد ۲ح=درویشان ۳ح=گفتند ٤ک=دادند ۵ک=گفتند
٦ک=بودند ۷ح=درویشان ۸ح=بستند ۹ح=بعد ازین بندگی
حضرت قطب زمان شیخ جهان دامت برکاته ۱۰معائنه کردیم=ک- ندارد

غلطیده بود بزرگے را در خواب دید که او را طپانچہا می زند و می گوید اے بے ادب سوی

شیخ احمد چرا پایۂ فراز کرده غلطیده نمیدانی که نشسته است و نان و رونون شکر[1]

انداختند پیش ما آوردند جوان مذکور را محلا آل بزرگوار پرسیده شد محلائی[2] گفت بمحلائی بندگی

بابو مانند بود دیگر مقدم او تیلیه اعمالے[3] دو هولقه اسمه ستپل[4] در سالی که موضع

مذکور را مقاطعه سنده بود بجہت تحصیل وجه مذکور بندگی شیخ حاجی برادر امیر یعقوب سوداگر

را فرستاده بودند درادای وجه مماطلت میکردند مدت گذشت با دیوان هم تعینت[5] داشت

بندگی قطب زمان شیخ جہاں داشت برکاته متفکر شدند که مبادا با شیخ حاجی مذکور بی

وضعی کند خواستند که شیخ حاجی را باخدمت گاران باز گردانند شب در خواب دیدند

که ستپل را بر تن سر نیست بیدار شدند فکر میکردند که این چه خواب است باز در خواب

شدند دیدند که سر ستپل مذکور بریده آوردند باز بیدار شدند شیخ تاج الدین را طلبیدند

گفتند دوبار در واقعه سر ستپل همچنین دیده شد شیخ تاج الدین عرضه داشت خواب

مخدوم درست است بارہا تجربه شده است تحقیق زوال ستپل قریب است هر که با

حضرت مخدوم بی وضعی کند سزائے او همین باشد شبا شب عبدالله سندهی را که چاکر قدیم

بود بر شیخ حاجی فرستادند که طعام و آب خوردنی[6] ندهی اگر نشسته اند بر کنی و اگر ایستاده

باشند بر راه کنی عبدالله مذکور بر ایشاں رفت نماز شام ماہی پخته بودند خوردن نداد

۱ک=سکر ۲ح=محلائی ۳ح=اعمال
۴ح=ستپل ۵ک=تعنت ۶ح=خورد

وکیفیت ع۱ اشارت بریں است که در راه ع۲ بیائید ہماں زماں رواں شدند صباح در حوض
وحولقه شد جامهائی شستند ناگاه دیدند سر ستل بریده در بازار می گردانند اگر ایشاں
دراں شب آنجا می ماندندی شبه ستلیاں ایشاں را می کشتند اما بندگی مخدوم
صاحب کشف بودند معامله ستل ہمچنیں معائنه کردند اول خبر او ہماں شیخ حاجی وخدمتگاراں
بحضرت شیخ ع۳ آمده عرضه داشت کردند خواہا مخدوم ایں چنیں بود **دیگر** سید اکرم در کھنٹو روزے
میان محفل نشسته گفت که شیخ آنرا گویند که میوهٔ زمستان در تابستان آرد
ومیوهٔ تابستان در زمستان وہمدراں سال رحلت بندگی بابو بود بندگی قطب زمان شیخ جہاں
دامت برکاته در عزلت می بودند با اصحاب کھنٹو مجالست اندک بود ع۴ سید را ازاں دشواری آمدے
درخواب دید که بندگی مخدوم در مقامی ع۵ مرتفع نشسته می فرمایند بیا سید بستان بر دست سید
میوه دادند بغایت ظریف تعریف ہر چند که سید احساس کردند که کدام میوه است فہم نتوانست
کرد چوں بیدار شد ازاں سخن که در محفل گفته بود پشیمان شد وایں خواب بر مخدوم باته بندگی
وعذر خواہی عرضه نمود **دیگر** ہم دراں ایام ملک احمد نام مقطع کھنٹو بر بندگی قطب زمان
شیخ جہاں دامت برکاته آمده بود بندگی مخدوم برنخاستند رنجیده بازگشت مولانا یوسف
صدر ع۶ را گفت که ما بر شیخ احمد بصحبت خدمت بابو می آیم بعد رحلت بابو چندروز پیش شده است
مارا تواضع نکرد، کد موئی کدوین ہوئی یعنی که مردوکے گفت ارشد وایں سخن در شریعت ممنوع است

١ ح=کیفیت ٢ ح=بباشد ٣ ک=شیخ احمد
٤ ح=بود ٥ ک=مقام ٦ ک=صدرا

در مذہب اہل تناسخ است که اگر گناه گارے می میرد[1] بروح او را در تن گفتارے یابد
کارے می[2] انداز نداد دیگراں را در تشویش می دارد آن سخن ناپاک[3] (ملاناک) در سمع بندگی مخدوم
رسید سخت شکسته خاطر شدند شب آینده ملک احمد مذکور در خواب دیگر[4] دید که
بندگی بابو بر و نفت شده اند و برآمده اند تو چه کسے دترا چه مجال سخن فضول راندن باشد
که در باب شیخ احمد برانی و دہشت بندگی بابو مقطعان را در حیات بسیار بودے ملک احمد
مذکور از غایت عفونت خدمت بابو لرزاں از خواب برخاست در خانهٔ مولانا یوسف آمد
شب بسیار بود کیفیت خواب گفت و گفت اشارت بندگی بابو برین است که بر و در پائے
شیخ احمد بیفت و د حجله[5] او آب نیست آب ہم بر برائے رضائے خدا تعالیٰ بیام ار در پائے
شیخ احمد بیند از ہر دو بر در جماعت خانه آمدند بندگی مخدوم بیدار بود[6] اند فرمودند کیست
مولانا یوسف عرضه داشت[7] که عرضه داشتی[8] دارم فرمودند از[9] احمد ناصر مگوی دیگر ہر چه
باشد بگوی در دل در آمدند تفحص کردند حجره[10] آب نبود ملک احمد پرسید که این چه کرامت
بابو است که بعد حمات ہم اعانت شیخ احمد چندیں میکنند در آوند با آب ریختند
مولانا یوسف عرضه داشت[11] که ملک احمد فرستاده بندگی بابو آمده اند[12] پشیمان و تائب
شده اند بندگی مخدوم را عفو میباید فرمود ملک احمد در پائے مبارک افتاد بندگی مخدوم عفو
فرمودند دیگر خانجہاں چوں در مسجد خود آمد بندگی مخدوم را ملاقات شد خواست

١ح=می مرد، ک=میرود ٢ک=که می ٣کذا در ہر دو نسخه شاید ناپاک باید باشد
٤ دیگر=ک۔ندارد ٥ح=حجله ک=حجلا ٦ح و ک=بوده اند ٧ک=کرد
٨ داشتی=ک۔ندارد ٩ک=از ١٠ح=حجلها ١١ک=کرد ١٢ک=است

کہ کنار گیر و بندگی قطب زماں شیخ جہاں دامت برکاتہٗ دست مبارک بر سینۂ او داشتند و فرمودند مصافحہ کافی است چوں بازگشت در قیلولہ بندگی بابو را در خواب دیدند کہ می فرمودند بابا احمد اگر بر دست ایں پسر[1] ترا چیزے بفرستند بستانی[2] ہمدراں وقت [مولانا اسمٰعیل از اقارب][3] قطب خواجگی کہ تسخنگی عمارت مسجد مذکور داشت رسید خواب مذکور بروے گفت[4] سلّمہٗ او گفت اے مخدوم ہمچو خانجہاں آمد چیزے نیاورد دیگر کہ[5] خواہد فرستاد ایں خیال بیش نیست بعد از دو سہ روز خانجہاں ظہر گذاردہ نشستہ بود مولانا مذکور پیش او رفت بر دست او[6] گرھے بزرگ بستہ بہدیہ[7] یا بود فرمود مولانا اسمٰعیل بیا[8] ایں وجہ برائے شیخ احمد ببر او ببرد آورد و گفت شمارات و خواب شمارا است چوں وجہ مذکور بر دست من داد خواستم کہ کیفیت خواب مخدوم بروے بگویم کہ نخواہد[9] ستد اما از جان خود ترسیدم کہ چناں خواہد زد کہ جان من بیروں خواہد آمد اگر مخدوم ایں وجہ قبول نفرمایند تعلق بر جان من باشد گفتیم ہم تو قسمت کردہ فقرا را بدہ دیگر در مسجد بیت الحرام[10] وقت خفتن اتفاق مصاحبان راہ مکہ بریں شد کہ ہر یکے نیت کردہ بخسپند تا چہ خواب بینند[11] صباح چوں برخاستند یکے را احتلام شد و ایں درویش را در راہ مکہ بازگشتنہ[12] گاہے احتلام نشد[13] مولانا احمد گفت من چیزے کہ دیدہ ام در [14] اشان شیخ احمد است [و ایں درویش ہم][15] چیزے دیدہ بود[16] ایں درویش گفت ایں خوابہا بر مولانا کمال الدین جداجدا بگویم[16] اوّل

١ک=پر ٢ک=مستانی ٣مولانا تا اقارب=ک۔ ندارد ٤ح=گفتہ
٥کہ=ک۔ندارد ٦ک=اورا ٧ح و ک=بہدیا ٨ک=بیان ٩ح=نخواہد
١٠ک=الحرم ١١ک=بیند ١٢ک=درمکہ ناکہ باکشد ١٣ک=نشدہ بود
١٤ح= درویشان ١٥واین تابود=ک۔ندارد ١٦ک=بگویم

مولانا احمد آهسته گفت گو نکه دو عورت خوبصوت پیش شیخ احمد آورده اند و میگویند که قبول فرمایند شیخ احمد گفت بابو[۱] ما قبول نکرده است ما چگونه قبول کنیم آرندگان گفتند از آنکه بابو تسار[رضا] می دید از دور بابو نمودند که بر سه دوزانو شده میفرمودند بابا احمد فرمان می شود قبول کن مولانا کمال الدین رخ برما کرد و شما چه دیده اید آهسته گفتیم بابو را در خواب دیدیم که میفرمودند که شیخ احمد فرمان می شود چرا قبول نمیکنی همه برخاستند ما را مصافحه کردند و قبول کردند که تحقیق شما شیخ هستید ثمرهٔ این خواب ماناک در آنکه از سمرقند باز گشته در سر گبیج آمدیم پیدا آمد سوداگری رسید دو عورت و یک غلام آورد گفتیم مجردی را حاجات است شیخ تاج الدین و شمس الدین سندهی گفتند که مخدوم دو نوع احتیاج است است یکے آنکه زایران که می آیند برائے ایشان کسے باید که طعام پزد[۲] دوم آنکه اگر عورتی در درون خانه باشد زایر یکایک بغیر اذن در نیاید ماناک بندگی قطب زمان شیخ همام دامت برکاته را نخواب ندکور یاد آمد هر دو عورت و غلام را به چهار ده تنگه زر خرید[۳] ند غلام را موجود نام نهادند و فرمودند تو پیش در باش تا از آینده خبر کنی عورت بزرگ را جامه دار کردند[۴] امین بود نماز بسیار گذاردی پیش از مخدوم پست چند سال پسرے شده موجود و عورت دوم تا سنه ۸۶۱ھ[۵] احدی و ستین و ثمانمائه در حیات اند **دیگر** بعد از رحلت بابو چون ما اختیار خلوت کردیم[۶] قاضی فخر الدین حاکم کھٹو در خواب دید گویا که بندگی شیخ معین الدین سنجری در دبلینه شیخ احمد آمده اند قاضی چون

۱ح و ک = بابو ۲ح = ببرد ۳ک = خرید نمود ند ۴ک = گردانید
۵ سنه ۸٦۱ھ = ک - ندارد ٦ بعد از کردیم "درسنه ستین وثما نمایه" = ک

شنید در دہلیز آمد دید بندگی شیخ معین الدین وضومی سازند [۱]یکتاء مبارک یک طرف بر دستارچہ برگرفتہ بستہ بودند قاضی عرضہ[۲] داشت کہ بندگی شیخ بجہ مصلحت آمدہ اند شیخ معین الدین فرمودند برائے شیخ احمد بساط آوردہ ایم قاضی عرضہ داشت چوں بگستر انید بندہ را اشارت شود یاری دہد فرمودند ما مرتب کردہ ایم صباح قاضی مذکور پیش بندگی قطب زمان شیخ جہاں دامت برکاتہ آمدہ عرضہ[۲] داشت کہ بشارت آوردہ[۳]ام و خواب مذکور گفت بندگی مخدوم بغایت منفرح[۴] شدند زیراچہ شیخ معین الدین مقتدا آفاق و مقبول عالم بودہ و اہل عزلت ہمہ در روضۂ مبارک ایشان می روند و می نشینند (پناہ ہند) و از انجا محلے نامزد می شوند[۵] چنانچہ[۶] خدمت بابو را در کھٹو نامزد فرمودند و این قصہ در کیفیت خدمت بابو بازدیدہ شدہ است

دیگر ہمیں قاضی فخر الدین ہمدران ایام در خواب دید کہ انبار ہست از کاہ بلند و پہنا [۷]وسیع و عورتی انواع زرینہ و مرواریدہا پوشیدہ باجامہا کبود پیش آں انبار نشستہ است قاضی او را گفت چیزے از چندیں کاہ برائے مادیان ما را بدہ عورت گفت این انبار شیخ احمد راست بغیر اذن ایشان مرا مجال دادن نیست خواب مذکور قاضی بر زن خود مسماۃ بیبی دولت گفتند بیبی دولت گفت قاضی خواہی دید کہ کار شیخ احمد تا کجا رسید

دیگر روزے در ابتداء ایام عزلت بندگی قطب زمان شیخ جہاں دامت برکاتہ در خواب آمدند[۸] کہ اسپی سبزہ خنگی بازین خوب انداختہ آوردہ اند

۱ ک=یکتاء ۲ ک=عرضداشت کرد ۳ ک=آوردہ ایم ۴ ک=منفرح
۵ ک=شود ۶ ح=چنچ ک=صبح ۷ ح و ک=اود
۸ کذا در ہر دو نسخہ محل دیدند است۔

تاویل کردند شیطان است لاحول فرستادند ناپدید شد **دیگر** بعد نقل بندگی بابو
مطربی در آخر شب هامی آمد و سرود ها میگفت بندگی قطب زمان شیخ جہان دامت
برکاتہ میفرمودند مارا ازاں حضور میرفت خدمت بابو را یکے از مصاحبان کسے در خواب
دید کہ میفرمودند ایں مطرب را بگوئید کہ فرزند[۱] آخر شب چرا تشویش میدہد آں مطرب را منع
کردند اعانتہا خدمت بابو بعد نقل ہم بسیار معاینہ شدہ است **دیگر** شبے ملک قطب
نجم در ناگور خواب دید کہ جوانی صوفی وش دامن او میگرد[۲] کہ چہار صد ٹنکہ من بدہ و محاورہ
چنین چنین دارد بدین محاورہ کیست ہمنشینان گفتند بدین محاورہ
شیخ احمد پیش نیست ملک قطب الدین را ہماں زماں یاد آمد کہ تحقیق شیخ احمد بر من
چہار صد ٹنکہ یافت[۳] دارند محرر را گفت چہار صد ٹنکہ را برات بنویس محرر برات نبست[۴]
ملک برات مذکور[۵] بر دست قاصدی در کھٹو بندگی قطب زمان شیخ جہاں دامت برکاتہ فرستاد
چہار صد ٹنکہ نقد دست دادہ و بروایت[۶] شیخ محمود ابو الفتوح کہ[۷] بر ایشاں ہم بندگی مخدوم
لطف داشتند سید اکرم التماس کرد کہ چہار صد ٹنکہ شما بر ملک قطب الدین یافت دارید
چرا طلب بدہ نمی آرایند بندگی قطب زمان شیخ جہاں دامت برکاتہ فرمودند چوں تارک
شدیم چہ طلب کنیم ملک خواب[۸] مذکور دید برات بر دست سوارے معتبر فرستاد سوار
مذکور وقت چاشت رسیدہ بود ناظر کسے علم[۹] نداد شخصے گفت از ملک یک نفرے کاغذے
آوردہ است اشارت شد مکتوب مذکور در فلاں فلاں طاق بدارید خواہیم دید گفت

۱ مراخر = ک ۲ ک و ح = میکرد تصحیح قیاسی ۳ یافت تائنگہ = ک ۔ ندارد
۴ نبست = ک ۵ ح = مذکورہ ۶ بروایت = ک ندارد ۷ ک = راکہ
۸ ک = خوب ۹ ح = غم

آن ع۱

این سوار برود یا بماند بعده مکتوب خواندند و او را باز گردانیدند سید اکرم رسید
او را فرمودند همچنین بهتر یا همچنان **دیگر** انفاس متبرکه بندگی قطب زمان شیخ جهان
دامت برکاته که در حیات معائنه شده است چندان است که لا یعد و لا یحصی و آنکه
بعد وفات در خواب فرموده اند یکے ازان این است ع۲ که مرید مونس ملک شیخن یونس
چندران که از آل خالد ولید بود در خواب دید در آنکه بندگی قطب زمان شیخ جهان
دامت برکاته دعوت حق را لبیک اجابت کرد و ملک متعلق شد که ما را هر گاه که دشواری
پیش می آمد پیش مخدوم عرضه میکردیم ع۳ اکنون کجا خواهیم گفت ناگاه یک شبے جمال با کمال
بندگی قطب زمان شیخ جهان دامت برکاته در خواب دیدم فرمودند که هیچ تعلق مکن چنانکه
در حیات اعانت کارها تو میکردیم همچنان خواهیم کرد اما سلطان محمد احمد را بگوئے که ضابطه
دهار محمود خلجی در گجرات خواهد آمد اما چنانکه ع۴ جنگ نخواهد کرد باز خواهد گشت خواب مذکور میر
سلطان عرضه افتاد سلطان مهم چانپانیر محمد قریب فتح شده بود که خلجی مذکور رسید سلطان
محضری ع۵ مذکور گذاشت مقابل خلجی رفت فرمان شد هست کسے در لشکر ما که در لشکر او
برود تشویش دهد و بما خبرها او برساند بنده مخدوم عرضه داشت این کار بنده را بنماید
فرمودند که ع۶ بندگی قطب زمان شیخ جهان دامت برکاته پیش ازین در خواب بنده را در کار
سلطان اختیار شوی سلطان هر نماز ذکر شب و روز گرد لشکر او می ماند ع۷ تعرض می رسید ع۸

۱ح=این ۲ک=ینست ۳ک=میکردم ۴ح=چنانک جنگ
۵ح محضری ۶ح=فرموده اند ۷ک=ماندیم ۸ک=رسانديم

بارہ ستور

وینبوع مغفرت بندہ را[1] شد چون در قصبہ بارہ سیتول[2] رسید شبے بندہ در لشکر او در آمد

غلغلہ در لشکر ایشاں افتاد مجبو ساں را خلاص شد سلطان محمد را خبر شد انعام و مراحم بسیار

در بارہ بندہ فرمودند فرمان شد دلاسا شما چگونہ است گفتیم چنانچہ[3] نفس بندگی قطب زمان

شیخ جہاں دامت برکاتہٗ در خواب شدہ است ہمان خواہد شد اگرچہ ملوک دیگر میگفتند کہ خلجی

جنگ خواہد کرد من باعتماد نفس بندگی شیخ میگفتیم کہ او را چہ اندازہ جنگ باشد چون از[4] بارہ سیتول[2] بارہ ستور

کوچ کرد بیرا[5] امفسد بر سلطان گفت او مستعد بر جنگ شد شما ہم مستعد شوید بر بندہ فرمان شد

شیخ[6] سخن ترا اثر کجا است گفتیم بندہ گویا نیدہ کسے گفتہ است کہ ہرگز نوع دیگر نشود فرمان شد

اگر ہمچنین است برو ببیں بیا[7] رفتیم[8] دیدم کہ در طرف مالوہ روئے نہاد[9] بندہ نزدیک[10] دم دار او[11]

بیست[12] سوار رفت ایستاد دمدار بادہ سلسلہ پیل و لشکر انبوہ ایستادہ بود

بندہ را اعتماد نفس شیخ دل خود را قوی کرد دو سوار از بیست[12] بر سلطان فرستاد تا

علم دہند[13] بامن ہژدہ[14] سوار بر دمدار حملہ کردیم ایشاں را شکست افتاد چندے را[15] اسیر کردیم

و چندے علف تیغ[16] شیخ گشتند و اسباب و اسلحہ ایشان بر دست ما آمد ہر ہژدہ[17] نفر ما

سلامت ماندند سلطان گفت ہر آئینہ نفس مشائخ جان دارد و انعام داد بعد چند گاہے

بار دیگر بندگی قطب زمان شیخ جہان دامت برکاتہٗ ما در خواب دیدم کہ میفرمودند

یک گاؤ میش شیر آور[18] در روضہ بفرست و سلطان محمد احمد را بگو کہ کوچ مکنید این بار

۱ را = ک۔ ندارد ۲ ح = بارہ سیتول ۳ ح = چنچ ۴ از = ک۔ ندارد ۵ ح = بیرا
۶ ک = سیخن ۷ بیا = ک۔ ندارد ۸ ک = رفتیم ۹ ح = نہاد ۱۰ ک = نزدیک
۱۱ ح = و ۱۲ ک = بیست ۱۳ ک = دہند ۱۴ ک = ہردہ ۱۵ ک = جندیرا
۱۶ ک = علف تیغ ۱۷ ک = ہزدہ ۱۸ شیر آور = ک

که محمود خلجی بیایند جنگ خواهد کرد اما شکسته باز گردد و شیخن تو در جنگ مقدمه شوی در وثنان

با تو[1]

بلبو خواهند بود ترا هیچ مضرت نخواهد بود چون بیدار شدم یک گاو پیش شیر آورده و خواب نامه

نبشته در روضه فرستادم سلطان را علم شد کوچ نکرد اما از حرامخوارگی بیرا[2] مفسد تا وقت

رحلت افسوس میکرد که ما او را چندان نوازش کردیم او با ما دغا باخت و تخلف نمود و در آنکه

شتر

مهر بیرا دفع شد پسر او ولایت ایدر[3] را قبض کرد حرامخورگی و سرکشی یکی بده کردن گرفت[4] بنده

مخدوم را دریغ آمد باعتماد نفس شیخ که تو وقت جنگ پیش شوی و در کار سلطان تقصیر

[5] یعنی شیخن چندران

نکنی دو بیست پیاده و صد سوار مستعد کرده و نراین داس[6] و سور داس را با دو بیست سوار

و سیصد پیاده با خود یار کرده در ولایت ایدر[7] در آمد پسر بیرا بضرور جماعت خود با پنج سلسله

پیل متابل آمد جماعت ما بر نسبت جماعت او مقدار نمک در آرد بود یاران ما را تردد شد

را

که حال ما چه خواهد شد و بنده التفات و تعلق نبود باعتماد نفس مخدوم با شصت سوار

بران کفار حمله کرد[8] سر غنه ایشان را سمه[9] جیسی سیلهٹ را کشتند و پیلان و پیلبانان

و شتر سواران و پیادگان را انداختیم کفار بهزیمت را غنیمت شمردند ما تعاقب کردیم کفار

هم[10]

را اینچنین هیبت افتاد که در بیجانگر که مقام ایشان بود ماندن نتوانستند مقام ایشان

نهب و تاراج کردیم و نراین پونجا را آنجا نصب کردیم باز گشتیم اول فتح در جلوس

سلطان قطب الدین آن بود بعده چنانچه نفس بندگی قطب زمان شیخ جهان دامت برکاته

---

١ ح=بابو ٢ ک=پیرا ٣ ک=ابدار ٤ ک=کردند

٥ ک= "یعنی شیخن چندران" اضاف دارد ٦ ک= نراین وسورداس

٧ ک=آیدار ٨ ک=کردم ٩ یعنی جے سنه=ک ١٠ ح=هم- ندارد

بود خلجی باز در گجرات رسید در قصبه ~~میرعو~~ بروده آمد[1] سلطان قطب الدین و خلجی در قصبه کپڑ بنج بر فرق اندک ماندند من بر سلطان حاضر شدم عرضه داشتم[2] که هیچ تعلق نیست شیخ احمد باتسما است چهار برادران ما پیش شما میدارم و من با جماعت خود بر صف خلجی حمله میکنم اگر خلجی برکت مخدوم شکسته نشود همان زمان همه برادران بنده را با خیلخانه در حوالۀ زها و انداخته شد فرمان شد سخن از کجا میگوئی عرضه داشتم[3] که من بقوت و جلدی خود نمیگویم فرموده شیخ احمد میگویم سلطان را هم اعتقاد شد فرمان شد[4] اکنون تحقیق جنگ باید کرد بعد دو سه روز او قصد کرد[6] بر لشکر ما رسید شیبه[5] حکم ~~چنانچه~~[7] بعضے خلق بنده باعثما[8] بجنبیده نفس[9] شیخ هم در معده بود روی نگردانیده بعده بنده با یاران خود دست بر شمشیر انداختند و حمله کردند چون خلق ما دیدند که حمله کردیم از هر طرفے یاران لشکریان چالاک[10] بتوفیق الله تعالی حمله کردند و مدد الهی بدوید از هر طرفے بانگ بر آمد که لشکر خلجی شکست یافت ما یک نیزه خلجی را آوردیم بعده بر پیلان او حمله کردیم برگستانیان او حایل شدند برگستانیان و پیلبانان[11] اسیر تیغ شدند پیلان او را از هر طرفے پیش سلطان آوردند میان دو لشکر لیبا[12] حایل بود سواران ما تا لب آب[13] رفتند اسپان در آب انداختند اسپ من بجو در آب مشغول شد از میان سواران با آواز بلند شخصی[14] گفت شما باز گردید که خلجی شکست خورد من در آن سوار نظر کردم از نظر من غایب شد مرا فهم شد که آن آواز شیخ جهان بود افسوس میکردم

۱ح=هرور در (ه) بروده وبرودره هر دو صحیح است- ۲ ک=عرض داشت کردم
۳ ک=عرضداشتم ۴ شد=ک-ندارد ۵ ح و ک=شیبه ۶ کرد=ح-ندارد
۷ ح=چنچ ۸ یجنبیده =ح- ندارد ۹ ح=نفس و ۱۰ ک=جالاک
۱۱ ک= پیلان ۱۲ ح=لبیا ک=لیباب ۱۳ ح=لبیا ۱۴ ح=شخصی ندا

که کاشکی در رکاب مبارک می افتادم و میگفتم که نفس شما و خواب شما راست شد
از کپیر[1] پنج تا[2] موضع با[3] باندرواڑه موازنه سی جند کروه[4] در تعاقب لشکر خلجی بودیم[5]
از هیبت ما کسی را از لشکر او مجال نشد که با ما مقابله کند **دیگر** قاضی بڈه مبارک
والوالجی[6] که موثوق و معتمد علیه حضرت بندگی قطب زمان شیخ جهان دامت برکاته بود!
روایت میکند که استازت شد بنویس بدار، شبی در خواب دیدند گویا که جای درویشان
مانند شهریان موئها آویخته هستند گمان آنست که امیر المؤمنین علی کرم الله وجهه هم هست
سقف[7] خانه باز شد چیزی دیدند فرمان شد سجده بکنید خواستند که سجده بکنند در
خاطر آمد که در خواب بوده وضو کجا داری همچنین بیدار شدند **دیگر** قاضی راجا ساکن
قصبه دهولقه[8] مردی متعبد و معتقد بندگی مخدوم بود قوت خود از وجه کتابت داشت
بعد رحلت در خواب دید که بندگی قطب زمان شیخ جهان دامت برکاته با لباس خوب
و پاکیزه در محلی[9] مرتفع نشسته اند بعده عرضداشت کرد که بعد رحلت با شما چه معامله باشد
فرمودند از اکل حلال و صدق مقال علو درجات و معلی مقامات شد **دیگر** خواهر ملک حسین
بلارامی[10] عورت پاک عفیفه مرید بندگی قطب زمان شیخ جهان بعد وفات در خواب دید عرضه
داشت که با شما چه معامله شد فرمودند مارا مرتبه شیخ فرید اجودهنی داده اند[11] **دیگر** در آنکه سلطان
احمد طاب ثراه را با ضابطه دکهن در سرحد مقابله[12] افتاد ملک خان شه خانو خواهر زاده ملک

١ ح=کپرپنج ک=کپرپنج ٢ ح=با ٣ ح و ک = باندرواڑه ٤ ح=گروه
٥ ک=بودم ٦ ح=والوالجی ٧ ک=شفقت ٨ ک=دولقه
٩ ک=محل ١٠ ح=بلارمی ١١ ک=دادند ١٢ ک=مقابل

جلال شد جائے در اثنائے راه برادرم طالب را ملاقات شد گفت بندگی قطب زمان
شیخ جہان دامت برکاته را در خواب دیدم می فرمودند که سلطان احمد را بگوی که
ہیچ تعلق مکن سلطان چون این خواب شنید در دیار او درآمد مظفر ومنصور باز گشت

فصل ہفتم فرائض

در عبادتہای بندگی مخدوم وصیام وذکر باخلاص
ودفع وسواس فرائض در اول[1] وقت می گذارندو این حدیث میخواندند که اول لها
رضوان ومنتظر جماعت می بودند قاضی عزیز[2] حافظ در امامت ملازمت داشت و
برادر بزرگ او قاضی منصور در عصر ومغرب وعشا سالها ملازمت گرفته بود[3] همو امامت
میکرد در صلوٰة جهریہ چون آیت مغفرت ورحمت می شنیدند[4] در رکوع وسجود دیگر
بودی وامام را تلقین میکردند تا آیت رحمت ورجا جنت بخوانند وبقرات امام تفول
میکرد[5] میفرمودند تفول عادت درویشان است یکبار درویشے خراسانی رسیده بود
او را بشارت دادند که در تفول شما انا اعطینا آمده وعمل باوراد شیخ الشیوخ شہاب الدین
سہروردی داشتند ونمازہائے که در مواسم منقول از ایشان است بکار می بستند
ودر صلوٰة حضور بسیار می داشتند ومیفرمودند ہرکہ در خیال نماز دیگرے شود
او را حظ از نماز خود نیست واز مریدان ہرکرا در صلوٰة حضور بودی بندگی مخدوم
را از ان آگاهی[6] می شد ومیفرمودند فلان را در صلوٰة حضور است ومیفرمودند چون تکبیر اول

۱ح=اول ۲ح=عزیز پدرک =عزبدر ۳ک=همون ٤ح وک="ودر" لیکن اینجا محل واو نیست ٥ک=میکرد ٦ح وک=آگاه

ببنند[۱] حق سبحانه وتعالی را برخود ناظر دانند ومقارنت در تحریمه با امام فوت نداشتند

وتحریمها بحضور تام باشوق بانگ هم وآواز بلندمی بستند وبنده را بارها بامامت میفرمودند

وبحضور یاران میگفتند که فلان را درصلوٰة حضوراست **وحکایت** که در تعرف

مذکوراست میفرمودند که امام ابوعمر علامه مقری را وقتی جماعتیان گفتند که امامت کنید

امام چون پیش رفت جماعتیان را گفت اِسْتَوُوْا یعنی برابر تسوید در خاطر امام من الله

الهام شد[۲] هَلْ اِسْتَوَیْتَ بی لی طَرْفَةَ عَیْنٍ حَتّٰی تَقُوْلَ لِلْخَلْقِ اِسْتَوُوْا یعنی تو برابر شده

از بهر[۳] یک پلک ما زدنی که میگوئی بندگان مرا که برابر شوید امام درحال بیهوش افتاد چون

بهوش یافت کیفیت حال گفت، ومیفرمودند که از لفظ صاحب تعرف[۴] که گفت

فَوَقَعَ لِیْ خَاطِرًا[۵] مِنَ اللّٰهِ کَانَ قَائِلًا یَقُوْلُ هَلْ اِسْتَوَیْتَ لِیْ بسیار مشکلات

مشائخ که گفته اند فلان را در سرا و چنین فرو خواندند با[۶] هاتف آواز چنین داد با مرا همچنین گفتند

مارا تمام حل شد ولِلّٰهِ دَرُّ مَنْ قَالَ، لَوْلَا التَّعَرُّفُ لَمَا عَرَفْنَا التَّصَوُّفَ یعنی شیخ ا

الشیوخ شهاب الدین سهروردی رحمة الله علیه فرموده اند که اگر نبودی کتاب التعرف[۴]

نمی شناختیم ماراه تصوف را وبعد فرض جمعه سنت همان شش رکعت میگذاردند چهار[۷]

که در بعضے نسخها مجرد ظهر افتاده است نه نیت سنت ونه فرض قبول میکردند واعادات[۸]

وتر هم قبول میکردند ومیفرمودند اول که گذارده است چه افتد علی الخصوص که مقبول شده است[۹]

۱ ک=شدند ح=بی ۳ ح=آنک یانگ زدنی ٤ ک=تعریف
۵ ک = خاطر ٦ ک=با ۷ ک=چهاری ۸ ک=اعادت ۹ ک=باشد

پس ثانی چه افتد و اگر گویند که نفل افتد سه رکعت نفل در مذهب
نیامده است و نیت تشفیع وتر بدوگانه که نشسته می گذارند نیز قبول نمی کردند که این امر[1]
ورای سنت و نفل است و محدث است و از بی بی عائشه رضی الله عنها درین
دوگانه نیت تشفیع مروی نیست و در سجده حاجات و مناجات با شوق دیر
ماندند دو طاس و زیادت هم میگذشت و روایت است از مولانا محمد خطیب خاص
که روزے شیخ زاده محمود ابوالفتوح در وقت چاشت حاضر شد بندگی قطب زمان
شیخ جهان دامت برکاته فرمودند چاشت ادا کرده[2] اید عرضه داشت خیر اشارت شد
بروید چاشت بگذارید بیائید شیخ زاده رفت چاشت ادا کرد باز رسید اشارت شد
چاشت بدین صورت (سرعت) چگونه بگذارید[3] دو طاس هم نگرفت اقل چهار طاس بایستی
که گیرد و نوافل شب را سه وقت داشتند یکے در اول شب چون همه در خواب می شدند
[4][در سرآن پلنگ آفتابه آب پُری بود همین که ملازمان در خواب می شدند] بندگی قطب زمان
شیخ جهان دامت برکاته می خواستند وضو می ساختند مشغول به نوافل
میشدند دوم وقت دوگانه نصف اللیل فوت نبود سوم نماز تهجد را چون ثلث
شب یا ربع می ماند می خواستند وضو[5] می ساختند بقراءت مطول میگذاردند[6]
و اغلب اوقات اکتفا بدوازده رکعت نمیکردند بسیار دوگانها میگذاردند

١ ح=این هری ٢ ک=کردند ٣ ح=بگذارند ٤ درسرتا شدند= ک-ندارد
٥ وضوساختند = ک-ندارد ٦ ک=میگذارد

وبعد وردِ فجر دو ساعتی پہلو بر بستر میداشتند بعده برائے اشراق می خاستند
ونوافل دیگر بسیار بعد اشراق می گذاردند چنانچه در پاہاء مبارک علامتِ مُردن خون
از غایت نشسته گذاردن نوافل " سیاہی در کعب وحوالی قدم ظاہر بود اَلعَظمةُ لِلّٰه
دراں سیاہی چه گویم که چه نوری تابید واوقات موضع (مزروع) بود ہیچ وقتی خالی از ذکر
خفی یا قرأت قرآن آنچه یاد داشتند نبود ومیفرمودند مقدار سه سیپاره یاد بود[1] است
در خلوت ابیات توحید (بسیار[2]) میخواندند ومیگریستند وسورۂ جمعه بسیاری خواندند
بلکه در آغازِ آن ذکر تسبیح وصفات باری تعالیٰ است ومیفرمودند[3] ہر دین خواندن
ور یک شفع تہجد البته بودی وبعد تہجد ذکر بجہر این چنیں بودے که در دیوار ہا ہمسایگان (ہم[4]) غزبدی[5]
ودرانکه بنده می دید سر مبارک درجنبش نبود ودر مراقبه سخت غلو داشتند وصورت
مراقبه میفرمودند که چشم بسته میانِ دو زانو سر افگنده بداند که حق مرا می بیند می فرمودند
مبتدی را در فکر غلو نباید کرد ونماز معکوس ہم درویشان گذارده اند وذکر خفی در
اول شب ہم بودی وروز را ہم یک شبے چوں ملازمان بازگشتند این مؤلف را رخصت نه شد
ماند وبے اذن کسے باز می گشت بر تخته چوکی تکیه بالشته کرده متصل جائے نماز بستر
در ذکر لَا اِلٰهَ اِلَّا اللّٰه مشغول شدند کاتب مقابل زیر درختِ انار بحکم اشارت نشسته
بود بعد دیرے اشارت شد بیداری بنده کله بر زمین آورد گفت بیدارم[6] وآہسته بذکر مشغول

۱ ح= بود ۲ ح= 'بسیار' ندارد ۳ میفرمودند= ک- ندارد
۴ ک= ہمه ۵ ح= غربیدی ۶ "و" = ک- ندراد

بود چوں نصف شب گذشت بنده را اجازت شد بازگشت و بر حکم اشارت هم در دهلیز مبارک خواب میکرد بارها برای تهجد گزاردن چنان آهسته می آمدند که بنده را خبر نشدی چوں وقت بیداری بنده شدی برمی خاست می دید که بندگی مخدوم در نماز اند نیز بنده شدیم و سید اکرم هم در کهٹو میگفت که ما را از کهٹو[1] مخدوم هیچ وقتی سبقت در بیداری شب نیفتاده است اگرچه کهٹو[2] کهتر میخاستیم و در کهٹو برای پیش از صبح در مسجدی رفتند[3] شبی سید مذکور خواست که سبقت کند چوں در مسجد آمد دید مسجد را روفته سید روفته در دامن کرده بیرون انداخت و بندگی مخدوم را قدری گرانی خاطر[4] هم از سید شده بود چوں سید را دیدند که روفته در دامن خود کرده سید را در کنار گرفتند و لباچه خود دادند بنده مؤلف در سر کهیچ بیرون دهلیز خاص نماز میگزارد گاه از گاهی برای ارشاد و تعلیم آداب تهجد و[5] مبکتر دندان طالع می شدند و در آستانه می نشستند و مواعظ و نصائح یا در بحث صفات بیچون جل جلاله مشغول می شدند تا طلوع صبح و گاهی بلطف آواز میدادند که فلان آن زمان بنده درون میرفت چیزی بر رمز و اشارت میفرمودند ببرکت صحبت ایشان بنده را فهم می شد خوش میشدند[6] اما هر کسی را فهم نشدی و میفرمودند که اطالت قرات تهجد بر حسب طول وقت تهجد است تا اگر وقت اندک باشد قرات مختصر بخوانند تا تهجد تمام شود چیزی ترک نشود چوں ضعف

۱ ح = ازکهٹو ۲ ح = چه کهٹو ۳ ک = رفتند
۴ ک = در خاطر ۵ 'و' = ح- ندارد ۶ ح = میشد

زور آورد پانصد دانه را سبحه گردانیدند دایم شسته و غلطیده بردست بودے سبحۀ[1] مذکور بذکر لا اله الا الله بسیار میگردانیدند و این مقام ازان اختیار افتاد که از تکلم ریا چنین روایتی[2] بیرون آمد از شیخ شهاب الدین سهروردی که بعضے از فقرا مغرب را در مکه دیدم که در سبحۀ او هزار دانه بود هر روز دوازده بار آن را گردانیدی بذکر لا اله الا الله و مریدان را هم بسیار جهد میکردند که بذکر لا اله الا الله مشغول شوند و فضیلت این ذکر در رساله مغز بیان که تصنیف خاصه بندگی قطب زمان شیخ جهان دامت برکاته است[3] به مبالغت دلائل کتاب الله و احادیث صحیحه و آثار صحابه مذکور است بجهت وسوسه در صلوٰة چون کسے التماس[4] کردے برانداز حال او جواب میفرمودند که بحروف آشنا بودے اورا میفرمودند که در خیال لفظ بباید داشت که من کدام لفظ خواندم و هر که بحروف آشنا بودے اورا میگفتند که در خیال ادا حروف باید داشت که حروف چگونه خواندم و کدام حرف خواندم و متعلم را میفرمودند که دل برین دار که مولا ترا می بیند[5] و فکر ترا می داند[5] هر کرا بوے از خوف و شرم است[6] دل او را قرار شود از هیبت ملک مجازی که مخلوق است میدانی که بچه حسن ادب ایستاده می باشی پیش خالق که در طرفة العین بیک صاعقه[7] محو و ناچیز کند چرا بے ادب و ناهموار باشی و چپ و راست چشم بگردانی و دل برقرار نداری و در ذکر چنانچه بعضے مشائخ بسته اند

1. ح=سجده 2. ک=رویتی 3. به=ح-ندارد 4. ح=انفاس
5. ح=بیند ک= دادند (داند) 6. است=ک ندارد 7. ک=ضاعقه

که شیخ را در مجلس حاضر داند ازین سخن هم بندگی قطب زمان شیخ جهان دامت برکاته
معرض بوده اند و میفرمودند مدخل غیر درین مقام نمی باید ولهذا الفظ محمد رسول الله
در آخر ذکر می گویند با با مشائخ دهلی مدتے درین بحث بوده اند آخر الامر همه اختیار مختار
ما کردند وآنچه بار با میفرمودند که ما در سلوک صاحب تولیم همین مؤید انست ومیفرمودند
بیداری سحر اول مرتبه درویشی است درصوم همه بندگی مخدوم دوام صوم
درحیات بندگی بابو اختیار کرده بود[1] تا[2] ثلاث وثمانمائه در دهلی
وخراسان وسفر حجاز فوت نبود وصوم اول سال وآخر سال بطریق التزام بود ومریدان
را هم درین دوروزه اهتمام میفرمودند وچون در غره محرم خلق را اشتباه شدی
قاضی منصور میگفتند تفحص کنید که مخدوم را نیت صوم[3] شده است یا نه اگر معلوم می شد
که ببست نهم ذوالحجه صوم داشته اند البته دوم روز غره واقع شدی و هیچ وقتی خالی
از عبادت نرفتی یا بنماز یا بذکر یا بفکر یا بتلاوت یا بمذاکره علم یا بنصیحت و
چون حکایت میکردند میفرمودند که در حکایت نصیحتها است و در مجلس
بندگی قطب زمان شیخ جهان دامت برکاته ذکر دنیا و تدبیر وے کمتر بودے درین
باب سلطان احمد هم بندگی مخدوم را پسندید[4] ندو وقتے شیخ موسی وراق را در ذکر بندگی
بابو ومخدوم غلبتے افتاد فرمان شد این بدگو مسلمان را کسی هست که منع کند

۱ح=بوده اند ۲ح=تا ۸۰۳ھ ۳ح='صوم' ندارد ۴ح= پسندید

ما چندین بار بخدمت شیخ احمد رفته ایم و وقتے ذکر دنیا نکرده اند و غیبت و عیب کسے نگفته

اند شیخ موسیٰ را بگوئید که در خانه باز گردد [ودر ع 1] شهر نهرواله بر و در رجوع و وداع آنگاه بهند

کرچه بگذاشته باشد روزے سلطان احمد اتفاق کرد که بندگی قطب زمان شیخ جهان

دامت برکاته در سرکهیج بیاید شیخ موسیٰ گفت فرمان شود من هم بیایم فرمان شد شما را

معتاد نیست روا نداشت [ع 2] که بیاید و فضولی کند و فرموده اند قَالَ النَّبِیُّ صَلَّی اللّٰهُ عَلَیْهِ وَسَلَّمَ

[تقوای ع 3]

اَلصَّوْمُ لِی وَاَنَا اُجْزِیْ بِه در این حکم است یعنی حواله بغیرے نکنم و صاحب حقی را از ثواب

صوم او ندهم و اجزی به هم یک روایت است و در اوائل صوم دوام داشتند و در گجرات

صوم خفی بسیار بودے ملازمان می دانستند که مگر مجلس درون تناول شد و می فرمودند هر که

در نوافل از گزاردن [ع 4] عادت کند و از نوافل [ع 5] موظفه اقل صد رکعت بر خود گیرد -

فصل هشتم

در توحید که بندگی مخدوم داشتند و ابیاتے که می خواندند و بیان مناسبت در

ابیات که می فرمودند بندگی قطب زمان شیخ جهان دامت برکاته در توحید علمی

و علمی نهایت راسخ بوده اند و می فرمودند ما را [بعنایت] بعنایت حق تعالیٰ در توحید درجهٔ قصوی [ع 6] داده

است در ابحاث عقلی و نقلی که در باب توحیدات خفائی نمانده است و آنچه خدمت شیخ

عثمان مغربی رحمة الله علیه فرموده اند [که گفت] عَتَقْتُ سَمَاعِیْ مِنْ حَدِیْثِ الْجِهَةِ فَلَمَّا قَدِمْتُ بَعْد

---

١ ک= باز گردند شهر ٢ ک= نداشت ٣ ح= تقوی، ندارد

٤ ح= ازکردن ٥ ک= نفل ٦ ک= قصوری

اِذَا دَانَ ذٰلِكَ عَلٰی خَلْقِیْ آں را میدانیم و کیفیت زوال هم میدانیم بار ها این بیت بر زبان مبارک می راندند شعر

در خلوت دل تا نبود لذت توحید	حق را نتوان یافت ازین قوم فعودے

و در استدلال باسمان و سیارات و نجوم و ابر[1] و باران و اعضاء بشریه و شاخ و برگ، درخت و سبزه و بهائم و حشرات و مخلوقات دیگر در فکر توحید دستی[2] تمام داشتند چنانچه روایت از شیخ زاده کرمانی است چون در تفرج صحرا و درختان سوار می شدند شیخزاده بهل می راند بوقت بازگشت بخانه می فرمودند قوت شما هم درین سواری دست داد و میفرمودند[3] در من سواری قوت شش ماه حاصل شد[4] میفرمودند روزے دانشمندے برین درویش رسید گفت یا شیخ شما مستدل هستید یا مقلد گفتیم مقلد مگوی و این لفظ ذو المعنیین و الثلاث می تواند بود[5] یکے آنکه مگوی مقلد دوم انکه مگوئید بصیغه جمع سیوم مرا مقلد مگو و آن دانشمند مردے پخته و صاحب تمکین بود گفت بس یک دلیل خویش در وحدانیت بفرمائید ما برهان تمانع[6] بر وے گفتیم آغاز کرد این برهان از ان دیگرانست شما ادعا[7] میکنید که من مستدلم دلیلے دیگر گفتم آن را هم گفت که این دلیل در فلان کتاب است از ان شما نباشد[8] جلهم هر دلیلے که گفتیم او حواله بکتابی[9] کرد و او را دلائل توحید که در کتب مذکور است همه یاد بود گفت

1- ک = ابروم 2- ک = دشتی ح = ودستی 3- کذا در هر دو نسخه باید اینجا فرمود مرا 4- (درمن تاشد) = ک ندارد 5- بود = ک - ندارد 6- ک = تماتع 7- ک = دعا 8- ح = باشد 9- ک = یک کتابی

شمارا دلیلے خاصه خود[1] باید گفت تا بدانیم که مستدل هستید گفتیم دو کس یا دو چیز که فرض کنیم[2] و یکے از ایشاں محتاج دیگرے باشد ایشاں را ثالثی[3] باید قطعاً که موجب باشد مرا[4] احتیاج هر دو را با یکدیگر گفت این هم در محلی است گفتیم کجاست آں را بیان نتوانست کرد اما ما را قلق اینچنین شد که طعام و آب اصلاً خوش نیامدی مدتے ترک طعام و آب بود زار و نزار گشته نشسته و[5] خاست با کسے نمانده بود دراں حزن و فکر مدت شش ماه گذشت بعد شش ماه جنبهٔ نفی گرفتیم بعنایت حق تعالیٰ در خاطر القا شد که همچنیں بگو همچنیں بگو در حال شفا پیدا آمد دل مجروح را[6] مرهم از غیب درآمد ~

هم یار بدست آمد و[7] هم کار فراهم[8] شد	:	المنة لله که همیں[9] شد و همان[10] شد

هر بار که این حکایت را می فرمودند آں سر را مکشوف نکردند که چه بود کسے را آں مجال نبود که طلب شرح کند و میفرمودند عَنْ اَمِیرِ الْمُؤْمِنِیْن عَلِی کَرَّمَ اللّٰهُ وَجْهَهٗ حِیْنَ سُئِلَ لِمَ عَرَفْتَ رَبَّكَ فَقَالَ بِفَسْخِ الْعَزَائِم[11] یعنی هر چه قصد کردم که همچنیں شود اغلب احوال همچناں نشد پس بتعیین دانستیم که کننده مالک الملک است و نیز در سمرقند یکے پرسید که معنی قول امیر المؤمنین علی کرم الله وجهه که فرموده اند مَنْ عَرَفَ نَفْسَهٗ فَقَدْ عَرَفَ رَبَّهٗ چیست گفتیم هر که شناخت نفس خود را بالعجز شناخت پروردگار را بقدرت معنی دیگر آنکه ~~چنانکه~~[12] روح مدرک و مفهوم نیست ذات پاک[13] باری تعالیٰ مدرک و مفهوم نیست چنانچه

چنانچه

۱ خود = ک ـ ندارد ۲ ک = عرض که ۳ ثالثی = ک ـ ندارد
۴ مرا ـ در هر دو نسخه تصحیح قیاسی ۵ 'و' = ح ـ ندارد ۶ را = ح ـ ندارد
۷ 'و' = ح ـ ندارد ۸ ح = فراهم ۹ آن = ک = ندارد ۱۰ = ح = لم ۱۱ ح = کردیم
۱۲ ح = چنانکه ۱۳ پاک = 'ک' ندارد

نہایت معنی قول امیر المومنین ابی بکر العجز عن الادراک ادراک سوم معنی آنست

کہ این تعلیق بمحال است سائل گفت شیخ جوابہا کہ میفرمایند بعضے ازانہا است کہ در

حال در کتابہا بیابند و بعضے ازانہا است بتتبع بسیار یابند و بعضے از اجتہاد نہاد است

امابر قاعدہ است[1] یعنی معرفت کنہ نفس [محال است[2] پس ہر کہ کنہ نفس] نشناسد

کنہ رب کجا شناسد فاضلے ہم ازین معنی در جواب سوال اشارت کردہ است بیت[3]

	ہم بحر یقین[4] دہم کان صفا	٭	در مشکل این حرف[5] جواب فرما
	گویند خدابود دیگر ہیچ نبود	٭	چون ہیچ نبود است کجا بود خدا
(جواب)	کیفیت حق زمن چرا می پرسی	٭ جواب بیت[6]	جان در تن تو بگو کجا دارد جا

مؤلف گوید اصلح اللہ شانہ قید کن ظریف افتادہ است بدین[7] قید معنی تعلیق

زود فہم می شود وانکہ بعضے مشائخ را میگویند کہ معرفت نفس بود اگرچہ غیر

ظاہر است امابقید نفی کنہ تحمل[8] جواز توان کرد حامل روح ہم در احادیث افتادہ است

کہ علم دارد[9] بدین معنی جایز باشد **دیگر** شخصے در مسجد خانجہان بریں درویش

رسید گلی برگرفت از و شاخی جدا کرد گفت مخدوم این چیست و آن[10] چیست سید کمال الدین

ملازم جواب داد این جز است و آن کل است مقصود سائل در خاطر سید نگذشت

درویشان گفتند این تمثیل باطل است فہم کرد سایل[11] بازگشت[12] شرح این سخن

۱- است = ک ندارد ۲- محال تا نفس = ک- ندارد ۳- ح = شعر ۴- ح = یقین
۵- ح = آن ۶- ح = ندارد ۷- ک = بدین ۸- ک = نحمل ۹- ک = دارد آن
۱۰- آن = ک- ندارد ۱۱- سایل = ح- ندارد ۱۲- بازگشت = ک- ندارد

از بندگی مخدوم سماع نشده است احتمال دارد سایل یک[1] وجودی بوده باشد هر بار این حکایت[3] میفرمودند آن سر را کشف نکردند[4]
بندگی مخدوم بدو[2] سخن سوال او از شیخ بر گشند یدند اخ اخ[3] بود در هر[5] بیتی و یا کلامی خوش[6]
که در باب توحید نوع قصور یا ترک ادب بودے آن بیت خوش نیامد چنانکه یک بیت افتاده است

ستار عیوب[7] و قاضی الحاجاتی[8]	ای زر تو خدائی ولیکن بخدائی

شخصی[10] همیں که مصراع ثانی میخواست که بخواند می فرمودند بس بس[9] دریں بیت هم ناخوش بود کہ کسی گفته است شعر

آمرزگار

نیست ما را حاجت[12] آمرزش[13] آمرز گار	با نعمتهائی پیر خود بنده[11] کرده ایم

روزے بنده مؤلف عرضه داشت که منقول است از نظام الدین اولیا که سلطان تغلق[14]
خواست که در حضرت[15] ایشان تعرضی رساند معتقدے رسید گفت دریں خیال است و
شیخ نظام الدین مسواک میکردند لختے مسواک را داشتند و این بیت میخواندند

بادشاهی از پے صد مصلحت یک خون کنند[16]	پادشاهان از پے یک مصلحت صد خون کنند

این بیت از شیخ[17] نظام الدین چگونه باشد بندگی قطب زمان شیخ جهان دامت برکاته فرمودند
موضوع است[18] مشائخ را هرگز این چنین نیفتد بعده بنده مؤلف از سخن شیخ نصیر الدین
محمود نیز استفسار کرد که شیخ محمود را چون خدام مزاحمت دادند که شما را چه مناسب گشت
که بنده یکبار سلطان محمد تغلق بدست خود بندید مانا که شیخ را جامه داری فرموده بود سلطان
را در خطه[19] تهته زحمت شده بود بر خدام نفس کشند[20] راندند که این بنده که ما بستیم خال بگشاید

۱ یک = ک ـ ندارد ۲ ک = بدان ۳ ک = اخ اخ ٤ (هر بار تانکردند) ح ـ ندارد
۵ هر = ک ـ ندارد ٦ ح = خویش ۷ ک = العیوب ۸ ک = الحاجات ۹ ک = که
۱۰ ک = خیسی ۱۱ ح = سنده ۱۲ ک = حاجتی ۱۳ آمرزگار = ح ـ ندارد ۱٤ ک = تعلق
۱۵ ک = مضرت بایشان رساند ۱٦ ح = کنند ۱۷ 'شیخ' = ح ـ ندارد
۱۸ ک = موصوعست ۱۹ ک = خط ۲۰ ح = راند

بندگی مخدوم فرمودند این سخن هم از ان شیخ نباشد و این هردو[1] حکایت ایماء میکنند
بر آنکه بندگی قطب زمان شیخ جهان دامت برکاته را در توحید درجه علیا بوده است ۔
واز کلمات بندگی قطب زمان شیخ جهان دامت برکاته است اے پیدا برہمه و اے پنہان
از ہمه پیدا برہمه بصفات کمال[2] و پنہان از ہمه بذات کمال و قتی شخصے دوہره خواند[3] ؎ دوهره

سائیں سرسی ساہ کروں تمہاری بالیا[5]	توں جان کرتار جی مجھ ساجن بیرہ[4]

بندگی مخدوم در حال برین نسق فرمودند دیگر (دوہرا[6])
توں جانمتا[7] کرتار جی منجھ سائیں نبیرہ[8] سائیں کی ہی سار با نجر ہانہ جو من بسنہ[9]
روزے در محل درون کنیزکی خود بود در چشم خود سرمه کرده پیدا شد بزرگ را[10] دشوار نمود رشک
در کار شد با وے بغضب بر آمد لت کرد بندگی مخدوم بر بدیهه فرمودند ؎

نہ ہیو دیکھن دینہ[11] مجھ نہ آپ دیکھہ سکینہ	دوکھا کا جل جی کروں تو سوکن دکھہ دینہ

وبندگی قطب زمان شیخ جهان دامت برکاته را دوہرها و مرموز[12] و مثنویات دلسوز می فتاد
شخصے پرسید که[13] بہوگی بوجہوں روز[14] پندتا[15] دو دن[16] کبستی[17] ماس ،، مناسب این مصراع ۔
چیزے فرماید بندگی مخدوم فرمودند دوہرہ

جی کن دیکھی دیس کی[20] برس نہ انت نہ ماس[21] ۔	دیسی[18] بجھتی ایک پل جانوں برس پچاس[19]

دیگر ۔ قاضی حاکم والد قاضی عالم در برج فرد خانه پرده[22] گاه می بست بندگی قطب زمان شیخ جهان

١ دو=ک۔ ندارد ٢ کمال=ک۔ ندارد ٣ ح=که ٤ ح=پیره ٥ ک=والا
٦ ح=دیگر ٧ ح=جانته ٨ ح=پیره ٩ ک=بسیء ١٠ را=ح۔ ندارد ١١ ک=دیه
١٢ ک=موزون ١٣ که=ک۔ ندارد ١٤ روز=ح۔ ندارد ١٥ کذا در هر دو نسخه
پونچهو بمعنی استفسار کنم ١٦ ح=بندتا ١٧ ح=رن ١٨ ح=دی ١٩ ح=تل
٢٠ ح=دیکهه ٢١ ح=برسنه ٢٢ ح=پرده گاه ک=بردگاه

دامت برکاته بربدیه این دوہرہ فرمودند، **دوہرہ**

تتی بدھی[1] کننری جوٹ[2] دہن اوجہل ہوئے ..	مورکہ[3] رکھی نین دو مُحہ[4] کہ رکھی کھوئے

دیگر۔ شاعری درمجلس نشستہ بود و بندگی مخدوم فقرا را مال می دادند در تعجب شد
گفت زہے[5] ایثار کہ حق سبحانہ تعالیٰ مخدوم را روزی کردہ است بندگی مخدوم فرمودند بیت

می برد ہرکس نصیبے[6] خویشتن ..	درمیاں احمد بہانہ بیش نیست

شاعر این بیت را غزل کردہ آورد او را انعام دادند و فرمودند تضمین کردن یک بیت را
غزل مشکل است چنانچہ سلطان محمد فیروز بیتی بتست و شعرا را گفت کہ تضمین کنید ہر یکے
چیزے بتست سلطان ازان کسے نہ پسندید بیت مذکور بریں درویش رسید در خاطر کرد
کہ شعرا بیت سلطان را خواستند مقدم دارند و مقدم خوب نمی آید این درویش موخر بتست
چون گفتار ہرکس[7] در ورق کردہ گذرانیدند ورق ما چون در نظر سلطان آمد تحسین کرد
فرمان شد این بیت ازان کیست حجاب گفتند بیت مذکور از بندگی قطب زمان شیخ جہان
دامت برکاتہ است فرمان شد بغایت طریف[8] است کَلَامُ الْمُلُوْكِ مُلُوْكُ الْكَلَامِ **دیگر** سید محمود
رکن نبیسہ سید رسول دار دہلوی درباب تحمل رباعی آورد ~~اینست~~[9] بیت

گر جفاکار از جفا بد را ندم از شخص[10] پوست	من نہ با او آں کنم کیں فعل مَن آن فعل اوست[11]
من مکافاتِ جفا با او کنم چنداں وفا	کو خجل گردد بگوید کہ این نکو کردن نکوست

۱ ح=بدھی ۲ ح=جوں ۳ ک=مورک ٤ ح=منہ ۵ ک=رہی ٦ ح=نصیبی
۷ ک=کسی ۸ ک = طریف ۹ ح=اینست ۱۰ ک=شخصی ۱۱ و=ح۔ ندارد

بندگی قطب زمان شیخ جہان دامت برکاتہٗ را رباعی مذکور خوش آمد ساعتی ہم درین رباعی

مشغول بودہ اند بعدہٗ فرمودہ اند کمالِ تحمل آن است کہ لفظِ خجل نیارند سید مذکور فی الحال

مصراع مذکور را اگر دانید گفت ع :- کو بجان و دِل بگوید کہ این نکو کردن نکواست

دیگر[1] بندگی مخدوم فرمودند : اخ ۔ اخ ۔ اخ سید در پائے مخدوم افتاد و گفت زہے ظرافت

طبع بندگی مخدوم سالہا ما این رباعی را در مجالس خوب طبعان خواندہ بودیم کسے بر سر این

نکتہ نشد دیگر شبے وقت سحر در آستانہ مبارک این مؤلف تہجد تمام کردہ نشستہ بود

ناگاہ درِ دہلیز باز کردند بندہ بجمالِ مبارک مشرف شد بیرون آمدند و زیر دیوار شدہ طرف

مسجد جامع نو کہ بنا ء خاص بندگی قطب زمان شیخ جہان دامت برکاتہٗ است روان شدند

و دران ایام بنیادِ مسجد ہنوز نہ شدہ است و مخدوم بہمان نیت می رفتند و بندہ را علم ندادہ

بودند فرمودند فلان و بندہ را بیشتر اوقات بدین لفظ آواز می دادند[2] تنہا بندہ بود

عرضہ آمد در سایۂ این دیوار بسیار دلہا ہر روز می آساید بر بدیہہ فرمودند ع[3]

در سایہ ہر کسے کہے[4] آسائید	زین روئے عمارت ار کنی می شاید

دیگر این ابیات بسیار بآواز بلند می خواندند در توحید ملک تیر ملک را[5] افتادہ است

مانا بکار و زما ہیچ کار نہ آمدہ

ا ح= دیگر بندگی ٢ 'درک' بعد از "دادند" چرا عمارت کردید

٣ ح= دیگر ٤ کذا در ہر دو نسخہ تصحیح قیاسی ٥ اضافۂ قیاسی

غزل بیت[1]

مانا بکار و هیچ ز[2]ما کار نه آمده
بیکار مانده ایم و[3] چه کاریم آه آه

رندان مفلسیم حریفان ناقصیم
جز نیستی و[4] جُرم نداریم[5] آه آه

نے در شمار مرد نه اندر شمار زن
معلوم نیست در چه شماریم آه آه

خواند اگر بلطف بیائیم شاد شاد
راند اگر بقهر برآریم[6] آه آه ٭

تا کئے از کوئے تو جدا باشیم
چند با درد مبتلا باشیم ٭

گر نیابیم[7] و بر درِ تو مقام
خود بگو جز درت کجا باشیم

فرد[8]

(در کلام شیخ افتاده است)

تا ترا یابیم دست گیرد دستگیر[10]
دست گیر و[9] دست گیر و[9] دست گیرا دست گیر

عالمی را تو کشته یک روز
چند کس را جواب خواهی داد

فرد

ای برما جو باز مانی زهمه
معشوقه روز بی نوائیِ منم

تو بارها ز دردِ دلم یاد کردهٔ
آن یاد میکنم دلِ من درد می کند

دیگر، چون در گورستان می گذشتند گفتند

برگذری و ننگری باز ننگر که بگذرد
فقر من و غناءِ تو جور تو احتمال من

گفتم شکایتے کنم از یار عقل گفت
تن را ز جان خویش چه جائے شکایت است

بدست لطفِ عنان را کشیده دار که من
ز خاک بوس رکابی تو باز می مانم

۱ ک=دیگر ۲ ک=زمان ۳ ح=در ۴ 'و'=ک-ندارد ۵ ک=ندریم
۶ ک=براریم ۷ ک=نیابم ۸ فرد=ک-ندارد ۹ 'و'=ح-ندارد ۱۰ ح=دست گیر

من آں کاکی بمردم (مردم) ہر آنچہ بدسند کردم	مکن چوں کاک رخ زردم دراں بازار یااللہ
ہستی یقین تو ہستی بے[1] بر بلند و پستی	روزے تو[2] می فرستی سبحان من یرانی
سو بہتر او کہاں غنچہ[3] جس ہوں بیسے ملانو[4]	[5] دندا کھیر ہا تکر ہکہ بھنونتی جانو

تعلیم نیست حاجت جز کرمت نیست مراد دستگیر از کرم تو نیستی مراد پذیر [6] بیت اے جو کرمت کہ دستگیر
گہ تو[7]
جز در گھیتو کجا است جائے

لی رزق کذ قیق وسط سوک بدوہ[8]	ثم قالوا الحقاہ[9] یوم ربح اجمعوہ
انّی قلت کلا ما تفقعوا[10] ان تسمعوہ	کل من اشتقاہ ربی لقد[11] ران تسعدہ
ادی حاجت الانسان قوتا وملبسا	وسائر حاجات الناس[12] فضولھا
وما العمر الا ساعتان فساعۃ	تولّت واخریٰ انت ترجوا وصولھا
فکم لذۃ تسعی حریصا لساعۃ	ولیس یقینا ان تنال حصولھا
اذا قلت ما اذنبت[13] ذالت محبتہ	حیوتک[14] ذنب لا یقاس بہا ذنب

واین رباعی بسیار در خلوت می خوانند، **رباعی**

بگذار جہاں[15] (جہان) را کہ زان تو نیست	وین دم کہ ہمی زنی بغیر[16] بان تو نیست
آں مال کہ گرد کردۂ مال تو نیست	برجان چہ کنی تکیہ کہ جان[17] (زان) تو نیست

[18] چوں در غور و فکر دنیا و بے وفائی او یاد می شدند این رباعی می خوانند رباعی

١ ک= نی ٢ سی = ک-ندارد ٣ ک=مجه ٤ ک=ملوں ٥ ک=دندا کھیر ہا بکھیا بانک جلوں ٦ "بیت" = ح-ندارد ٧ ح=درگھیتو ٨ ح=بدورہ
٩ ک=الحقا ١٠ ک=فقفوا استمعوا ١١ ک=تقدروا ١٢ ک=الاناسی
١٣ ک=ماذاتبت قال مجیبه ١٤ ک=حیویک ١٥ ح=ندارد ١٦ ح=فرمان
١٧ ح=ندارد ١٨ ک= بیت

گر آمدنم زمن بدے نامدمے[1] | یا[2] خود[3] شدنم زمن شدی نہ شدمے
بہ آں بودی کہ اندریں عالمِ دوں | نے آمدمے نے شدمے نے بدمے دیگر[4]

در عدم آسودہ بودم ایں زماں از بود خود | رنجہ دارم کاشکے ہرگز نہ بودے بود من

غنیمت دان حضورِ دوستاں را | کہ دوراں می نماید بے وفائی
ازاں ترسم وفا از وے نہ دیدم | بسا[5] گوئی کہ ای[6] دوراں کجائی

صحبت گیتی کہ تمنا کند | با کہ وفا کرد کہ باما کند

سام کہ سیمرغ پدر پیر داشت | بود جواں گرچہ پدر پیر داشت[7]

ہر ورقے چہرۂ آزادہ ایست | ہر قدمے فرق ملک زادہ ایست

ہر کرا سودائے لیلے نیست مجنوں آنکس است | ورنہ مجنوں راچہ نیکو بنگری دیوانہ نیست[8]

فرد

صبا گر بینش[9] جای زمن روی بر زمیں آری | گرت پرسد زحالِ من بگو دررازِ[10] تو مجنون شد

قد شرف اللہ ارضاً انت ساکنہا | وشرف الناس اذ سواک انسانا[11]

خیالم آنچناں اندر خیال تو فرو تند[12] (فرد باشد) | نگر اندر ازل بودست خیالم باخیالِ تو

فصل نہم

در نصائح برائے مریداں و دوستاں و من نصائح[13] رضی اللہ عنہ[14]

کُن ذنباً ولا تکن راساً = کن کاحدٍ مِنَ النّاسِ کن طُفیلیاً = التبح لا یکون طامعاً

١ ک = نامدی ٢ با = ک ٣ خ = خود ٤ ح = "دیگر" ندارد ٥ 'بسا' = ک ۔ ندارد
٦ 'ای' = ح ۔ ندارد ٧ ک = داست ٨ ح = است ٩ ح و ک = بینش
١٠ ک = درزاریت مجنون ١١ ح = انسانا ١٢ ح = شد ١٣ ح = نصایح
١٤ ک = رحمتہ اللہ علیہ

صاحب تنزل بعد سیصد[1] روز بمجاہدات بمقام عروج رسد، دیگر بعد چہل سال ولی در ولایت رسد اما صاحب ولایت نشود۔ دیگر[2] درویش را شورت خیانت است

دیگر[3] ہیچ دوستی از دوستانِ خدا تعالیٰ بے ادب نباشد و دروغ نگوید **دیگر** چون بندہ مؤلف را کلاہِ صوف از سر مبارک روز پنج شنبہ آخر ماہ شعبان سنہ تسع عشر وثمانمائیہ عطا کردند اول برائے معاہدہ[4] و بیعت کہ پنجہ کشادند بزرگی آں پنجہ در تقریر نیاید[5] و بدست مبارک کلاہِ ناگوری[6] بر سر بندہ نہادند نصیحت فرمودند حلال و حرام را[7] شما[8] می دانید اما دروغ نگوئید فقط و آخر شب برائے تہجد برخیزید کہ اول مرتبہ شیخی بیداری آخر شب است و ہر کہ بخدائے رسید[9] بدین چیز رسیدہ است کہ شاعر گوید مصرع[10]

جوع و صمت[11] و عزلت و ذکر بدوام[12]	ناتمامانِ جہاں را بکنند[13] کار تمام

فرمودہ اند درویشی صعب کارے است کانسکہ کہ کاسب[14] تا از خود برنخیزی[15] و شہوتِ خود برکندن[16] موی[17] بیضہا قطع نکنی[18] کار پیش نشود سوختہ رباعی گفتہ است **رباعی**

برنکنی و[16]

نوخاستہ ز خویشتن می باید	برخاستہ ز جان و تن می باید
در ہر قدمی ہزار بند افزون است	زین گرم روی بند شکن می باید

دیگر[19] فرمودند چون از احرام صبح فارغ شدند سر بر خالق[20] داشتند شخصے از مسجد الحرام بانگ کرد و این دوہرہ خواند **دوہرہ**[21]

۱ ہفصد=ک ہیصد بمعنی ہشتصد ۲ ک=مشو ۳ ک=دیگر فرمودند
۴ ک=معاہد ۵ ح= نیامد ۶ ح= ناگور ۷ را=ح۔ ندارد ۸ ک=شمارا
۹ ک=رسیدہ است ۱۰ ک= مصرع ۱۱ ح= دسہروطبی وشہرو ۱۲ ح=ذکر بداوام' ک=ذکری بدوام ۱۳ 'بکند'=ک۔ندارد ۱۴ می بودیم = ح۔ندارد
۱۵ ک= برنخیزد ۱۶ ح=برکندن ک=برنکند ۱۷ ک=قوی ۱۸ ک= نکند
۱۹ دیگر=ح۔ ندارد ۲۰ ک=خالق ۲۱ دوہرہ= ک۔ندارد

آری مینین ایشان بهیران مینیان سر در نجاوی کوی

اہیین مناء ہوں سر نین کیھا ہوئے ~~ایشان بہیدان مینا سر لک نکی کوئے~~

بندگی قطب زمان شیخ جہان دامت برکاتہ سر از حالق کشیدند و فرمودند سر آنگاہ حلق

بلنائیم کہ دل از لوث دنیا پاک کنیم چوں در سر کھیچ آمدند سر مبارک نشستہ بر جھجہ نشستہ

موی خنک میکردند عورتی را از محلت نظر بر موہا مبارک افتاد گفت این چہ

درویشی است کہ موہا کنادہ بر جھجہ نشستہ اند در سمع مبارک این سخن او رسید ہماں

زماں حالق را طلبیدند و موہا دور کنانیدند و میفرمودند تا از غیب تنبیہی لایح

نمی شود کاری نمی کنند **دیگر** بارہا میفرمودند ہر کہ چہل روز در صحبت این

درویش بنشیند و آنچہ این درویش میگوید بکند اگر شیخ نگردد ما درویش نباشیم بگوید

ذٰلِكَ فَضْلُ اللّٰهِ يُؤْتِيهِ مَن يَشَاءُ **دیگر** بندگی قطب زمان شیخ جہان دامت برکاتہ

میفرمودند مصاحب کہ آخذ باشد و اگر آخذ نیست او را صحبت نفع نکند چنانچہ

ابو طالب را نفع نکرد اگر پسر را خود متابعت پیغامبر صلی اللہ علیہ وسلم تحریص

میکرد و لعاب پیغامبر صلی اللہ علیہ وسلم بر ظاہر وجود خود مالید و پیغامبر گفت

صلی اللہ علیہ وسلم تو یکبار در گوش من کلمہ بگو نگفت زیرا چہ آخذ نبود **دیگر** بارہا فرمودند

کہ دروغ گوئی پیش خود خوار است یعنی میداند کہ آں سخن مرا دروغ افتاد و میفرمودند

دائرہ دروغ وسیع است و دائرہ صدق تنگ است **دیگر** روزی خادمی را فرمودند

---

۱ ح = ار ۲ ح = بہیدان مینا ۳ ح = نکئیے کوی ٤ ک = خالق ۵ ک = حالف
٦ ک = آنجہ ۷ ح = میگوید ۸ ح = چنانچ ۹ ح = درمتابعت ۱۰ 'دیگر' ک ـ ندارد

۳ع

که درچاه کها بریه گندم که زراعت کرده اند[1] به بینند[2] چون او بازگشت[3] آمد فرمودند بالهای

گندم چه مقدار است عرضه داشت که مقدار یک بدست وچیزی زیادت است موجود

خدمتگار چون حاضر شد پرسیدند بعضی میگوئید که بالهای گندم چاه[4] بریک بدست وچیزی زیادت

است موجود عرضه داشت که درازی بالها[5] بدین حد دروغ محض است تعجب کردند و از خادمی

دور کردند المقصود از دروغ و از دروغگویان سخت کاره بوده اند و از ملقی سخت می رنجیدند

دیگر میفرمودند که بر لطف سلطان و بر هیچ کس اعتماد نباید کرد چنانچه[6] مولانا ابراهیم کیتهلی بصحبت

سلطان محمد فیروز مغرور شد با وجود اتحاد و محبت و انبساط بحدی که یک پلنگ می خفتند[7]

بسبب سهلی سلطان تغیر شد فرمان داد که مولانا مذکور و مولانا نظام الدین که وقتی طعام

در خانه می پخت اگر از[8] غیب چیزی رسیدی خوردی فقط هر دو از دهلی بیرون آیند مولانا

ابراهیم راهیمین کسیر شد کفش در پای کرده[9] بیرون آمد و مولانا نظام الدین بر با چه گفت[10] گفته

فرستاد که در باب ما اینچنین فرمان شد شما چه میکنید گفتیم بر ما کسی نیامده است و ما خود

رختی هم نداریم مسکین مولانا نظام الدین رخت نهاد داشت بدستواری بیرون شد بعد دو سه

روز سلطان را سواری شد نظر بر در مسجد خانجهان افتاد فرمان شد در مسجد چرا بسته است اند[11]

عرضه داشت که تحریب این در شیخ احمد کهتو مشغول می شوند سبب آن بسته می ماند

فرمان شد ایشان بزرگانند دخل در کار کسی ندارند و میفرمودند[12] سبب نفر خود با کسی از ایشان

١ اند=ک- ندارد ٢ ببیند و بیاید =ح-ندارد ٣ ح=باز گشت ٤ چاه= ح- ندارد
٥ ح= درازی باد ٦ ح=جنچ ٧ ک= می خفتند ٨ از=ح-ندارد
٩ ک=کردو ١٠ ح= چه گفته ١١ اند=ح-ندارد ١٢ میفرمودند =ح- ندارد

بجهت حد کشت

که در کیتهلی زراعت داشت[2] کیتهلی

دیوان زیادتی نیاید کرد چنانچه مولانا ابراهیم کرد[1] سبب پسر وای مقطع درافت دگر

نفران مقطع او ر الت[3] کردند وایه بر مولانا آمد فریاد کرد مولانا در غصه شد بر مقطع

گفت فرستاد مقطع نفر خود را بسته[5] بر مولانا فرستاد نفر خود را مولانا[6] مذکور لت بلیغ

کرده داشت مقطع بخدمت آمد و گفت من پسر دایه خود را بستم و بخدمت شما فرستادم

بتوقع آنکه ازو بگذرید و شما او را چندان لت کردید که شبه در حیات اوست

بر آن پسند[7] نکردید او را داشته بلکه[8] آید[9] اگر بگذارید تداوی کنیم هم مولانا باز نه گشت[10]

مقطع فسرده شد خشم کرد اقاربان خویش را که در نواحی کیتهل بوده اند طلب

فرستاده با جماعت انبوه مستعد آمدند و در خانه مولانا در آمدند نفر مقطع رها کردند[11]

پسران مولانا مقابل شدند هر دو را به تیغ گشتند مولانا بر مصلی رفت مقابل قبله

نشست او را بر مصلی کشتند خانمان را[12] غارت کردند ایام فرت سلیمان محمد فیروز

بود هیچ سر دیائی نشد بارها این بیت در نصیحت تحمل می‌فرمودند بیت[13]

تحمل کند هر کرا عقل هست	.	نه عقلی که خشمش کند زیر دست

و بنده مؤلف کرات معاینه کرده است که تا بیکان[14] سر هیچ با نفران بندگی قطب زمان

شیخ جهان دامت برکاته زیادتی ها کرده اند و تحقیق شده است که نفران مظلوم اند

با آن هم ظالمان را از دست خود چیزها میدادند و بیدادی ایشان تحمل کردند و قتی انتقام

1ح= چنچ 2 کیتهلی =ح- ندارد 3 (که در تا نفر)=ح- ندارد 4 ح=بست
5 ح=بست 6 ک=مولا 7 ح=پسند ک=بس 8 بلکه=ح-ندارد 9 ک=آمد
10 ک=بگشت 11 ک=نکردند 12 'را'=ح-ندارد 13 بیت=ح-ندارد 14 ک=لیتکان

نکشیده[1] اند وکذالک بامقدم موضع اوتیلیه که هر سالی در[2] وقت زراعت
وقسمت غله چه نوع بیدادی ساوظلم بررعیت وباخدمتگاران[3] شیخ
شکر[4] دمها ازطرف شیخ تحمل بود وملوک[5] واکابر بسیار خواستند که اوراگوشمالی
دهند رضای مخدوم نشد[6] وقتی ملک جلالت بر سلطان احمد گذرانید
که پادریه با نفران شیخ سخت بی وضعی میکنند فرمان شد لشکر بستان
وبدوبکش وخانمان او نهبت[7] کن بندگی قطب زمان شیخ جهان دامت برکاته
راچون علم شد در هوای اشکال بلب آب رسیده[8] بود بنده مؤلف را فرستادند
که نباید ملک بر پادریه سواری فرماینده ودرویشان رابرای خون ریزی درجهان
نیاورده اند اگر ملک برای این معنی سوار شده[9] ماخواهیم رنجید مؤلف بر حکم اشارت
بندگی مخدوم برخواجه[10] دبیر ملک مذکور رفت خواجه مرید مخلص مخدوم بود صباح
بر ملک مذکورات بندگی مخدوم رسانید ملک گفت من بنده فرمانم تا دوست چه فرماید.

دیگر روزی سلطان مظفر طاب ثراه بزیارت بندگی قطب زمان شیخ جهان
دامت برکاته رسید ملک شه ملک فخر هم برابر بود سلطان آب طلبیده بندگی مخدوم
آب بدست خود کرده بسلطان دادند ملک گفت پس خورده کرده بدهید بندگی
مخدوم کتوره گرفته آب تمام خوردند پس خورده نگذاشتند سلطان را این معنی

۱ ک=نکشیدند ۲ در=ک-ندارد ۳ ح=خدمت داران ۴ ح=میکردند
۵ ملکوک=ح-ندارد ۶ ح=نشد ۷ ح=نهیب ۸ ک=رسیدند
۹ ک=شوند ۱۰ بده=ح-ندارد

دل پسند نیفتاد که مبادا شیخ را حملی دیگر در خاطر بگذرد که سلطان را آب غیرے
نا آزموده ندهند[1] ملک را[2] سلطان پیش در فرستاد بندگی مخدوم سلطان را
نصیحت کردن گرفتند و[3] درباب شخصے که او را سلطان داشته بود شفاعت
کردند سلطان در تعریض بے وفائی او گفت چون مخدوم میفرمایند او را لعبه
باز گذاشتن رها خواهیم کرد اما ما هم یک نصیحتی عرضه میکنم آدمی را هم بدو[4] نباید گذاشت
وا[5] زو ایمن نباید شد زیرا چه ذو الحال است بندگی مخدوم را این سخن در دل نشست
و هر بار که از نصرت بر خلاف مزاج چیزے صادر شدے یاد میکردند که سلطان مظفر
ما را این نصیحت کرده بود دیگر میفرمودند که اگر درویشے و شیخی نخواهند[6]
تنها طعام نخورد[7] و در نشست و خاست با آدمی عادت نکنند که[8] صحبت
با کسے خالی از غیبت و میمنت (نمیمت)[9] نباشد و بندگی قطب زبان شیخ جهان دامت برکاته
با زائران هم بسیار نمی نشستند اگر چه کسی آرزو بسیار داشتی و پیش آوردن کسے
که مقصود او اخذ چیزے بودے مرضی نبودے و همت و نهمت در ایثار داشتند
و نصیحت میکردند مریدان را که تنها طعام مخورید اگر کسے نباشد همسایه
طلبید[10] و زائر را زود باز گردانیدند و گفتار دنیاوی و دیوان[11] و سلطان
و دیوانیان در مجلس کمتر بودے و چون ذکر توجه افتاد میفرمودند بعضے را توجه

١ ح=بدهند ٢ را=ک-ندارد ٣ 'و'=ح-ندارد ٤ بدو=ک-ندارد ٥ ک=از
٦ ح=بخواهند ٧ ح=نخورند ٨ که=ح-ندارد ٩ ح=میمنت ١٠ ک=طلبند
١١ ک=دان

جعلی است یعنی خود را بتکلف[1] درین می آرند پنهان باید کہ توجہ لہ عادت گردد تجلی زود
تر می رود و اگر در طعام مشغول باشند و کسے بر در بیاید اگر او را آن طعام نخورانند
درویشی نباشد و چون کسے را تعلق[2] دنیاوی پیش می آمد و او بہ بندگی قطب زمان شیخ جہان
دامت برکاتہ عرضہ میکرد[3] کہ بندہ را این تعلق پیش آمدہ است چہ کنم می فرمودند
کہ تعلقاتِ دنیا[4] بموجہاءِ دریا مانند ناگاہ یک موجی پیدا شود[5] اصحاب کشتی متحیر
شوند[6] کہ یارب ازین موج حال ما چہ خواہد شد[7] موج مذکور بعنایت اللہ فرو کشتی
می شود و کشتی بالا او میگذرد و باز موجِ دیگر زیادت تر و مہیب[8] تر پیدا می آید
کہ ایشان امید خلاصی[9] منقطع می شود باز بکرمِ حق سبحانہ و تعالی آن موج زیر کشتی
می رود و کشتی بالا او شدہ سلامت می ماند حاصل آنست کہ صبر پیش می باید کرد
و بہ خدائے تعالی[10] می باید پناہید[11] حق تعالی از آن تعلق مخلص دہد قال اللہ تعالی
وَمَنْ يَتَوَكَّلْ عَلَى اللهِ فَهُوَ حَسْبُهُ وقال وَاُفَوِّضُ اَمْرِىْ اِلَى اللهِ
اِنَّ اللهَ بَصِيْرٌ بِالْعِبَادِ **دیگر** فرمودند خمس لا یکونون کفوا لاحد ط
الحجام والدباغ والحایک[12] والکناس وجنس خامس لم یذکر
فی الکتاب استنکافا منهم استکبارا وهم العونة الذین یبتغون
دینهم بدنیاهم یعنی سرہنگان **دیگر** بارہا بندہ مؤلف را فرمودند کہ

١ح = بتکلیف ٢ح = تعلقی ٣ک = عرض میکردند ٤ک = دنیاوی
٥ح = شد ٦ح = شدند ٧ک = بود ٨ک = محیب ٩ک = خلاص = ک
١٠ک = خدیتعلی ١١ح = نباهید ١٢ک = لحایک

فلاں مال بدست زن مدھی ای باعتماد او مگذاری و بدو مسپاری وچون از دیہ غلہ
دیا از سلطان یا از ملکی فتوحی آمدی اول بصلحا میدادند و اگر بندہ حاضر بودے
ابتدا از بندہ می کردند و این حدیث میفرمودند عَنْ عُمَرَ رَضِیَ اللّٰہُ عَنْہُ اَنَّہٗ قَالَ قَالَ
رَسُوْلُ اللّٰہِ صَلَّی اللّٰہُ عَلَیْہِ وَسَلَّمَ اِذَا اُعْطِیْتَ شَیْئًا مِنْ غَیْرِ مَسْئَلَۃٍ فَکُلْ وَتَصَدَّقْ
یعنی چون دادہ شوی چیزے ناخواستہ پس[1] بخور و صدقہ کن **دیگر** بندگی قطب زمان
شیخ جہان دامت برکاتہ فرمودہ اند اسباب مغفرت بسیار است و این ہم
میفرمودند الارجاف مقدمۃ الکون دیگر میفرمودند کُلُّ مَمْنُوْعٍ مَطْبُوْعٌ بجز عین ہر بار
بندہ مؤلف را دشوار می[2] نمود کہ "مطبوع" برفع بایستی خواند[3] زیرا چہ خبر مبتدا است
اما از خوف بے ادبی عرضہ نمی توانست کرد بعد رحلت در خاطر[4] یکایک گذشت
کہ الحمد للہ خوب شد کہ عرضہ نشد زیرا جر جوار[5] مشہور است چنانکہ "جحر ضب خرب[6]"
معنی آنست کہ ہرچہ در شرع ممنوع است طبیعت آدمی میل بران دارد خداشناسان
ازاں احتراز می کنند **دیگر** میفرمودند بزرگان گفتہ اند ارسل الحکیم ولا توصیہ
او ولا[7] توصیہ چون کسے را نصیحت میکردند برائے زجر نفس خود میفرمودند
اب تجاوی[8] ساہری لوکن کون[9] بدہ دیکی[10] :-

١ ک= بس ٢ می = ک۔ ندارد ٣ ک= خواند ٤ ک= یکایک درخاطر
٥ ک= جار ٦ ک= صحر صب خرب ٧ اوولا = ک۔ ندارد ٨ ح= تجاوی
٩ ح= لوکنہ ١٠ ک= بدہ

فصل دهم

در قلت طعام بندگی قطب زمان شیخ جهان دامت برکاته و در

مجاهده و ریاضت و اربعین که ایشان برآورده اند قلت طعام این چنین بود، که

وقتی نان درست نمی خوردند زیراچه اغلب اوقات در طعام خوردن بنده

برابر بود[۱] ازان معاینه شده است و لقمه کوچک میکردند و روغن در کهچری بسیار

می انداختند لقمه چندے[۲] شتاب می خوردند و میفرمودند شما عیال[۳] دارانید[۴]

تقلیل نباید کرد که در حدیث صحیح است اِنَّ لِنَفْسِکَ علیک[۵] حَقًّا وَلِزَوْجِکَ عَلَیْکَ حَقًّا.

پیش بنده روغن بسیار می ریختند و میفرمودند عَلَیْکُمْ بِالدُّهْنِ و همین که مزه[۶] در می یافتند،

از طعام دست می کشیدند و پس خورده مبارک خوشبوئی اینچنین داشت گوئی

که مشک و عنبر و گلاب در وے آمیخته اند و آن مزه[۷] در هیچ طعامی نیست و گاہے.

و تقلیل طعام برین صورت بودی که محل درون میدانستند که طعام بیرون خوردند

و بیرونیان قیاس می کردند که درون و در واقع دوکان سکان وقت نانه در طعام افتادی

و در سعی برآمدن[۸] حاجت متوجه[۹] طعام مطلق میدانستند و ملازمان را هم می فرمودند بدعا[۱۰] می شدند و دست از

باشید و از بندگی قطب زمان شیخ جهان دامت برکاته مسموع است که گاہے شخصے

در کھٹو سبزی سرسوں[۱۱] آورد، سید اکرم را گفتند برین هم اکتفا توان کرد چون نمازشام گذاردند[۱۲]

۵ رسوں

۱ ک = میبود ۲ ک = چندین ۳ ک = عیال دارید ٤ "را" = ح - ندارد
٥ علیک = ح - ندارد ٦ ح و ک = مژده ۷ ک = مزه ۸ ک = برآمدی
۹ ح = متوجهی ۱۰ (بدعا تا از) = ح - ندارد ۱۱ ح = شرسوں ۱۲ ح = گذاردن

رسید سید را اجازت بود که بوقتِ طعام حاضر می شدند[1] چوں حاضر شد فرمودند
ما افطار کردیم و بندگی مخدوم مقداری ہماں سبزی خوردہ بودند دوم روز سید را
معلوم شد که در ادینه[2] روز مخدوم چیزے نخوردہ اند و تدبیر ہم نشد بعدہ سید در خانه
خود رفتند بر بی بی نصرت منکوحه خود[3] فرمودند که شیخ احمد ادینه روز باز چیزے نخوردہ
اند بی بی نصرت طعام پخته بر دستِ پسر خود فرستاد و سلام گویانید[4] پسر را
فرمودند پدر ترا با کارِ درویشاں چه کار است طعام مذکور باز گردانیدند[5]
سید سیوم روز پوپا[6] بقال را فرستاد که او بندگی بابو را ہم قرض می داد عرضه داشت
ہر روز آں قدر که بفرمائید طعام برسانم بندگی مخدوم سخن وے نیز قبول نه کردند
پوپا عرضه داشت که من باسم بندگی بابو از وجوہات دیوانی[7] خلاص می یافتم اکنوں ہم
بندگی مخدوم خلاص خواہم [یافت[8] بندگی مخدوم این سخن ہم] قبول نکردند که ابہام
دارد بعدہ سید رسید عرضه داشت که از بقال مذکور قرض بگیرند بعدہ بندگی مخدوم
فرمودند ما که قرض بستانیم مال از کجا بدہیم بقال گفت من از دیوان مجری خواہم
کنانید اشارت شد دو نیم سیر منگ[9] و دانگ[10] سیر روغن کنجد ہر روز برساں آں
دو نیم سیر منگ می پختند و سید و یک درویشی دیگر و عبدالرحمٰن را می طلبیدند
و نه درم روغن کنجد در منگ می انداختند و نه درم را چراغ می افروختند بندگی مخدوم

١ ح=شدند ٢ ک=دینه ٣ ک=خودرا ح = ندارد ٤ ک=یانید
٥ ح=گردانید ٦ ک=بویا ٧ ک=دیوالی ٨ (یافت تا ہم)=ک۔ ندارد
٩ ک= مونگ ١٠ دانگ = ک۔ ندارد

راهمان که با ایشان تناول بودے اکتفا می بود[1] وآن سه نفر در خانه نبود طعام هم می خوردند
روزے پویا[2] مذکور محلے رفت بسر او خورد بود مال طلبید منگ[3] نداد شخصے را خبر شد[4]
بر کاله کنجاره وقتِ افطار[5] آوردی بدان افطار میکردند روزے[6]
زن روغن گر او را پرسید که این قدر کنجاره برائے چه می برید گفت برائے افطار
شیخ احمد عورت مذکور افسوس کرد که شیخ احمد اینچنین مجاهده پیش گرفتند[7] کو بر[8] کاله کنجاره
خود را میدارند[9] دران روز مقدارے قند یار کرده کوفته[10] داد چون بندگی قطب
زمان شیخ همان دامت برکاته آن را در دهن انداختند دریافتند که[11] قند انداخته اند از دهن بیرون
انداختند وآن کنجاره را هم ترک دادند چون پویا[12] بقال در قصبه آمد وکیفیت کنجاره
شنید گریه کنان بخدمت مخدوم آمد چراغ آورد و[13] دو سیر جوز مغز هندی[14] پیش داشت
و عذرخواهی بسیار کرد عذرها مسموع نداشتند باز سید اکرم را شفیع آورد بندگی
مخدوم فرمودند جوز ما را چه کار می آید همان منگ[15] بیار چون مدتی گذشت خواستند که در
اربعین بنشینند چند روز هرچه نفس آرزو می[16] کرد او را آورده دادند چشید[17] بشرط آنکه
چهل روز تشویش ندهد کانجی نیاورده بودند در اربعین هربار کانجی
در خاطر گذشتی بعده چهل خرما آوردند چند خرما باریک بود بقال
برائے بدل کردن رفت تا بزرگ بسیار د بقال هنوز نیامده بود.

۱ک=بودی ۲ح وک= بویا ۳ک=مونگ ٤شد=ک-ندارد ٥ک=افتار
٦ک=روز ۷ح=کرد ۸اضافهٔ قیاسی ۹ح=میدارد ۱۰ح=یارکرد وکوفت
۱۱دریافتند که=ح- ندارد ۱۲ح وک= پویا ۱۳'و'=ح- ندارد ۱٤ هندوی=ح
۱٥ک=مونگ ۱٦می=ک ندارد ۱۷ح=چشید بشرط

کار بعین شروع کردند و در حجره مسدود کردند و چهل خرما برابر بردند و دو مجلد[1] آب
بعده سید مبارک او را رسید اکرم مردے بزرگ بود شیر گرم کرد آورد ذکر مخدوم همه
وقت نعمت خوار بودند مجاهده نخواهند توانست خلق را[2] جمع کرد گفت زود در حجره
بگشائید مولانا یوسف و بعضے یاران گفتند که سید همچنین منفرمائید
ایشان تارک شده اند و مجاهده اختیار کرده اند[3] مزاحم ایشان نباید شد
سید محزون شده بازگشت بندگی قطب زمان شیخ جهان دامت برکاته
میفرمودند سه روز نفس را در حجره چیزے ندادیم چون چهارم روز شد نفس سخت
کردیم یگان یگان بر کاله[4]
عاجز شد یک خرما را چهار پرکاله تا چهار روز دادیم هشتم روز ضعف این چنین پیش آمد
که میان نماز مغز سر در وقت سجده در پیشانی می آمد و می خلید نهم روز بعنایت حق
قوتی پیدا شد که همه فرائض و نوافل ایستاده میگذاردیم[5] چون چهله تمام شد یازده[6] دوازده
خرما بیرون آمد[7] در دوله شستند یاران گرد دوله پرده کردند[8] در نماز عید بردند
بنده را این یک چهله از زبان دو بار بندگی مخدوم یاد داست اما راویان یک دو
چهله میگفتند روزے مولانا یوسف صدر همدانی دید که در روے مبارک [illegible]
مخدوم زردی بسیار می زند پرسید موجب زردی چیست هیچ جوابی نگفتند
آخر مولانا مذکور بنوعی دریافت که سیخی آهنین در قلب آلت رجولیت از یکطرف

۱ ح و ک= حجله ۲ "را"= ک- ندارد ۳ اند= ک- ندارد ۴ کردیم تاکاله= ح- ندارد
۵ میگذارد= ح ۶ ک= یازده و ۷ ح= آمدند ۸ ک= کرده

بدوم طرف گذارا کرده‌اند[1] و رشته در رخنه آن شیخ[2] در آورده اند و از غایت درد

ضعیف و نزار گشته مولانا یوسف مذکور عرضه داشت که این چنین مجاهده

در شرع محمدی هیچ محلی سطور نیست مجاهده بیش گیرند[3] که معمول مشایخ است این مجاهده

عمل قلندران و تارکان سنت پیغامبر است اگرچه از بعضی حیدریان معاینه

نده است که چند سیر را در[4] حلقه در سوراخ کرده بود اما بدعت است و مقصود

از آوردن این کیفیت بیان آنست که در تحمل متابعت[5] اتباع[6] و تجرع مرارات

انقطاع و اختیار، اختیار نفس ستیزه کار و کسر و زجر آن مکابد بندگی قطب

مصرع[7]

زمان شیخ جهان دامت برکاته را در وقت ثانی نبود ۵

مرو در ره نفس کش کافر ز بهر کشتن است، بیت[8]

تا سود و زیان همت[9] در اندیشه تو	عشقت نه بدست که سود است هنوز

حال را اهل حال فهم کنند قالی حاید در مقال چه شناسد از تعصب تغضب

عذر هم ملحوظ نمی کنند، ۵

ای تراخاری بپا نشکسته کی دانی که چیست	حال شیرانی که شمشیر بلا بر سر خورند

و این هم احتمال دارد که از قبیل فعل بازگونه زدن باشد بعده رشته مذکور ازان سوراخ

بیرون آورده‌اند به هزار حیله جراحت مذکور مندمل[10] شد، مجاهده بندگی مخدوم

١ ک=گذارد ٢ ک=شیخ ٣ ک=گیرید ٤ "در"= ک ندارد - معنی این جمله واضح نیست ٥ ک= متابعت ٦ ک=ابتلاع ٧ "مصرع"=ح- ندارد ٨ ح=شعر ٩ ح=نیست ١٠ ح= میدمد

بغایت عجیب بود کاتب از صد یکی هم نبود اند وقتی سید اکرم میان خلق نشسته
می گفت که شیخ احمد خود را در مجاهده آنچنان می سوزد که هیچ کس در سوختگی همتای
خود خود را نه سوخته است و بندگی قطب زمان شیخ جهان دامت برکاته بارها
می فرمودند که نفس این چنین مرتاض نشده است که چون سخت گرسنه می شود مقداری
سپاری در دهن میکنم هم بدان صلح میکند وقتی بسید اکرم از غایت ملازمت
بی سرفه عرضه داشت که حق سبحانه و تعالی را نشسته نیابند مسافرت باید کرد
بندگی مخدوم فرمودند سید این سخن از کسی شنیده یا از خود می تراشی
سید گفت از مولانا رضی الدین ابو الفرح شنیده ام و بندگی مخدوم را با مولانا مذکور
در قصبه دینده‌وانه ملاقات بسیار بود[1] و مولانا مذکور معتقد مخدوم بوده[2] وقتی
برهان نام نبیره مولانا مذکور هم دران ایام در لکهنو آمد بندگی مخدوم او را فرمودند که مولانا
رضی الدین را با[3] کار درویشان چه کار است برهان مذکور این تمام کیفیت بمولانا رسانید
مولانا عرضه نبشت که دیباچه او این بود من بنده معتقد[4] درویشانم و بجان و
دل مخلص ایشانم گاهی در قصبه لدنو[5] عورتی هندیه را کار خبر شده بود از شرم با شوهر طعام
نمی خورد و [illegible] هم جهدی میکرد بگمان آنکه با شوهر طعام می خورد شوهرش[6] هم جهدی
نمیکرد بگمان آنکه با مادر من طعام می خورد بعد چند روز عروس مذکوره برای جل[7]

١ ک = بود ٢ ح = بوده اند ٣ ک = یا ٤ ک = معتقدان
٥ حالا این قصبه را لادنون میگویند ٦ ک = شوهر ٧ ک = جلی

دادن تنکان بر در آمده یک دانه ازاں تنکاں در دہان انداخت درحال او را کشف

شده دید که از دور دست لشکرے برائے تاختن قصبہ لڈنو سوار شده است خسرو

خوشدامن
خشوا دبزرگان آں مقام را طلبیده گفت کیفیت دیدن لشکر گفت دانایان ع۱

رخت و اسباب خود کشیدند صباح لشکر رسید لڈنو را تاخت کرد کسانیکه مانده بودند

اسیر شدند اکنوں عورتی ہندیہ را که خبر از غسل و وضو نداشت و منتظر که بود از ترک طعام

ہمچنیں کشف شده اگر مومنی موحدے تارکی جوانی متعبدی صالحی پاکی که لله فی الله ع۲

ترک طعام کند و مجاہده اختیار کند عجب نباشد که زود بحق رسد و او را ع۳

کشف شود هر که به بندگی مخدوم از من گفته است از بنده نیست کاغذ مولانا

رضی الدین را بندگی مخدوم مطالع نموده داشتند در مسجد خانجہاں بندگی قطب زماں

شیخ جہاں دامت برکاته چوں رفتند میسر نمودند دو سه روز گذشته بود که چیزے نخورده

بودند از غایت بے طعامی در ہوش فرق افتاد بعد ادا بین بچشم پیش کرده بودند

چوں بیدار گشتند موذن را فرمودند مگر روز شد موذن عرضه داشت که نیز مخدوم

ہنوز اول شب است عشا ہم ادا نکرده ایم موذن دریافت که مخدوم را از غایت

جوع در ہوش فرق شما ناکه چیزے آورد آں را تناول کردند موذن مذکور

دریں خیال پیش ازاں بود که از کجا می خورند و که می آرد کسی را ندید که چیزے آرد

۱ح= حشورا ۲ک=که=ک۔ ندارد ۳ک=رود

مجاهده[1] بندگی مخدوم را اگر در قلم آرند مجلدات شود و کاتب را از جمیع مجاهدات ایشان خبر نیست آنچه معاینه کرده است و یا از مصاحبی شنیده است آن را در قلم آورد - در مزاجها[2] بندگی قطب زمان شیخ جهاں دامت برکاته پیشتر مزاج[3] بندگی مخدوم در اثنا طعام بودی یکبار بنده مؤلف را میفرمودند که فلاں[4] تو حکایت میکنی و قاضی بده خاموش شده طعام می خورد همه خواهد خورد و چون خدمتگاران طعام می خوردند میفرمودند میاں شما لقمها بزرگ که برمیدارد و چون خواجه حسام الدین مقدم بچه سرکهیچ در اثنا طعام حاضر می شد میفرمودند خواجه شما را در علم رمل و نجوم مگر حوایتی[5] است و بنده مؤلف را بارها فرموده اند که فلاں شما طرف می شنید که صحنک میل دارد تا روغن که باشیں بیند از یم طرف نشیب آید و بندگی قطب زماں شیخ جهاں دامت برکاته را عادت بود که از کتوره بدست مبارک روغن بسیار پیش هر یکے می انداختند روزی مولانا خطیر الدین خالوی که یکے از جلساء و قربای بندگی قطب زمان شیخ جهان دامت برکاته بوده است بحضور طعام میخوردند[6] و دو نفر نایکان[7] یکے علی رومی و دوم خلیل ایدهات[8] حاضر بودند مولانا گفت مخدوم این نایکان عجب شرم دارند اگر در طعام خوردن حاضر شوند طرف طعام نظر نکنند[9] و اگر ایشان را طلبند طعام نخورند و اگر بخورند لقمها کوچک کنند

۱ح=مجاهده ۲ح و ک=مزاجها ۳ح و ک= مزاج ۴ح=فلان
۵ک=حویتی ۶ک=میخوردند ۷ک=نایتگان ۸ک=ابدهات ۹ک=نکنند

بندگی مخدوم دریافتند که مولانا ایشان را تحمیق میکنند[1] در خنده بیهوش شدند
نائیگان[2] مذکور بیرون رفتند بندگان بندگی مخدوم و مولانا در خنده حیران[3] شدند بار دیگر
هم چون مولانا هم بران نهج گفت غلیل اید بات گفت مولانا دغا همان یکبار
پنیس نباشد نه رفته مانند شریک مولانا شدند بندگی مخدوم فرمودند
گفتار مزاح است شَرِیکُ الاَکْلِ مُبَاحُ الدَّمِ وَ[4] حَقُّ المِلْحِ مَحَقٌ مِنَ الاَبَوَیْنِ ط

فصل یازدهم

عنوان

در خوارق و[5] کشف و کرامات و عجائبات بندگی مخدوم خوارق خدمت
ایشان [در تحریر محرران[6] و تقریر مقرران نه بدان اندازه است که بگنجد] ولیکن آن مقدار که با
تجربه این کاتب را معاینه شده است بقدر وسع نبشته آمد دران که خدمت
بابو سید عبد المجیب[7] بن محمد نایب زاده قاضی دیندوانه را در طلب بندگی قطب
زمان شیخ جهان دامت برکاته از قصبه کهٹو در قصبه دیندوانه فرستادند شیخ
در عنفوان جوانی با یاران بر سر جای وجود مبارک می نشستند چون آینده[8] را از دور دیدند
فرمودند اینک[9] می آید از کهٹو آید [بعده گفتند[10] بر ما می آیند] بعده گفتند از خدمت بابو
می آید چون رسید خبر طلب گفت هم ازان جا طرف کهٹو روی آوردند اما قدم مبارک
بر زمین نمی رسید در هوا می رفتند سید[11] عبد المجیب را گفتند سیدا چیزی می بینی

---

۱ ک= میکنند ۲ ک= نائیگان ۳ ک= بسیار ۴ "و"= ک۔ ندارد
۵ "و" =ح۔ ندارد ۶ ک= نه بدان اندازه است که در تحریر محرران و تقریر مقرران بگنجد۔ ۷ ک= عبدالمجید ۸ سید= ک ۹ یعنی این که
۱۰ بعد تا می آیند= ک۔ ندارد ۱۱ سید عبدالمجیب= ک۔ ندارد

سید گفت آرے مخدوم سیر تماد رہوا می شود و مصاحبان دیگر ہم معائنہ کردند
کہ اقدام مبارک در ہوا سایر[1] ست کاتب نیز سید را پرسید سید گفت تحقیق
ہمچنیں بود و من دران ایام با مخدوم کتاب پنج گنج بحث میکردم **دیگر** درایام صغر
شخصے را در کھٹو دیو مسخر شدہ بندگی مخدوم فرمودند برائے دیدن در خانہ او رفتیم دیو را علم
شد کہ ما می آئیم دیو گفت من می روم مرا مجال نیست کہ جائے کہ شیخ احمد بیاید ماندن
توانم[2]
در حال کفش در دہاں گرفت رفت [**دیگر**[3] روزے بندگی بابو را بر بام مزاج
گرم شدند بالائی دروازہ نشستہ بودند و پیش ایشاں کرسی ریسمان بافتہ افتادہ
بود آں کرسی بر ما بر تاتت کردند مخدوم می فرمودند مرا ازاں چنداں زخم نرسید
ولیکن پای مبارک خدمت بابو لغزید از بام در صحن خانہ افتادند من ہم از بام خود را
انداختیم خدمت بابو را در پاے مبارک قدرے آزارے رسید فریاد بر آوردند چوں
مرا افتادہ دیدند فرمودند تو چرا افتادی عرضہ داشتیم چوں خدمت بابو را افتادہ دیدم
مرا طاقت نماند من ہم خود را انداختیم فرمودند یک جان در دو قالب است دراں زماں
نفس آری ہر کہ بر شیخ احمد بر آید ہم چو افتہ چنانچہ اسحٰق یافتند بابا احمد شیخ است
وما ابدال ایم [**دیگر** روزی[4] بندگی قطب زمان شیخ جہان واست برکاتہ می فرمودند
شبی در سفر بہ رکاب بندگی بابو بر گردون ایں درویش خفتہ بود چوں بیدار شد[5]

۱ح=سایند ۲ح و ک = نتوانیم ۳ک= این جا این حکایت راندارد
۴روزی=ح- ندارد ۵ک=شدم

بابو را ندیدیم[1] یاران را پرسیدیم[2] که[3] بابو کجا اند گفتند درون مسجد اند[4] درویشی آمده بود
با او رفتند ما هم وضو ساختیم در مسجد رفتیم دیدیم که خدمت بابو در یک گوشه اند[5] و در گوشهٔ دیگر آن درویش اند هم
مشغول بود محلی[6] ما هم مشغول شدیم شب بسیار رفت بابو و آن درویش از مسجد بیرون
آمدند خفتند ما را حالی پیدا آمد گویا که سقف مسجد حائل نماند نظر به بالا افتاد هر چیز[7] دیده هم
می [illegible] هر چند که استفسار کرده شد بیان نکردند فرمودند متحیر شده[8] از مسجد
بیرون آمدیم بخدمت بابو کیفیت عرض کردیم خدمت بابو برخاستند ما را کنار
گرفتند دل ما برجای آمد فرمودند حالتی خوب است تعلق نیست بعده در حیات
بابو نیز آن حالت در بیشتر احوال می آمد هم درین سفر با سفر دیگر بر گردون خفته حالت
مذکور پیدا[9] شد بی خبر از گردون فرود آمده[10] شب تاریک بود[11] در جنگل رفتیم ناگاه آواز
جرس
ستوران در گوش افتاد هوش باز گشت جنگل هامون بود[12] متحیر شدیم که کجا رویم هم بر رخ
آن جرس رفتیم مکاری[13] ستوران می چرانید گفت شیخ احمد کجا می روید گفتیم گردونها
کجاست گفت درین راه بیائید تا[14] در گردونها برسید بر گردونها آمدیم خدمت
بابو در استراحت بودند مزاحمت جایز نشمردیم و در مسجد خانجهان هم حالت مذکور
بارها می آمد در ملوک خانه درے کشاده بودند متصل مسجد طرف قبله برای دختر قاضی
حاکم پدر قاضی عالم که در سر کهیج آمده بود چون در ملوک خانه حالت مذکور می آمد در حال

۱ ک=ندیدم ۲ ک=پرسیدم ۳ که=ح- ندارد ۴ اند= ک-ندارد
۵ اند= ح- ندارد ۶ محلی =ک-ندارد ۸ ک= شدم ۹ ح=براه
۱۰ ک= آمدیم ح="آمده" ندارد ۱۱ بود=ح- ندارد ۱۲ بود=ح-ندارد
۱۳ ک=مکاری شبی-مکاری بمعنی ستوربان ۱۴ ح=ما

عورت مذکور می رسید کُرمی[1] گرفت، چون به هوش می آمدند باز میگشت یک بار
بالائی بام[2] مسجد مذکور آں حالت پیدا شد در افتادن از بام چیزے نمانده بود
بعنایت حق تعالی[3] او را علم شد رسید فرود آورد در ساعد بازو جراحتے رسیده بود
خون[4] بسیار رفته بود[5] چون آلودگی خون در اندام رسید بهوش باز گشت[6] و این
حالت در سر کهیچ هم بسیار می آمد صباح را می فرمودند مشب آن حالت آمده بود
و بارها دراں حالت هیبت میزدند عورات خادمه در می یافتند در حال می رسیدند
و میگرفتند و در شبی که آں حالت می آمد روئے مبارک دراں روز مخمور[7] شکل فراق
زده می شود کاتب را ازبیانِ ایں حالت چیزے نفرمودند بعضی مریدان
می گفتند که چنیں دیدند و چناں دیدند کاتب را براں[8] اعتبار نیست زیرا که هم
از حضرت بندگی قطب زمان شیخ جهاں دامت برکاته مسموع ست که سر حالی را و هر
متعالی را علامتی[9] است که آں علامت مصداق او باشد و هر بیانی را هنجاری است
که بدان دانسته شود که راست است چنانچه در کتاب تعرف آمده است که روزے
حارثه نام صحابی بر پیغامبر صلی الله علیه وسلم رسید گفت اَصْبَحْتُ مُؤْمِناً حَقّاً
فَقَالَ النَّبِیُّ صَلَّی اللّٰہُ عَلَیْہِ وَسَلَّمَ وَمَا حَقِیْقَةُ[10] اِیْمَانِکَ فَقَالَ عَرَفْتُ نَفْسِیْ عَنِ الدُّنْیَا
فَاَظْمَاءْتُ نَهَارِیْ وَاَسْهَرْتُ لَیْلِیْ[11] و در نسخه از سلوک ایں قدر زیادت است

۱ ک=مکری ۲ بام=ک- ندارد ۳ تعالیٰ=ح- ندارد ٤ ح=چون
۵ ک=بود ٦ (چون تا آمد)=ک- ندارد ۷ ک=مخول ۸ ک=برا
۹ ح=علامت ۱۰ علامت=ح- ندارد ۱۱ ح=لیل

وَ اَبِیتُ عِندَ رَبِّی یُطعِمُنِی وَ یُسقِینِی فقال النبی صلے اللہ علیہ وسلم[۱] اصبت فالزم

اکنوں ازیں حدیث تمام کیفیت وصال حق تحقیق شد اگر نادانی برای ~~لت~~ بی پرهیزی[۲] لت ازان عا

بیان کند محققانِ سلوک صدق و متشرعان اہل معنی کجا باور کنند و نادر سری

باشد کہ از بندۂ خود کہ یک قرن ملازم بود مخفی داشتہ باشند و در استغراق

و مشاہدہ بارہا این کاتب حاضر بودی[۳] مخدوم[۴] را ہرگز این عادت نبود کہ کشف اسرار کنند اما نکردندی[۵]

[در ؟]

زیراچہ انفاق اہل[۶] سلوک است کہ افشاء سِر ربوبیت خوف کفرات زیاعی[۷]

	قلندری زکوتہ نظر ~~نیست~~	تمکین و ادب زغایت را ہبرنیست[۹]	
	سِرّے بزبان شرع می باید گفت	گفتن بزبان دیگر از بے ہنر است	

افشای[۸]

دیگر چوں خیلخانہ خدمت نبیا این مؤلف مولانا عبدالسلام از ولایت سورتھ

[۱۰] بازگشت ایام صیام عاشورہ بود پسران و اقارب مولانا و این مؤلف بحضرت بندگی

قطب زمان شیخ جہان ادام اللہ برکاتہ برای پابوس آمدند ہر یکے در راہ نیتی کرد

یکے گفت اگر بندگی مخدوم امروز مارا افطار بکنانند چہ خوب باشد

دیگرے گفت ~~کہ~~[۱۱] نان و گوشت گرم بخورانند خوب تر باشد سوم گفت تنکہا بقرہ

ہمہ را مرحمت کنند اولی تر باشد[۱۲] چہارم گفت بوا نغزگان است اگر نغزک بسیار

رسد کرامت شیخ باشد چوں دولت پابوس حاصل شد ہمہ را پیش خود در دہلیز مبارک

۱ ک= سقیننی ۲ ح= پرہیزی ۳ ک= بود ٤ مخدوم تا نبود= ک- ندارد
۵ اما نکردندی= ک- ندارد ٦ اہل= ک- ندارد ۷ ک= دیگر ۸ افشای= ح- ندارد
۹ ح= بریزی است ۱۰ ک= بار ۱۱ ح= و ۱۲ ح= او بہتر

شاناند قضارا کار خیر نائبه بود و برای بندگی شیخ بر خبسی طعام فرستاد از کرامت فرمود
شما مسافرید صوم افطار کنید طعام مذکور را با ایشان در جماعت خانه فرستادند
و فرمودند بفراغ خاطر بخورید در عقب نعمت کهای بسیار فرستادند بعده طبق براز
تنکهای نقره مرحمت فرمودند هر یکی چنانچه نیت کرده بود مراد خود یافت و اینچنین
خوارق بندگی مخدوم را هر روز چند بار افتادی هم ازین جهت سلطان احمد طاب ثراه
میگفت شیخ احمد شرف باطن اند و سلطان احمد بر هر درویشی اعتقاد نکردی
اما برای همین که از بندگی قطب زمان شیخ جهاں دامت برکاته چوں معاملات متواتر
و متوالی دید مخلص شد **حکایت** شیخ زاده احمد کرمانی میگفت چوں پسر
پرواز کهنبایتی اسمه علی از بندگی قطب زمان شیخ جهاں دامت برکاته باز گشت
باران خود می گفت که چشمهای شیخ احمد از چشمهای اهل واردات است یکی آغاز کرد
با مدار ایشان گاهی چیزی ندیدیم شیخ علی گفت چشمهای تو مرض دارد **روزی**
مولانا علاء الدین چهابکله مخصوص از شهر نهرواله قصد کرده در سرکهیج رسید تا ملاقات با
مخدوم کند روز جمعه بندگی مخدوم در مسجد جامع خاص بودند مولانا مذکور از
در جنوبی نظر بر مخدوم کرد همان زمان باز گشت یاران گفتند چندین قصد کرده آمده
بودید ملاقات چرا نکردید گفت ترسیدیم نظری دارد که از سر که سخنی بی مزاج

۱ طعام = ح - ندارد ۲ ح = چنچ ۳ ح = خارق ۴ ک = همین که از برای
۵ حکایت = ک - ندارد ۶ ح = پسر پیر پرواز ۷ ک = چهابکله

بشنود او را بسوزد **دیگر** در آنکه سلطان محمد تاتار خان در بادشاهی شست خلق ناگور

از محصری چوں نفسہ عامے[1] خلاصی یافتہ در گجرات آمدند ایں مؤلف ہم در رکاب استاد

خود ملک بدہ بدین جبال با کمال و بوسید ن نعال بے مثال بندگی شیخ رسیدند

خواجہ خضر سعید[2] کہتووال ہم بود چوں نزدیک خانہ قاضی منصور و قاضی حسین رسیدیم

ملک بدہ گفت ہوا گرم و تشنگی زور آوردہ است چہ خوب اگر بندگی مخدوم

بجرد پا بوس آب سرد بخورانند چوں بپا بوس مشرف شدیم در حال موجود خدمت گار

را اشارت شد برائے ملک زادہ[3] آب سرد بسیار ہوا گرم است و تشنہ آمدہ اند

و کشورہ پر کردہ بخورانید[4] **دیگر** گاہے خطیب مسجد جامع خاص بندگی قطب زمان

شیخ جہاں دامت برکاتہ اسمہ محمد علی در احمد آباد رفتہ بود مشایخ و اکابر شہر را

شخصے در ولیمہ خود دعوت کردہ بود سماع در دادند خطیب مذکور را ہم در سماع وقتی

شد شیخ ابو الفتح باری[5] و مولانا نظام الدین سر خرہ در حلقہ سماع می گشتند سر خرہ را نظر

بر خطیب افتاد ایں را ہم در حلقہ در آورد چوں فارغ شدند خطیب را سر خرہ گفت ارادت

کجا داری گفت بر بندگی شیخ احمد کھٹو گفت پیر اوریش می تراشید خطیب بحضرت بندگی

قطب زمان شیخ جہاں دامت برکاتہ کیفیت مذکور ہمیں کہ عرضہ داشت در حال بر زبان

مبارک راندند اے گردن مہرۂ او شکستہ کہ بابو را در مجمع ہمچنیں گفت دوم یا سوم روز

---

[1] ح = مفسدی [2] ح = سید کہتوال [3] ح = ملکزادہ را
[4] آوردہ = ک۔ ندارد [5] ح = ماری

مادیان سوار در بلندی یا نشیب خانه برمی آمد از مادیان افتاده[1] گردن مهره شکست و کمر هم[2] ماند دوله بکردند بخانه بردند سپری شد **دیگر** مولانا قاسم بن محمد سنبهری دانشمند ان بنده بود بزدوی[3] ضبط داشت با کاروان ناگور بصحبت بدر آمده بود و بر بندگی مخدوم آمد[4] و چیزے بحث بزدوی[3] برکرد سفره زبان نداشت تربیت نیافته بود ادب مجلس مشائخ رعایت[5] نکردی[6] بی محابا سخن گذار کرد بندگی قطب زمان شیخ جهان دامت برکاته هیبت زدند و فرمودند باندیشه سخن گوئی همان تپ کرد قاسم مذکور را گرفت در دو سه روزے جان داد **دیگر** روزے سید رضی[7] بر سید خاصه نیز از دینه وانه آمده با خیلنی نه خود در بصر و بج سکونت گرفته بودند و سید رضی مذکور نوافل بسیار گذاردی یک روز در خیال او آمد سوالی بنشست که تسما روشن است که این[8] سائل چندین صلوٰة دارد دلی است سادات خیلنی نه از اخوان واو[9] در آن گواهی بنشستند بعده در سر کهیج آمد بندگی قطب زمان شیخ جهان دامت برکاته را مزاحم شد که شما هم کتبه کنید بندگی بر حکم حدیث قدسی که اَولیائی تحت قبائی لا یعرفهم غیری یعنی غیر حق ولی را کسی بتحقیق مدرک نشود و آنکه بخصلتی با اعتقاد در وهم کسی در آید از مبحث خارج است سید رضی را منع فرمودند سید سخت گو نه بودند مذلق گوئی آغاز کردند و الفاظ بیرون افتادگان گویان از مجلس برخاست مخدوم را سخت رنجانیده

۱ ک= ندارد ۲ ح=کتر ۳ ک=پزدوی ۴ ح و ک = "آورد" تصحیح قیاسی
۵ ک= اعانت ۶ ح=کردی ۷ ک=رضی الله ۸ ک=آن ۹ ک-واو= ندارد

در بھروچ بازگشت، همدرین ولوله از خانه بیرون آمده راه جنگل نوساری گرفت ناپیدا نه، کسے را معلوم نشد که کجا رفت برادران بسیار داشت، هرچند که در قصبات و قریات دور و نزدیک تتبع کردند کسے نشانی[1] نگفت و نیز بندگی قطب زمان شیخ جهان دامت[2] برکاته میفرمودند که درویشان تیغ برهنه اند یعنی چون تیغ[3] برهنه در مقام تاریک[4] باشد، هرکه از بیرون بیاید دست و پاے او[5] بران تیغ بیفتد، ضرورت خراشیده گردد، تیغ راچه گناه نهند سخن فضول بیش مشائخ همیں بار آرد **دیگر** قاضی خاصه عبدالملک[6] که یکے از قاضی بچگان قاضی فخر الدین حاکم قصبه کهٹو بود بر والدهٔ خود مسماة بیبی خواندا[7] گفت، پیراهن من[8] پاره شده است، در سرکهیج بروم از مخدوم نه گز جامه بستانم، واگر ناگفته بدهند کرامت ایشان ظاهر شود والدهٔ او معتقدهٔ بندگی مخدوم بود هر[9] چند منع کرد او نماند در سرکهیج آمده پابوس شیخ کرد، مخدوم عبدالحی را گفتند در صندوق جامه که هست بیار، آورد هشت گز بود فرمودند یک گز دیگر را وجه بده اجرت دوختن پیراهن هم تسلیم بکن تا[10] قاضی خاصه پیراهن بپوشد و قاضی را بدست مبارک گوشمال دادند و فرمودند درویشان را امتحان مکنید **دیگر** بندگی قطب زمان شیخ جهان ادام الله برکاته[11] بر مؤلف در خلوت میفرمودند که شبے در خواب بودم[12]

۱ ح = بنشانی ۲ ح = دام الله ۳ ح = شیخ ٤ تاریک = ح - ندارد
۵ او = ک - ندارد ٦ ک = ابولمحک ۷ ح = خواندا ۸ من = ک = ندارد
۹ ک = هم ۱۰ تا = ک - ندارد ۱۱ ح دامت برکاته ۱۲ ح = بوده ایم

چشم کشادیم چه بینیم جانورے بر روی ما آمده در بوالرزان می پرید مؤلف
عرضه کرد مگر آن همائی بود که بر سر پادشاهان سایه می[1] افگند فرمودند قضیه هم چنین
بود والله اعلم واعجب الخوارق[2] ما وقع فی سفر الحج بموضع لا دره[3] وفقد الثیاب بجزیرة[4]
عدن وغیرها. **دیگر** یک بار ماری سهمناکے که در خانه بدابوهره
پیدا شد چندروزی نمودار گردید و غایب شدی یک شبے برای تهجد برخاستیم
مار مذکور در دوم پایه[5] نردبان دروازه از بالا آمده نشست هرچند که گفتیم بر و نرفت
ضرورت تیر او بکفایت رسانیدیم زدیم و بیرون انداختیم هر که میدید تعجب میکرد
که این چنین مار بزرگ قوی را جز شیخ کسے نکشته بار در خانه نو که آمدیم کژدمی بزرگ
پیدا شد در پاے نیشش زد بعنایت الله زهر او هیچ اثر نکرد و ما در ساعت جان داد
کما ورد لحوم الاولیاء مسمومة و قریب سنه ۸۴۰ھ اربعین و ثمانمایه خارشی[6]
بالاے ارنج مبارک پیدا شد خاریدند و مؤلف را فرمودند ملاں نظر کن چیست
بنده دید که نار و سر کشیده بنده را سخت اندوه بیش آمد فرمودند[7] تعلقی نیست
قدرے لعاب مبارک بر پا مالیدند نا پیدا شد و هیچ تشویش نداد روایت هم
از خطیب است که او را چهار پسر شدند و در خوردگی فوت گشتند روزی بندگی
قطب زمان شیخ جهان ادام[8] الله برکاته میانه روز در حوض مبارک غوط در آمدند

۱ می = ک - ندارد ۲ ک = الخورق ۳ ح = لاودره ٤ ح = الجریدة
۵ پایهٔ = ح - ندارد ٦ خارشی = ح - ندارد ۷ ح = وفرمودند ۸ ک = دامت

وجود مبارک می شستند چون بیرون آمدند من رسیدم شکسته خاطر بیمار بچه گم کرده عرض داشتیم که چندین معتقدان را به برکات انفاس متبرکه فرزندان نرینه دراز عمر شده اند در باب این شکسته هم دعا باشد که پسری دراز عمری روزی شود در رومال مبارک قرنفلی چند بسته بودند کشادند و منظور خود گردانیدند بعده بدست من دادند و فرمودند امشب شما هر دو بخورید و بخسپید چون در خانه باز گشتم والده[1] خورد کان صفه را در احمدآباد می برد گفتیم این را بگذارید علی الصباح من خواهم برد همچنان کردیم ماه دوم بندگی قطب زمان شیخ جهان دامت برکاته بنده را خود پرسیدند چیزی از هست خانه را پرسیدم گفت پنج روز بر نوبت بر رفته است بحضرت مخدوم گذرانیدم شکر خدای بجا آوردند دران بار شیخ فرید تولد شده و کرامتهای بندگی قطب زمان شیخ جهان ادام الله برکاته[2] هر روز میان عامه مؤمنان ظاهر می شد، حکایت سلطان احمد طاب ثراه دو بار در استسقا التماس کرده[3] فرستاد فرمودند امید است درین جمعه ببارد همچنان شد **دیگر** مولانا حافظ الدین را که یکے از اکابر دہلی بود میان خطۂ ساول در سلوک اشکالے شد که مردم اگر فکرے پیش آید که من از کدام زمره ام چه کنند شیخ دیگر از فرزندان شیخ بهاء الدین زکریا[4] که سلطان محمد مظفر او را شیخ اسلامی[5] داده بود مولانا را گفت

١ح = ویلده ک= ویللد ٢ک=دامت برکاته
٣ح=کرد ٤ک=ذکریا ٥ک=اسلام

که این معنی از بندگی قطب زمان شیخ جهان دامت برکاتہٗ شیخ احمد کھٹو تحقیق شود

مولانا او را گفت ایشان[1] را چیزے پیش می آرند از ان نمی رسد گی بخدمت ایشان

رفته نمی شود شما هم بیایید این بار[2] بردیم و این مقام تحقیق کنیم و برهان ایشان

همین باشد که ما را چیزے ندهند ملاقات شد مولانا اشکال مذکور گذرانید

مخدوم فرمودند در خود نظر باید کرد که اعمال کدام زمره رجحان دارد بران حکم کنند

مولانا گفت اگر هر دو دارد مخدوم فرمودند هر دو را از نظر خود طرح کند و[3] از سر متوجه

حضرت شود و به پناه او در آید که اِنّی وَجَّھْتُ وَجْھِیَ لِلَّذِیْ فَطَرَ السَّمٰوٰتِ وَالْاَرْضَ

حَنِیْفًا وَّمَا اَنَا مِنَ الْمُشْرِکِیْنَ اَنَا اَوَّلُ الْمُسْلِمِیْنَ مولانا را در جواب ذوقی دست

داد و بندگی مخدوم را از نیت مولانا وقوف شد که چیزی نخواهد ستد یک تنکه زر

علائی بزرگ آوردند و فرمودند این را بکسے بدهند مولانا در تحیرشد که زہے کشف

و صفاء باطن که مخدوم راہست دل ایشان بجام جهان نمای مانند تنکه مذکور

گرفت بازگشت مخدوم هم بغیر کفش تا آستانه مولانا رسانیدند مولانا چون

مخدوم را پای برهنه دید دوید کفشها مخدوم را از مقام آورد و پیش داشت[4] بر

مصاحب گفت تنکه فقرا را دهانید تا مرا جاے افتراض نماند **دیگر** برهان کشف

مخدوم آن خوابی که سر مقدم موضع او تیلیه شب را نجواب برید[5] دیدند چون روز شد

1ح = ایشا 2ک = بار 3ک = ندارد 4 'و' = ح - ندارد 5 دیدند - ک - ندارد

سراو برید ند ملک اودهرن ناک[1] کارکن قصبه دهولقه سراو برید چنانکه در فصل
خوابها مکلف[2] مذکوراست **دیگر** درآنکه در بلاد گوجرات خلق را کرمها بیرون آمدن
گرفت از قصبه مهراسه[3] داماد این مؤلف آمد گفت پسر بزرگ تمارا سم علامت
بیرون آمده است مؤلف را پای از ته رفت کم ماند[4] بر بندگی قطب زمان شیخ جهان
دامت برکاته گذرانیدم برای[5] وداع پیاده بیرون آمدند[6] داماد بامنی را در موضع باسنه
آورده[7] رسانید و گفت نفس بندگی شیخ هم چنین شده است که[8] پسر ترا باکی نیست
تعلقی مکنی اما[9] مؤلف را[9] میان راه قرار وآرام نبود طعام وآب خوش نمی آمد چون نفس
مخدوم شنیدم[10] امدا خاطر شد سید نصیر قاسم ناگوری دوم روز در راه مهراسه رسید
بخوف نه پرسیدم سید خود آغاز کرد پسر تمارا استفا[11] شد کنیزک گفت خدایا
بلا در میان[12] ما در ابده همان زمان کنیزک را علامت بیرون آمد سیری شد علامت
میتهن[12] در بخت آمد صحت شد و این مقام کشف از بندگی قطب زمان شیخ جهان
دامت برکاته این مؤلف را و خلق دیگر را بارها معاینه شده است صحیح چنانچه[13]
میان بابو پسر قاضی بده از اولاد شیخ جیلانی[14] میگفت که سلطان احمد درآنکه مهم[15] ناگور
کرد خبر آمد که ذا انفر از لشکر محلی[16] تلف شدند یکی از ایشان قاضی بده بود من ترسان
ولرزان بر پیر خود قطب زمان شیخ جهان دامت برکاته[17] رفتم خادم را اشارت شد که میان بابو

۱ ح = ناک ک = ماک ۲ ک = میگفت ۳ ک = موراسه ۴ ک = وقوة کم ماند
۵ برای = ح - ندارد ۶ ح = آمده ۷ ح = آورد ۸ که = ک - ندارد ۹ اما - را = ح -
ندارد ۱۰ ح = شنید ۱۱ ازینجا تا ورق نسخهٔ ک افتادگی دارد ۱۲ ح = مستن
۱۳ ح = چنچ ۱۴ ح = جیلا ۱۵ ح = سهم ۱۶ ح = مجله ۱۷ دامت برکاته = ح - ندارد

درست

بتیس بطلب چون بجمالِ جہان آرای لقای مبارک مشرف شدم قصه مذکور آغاز کردم اشارت شد با ما کیفیت معلوم شده است شما خاطر جمع دارید پدر شما بصحت وسلامت است هیچ تعلق نیست چون سلطان در شهر نهر واله رسید باز فرمودند بابا پدر شما با لشکر در شهر پتن بصحت وسلامت رسیده است همچنان[۱] خدمت والد بصحت وسلامت رسید الحمد لله علیٰ ذلک بندگی قطب زمان شیخ جهان ادام الله برکاته[۲] را عجب عادتی بود چون کسی چیزی از مغیبات پرسیدی دو انگشت مبارک ابهام و بنصر[۳] در مقدم دو چشم مبارک می نهادند وسبابه و وسطی را درمیان بینی میداشتند و در استغراق ساعتی می ماندند طالب را حاجتی که می بود من الله تعالیٰ در زمان در باطن مبارک ایشان تلقی[۴] می شد بشارت می دادند دیگر سید خاصه و سید اسمٰعیل ساداتِ دینه وانه برای مقرر داشت[۵] در دهلی رفته بود ند کار ایشان حواله قاضی نصر الله حاکم شهر سمندهی[۶] سلطان محمد فیروز شد قاضی ایشان را رد کرد که شما صدر الدین میت را که او در شما باشد پسران چگونه بنویسانید سید خاصه در مسجد خانجهان دست بر کمر نهاده دور می زد و می گفت الٰهی ببرکت فلان شیخ و ببرکت فلان پیران حاجت ما را آر بندگی قطب زمان شیخ جهان دامت برکاته می گفتند که سید خاصه را گفتیم شما یگان بنفته

۱ک = ندارد ۲ک = دامت برکاته ۳ک = بنصره
۴ح = ملقی ۵ک = مقرداست ۶سندی = ح

هر پیری[۱] را تشفیع آرید درنفقه عرض شما حاصل شود بدانید که برکت آن

پیر شد سید فصیح[۲] دانا بود درحال عرضه داشت که ما اول هم شما[۱] تشفیع می آریم

ملکی بود ابراهیم نام سرجامداران سلطان محمد مذکور را ور طلبیدیم عرضه داشت ایشان

بردست او دادیم که بر سلطان بگذران و متعرر داشت ایشان بردست بیار

ملک ابراهیم همان روز گذرانید فرمان شد بر قاضی نصرالله فرمان برسان

قاضی گفت ایشان را تصحیح بکنم ملک گفت ایشان هدایه[۳] بزدوی[۴] تصحیح شده

اند قاضی گفت چگونه گفت شیخ احمد کهتو مبینت کرده اند فرمان شد چنانچه[۵] رضای

شیخ است بر وفق بنویس قاضی کار در تعلل انداخت ملک ابراهیم گفت

اگر اشارت مخدوم شود جامها که دوم سیوم روز که اورا میدهانید[۶] من هم در تعلل

اندازم گفتیم سوم همچنان کرد قاضی گفت تو تعلل میکنی من بر سلطان خواهم گفت

ملک گفت شما در پروانگی چرا تعلل میکنید قاضی بر سلطان گفت جامها

که فرمان شده بود ملک ابراهیم هنوز نداده است ملک ابراهیم از فرمان شد

چرا نمیدهی عرضه داشت کسوت خاص هنوز مرتب نشده است قاضی دید که

عنه محکم آورد. درحال پروانگی نبشت داد میان دو سه روز ملک ابراهیم

فرمان مرتب کرده برما آورد سادات را دادیم و خرج راه هم[۷] پیش آوردیم

---

۱ ک= پیر ۲ 'و' = ح- ندارد ۳ "و" = ح- ندارد ۴ ک= پزدوی
۵ ح= چنچ ۶ ک= میدہانند ۷ ک=راه که

شادان وخوشحال بازگردانیدیم **دیگر** قاضی عبدالرزاق مبارک والوالجی[2] را
که یکی از ملازمان مخلص بود و عهدهٔ کتاب خانه وکتابت داشت واورا قاضی بدهٔ
مبارک میگویند در انگشت بنصر[3] پایه رشته بیرون آمد بندگی قطب زمان
شیخ جهان دامت برکاته در[5] یک روز تقصیر افتاد دوم روز بخدمت[4] آمد
فرمودند کجا بودی کیفیت نار وعرضه داشت اشارت شد پیشتر آی پیشتر آی
مرا نیمای از حسن ادبی که دران درگاه داشت پیشتر نمی شد چون جهد بلیغ
فرمودند بضرورت نزدیک آمد لعاب مبارک بانگشت مبارک بر نارو
نهادند درحال شفا شد **دیگر** عبدالرحمن مولی اسلام خدمتگار قدیم
را مارگزید[6] در حضرت بندگی قطب زمان شیخ جهان دامت برکاته آمد[7] فریاد کرد
لعاب مبارک برکاز او نهادند در زمان شفا شد **دیگر** خدمت سید مکرم
اکرم را هم در راه دهار مارگزید سید بندگی قطب زمان شیخ جهان دامت برکاته را[8]
شفیع آورد که مرا با مان حق سپرده اند که سلامت خواهی رفت هلا شیخ احمد زهر که
بالا شده بود فرو شدن گرفت در حال شفا شد هیچ زهر مار اثر نه کرد
دیگر مریدی بود از قصبه پتلاود شنید که برادر اورا که در دیهه بود علت خنازیر
پیدا آمد سخت محزون شد شخصی اورا گفت که از کاچک سر آدمی قدری رسانید

۲ ح = والوالجی ۳ ک = بنصره ۴ بخدمت = ح ـ ندارد ۵ آمدند در
۶ ک = گذید ۷ آمده = ک ـ ندارد ۸ را = ح ـ ندارد

بر خنزیر بہ بالین شفا نشود محلے کاچک آدمی افتادہ بود از ان قدری

شکستم شدم و بندگی قطب زمان شیخ جہان دامت برکاتہ آمدم و کیفیت

علت آن برادر گذرانیدم و ہیچ کاچک نکردم بندگی مخدوم فرمودند

تعلق نیست و خنزیر نباشد شفا نخواہد شود اما از آدمی بعد مردن تعرض باعضاء

او نہ رسانید کہ در حدیث است میت را ادراک باقی است شرمندہ شدم

بہ یقین دانستم کہ شیخ را از کیفیت کاچک کشف شد توبہ کردم پشیمان شدم

دیگر یکبار جوگی بعد وفات خدمت بابو در کھٹور سید بر کوہ کھٹو بر آمد بالا ہنگی

پاہا لسان گذاشتہ نشست ہر کہ او را ملاقات می شد بر فور نام او و نام مادر وپدر و برادران

او میگفت خلق کھٹو تمام بر وے رفتند دیدند ہر یکے از و در تعجب شدہ کہ ما و

ناحہا از کجا می ہٰذا اند و حی گوید در خانہ فلان غنیمت است و در خانہ فلان

فقیر است سید اکرم بندگی قطب زمان شیخ جہان دامت برکاتہ آمد عرضہ داشت

کہ فتنہ در کھٹو قایم شد اینچنین جوگی آمدہ است خلق را از راہ می بر د بندگی مخدوم

قاضی نیکو نام خادمی داشتند بر دست او پنج خرما دادہ فرستادند قاضی نیکو را

چون جوگی دید گفت شما را برمن شیخ فرستادہ و پنج خرما فرستادہ اند و طلبیدہ اند

شما باز گردید صباح را می آیم ہوشیار باشید صباح را رسید بر تختہا در لکد محکم زد

۱ ک = برنیش ۲ بخدمت = ح ـ ندارد ۳ مذکور = ح ـ ندارد ۴ ح = نرساند
۵ ک = درک ۶ ک = لقان ۷ و برادران = ح ـ ندارد ۸ ک = عجب
۹ ح = غنیست ۱۰ ح = فقر ۱۱ بخدمت = ح ـ ندارد

بچنانچه دیوارها شنیده و نعره برآورد[1] همسایگان را هیبت افتاد بندگی حضرت

شیخ جهان قطب زمان در کت دنده درون طلبیدند[2] فرمودند بااو تا اشراق

فارغ نشدیم تکلم نکردیم چون فارغ شدیم هرچه اوگفت جواب اوگفتیم

اصطلاح

و از خدمت بندگی حضرت بابو در ابتان حوایت شده بود و خللی که

در قواعد ایشان بود ثابت کردیم و دلایل[2] توحید گفتیم ملزم شد و بروایت

قاضی بده والواجی[3] مذکور شاگردی ذات مسلم نیس در بود درون طلبیدند گفت

چیلا حضرت شیخ مرد بزرگ مرد است چه باید کرد گفت هرچه بفرمائید باید شنید

اسلام عرض کردم مسلمان شد باز گردانیدم و بروایت شیخ احمد کرمانی[4] سه روز

در حجره بود **دیگر** بندگی حضرت شیخ جهان قطب زمان داعت برکاته[5] بفرمودند گاهی بتفرج[6]

از کهتو بیرون رفتیم در جنگل جوگی را دیدیم بی تاب افتاده بر سیر او رسیدیم

برحمت[7] رشته پای سخت آماس کرده سخن نمی توان گفتن[8] اشارت کرد که آب بخورانید[9] چیاو

راستا یاران[10] را فرستادیم یکی خبر جای بیاورد در حال کهیپ[11] بریدیم رسنی تافتیم

سبو بود جا بها برسن بستیم تر کرده کشیدیم آب خورانیدیم چون بهوش آمد

در خانه آوردیم تدوی کردیم شفا یافت عذر خواهی بسیار کرد گفت علمی

داریم بندگی شما را مخفی بنمایم سفالی[12] گرم کرد مس انداخت مواز نه چند تولچه[13]

برگی از گیاهی آورد شیلید بر آن مس انداخت مواز نه یک کرلیه[14] زر خالص شد

1. برآورد که ک 2. ک= دایل 3. ح= والوالجی 4. کرمانی =ح= ندارد
5. داعت برکاته= ح- ندارد 6. بتفرج =ک 7. برحمت = ح- ندارد
8. ک= نمی توانست گفت 9. ح= بخورید 10. را= ح- ندارد
11. ک=کهیت 12. ح= سقابی 13. ح= تولچه چند 14. ک=کرماله

بنده[1] مولف عرض داشت بندگی حضرت مخدوم آن گیاه را می شناسند فرمودند آری می شناسیم اما کسانی را که گنج ها غیب[2] خود حق سبحانه وتعالی همه نعمتها[3] نقود آماده برساند او در آتش چرا بیفتد در مقام توکل چگونه بگذارد دیگ فرن بنده ملازمت داشت هیچ وقتی ازین حکایتی و ملامتی ندید پیش سلطان احمد بعضی حساد گفتند که شیخ احمد علم کیمیا دارد همین که مولانا سیف الدین معلم حاضر شد فرمان شد مولانا بعضی امروز می گفتند که شیخ احمد کیمیا دارد عرض کرد کیمیاء حضرت شیخ دعاگوئی بندگی حضرت تخت اعلی است فرمان شد راست میگوئی چون مولانا سیف الدین این کیفیت پیش بندگی حضرت مخدوم گذرانید بازگشت در خلوت به بنده[3] را فرمودند درویشان[4] بعنایت حق سبحانه[5] تعالی همه هست کیمیا هم مانند کیمیا هم یکی از[6] خوارق است:

یک ذره عنایت تو ای بنده نواز	بهتر ز هزار سال تسبیح و نماز

دیگر گاهی سلطان احمد بر دست شهزاده شادی خان و شنکر خان هزار تنکه زر و نقره خلط کرده[7] بخدمت بندگی حضرت شیخ جهان قطب زمان عز رستا دامت برکاته فوطه وار[8] را فرمان شد برابر ایشان برود تسلیم کند شادی خان نیت کرده بود[9] که اگر شیخ مرا لقمه کهچڑی و یا چیز دیگر پس خورده خود مرحمت کنند[10] چه خوب باشد و شنکر خان نیت کرد که مرا تنکه نقره بدهند فوطه دار گفت من هم

---

۱ ک= بعده ۲ ح= گنج از غیب ک = ازغیب گنج ۳ ح= بربنده را
٤ ح و ک = ندارد۔اضافۂ قیاسی ۵ ح= ندارد ٦ ح = ندارد ۷ ک=خواق
۸ ح= ندارد ۹ ک= پوطه دار ۱۰ ح= ندارد ۱۱ ح=کنند

بیک خرما اکتفا میکنم همیں که شادی خان پرسید (رسید) اشارت شد شمار نان و گوشت می برند دو تنکه نقره شکر خان را[1] دادند فوطه دار وداع خواست دو خرما مرحمت کردند و فرمودند درویشان را امتحان نه کنند این حکایت از خطیب مولانا محمد است که بر من همیں فوطه دار گفته بود در آنکه من برای وظیفه رفته بودم[2] گفت شما از کجا ئید گفتم از سر کهیچ گفت چه هنر دارید گفتیم[3] من خطیب مسجد جامع بندگی حضرت شیخ ام عادت بندگی حضرت مخدوم این بود چون کسے التماس فرزند می کرد اگر همان زمان دست مبارک برآورده سوی آسمان هُوَ الْمُعْطِی می گفتند و فاتحه می خواندند تحقیق غرض و حاصل شدی و اگر میفرمودند برای خیریت ایشان فاتحه بخوانیم حصول مقصود اندک بودی و بارها میفرمودند که کسانے را که فرزند نمی شود و ایشان[4] جهد[5] گوشش میکنند[6] که بنوعی فرزند شود بجبرد شود[7] که فرزند یا[8] پدر را خطر وجود پدید میشود[9] یا[8] مادر را[10] این معنی بارها معاینه شده است بهتر آن ست که راضی بقضاء الله شوند و این بیت را بلفظ کرم کرده بنده[11] می خواندند

بر دست ما نیست عنان ارادتی	بگذاشتیم تا قضا[12] او چه میکند

دیگر[13] از کرامت های بندگی حضرت شیخ جهان قطب زمان[14] دامت برکاته آن بود که دستار از غیب ایشان را رسیده بود و کیفیت آن آنست که بندگی حضرت مخدوم بعد وفات بندگی حضرت بابو اسحاق همان طاقیه که در ایام وقت وفات بدست

١ ک = برای شکرخان ٢ ح = بودیم ٣ ک = ندارد ٤ ک = اوشان ٥ ح = ندارد ٦ ح = میکند ٧ ح = ندارد ٨ ح = یا ٩ ح = بدید ١٠ ح = ندارد ١١ ح = بنده بلفظ ١٢ کذا درهردو نسخه اینجا شاید "که قضایش باشد ١٣ ک = ندارد ١٤ ح = ندارد

مبارک خود خدمت بندگی حضرت[1] بابو برسر بندگی حضرت مخدوم نهاده بو[2]

بوشید[3] می مانند دستار نمی بستند روزی در مسجد خانجهان وقت قیلوله شخصی

بارانی پوشیده دراز قد و پهن ریش خوش اندام در آمد گودکی برابر داشت بدست او

موازنه[4] بیست گز کرباس و گفت مخدوم این دستار به بندید بندگی حضرت مخدوم میفرمودند

ما گفتیم که هنوز شایان[5] دستار نشده ایم گفت خیر مخدوم دستار بپوشید بسیار

خلق از تعظیم شما محروم می شوند[6] شما سبب فرمان[7] می گردید دستار بپوشید

تا خلق از سعادت[8] ملاقات شما بهره مند شوند هر چند که ابا می آورد

او از جهه باز نمی ماند ملک برطریق امر می گفت بپوشید چون خیلی جهد نمود دستار

مذکور بسته شد او بسرعت برخاست رفت شخصی را در پی او بهمان زمان فرستادیم

در نظر وی غایب شد بسیار تتبع کرده آمد که او از کجا بود و که بود کسی نشان[9]

نگفت همه گفتند ما را که خواجه خضر باشند[10] والله اعلم دیگر[11] و پیش ازان هم بندگی

حضرت مخدوم در صحرائی بر[12] چشمه آب بر برسر[13] سنگ تکیه کرده بودند و بر خود درون

خریطه مهری هر جنس داشته بود[14] بعد چند روز یک درویشی آمد در دل گذشت

که او را ازان مهری[15] که بدبند ازگرده[16] یکی[17] مهر کشید[18] و از امید او ندا و نگرفت آغاز کرد مهر

این جا آید او مهر چه کند دبردست او عصا[19] بود بر سنگ زد تمام سنگ

وزمین زر شد و بندگی حضرت مخدوم در دل دانستند[20] که خواجه بود و بندگی حضرت مخدوم

---

۱ ک = ندارد ۲ ح = بود ۳ ک = بوسیده ۴ ک = موزنه ۵ ک = شان
۶ ح = می شود ۷ ح = فرمان ۸ ک = سعادوت ۹ ح = بنشان ۱۰ ح = باشد
۱۱ ح = زاید ۱۲ ح = بر ۱۳ ک = برسر ۱۴ ح = بود ۱۵ ح = ذران ۱۶ ح = کردهٔ او
۱۷ ح = یکی ۱۸ ح = کشید ۱۹ عصائی ۲۰ ح = دانست

همه مهر را بی تاب کردند و الله اعلم دیگر بندگی حضرت شیخ جهان قطب زمان می فرمودند که وقتی مولانا ابراهیم کیتهلی که یکی از کبار مشائخ دهلی بود از مریدان خدمت سید جلال بخاری رحمة الله علیه و دانشمند صاحب وقت بود بریں درویش بسیار آمدی روزی می گفت که شیخ شمس الدین نامے[۱] مردی ست که شبها بملاقات مشائخ می آید و او را مشائخ مرد غیب می گفتند[۲] انتسب با او مجالست بود از و استفسار کردم که در وقت صبا هم کسے را ولایت تواند بود گفت آرے چنانکه شیخ احمد کهٹو که در مسجد خانجهان میماند[۳] که او از خوردگی باز صاحب ولایت است[۴] دیگر از کرامت بندگی حضرت شیخ جهان قطب زمان دامت برکاته[۵] آنست که[۶] سلطان احمد در بادشاهی گجرات نشسته برصورت[۷] امتحان نیم شبی با سواران معدود لغیر میدان[۸] بر در بندگی حضرت مخدوم آمد و کسے را اطلاع نه شد خلقی که در آستانه مبارک خفته بودند همه را مانع شد که کسے حلقه در نزند و علم ندهد بندگی حضرت مخدوم میفرمودند که حق سبحانه و تعالی دران شب ما را این چنین فیض کرد که خواب معتاد هم دست نداد خدمت گار[۸] را فرمودند که[۹] بالاء بام صفه چراغ ببر بمقام مروح است تا باید که دران بسطی دست دهد آنجا هم قرار نه گرفتند در دهلیز آمدند هم انشراح نشد تختها را در باز کردند ناگاه سلطان احمد را دیدند که نشسته اند گفتیم درون[۱۱] دهلیز بیائید[۱۲] دیر[۱۳] باز انتظار[۱۴] این درویش دانسته اید[۱۵] چنین امتحان

۱ ک= ندارد ۲ ک= میگویند ۳ ح= میماند ۴ ک= اند ۵ ح= ندارد ۶ ح= آنکه
۷ ک= برصورت را امتحان میکرد وقتی ۸ ک= آن خدمت گاران
۹ ح= ندارد ۱۰ ک= ببرند ۱۱ ک= درو ۱۲ ح= بیایند ۱۳ ح و ک= دیربا
۱۴ ح= انتظار تو بود ۱۵ ح= اند

چیست که حلقه بر در زدن[1] ندهید[2] سلطان ساکت شد عذر پیش آورد
که ما برائی پابوس بندگی حضرت مخدوم آمده بودیم و چیزے که نیت در دل
کرده شاید شیر برنج یا کھچڑی و چهار کسان دیگر هم چیزے[3] در دل نیت کرده بودند
همان پیش ایشان آوردند سلطان در تعجب ماند و بندگی حضرت مخدوم
فرمودند که پادشاهان را نشاید که با[4] معدود نفران بیرون آیند[5] دیگر در آنکه در
سرکھیچ بندگی حضرت شیخ جهان قطب زمان را کناک زور آورده سلطان احمد
طاب ثراه شنید[6] طبیبی حاذق فرستاد که برو تداوی بکن طبیب نبض مبارک
گرفت گفت منشاء این کناک از خوردن خربزه شده است طبیب را انعام
فرمودند
دادند و باز گردانیدند و[7] خربزها بیارند خربزها همین که خوردند کناک بکلی دفع شد
الحمد لله علی ذالک شفاء تمام شد دیگر از مریدان بندگی حضرت شیخ جهان
دامت برکاته[7]
قطب زمان[7] قاضی عبد الغفار بن طیب می گفت[8] کیے بحضور من[8] مولانا صدر الدین بنبانی
طاب ثراه بخدمت شیخ یک بار رسید گفت امروز با[9] بندگی مخدوم بحثی کنیم
[10] معتقد مائید باشما بحث نمی شاید کردن باز گفت چیزی بحث کنم باز بندگی مخدوم فرمودند شما
بندگی حضرت مخدوم فرمودند شما استادید باشما چه بحث سیوم بار چون مزاحم شد
که
اشارت شد کدام بحث است مولانا بحثی از طوالع آغاز کرد بندگی حضرت مخدوم
متعجب شدند و بنده را اشارت شد که بابا عبد الغفار بشنو مولانا چه می گویند بنده
از خود برفت در مباحثت شد نمیدانم چه گفت اما بحث تمام کرد مولانا گفت[11]

۱ ک= دروازه زدند ۲ ح= ندهند ۳ ک= ندارد ۴ ک= ندارد ۵ ح= آید
۶ ح= شنید ۷ ح= ندارد ۸ ح= ندارد ۹ ک= ندارد ۱۰ ح= ندارد
۱۱ این جمله تمام در نسخهٔ ک، نیست۔

از کجا میگوئی بعده بندگی حضرت مخدوم فرمودند هم از طوالع مولانا گفت
طوالع بسیار اند اشارت شد درون[1] صفحه[2] جلد لعل است بیار این مؤلف بیاورد
اشارت شد بکشا چون بنده بکشاد همان محل بیرون آمد بندگی حضرت مخدوم
مطالعه نمودند و بمولانا دادند مولانا مطالعه کرد بعده اشارت شد در پای مولانا بیفت
مولانا گفت این بحث این[7] خرد کس نیست نبود بود آز آنجا که بود[3] بعده روغن و کهچڑی
آرانیده اند و مرا نیز اشارت شد که با مولانا طعام بخور بنده صایم بود و آفتاب
از سر گذشته بود اما نگفت که مرا صوم است با مولانا طعام خورد بندگی حضرت مخدوم
مولانا را یک تنکه نقره[4] و دو تنکه را خرده و یک قطعه بهیرم[5] دادند باز گردانیده اند
بنده را گفتند که اگر صوم باشد مرا اعلم باید داد[6]
بنده ایستاده عرض نمود که صوم را قضائی و کفارت نیست و صوم نفل[7] را
قضا نیست که بدان مستحق گردد اما در نفس پیر را نه قضا و نه کفارت که بدان ایجاز شود
پس لاحماله اطاعت باید کرد بندگی حضرت مخدوم بغایت خوش شدند و[8] دعا کردند
قاضی عبد الغفار مذکور می گفت این فقیر را مهم کار خیر دو دختر پیش آمد بندگی
حضرت شیخ جهان قطب زمان دامت برکاته عرض داشت دو تنکه زر و چهار قطعه
فرنگی[9] فی[10] الحال مرحمت کردند و فرمودند از احمد آباد که باز گردی این جا باز بیائی بعد
چند روز از احمد آباد این فقیر باز گشت بحضرت بندگی مخدوم آمد دو طاقه سالو
و دو بهیرم[11] و دو تسر بتی و چهل پهدیه و سی هشت تنکه را خرده دیگر دادند و دعا برکت

[1] ک = درو [2] ح = ندارد [3] ک = از آنجا بود [4] ک = ندارد [5] ک = بهیرو
[6] ح = ندارد [7] ک = ندارد [8] ک = ندارد [9] ک = فرتکی [10] ح = ندارد
[11] ک = بهیرو [11] ح = ندارد

کردند باعتقاد تمام این فقیر ستده در شهر نهرواله رفت و در خریطه سی[1] و هشت تنکه
خرده و چهل پهده[؟] فیروزی انداخت و در کار خیر ها شروع کرده خرچ ازان
می کرد و کتابت می آورد موازنه[2] هفت صد تنکه در حساب آمد چون خریطه نگاه کرد هنوز
چیزی هشت[3] خریطه گشت دشمار کرد آن چهل پهده[؟] فیروزی و سی هشت[1] را خرده موجود
یافت بر والد خود قاضی طیب کیفیت مذکور عرض کرد فرمودند اگر آن را شمار نمی کردی
و خرچ میکردی تا روز قیامت برکت همچنین می[4] بود مؤلف بیچاره مثل آن کرامت
از زبان بندگی حضرت مخدوم در کیفیت سمرقند در قلم آورده است که نسخهٔ
سمرقند را معاینه شده است نظر باید کرد دیگر[5] بتاریخ دوم بماه شوال سنه تسع و
اربعین دتمانمایة[؟] سید احمد عرب بحضور ملک عمدة الملک ابو المعالی د
دلاورخان[6] و مولانا امام بن شیخ امام سلطان محمد بن سلطان احمد طاب ثراه
و حسام الدین قندزی[7] و معارف دیگر گفت مدة دو سال باشد شیخ یحیی
خلیفهٔ شیخ عمر جبیلی در کهنبایت[؟] آمده بود میگفت چون طرف هند مسافرت
اختیار کردم شیخ عمر جبیلی فرمود سرکهیج نام قصبهٔ در گجرات است بندگی
حضرت شیخ جهان قطب زمان دامت برکاته قدوة السالکین بندگی شیخ احمد
آنجا اند سلام من برایشان برسانی و بگوئی چهار سال و[8] چند ماه شده است
که شما را قطب گردانیده اند حق سبحانه و تعالی جهانیان را به برکت[9] شما

۱ ح = ندارد ۲ ک = موزنه ۳ ک = هشت ٤ ک = ندارد ۵ ح = دیگر
٦ ک = دلاوخان ۷ ک = قندوی ۸ ح = ندارد ۹ ح = برکت

قایم میدارد و کیفیت مذکور بر علما و معارف رسید دیگر نیز سید احمد

ع۱ مذکور بر ملازمان

مذکور تقریر تخت ملک رفعت هم گذرانید و سید احمد

مذکور بحضور بندهٔ مؤلف میان دو نماز بملاقات بندگی حضرت شیخ جهان

ع۲ دامت برکاته

قطب زمان آمده بود بست ٹنکه مرحمت کردند دیگر بروایت قاضی بدهٔ مبارک

ع۲ دامت برکاته بد

که یکی از ملازمان بندگی حضرت شیخ جهان قطب زمان معتمد و موثوق

ع۳

بود وقتی مولانا صدر الدین نبهانی بخدمت شیخ آمده نوازش بسیار فرمودند

ع۴ شاید تنگیا

معتاد ایشان بیشتر احوال ده ٹنکه دوازده ٹنکه بود موجود نه بود یک جوره پیرم

بر دست مبارک کرده آوردند فرمودند قاضی بستانید تنها را کار خواهد آمد

ع۵

قاضی بازگشت قاضی را باز ملاقات میسر نشد بعد چند روز رحلت بکردیم

ع۶ بدان

از جامه پیرم تکفین کردند دیگر یک مرید مختص و مونس ملک شیخن یونس چندران

آل خالد ولید بر بندهٔ مؤلف باز نمود در آنکه از سلطان محمد طاب ثراه بنده

ع۷ ع۸

مخلص تهانه موضع چاره یافت مقدم او قوی سرکش بود کسی از ملوک آنجا

تهانه کردن نتوانست متعلق شده بحضرت بندگی شیخ جهان قطب

زمان عرض داشت که بنده را اجماعت مختصر است آن تهانه چگونه قبول کند

ع۹ خواهند

اشارت شد تعلق مکن تهانه مذکور اختیار کن درویشان در کار تو بود

از مقدم هیچ التفات مکن در هر جنگی ترا نصرت است نفس مبارک در کار شد

ع۱ح = میکرد و بندگی ع۲ح = ندارد ع۳ک = نوزش ع۴ح = ندارد
ع۵ کردیم ع۶ح = ندارد ع۷ح = مخلص را ع۸ک = چاده ع۹ح = خواهد

هر بار بمقدم برای جنگ آمد مخذول و مقهور گشت و تهانه مذکور
مستقیم و معمور شد دیگر چون مذاکره دوستی یا معتقدی یا آشنائی
می[1] افتاد و بتقضاء الله تعالی او در عین مذاکره یا بعد ساعتی پیدا شدی[2]
بندگی حضرت شیخ جهان قطب زمان[3] میفرمودند سبحان الله همین مذاکره
این عزیز بود با کشف تقریب[4] گویند روزی خطیب بالنهیور[5] بحضرت بندگی
مخدوم شیخ احمد آمده بود برابر او یک ملا بود او هنر[6] کیمیا داشت هر بار خطیب
مذکور را گفت اگر اشارت بندگی حضرت مخدوم باشد چیزی راست
کرده پیش بندگی حضرت مخدوم بگذرانم سخن آن ملال[7] بسمع مبارک رسید
فرمودند این عزیز چه می گوید خطیب آغاز کرد این زا بر هوس کیمیا دارد
و میگوید اگر اشارت شود چیزی راست کنیم بندگی حضرت مخدوم
فرمودند بابا درویشان را این هوس نیست در آتش نمی افتند در
جمعه آینده که در آستانه این درویش آیند دو سفال آب نارسیده
بیارند ایشان را چیزی عطا شد باز گردانیده ند ایشان در احمدآباد
رفتند و بعد چند روز جمعه آمد بمعتاد خویش بحضرت بندگی مخدوم
رخ نهادند و در دل گذشت که بندگی حضرت مخدوم دو سفال آب
نارسیده طلبیده بودند یک جیتل داده دو سفال در[8] بازار خریدند بحضرت

۱ک= میان ۲ک= میشند ۳ح= ندارد ٤ک= تقریر
۵هالنیور= ک ۶ح= نیز ۷ک= ملا ۸ک= از

بندگی مخدوم آمدند و سفال مذکور درون مصلا بپیچیده بر دست نفر داده
ایشان هر دو پابوس کردند و طعام خوردند و بندگی حضرت مخدوم
چیزی نقد دادند وقت بازگشت فرمودند[۱] خطیب درویشان چیزی
طلبیده بودند ایشان عرض کردند که آورده اند فرمودند بیارید[۲] ایشان از[۳]
دست نفر خود ستده آمدند[۴] دران وقت هر دو بطریق سفال[۵] میان خود آواز کردند
و پیش حضرت بندگی مخدوم بردند همان که نظر بندگی حضرت مخدوم بران افتاد
فرمودند باز گردید چون بیرون آمدند چه بینند هر دو زر طلا شده و بارها فرمودند که نظر
درویشان کیمیا دارد اگر بر کوه نظر کنند همه زر شود و پیش درویشان
جوی زر میرود نمیگرند بسبب آنکه حساب دادنی است

فصل دوازدهم

درسماع بندگی حضرت شیخ جهان قطب زمان دامت برکاته و بکاء
ایشان گاهی[۶] خدمت بندگی حضرت[۷] بابو در قصبه لدنو مضافات ناگور
رفته بودند ملک علاؤ الدین نومسلمان مرید خدمت سید جلال که نام او
بود مقدم قصبه مذکور برای خدمت بندگی حضرت بابو فتوح آورده — میسنگ
خدمت حضرت بابو مالیده کنانیدند و اکابر قصبه لدنو که مسلمان بودند
طلبیدند و مالیده خورانیدند[۸] بعده کسے گفت دست بشوئید قاضی ترک

۱ ک = ای ۲ ک = بیارند ۳ ح = بر ٤ ح = آمد ٥ ک = ندارد
٦ ح = ندارد ٧ ک = ندارد ٨ ک = کنانیدند

حاکم قصبه مذکور خوب طبع بود گفت ازین نعمت دست نشویم بعده بندگی حضرت شیخ جهان قطب زمان دامت برکاته در نظاره با آنکه[۱] قصبه مذکور بود رفتند صفت بایمن مذکور دراں ایام در دیار روش[۲] ... درون در آمدند در کناره آب نشستند عورتی برای آب آمده بود نواخت سهیلا[۳] کرداں نواخت بندگی حضرت مخدوم را سخت گرفت مست شدند و در آب افتادند همان عورت دست گرفته از آب کشید:

ترک خون ریز مرا کشت طبیبان چه کنند .	ور کسی زنده کند کار همان قتال است .

و این دلیل معقول خاصه بندگی حضرت مخدوم است که[۴] اگر گوینده گاهی بر در بندگی حضرت مخدوم صوتی و یا غزلی و یا سرودی میخواندند یا میگفت در دهلیز آمدند و می نشستند و چندان می گریستند که رومال دو سه بار تر می شد و می بشنیدند[۵] و بعضی اوقات[۶] بی هوش می افتادند از غیری این چنین گریه و زاری در صوفیان معاینه نشده و هر که گوینده را مانع شدی از وی سخت می رنجیدند و ذکر سماع و ایجات او در فصل چهاردهم در سمر قند رفتن نبشته شده و گوینده را چیزی نیکو می دانند و گستی و دست و پای زدنی نه داشتند .. اما در آخر سال عمر از شنیدن سرود و غزل از گوینده[۷] مطلق مانده بودند چنانچه بنده مؤلف یک بار عرض داشت که چون بیشتر ازین چیزی

۱ح = ندارد ۲ح = است ۳ح = سولها ک = سوی تصحیح قیاسی
۴ح = ندارد ۵ح = شیلیدند ۶ک = ندارد ۷ح = گویندگان

می شنیدند درین وقت چرا نشونند اشارت شد این زمان حالتے دیگرست
مجنونِ عشق را دگر امروز حالت است کاسلام عشق لیلےٰ[1] دیگر[2] ضلالت است

فصل سیزدہم

در روان شدن مخدوم برائے حج گذاردن[2] وکیفیت حج رفتن بندگی حضرت شیخ جہان قطب زمان میفرمودند کہ بعد نقل بندگی حضرت بابو بیشتر شغل ما برکوہ کھٹو بربالا می بود[3] یک بار در خاطر گذشت کہ حضرت رسالت صلی اللہ علیہ وسلم درزمین اند چہ بے ہمتی است کہ مشرف بزیارت نشوند بر سنگ نشستم کہ اگر دہم روز روان نشویم[4] دروغ زن باشیم[5] بعد ہشت روز بر قاضی نیکو کہ ملازمت بر ما داشت سر کشادیم[6] کہ درویشان نیت زیارت پیغامبر صلی اللہ علیہ وسلم جزم کردند آنا ہشت روز برآمد کہ خواب چیزی نمی بینیم[7] قاضی نیکو گفت بندگی مخدوم اصلا خواب نمی کنند[8] اگر خواب کنند[8] بہ بینند[9] ہم دران وقت استراحت فرمودند و بیدار شدند فرمودند کعبہ و راہ کعبہ تمام دیدم شب آیندہ بندگی حضرت بابو در خواب[10] آمدند در دہلیز نشستہ اند ما استقبال نمودیم و بملاقات مشرف شدیم بندگی حضرت بابو فرمودند در ناگور صحبت جمع شدہ است روان شوید و حج گذارده[12] سلامت باز گردید ما بخوشی و خرمی بیدار شدیم کہ الحمد للہ رضا بر بندگی حضرت بابو وداع ایشان ہم شد

۱ اضافہ مرتب ۲ ک = ندارد ۳ ک = بالائی بودند ۴ ح = نشوند
۵ ح = باشند ۶ کشادند ۷ ح = بینند ۸ ح = کنند ۹ ح = بیند
۱۰ ک = ندارد ۱۱ ح = نمودند ۱۲ ح = ندارد

دواتی نقره بود سید اکرم را دادیم و بر مقطع گویا ماندیم که ما را اتفاق عزیمت
حج است دوستان مزاحمت خواهند[1] نمود اگر شما صباح سواری فرمائید[2]
بدان بهانه بیرون آییم مقطع عرضی داشت کنانید اسپی دارم اگر آن را قبول
فرمایند اطاعت کنم اسپ مذکور قبول کردیم صباح او سوار بر ما آمد و اسپ
زین کرده فرستاد ما هم سوار شدیم علما و سادات و قضاة و شاهیان[3] و بیشتر ایشان
را معلوم شد که فلان در حج می رود همه پیش دروازه می آمدند عرض کردند که بغیر
وداع چرا سوار می شوید[4] فاتحه سوار شده خواندیم ایشان گفتند ما امشب
در رکاب خواهیم آمد هر جا که نزول خواهید[5] فرموده از آنجا وداع کرده آید[6] در
موضع ترناو موازنه دوازده کروه از کهتور قیم ماندیم تمام خلق آنجا رسید[7] (دیو) راج
مقدم موضع مذکور بسیار تکلیف در ضیافت کرد آخر شب چون از آنجا
سوار شدیم خلق مذکور چنان گریستند که آواز گریهٔ ایشان در قربات جوار
رسید ایشان هم آمدند وداع کردند در ناگور رسیدیم بسرای ملک چوبان[8]
[9] و بیش از ما جماعت دران سرای یکی[9] از ان جماعت
فرود آمده بودند مولانا کمال الدین دانشمند محقق امام خانجهان دوم مولانا شیخ
صاحب سجاده از خضر حوض خاصی[10] سیوم مولانا احمد ماناند خادم شیخ نصیر الدین محمود
چهارم شیخ شمس الدین بزرگواری[12] از گوشه نشینان دهلی ان همه اکابر
بملاقات ملک قطب نجم مقطع ناگور داماد ملک رضی الملک دهلوی[13] رفتند

١ح=خواهد ٢ح= فرمایند ٣ح= شامیان ٤ح= شوند ٥ح=خواهند
٦ک= خواهیم کرد ٧ح=سرراج ک= برراج- اسم مقدم درجای دیگر در
هردو نسخه دیوراج آمده است- به بینید صفحه ١٨٦ ٨ح= جویان ک=جوبان
٩ح=ندارد ١٠ خاصی درهردونسخه تصحیح قیاسی ١٢ک=بزرگوار ١٣ح=دهلی

ملک قطب الدین بغایت سخی بود بخدمت ایشان چیزی نیکو پیش آورد
پرسید دیگر مصاحب کیست ایشان گفتند بندگی حضرت شیخ احمد کهتو
هم امروز رسیده اند[1] ملک گفت بندگی حضرت شیخ احمد را یافتن نخواهم
داد او سخت ضعیف شده اند از غایت مجاهده این مشقت چگونه توانند[2] کشید
نفران را تعیین کرد که تتبع کنند کجا نزول فرموده اند آن بزرگواران از ملک
بازگشته[3] آمدند و ما را گفتند که ملک شما را نمیگذارد آشنایان ناگوری ما چنانچه
قاضی امام الله حافظ و متعلم با ... خود قاضی منصور ناگوری که به ملاقات
آمده بودند وداع کردیم و از آن سرای بمحلی دیگر رفتیم نفران ملک در سرای
مذکور ما را نیافتند آخر شب چنان سوار شدیم که کسی را[4] خبر نشد
چون در موضع مهوبه غرق[5] تلواره رفتیم رائی مندلک را خبر شد به ملاقات ما آمد
سوار کرد در خانه خود برد اسپ ما را بر سر طویله خود به بست به نیت تبرک و انواع
تواضع و ضیافت نمود سه روز مهمان داشت قافله بسیار جمع شد چهارم روز با ما
وداع کرد چند گلیم و خرچ پیش ما آورد از آنجا در موضع لادروه رفتیم در خانه عورتی
غریبه فرود آمدیم[6] خانه او در کناره آب بود عورت منازعت کردن گرفت
که چون متقدم نشنود که مسلمان را جای داده مرا زیان کنند هم درین بودیم ناگاه
سیل آب آمد آن عورت رخت از خانه کشیدن گرفت و همسایگان هم رختها

۱ح = است ۲ح = تواند ۳ح = گشت
۴ک = ندارد ۵ح = غرق ۶ک = آمده

می کشیدند سبب آنکه آن خانها در[1] سیل بود در وقت سیل ثلث دیه غرق [2]شدی بدان سبب خلق دیه رخت خود از خانه خود[3] کشیدند عورت گفت که شیخ آن زمان هم[4] جای خود خواهد گذاشت ما چون دیدیم سیل غالب می شود یک چوب را در کنارهٔ لب آب نصب کردیم و گفتیم آب ازین هیچ تجاوز نکنی سیل سخت رسید آب از ان هیچ تجاوز نکرد غونامیان کفار افتاد اینچنین شیخی آمده است در تماشا آب آمده بودند عجبی دیدند بر ما هجوم کردند و پایهامی بوسیدند در اثنا آن درویشی با زخمها خون چکان آمد پیش ما گفت که دو تنکه زر از من تقدم این مقام کرن نام شده ومرا زجر کرد راج [5]پتیری از هم نشینان او بر ما آمده بود او را گفتیم اصیلی که شما دارید کم[6] اصلان از ان [7]استنکاف نمایند زیرا که هیچ کسے طائفه جوگی و درویش را دست نبینند از دشمان چه قومی که [8]ایشان را هم نمیگذارید برو کرن را [9]بگو دوجه این درویش را [10]بدبند راج پتیر ندکور گفت مرا مجال نیست که این سخن برکرن بگویم اگر نفر خود بفرستند بگذرانم ما خود سوار شدیم طرف خانه او روان شدیم راج پتیر مذکور شفقت کرد برکرن رفت که این چنین شیخی آمده است، دکیفیت نصب کردن چوب برکناره لب آب دکیفیت درویش و زخمها او برکرن گفت چون ما نمودار [11]گردیدیم زنار داران که در مجلس او بودند گفتند این شیخ که در خانه تو می آید این جا آوردن مصلحت نیست

۱ح = ندارد ۲ح = می شود (= می شدو) ۳ک = ندارد ٤ح = ندارد
۵ک = نیر ٦ح = کم اصل از ۷ اشکاف ۸ح = ازشان ۹ک = بگویم
۱۰ح = بدهند ۱۱ح = گردیم

هر جا که قدم او بیاید اسلام شود ترا پا بر دے باید رفت کرن در حال
استقبال نمود ما بهلشته[1] برگرده می رفتیم او از آمدن باز ماند در میان راه
رسید خدمت کرد ما از اسپ فرود آمدیم نشستیم گفتیم میدانی برائے چه آمده ایم
کرن گفت میدانم گفتیم بیار نفرے را فرستاده و هر دو ٹنگه زر طلبیده
نفر یک ٹنگه آورد کرن آن را پیش ما داشت گفتیم دوم کجا گفت
تفحص کرده آن هم می آرم باز گشتیم شب بسیار گذشته بود که خود در وثاق
ما آمده دوم هم پیش داشت فقیر که زخم خورده بود حق او را رسانیدیم کرن گفت
برادرے دارم سوہر[2] نام پسران او رهزنی میکنند[3] و او مانع نمیشود در خیال افتاده
است که تلف کنند بعد ازین حکایت سوهر مذکور با جماعت خود پیدا شد
کرن متعلق شد که مگو برائے جنگ آمده است برخاست کرن را گفتیم
تعلق مکن سوهر برای ملاقات ما آمده است نشین[4] سوهر آمده در پای ما
افتاد و دور رفت بزانوی ادب نشست ما کرن را گفتیم هیچ تعلق[5] مکن
میدانی ترا چه قرابت باشد کرن گفت همواره پرسند سوهر گفت پیشوایان
این میخواهند که پسران بنده را تلف کنند[6] گفتیم هر دو برخیزند آشتی کنند برخاستند
کنار گرفتند میان ایشان بعد مدتے مدید و عهدے بعید اصلاح دادیم
هر دو برادران در رکاب شدند تا لب آب آمدند ایشان را باز گردانیدم

١ ک= بهلشته ٢ ح=سوم ٣ ح= میکند
٤ ک= پشنین ٥ ک= ندارد ٦ ح=کنند

وگذرانیدیم در شهر نهرواله رسیدیم ملک فتح الملک پدر راستیخان
در شهر بود ملاقات کرد تعظیم و تکریم نمود و خیلی خدمتی پیش آورد و بر پسر
راستیخان که در کهنبایت بود پروانه نبشت که این بزرگوار در حج میروند باید که
جهاز خوب بدهند و مراعات تعظیم ایشان بکنند چون در کهنبایت
رسیدیم موسم نبود جهازات روان شده بودند یک جهازی ازان خواجه محمد مراد
مانده بود راستیخان پدر شیخ زاده کرباتی[1] و قاضی تاج الدین عباسی حاکم خطه کهنبایت
را فرستاد تا بابا او از جهت کرایه[2] قرار دهند او مال نول[3] بسیار میگفت
گفتند این شیخ هستند نول[4] اندک باید گرفت گفت اگر این شیخ اند
من مرید مانم بندگی حضرت شیخ جهان قطب زمان فرموده‌اند که او نامراد است
در جهاز او نخواهیم نشست از تاثیر آن نفس فرزندان او تا غایت بنامرادی
گرفتار اند بعده عزم مهایم شد راستیخان پانصد تنگه پیش آورد در مهایم رفتیم
در مسجدی فرود آمدیم[5] در تتبع جهازات بودیم همه جهاز روان شدند گفتیم اگر جهازی
به بها یافته شود تحریم[6] خواص ازان راه نصرت صاحب مهایم [این][7] را شنید برای
نصرت گفت اینچنین بزرگی شیخی در مسجد نزول کرده است اینچنین سخنها
می فرمایند رای گفت تفحص کنید که کیستند چون نام[8] ما شنید در خانه خود
برد و بسیار نوازش نمود و وزیر خود را گفت ما او را[9] نام بزرگی که برای ملاقات

١ ک = ندارد ٢ ح = کرا ٣ ح = مال نویس ٤ ک = ندارد ٥ آمدایم
٦ ح = تحریم ٧ اضافهٔ قیاسی ٨ ک = ندارد ٩ بعد ازین در 'ح' = ما او را نام واین کلمه هاربطی ندارد.

ایشان مارا درناگور می بایست رفت حق تعالی مارا درخانه نشسته ملاقات
روزی کرده شکر خدا تعالی بجا می آورد و کاشتهای اجناس طعام بدست خود
بنیس بانها دبعده جهازی[1] را به پانصد تنکه خریدیم و سوداگران پانصد تنکه بول
او دادند هم دران جهاز نشستیم رخت خویش هم انداختیم در عدن رسیدیم
شیخ فرضه[2] و ناظر در قصبه نشسته بودند آن هر چهار بزرگواران میان خود اتفاق
کردند که عربی دان نخوانند و پیرانیم مناسب ما نیست که دنبال این جوان
برویم مولانا کمال الدین گفت در کدام خیال افتاده اید[3] این فکر خوب نیست
مارا اتفاق ایشان[4] نشد علاحده طرف قصبه متوجه شدیم[5] شیخ فرضه[6] و ناظر را نظر برما افتاد
در محل بلند نشسته بودند فرود آمدند استقبال نمودند مولانا احمد چون دید که چون
شیخ[7] فرضه و ناظر بتعظیم ملاقات بندگی حضرت شیخ همان قطب زمان
کردند در حال پیش آمد ایشان گفتند رخت بندگی حضرت مخدوم کسی[8] که بیارد
در راه فرضه بیارد تا[9] چیاور استا تلف نشود مولانا احمد مذکور گفت رخت بندگی
حضرت مخدوم من خواهم[10] آورد گفتند مبارک باشد رخت این چهار اکابر
چند هزار تنکه را بود و مارا در یک بقچه چند تفصیل بیش نبود با تمام رخت ایشان
معاف گشت[11] دانگی و درمی اخراجات نشد در محلی خوب فرود آوردند
مولانا کمال الدین گفت بندگی حضرت مخدوم[12] شما را می باید که شیرینی خوب بسیار

۱ ح= ندارد ۲ ح= قرضه ک= قرصه ۳ ح= اند ٤ ح= ندارد ۵ ک= شده ایم
٦ ک= قرضه ۷ ک= ندارد ۸ ک= کسی ح= کسی که ۹ ک= ندارد
۱۰ ک= خواهیم ۱۱ ک= شد ۱۲ ک= ندارد

بسیار ند اگر علیحده ملاقات میکردند اول ربعی میدادند اکنون ثمنی[1]

بحضرت مخدوم خدمتی بکشید باد غرور از سر ایشان باقبال بندگی

حضرت مخدوم فرود آمد مقر و معترف شیخی بندگی حضرت مخدوم[2] (شدند و) بمقتدائی

قبول کردند و بخطای خود شرمنده[3] شدند ما جهاز خود را بانصد تنگه فروختیم

دوم روز شخصی از جهازیان عدن بر ما آمد و گفت[4] اگر شما را حاجت به جهازی

باشد بنده جهازی خوب[5] دارد با او قول خود قرار دادند او گفت که رخت

شما چند است گفتیم همان یک بقچه رخت ماست چند دراهم نقره او را دادیم

و بقچه تسلیم او کردیم او وعده کرد که نماز شام را بندگی شما خواهیم آمد بقچه برد اما او بر وعده

نیامد مولانا احمد رسید گفت شما چرا تسلیم نمودید[6] مردی بیگانه[7] خانمان او معلوم

نه این چه معقول بود گفتیم در خاطر داشتیم بچند دفعت فقرا را بدهیم گو یا که یکبار دادیم[8]

هیچ حیرتی[9] نشد شب بقرار باطن میتوان[10] نشد اما البته تهجد دل گرانی کردن گرفت

مصاحبی بود جمال نام او را گفتیم بیا در ساحل برویم جمال برابر شد از دور در نظر ما

آمد که دو نفر پیش دهلیزی[11] حکایت میکنند جمال را گفتیم که مقابل ایشان می رویم

تو برابر دیگر در خیال ایشان شو (ایشان[12]) هم در حکایت بودند که ما بر ایشان رسیدیم

یکی را گفتیم که وعده جهاز که شما کرده (بود ید کجاست[13]) دوم شخصی آغاز کرد[14] کیفیت

چیست گفتیم[15] نحنُ رجالٌ غربا جئنا من بلادِ الهند این عزیز ما را[16] ملاقات نند

۱ک= ندارد ۲ح= ندارد ۳ک= شرمنده ۴ح= ندارد ۵ح= خوبی ۶ح= نمودند
۷ک= بیگانه بود ۸ک= داده ایم ۹ح= حیرتی ۱۰ک= میتونه ۱۱ک= دهلیز
۱۲ح= ندارد ۱۳ح= بود کیا نند ۱۴ح= ندارد ۱۵ک= گفتم ۱۶ح= مارا

بود گفت اگر شما را حاجت بجهازے باشد ما را بفرمایند[1] تمام کیفیت
چنانچه بود بران شخص باز نمودند[2] این شخص بروے گفت اگر قول[3] کرده جهاز شمای
دبا بقچه هر وجه ستده واپس بده او گفت چه حکایت است وچه نیست[4] سوگندها
خورد[5] که نمی شناسم و نمی دانم شخصے دوم گفت شیخ این سوگندها اینچنین
می خورد چکنم بیا[6] جمال مصاحب را گفتیم که تو درون خانه در آی و تتبع کن جمال درون
خانه رفت خالی بود یک عورتی زال نشسته [ریسمان[7] میریسید جمال در حجره
درآمده[8] بقچه عین موجود یافت یک تفسیله[9] درون کشیده دیده بود با زشتاب
که داشته بود چیزی تفسیله درون بقچه رفته بود و چیزی بیرون مانده بود جمال بقچه عین
پیش ما آورد ما مصاحب او را[10] گفتیم بدا متاعی و یک طپانچه او را زدیم دستار از سر افتاد
دران[11] درم (افتادن) بول از دستار بیرون آمد گفتیم هذا دراهمی او را گرفتیم پیش کردیم باز او
گفت رخت شما ببرکت شما پیدا شد وبعض آمد اکنون فضیحت چرا میکنید
ما چند درهمی ازان دراهم بر دست او دادیم و گفتیم هذا اجر محافظت که یک
بقچه[12] (نزد) ما چهار رفیقان آوردیم ایشان تعجب شدند گفتند این الهام حق
سبحانه[13] (و تعالی است) کشف و کرامات بندگی حضرت شیخ جهان قطب زمان داگر نه
کسے چه داند[14] (او را که) که بود و خانهٔ او کجا باشد چون از عدن عزم عزیمت شد
چیزی توشه[15] تسلیم ناظر مذکور کرده آمد و در جهاز نشستم آبی گرمی رسید

۱ ک= ندارد ۲ ک= نموده شد ۳ ح= قولی ۴ ک= جه نسبت
۵ ح= خوردند ۶ ح= با ۷ درنسخهٔ ک از اینجا تا صفحهٔ ۱۹۱ سطر ۱۲ درورق
۱۱۳ الف تا ورق ۱۲۰ ب آمده است ۸ ح= در آمد کشیده ۹ ک= تفصیل
۱۰ ک= ندارد ۱۱ ح= ندارد ۱۲ ح= ندارد ۱۳ ح= ندارد ۱۴ ح= ندارد ۱۵ ح= نوشته

وهوا آنچنان گرم شد که توت قوت داشتن کسے نماند همه کس مردهها از دست رها میکردند[1] و بادهم کم شد چند روز گذشت توته هم کم شد دو سیر جرت بود بر خباز فرستادیم خباز گفت اصبر بعد ساعتی باز فرستادیم باز گفت اصبر بعد سوم کرت جرت طلبید گفتیم مصروف شد خباز پشیمان بازگشت اهل جهاز را خبر شد که بندگی حضرت شیخ را روزه طے شد یک خریطه آرد و یک خمره عسل پیش آوردند هر چند که امتناع کرده شد بالحاح[2] پیش آمدند ضرورت ستده شد ناگاه میان دریا پشته یکی پیش آمد جهازبان برای پختن[3] طعام و جز آں فرود[4] آمدند خلوت شد در خاطر گذشت که ما هم بفراغ فرود آئیم و وجود بشوئیم از جهاز رسن گرفته فرود آمدیم در اثنای مالیدن اندام رسن گرفته از دست رها شد جهاز قدرے پیشتر رفت شنا کردن میدانستیم اما قوت نمانده بود سست شدیم مستعد گشتیم که موت رسید این اسماء اعظم در دل الهام شد یا حافظ یا حفیظ یا رقیب یا وکیل یا الله یا الله یا الله بزبان راندیم زیر پای تکیه پیدا شد قرار وجود بازگشت نظر خورندگان[5] جهازبان بر ما افتاد ایشان نعره بر آوردند که الشیخ یغرق جهاز نزدیک آوردند[6] در جهاز در آمدیم شکر خدای عز و جل بجا آوردیم از آں روز باز[7] که تعویذے[8] از بندگی حضرت مخدوم طلبیدی برای هر زحمتی که بودی همیں اسمای نبشتندی[9] روزے بنده مؤلف عرضه داشت

۱ ک = می کردند ۲ ک = بالحاج ۳ ک = ریختن ۴ ک = ندارد
۵ ک = جورندگان ۶ ح = آوردید ۷ ح = ندارد ۸ ک = تعویذ
۹ ک = اسامی نوشته اورا سی دادند

ع۲ بسم اللہ رب الارض والسماء

برای تعوید نبشتن ہیچ تمسکی ہست فرمود ند بسم اللہ خیر الاسماء بسم اللہ الذی لا یضر مع اسمہ شیئ فی الارض ولا فی السماء وھو السمیع العلیم بعدہ بندہ مولف عرضہ داشت کہ روزی صحاح لغت امام جوہری مطالعہ میکردم لغتی دیدم کہ معنی او این بود کہ این اسم ماہی است کہ دوستان حق تعالیٰ را در دریا اگر مزاحمت آب می شود آن ماہی پشت خود را زیر پای ایشان می نہد ازین کیفیت بندگی حضرت شیخ جہان قطب زمان بندہ را معنی او یاد آمد اما لفظ یاد نماندہ است بندگی حضرت مخدوم فرمودند این از حسن اعتقاد شما است چون جہاز پیشتر روان کردند باد ماند و زاد کم شد جہاز بان را سخت تحیر پیش آمد کہ مکیم و ما در خواب منارہای مکہ مبارک معائنہ کردیم بیدار شدیم واقعہ مذکور بر جہاز بان گفتیم ایشان را تقویتی شد سخت معتقد بودہ اند ناگاہ بادی موافق آنچنان پیدا شد کہ نماز عصر در جدہ ادا کردیم از آنجا بر شتران سوار شدیم در مکہ مبارک رسیدیم آن سال سنہ ثلاث و ثمانمایہ بود

ع۹ یک تفسیلہ از ان بقچہ شیدیم دو عورات از شہزادگان مصر چون تفسیلہ را دیدند گفتند ما نتمنہ گفتیم ما اعطیتنا فھو ثمنہ ایشان گفتند ھذا کلام عجیب نحن لو نشتری بثمن قلیل گفتیم الکلام واحد جمال کہ در رکاب بود گفت این چہ سخن است ایام ہنوز بسیار است در مدینہ می باید رفت بندگی حضرت مخدوم فرمودند بہر چند درم سخن خود چگونہ بگردانیم عورات این مذاکرہ دریافتند مر دبر دلالت

ا ک = دیگر ہم ۲ ح = ندارد ۳ ح = ندارد ۴ ک = ندارد ۵ ح = ندارد ۶ ک = ندارد ۷ ک = آمد ۸ ک = تقوی ۹ ح = ندارد ۱۰ ح = کردہ ۱۱ ح = ندارد

در وتاق بزیارت آمدند دو صحنک تیسر برنج از بازار آرانیدیم پیش ایشان
آوردیم ایشان هر دو[1] [illegible] دران کوشیدند که یک نفر[2] برما عرض کرد که قدوم
مبارک بندگی مخدوم اگر در وتاق ما برسد و مشرف کنند[3] یمنی و برکتی در اسباب
املاک ما شود و ثمن تفسیله از رخت کشیده برسانیم بسیار عجز کردند بردند
یک کوزه آب بو العجب خوشبو معطر ما را خورانیدند دو صندوق پر نقره نگها نمودند
گویانیدند که بندگی مخدوم اگر یکی را بخدمت قبول فرمایند هر چه با ما اینجا و در مصرفست[4]
صاحب آن بندگی حضرت شیخ باشند یاران گفتند که ما چهار نفر کالبدیم و جان مایان[5] حضرت
شیخ اند کالبدی بی جان چون بماند باز گویانیدند که شما هم بباشید زهی
سعادت ما که درین زمره باشیم یاران گفتند ما هر یکی را در دهلی خیلخانه بسیار اند
یک طوافی کنیم بعده طواف ما در مقام خود رفتیم[6] و ایشان در وتاق خود رفتند[7] چون
کیفیت این درویش در جماعت مشائخ مصر شائع شد شخصی را بما فرستادند
که همه بلقا بندگی حضرت مخدوم باشوقیم اگر قدم رنجه فرمایند همه بسعادت مشرف
شویم آینده را گفتیم که طلب درویشان از که صادر شده است کسی را مجال نشد که
بگوید که از من بعده خود در تکیه ما آمدند و ما را باعزاز و اکرام مقدم کردند و همه دنبال
ما شدند و ما رخ مقام ایشان نمی دانستیم ناگاه دو راه پیش آمد ما بحکم حدیث
راه راست پیش[8] گروه در مقام ایشان رفتیم همه معتقد شدند و بسیار تعظیم نمودند مصافحه

١ ح= هر دو فرمودند ٢ ک= یک نفررا برما عرض کردند ٣ ح= کنند
٤ ک= مصرف ٥ جانی مایان ٦ ک= رویم ٧ روند ٨ ح= ندارد

ومعانقه با تواضع کردند بنده مؤلف را[1] معلوم نیست که از آنجا چون بازگشتند
بندگی حضرت شیخ جهان قطب زمان میفرمودند شخصی مارا یک جفت کفشها
ظریف در مکه آورده بود هندوستانی رسید گفت شیخ جای کار دارم اگر
اشارت باشد ساعتی این کفشها بپوشم آنجا روم باز برسانم از شرم از و منع کردم
او بر وعده نیامد مولانا شیخ را علم شد بسیار اندوه کرد دوم روز که برای
طواف میرفتیم هندوستانی در نظر مولانا شیخ افتاد کفشها از و ستد هر چند
که هو گفتیم ستان گفت این چه وقت است که کفشها بگذارند فردا در مدینه
روان[2] باید شد برهنه پای چگونه بمانند بعده جمال را گفتیم که[3] مهرے بر تو مانده است
خورده او بسیار جمال خورده اندک آورده وگفته که مولانا شیخ چندین مسعودی
از جمله این خورده از من بر ور ستده گفتیم تعلق نیست از ایشان طلب مکنی[4] چون
قافله سوی مدینه روان شد ما پیاده اختیار کردیم شب بدشواری در ارد گاه رسیدیم
آخر شب چون قافله روان شد پا بیمار را دیدیم که کار نمیکند مولانا شیخ را گفتیم شما
روان شوید ما آهسته خواهیم آمد مولانا گفت جای شتر می آرم و در قافله ندا کرد جمل[5] بکری
جبل بکری شخصی شتر آورد مولانا گفت سوار شوید گفتیم وجه کرایه نیست گفت از ما قرض
بگیرید[6] گفتیم خدمت با بوزنده نیست که قرض بگذارند گفت ما خرج شما برخود میگیریم
بشرط آنکه هر فتوحی که شما را برسد ما بستانیم گفتیم مولانا این شرط جایز نیست ایشان

۱ ک = ندارد ۲ ح = روان ۳ ک = ندارد
۴ ح = کنی ۵ ح = جبل ۶ ح = بگیرند

بسیار جهد کردند قرض از ایشان چیزی نگرفتیم چون قافله روان شد بر خاستیم در پایها قوت نیکو پیدا آمد شکر خدای تعالی را گفته روان شدیم باز مولانا شیخ آمد گفت بندگی حضرت مخدوم امروز شما را مهمان میگیریم گفتیم شیخ احمد مهمان کسے چگونه شود گفت چیزی وجه شما از جمال گرفته بودیم بر من است وجه مذکور آورد و[۱] او را بر خباز فرستادیم پیگاه شده بود خباز را دشوار نمود اما چون شنید که از آن این درویش است درحال برخاست نان پخت و دو کوزه آب سرد معطر بمشک و زعفران فرستاده مزه[۲] آن آب در دهن تا خیلے شب مانده بود صباح چون قافله روان شدن گرفت مارا ماندگی زور آورده بود شخصے با پنج شتر پیش آمد گفت یا شیخ ارکب سوار شدیم دوم روز او با دو نفر شیخ زادگان آن دیار که بر شتران او سوار شده بودند صاحبان بسیار[۳ رخت] بودند تقاضای طعام کردن گرفت ایشان گفتند لِمَ لکم تطلب مِن هذا الشیخ او گفت لیس مَعَہ شیءٌ فماذا اطلب ذهب یومانِ وما اکل شیئًا ولا یترک الوضوء بیک وضو پنج وقت نماز می گذارد[۳] بمنزل فرود آمدیم شیخ زادگان [۴ مذکور] بملاقات ما آمدند بسیار جهد کردند[۵] که شمارا ضیافت کنیم قبول نکردیم چون بمدینه رسیدیم مولانا شیخ آمد گفت امروز مهمانِ ما شوید گفتیم امروز مهمان حضرت مصطفےٰ ایم صلی الله علیه وسلم چون گنبد حضرت رسول صلی الله علیه وسلم از دو سه کروه در نظر افتاد خود را از شتر انداختیم

۱ک= وداد ۲ک= مزه ۳ح= ندارد ۳ح= گذارد
۴ح= ندارد ۵ح= نمودند

و بشوق و آرزومندی بآواز بلند متوجه بگنبد شده می گفتیم[1] یا رَسُولَ اللّٰه یا نبیّ الحَرَمَینِ الشَّرِیفَین و یا سَیّدَ الثَّقَلَین و دیگر اوصاف حضرت رسالت صلی اللّٰه علیه وسلم تکرار کنان چشم بر گنبد داشته می دویدیم چنانچه کف از دهن بیرون آمده چون بگنبد مبارک رسیدیم بآواز بلند می گفتیم الصَّلوٰةُ وَالسَّلامُ عَلَیکَ یا رَسُولَ اللّٰه هجوم بسیار بود مقدم مجاوران را نظر برین درویش افتاد[2] خرما بر رومال خود بسته طرف این درویش انداخت و گفت یا شیخ هذا[3] من ضیافة النبی صَلَّی اللّٰهُ عَلَیهِ وَسَلَّمَ لکَ و این سخن ثمره آن بود که به مولانا شیخ بندگی حضرت مخدوم فرموده بودند[4] که ما ام وز مهمان حضرت مصطفی صلی اللّٰه علیه وسلم ایم[5] بعده باز گشتیم در عدن آمدیم بر ناظر یکے را فرستادیم تا نوشته که بر ایشان رفته امانت داشته بودیم بیارد ناظر نه داد گفت امانت تا خصم را نه بینم ترا نخواهم[6] داد و[7] باز گشته[8] آمد دانستیم[9] که باز می طلب بعد ز بیشتر آمد گفت که مقصود من همین بود که قدم مبارک شان در خانه من سعادت بیارد بعده سید مسعود ناگوری برادر[10] سید قاسم و سید مهدی از سادات ناگور برای ملاقات این درویش آمد[11] و چیزی آورد[12] گفتیم سید شما آشنایان قدیم در عدن ملاقات بما شد نشاید که پیش شما تحفه بیاریم گفت بندگی مخدوم شما در احسان[13] سابق هست[14] سید زیرا چه برادران مرا باز پرس بسیار

۱ ک = گفتم ۲ ح = انداخت ۳ ک = خذ ٤ ح = بود ٥ ح = ندارد
٦ ح = بخواهد ۷ ک = اما ۸ ح = گشت ۹ ندانستیم ۱۰ ح = برنمود
۱۱ ک = آمدند ۱۲ ک = آوردند ۱۳ ح = اجسام ۱٤ ح = هستند

کرده اید[1] سید مسعود مذکور بر تجار مدن رفت، ذکر این درویش کرد[2]
ایشان در محلے یکجا نشسته بودند همه گفتند اگر می توانی تو شیخ
را بوعی اینجا بیار و سید بر ما آمد[3] گفت سوداگران مشتاق لقا
بندگی مخدوم اند[4] برائے حرمت داشتن این غریب قدم رنجه فرمایند
بضرورت رفتیم ایشان همه تواضع بسیار نمودند ماهیان تسبیح بریان از
تنور کرده پیش آوردند خورانیدند و یک خریطه توشه و یک خمر[5] عسل و یک
گره وجه وقت[6] باز گشتن برابر ما کردند. بعده ملاقات شیخ المشایخ
شیخ عبداللطیف کردیم شیخ یکے از واصلان حق بود با او صحبت شد
چنانچه در شجره مذکور است بعده در جهاز ٹهٹه نشستیم بخطه ٹهٹه رسیدیم
از آنجا موضع ترناد جوار کھٹو آمدیم آن دیو راج مقدم را که در وقت
رفتن چندان ضیافت کرده بود خبر کنانیدیم شب بود[7] مقدم مذکور مخبر
مذکور را تکذیب کرد گفت کجا شیخ احمد کھٹو آمد[8] این جا مدتی شد ایشان رفته اند
ما خود در رفتیم آواز دادیم شناخت[9] آمد ملاقات کرد لیکن سخن[10] عقل[11] حال
زده بود قحط سال بیتال[12] خانه خراب نمود که این جا فرود آیند باز نفر رفت
بروے گفت چیزے تدبیر طعام خواهد شد یا نه گفت چیزی خواهیم کرد اما مگر تدبیری
نشد آخر شب پکیهر[13] برخاستیم روان شدیم تا شرمنده نه شود روز تمام قصد

١ح=اید ٢ک=نکرده ٣ح=ندارد ٤ک=ندارد ٥ زخمر ٦ح=نقد باز گشت ٧ک=بودم ٨ح=آمد ٩ک=شناختیم ١٠ این کلمه مخدوش است، فهمیده نمی شود ١١ک=مقل ١٢ احتمالاً این اشارت است به اصطلاح مروجه درزبان گجراتی یعنی قحط سال چهل دو (بیتالیس) ١٣ح=کهتر ک=بکهتر

کردیم بدشواری قریب یکپاس شب درکھٹو رسیدیم نظر بی بی مبارک زن شہاب دوعکہ مقدم کھٹو درمیان کوچہ بر ماافتاد بہادر غلامی داشت بروگفت درمقام خدمت بابا اسحاق تفحص بکن مانگہ بندگی حضرت شیخ احمد آمدہ اند غلام گفت این چنین شب تاریکی شیخ احمد[۱] کجا این چہ گفتار است بی بی گفت اگر این رفتار بندگی شیخ احمد نباشد دیدہ مرا بکنند بہادر درمقام آمدہ وما بنیش قبر بندگی حضرت بابو خود را چنان افگندہ بودیم کہ زمین[۲] دور گشتہ در نظر کسے نمی آمدیم بہادر رفت گفت کسے نیست بی بی نفرے دیگر فرستاد ما چون دم سرد کشیدیم[۳] آنگاہ نفر دانست بی بی را خبر کرد امیر شہاب الدین وہمسائیگان دیگر آمدند ملاقات کردند ایمۃ وسادات تمام شب بخوشی وخورمی ایشان را گذشت روز را ہمہ پابوس بندگی حضرت شیخ جہان قطب زمان مشرف[۴] شدند وخوشی کردند +

فصل چہاردہم

روان شدن در سمرقند بندگی حضرت شیخ جہان قطب زمان برای امر معروف کردن بر بادشاہ تیمور ومغلان چون غلغلہ رسیدن مغلان وزلزلہ آمدن بادشاہ تیمور در دہلی افتاد بندگی حضرت مخدوم میفرمودند ما خواستیم کہ سر از سجدہ آنگاہ برکنیم کہ دفع شوند بعدہ

۱- ح = ندارد ۲- ک = ندارد ۳- ک = کشید ٤- ح = ندارد

ودر دل افتاد که فال مصحف به بینم در مصحف این آیت آمد که وَذَرُوا الَّذِينَ
يُلْحِدُونَ فِي أَسْمَائِهِ سَيُجْزَوْنَ مَا كَانُوا يَعْمَلُونَ ۞ و شب در خواب
دیدم که زلزله پیدا شده است بندگی حضرت بابو اسحاق طیّب (لله) مرقده
از یک طرف میفرمایند که شیخ احمد این سوی بیرون آیند چون صباح شد
ایشان در شهر در آمدند[1] غارت کردند خانها کاویدند[2] و خلق را اسیر کردند
این درویش از مسجد فرود آید خواست که بر تیمور بادشاه برود و ام معروف
کند سید کمال الدین پسر سید رسولدار رسید و گرهی[3] که ازان خود آورد
مانا نکه دران جواهر بود گفت بندگی حضرت مخدوم ایشان از من خواهند[4]
ستد برنو و بدارید گفتند درویشان کجا بدارند از سید گره مذکور ستدند و
در ناودان سقف مسجد انداختند چنانچه در میان مهر ناودان افتاد
غلامی بود ازان بندگی حضرت مخدوم مسکین نام او گفت بندگی حضرت
مخدوم بر من پنجاه تنگه را بهدیه[5] است حکم فرمودند بیش نردبان
مسجد مذکور ببینداز و خاک بالا کن او همچنان کرد ازآنجا روان شدند
محلی که میر تیمور فرود آمده بود[6] رفتند گفتند کجا است آن اعرج[7] متروک کجا است
آن ظالم ملعون کذا و کذا یکی ازان جماعت گفت مخدوم صبر کنید او می تواند
که جواب[8] شما را به زبان تیغ بگوید یعنی بکشد گفتیم در قیامت چه جواب

۱ ک= ندارد ۲ ک= ندارد ۳ ح= گروهی که ٤ ک= خواهد ٥ ک= بهدیه
٦ ک= بودند ۷ ک= میرو ۸ جواب شمارا بگوید یعنی به زبان تیغ بگوید

خواهند[1] گفت ازاں وزرا که نشسته بودند یکی سید علاء الدین سمنانی
و دوم عبدالملک و غیر ایشان بتعظیم گفتند بندگی حضرت مخدوم
بنشینند تا علم داده شود کودکان را محل درون فرستادند ایشان آمدند گفتند
امیر در خواب است وزرا گفتند برای حضرت مخدوم خیمه بر آرند که[2] تا امیر بیدار شوند
مشغول باشند سید کمال الدین مذکور بر وزرا التماس کرد چیزی وجه محلی داشته
ام اگر امیر برا مرحمت اشارت شود برابر او شده برویم بیارم[3] در حال وزرا
امیر برا حکم کردند[4] امیر عرض داشت که بندگی حضرت شیخ[5] هم اگر باشند[6] کسے را مجال
اخذ نباشد وزرا[7] را این سخن قابل افتاد همه متوجه با حضرت مخدوم شدند
حضرت شیخ را[8] سوار کردند [9] بندگی حضرت مخدوم عزم در لشکر تیمور کردند سبب
خلق دهلی که اسیر شده بود رها میکنانند[10] بدان سبب قصه همراهی[11] کردند]
امیر برابر شده بر در مسجد آمدند چه بینند که[12] جوار مسجد زمین و خانها همه یکساں دوگان
گز کاویده اما برکت میں دست مبارک حضرت شیخ آن گره همانجا میان ناودان
سقف مانده بود کسے را قدرت اخذ نشد گره مذکور تسلیم[13] سید مذکور
کردند آن بهیدیها هم از قریب نردبان مسجد سلامت یافتند بازگشته
چون آمدند تیمور بادشاه کوچ کرده بود کوچ در کوچ طرف سمرقند باز گشت
امیر حسین[14] نام مغلی بود[15] در وثاق خود حضرت مخدوم را جاے داده بود

۱ک = خواهید ۲ک = تا، ح = تاکه ۳ح = بیارم ۴ح = آوردند ۵ک = مخدوم
۶ک = برابر باشند ۷ح = ندارد ۸ک = ندارد ۹ درحاشیه نوشته شده
۱۰ح = میکنانیدند ۱۱ح = همراه ۱۲ح = بیند ۱۳ح = بتسلیم ۱۴ح = جان
۱۵ درنسخه 'ح' بعدازین "فردسی آورد" آمده که ظاهراً کاتب اشتباهاً نوشته است۔

در وقت کوچ بدست خود اسپی زین میکرده[1] سوار میرامی داد و در خیمه خود
فرود می آورد و لشکر تیمور بادشاه سی تمن[2] بود دوازده گروه را عرض میرفت
و قحط این چنین افتاده که هر که پنجاه نفران داشت نیمی[3] او (هم) بسلامت نه رفت و
کذالک اسباب [4] خلقِ دهلی هر گرا بندگی حضرت مخدوم می شناختند
رها کنانیدند و بیشتر خلق که اسیر بود رها کنانید[5] (ند) و شکرانه حضرت بی نیاز
بجا آوردند[6] روزی امیرزاده پیر محمد محلی در کوچ بر بلندی سوار ایستاده
بود کسی او را نمود که اینک شیخ دهلی در کوچ میرود و در تمام لشکر تیمور آوازه کرامت
و بزرگی حضرت مخدوم شهرت یافته بود چنانچه در وثاق امیر حسین مذکور
یک ساعت بندگی حضرت مخدوم را از[7] زائران فرصت نه بود الغرض امیرزاده
حاجب خود را فرستاد که شیخ را بیار[8] امیر حسین دریافت که حاجب امیرزاده
برای طلب حضرت مخدوم می آید بندگی حضرت مخدوم را عرض داشت
که اگر امیرزاده چیزی ذکر وثاق من کند باید که شما تشنیع من[9] فرمائید بندگی
حضرت مخدوم چون رفتند تواضع بر موازنه کرد پرسید شیخ چند ساله[10]
حضرت مخدوم فرمودند تو چند ساله گفت من نمیدانم بندگی حضرت مخدوم فرمودند
ما که در این چنین بلا افتاده ایم ما را چه یاد آید سرا یچها نصب کرده بود[11] فرمود
که این جا باشید همانجا ماندیم گفت امیر حسین را چه مجال باشد که این چنین

۱ح = میکرد ۲ک = ثمن ۳ح = ندارد ۴ح = از خلق ۵ح = میکنانید
۶ک وح = بجا آورد ۷ک = ۱ ۸ک = ندارد ۹ک = ندارد
۱۰ک = سال اید ۱۱ک = بودند

بزرگے بروی فرود آید پلنگ وجامخواب خود برای بندگی حضرت مخدوم فرستاد
نہالی وبالشت سخت بلند بود بندگی حضرت مخدوم بران [1] پنہ غلطیدند مشغول
مع الله بودند صباح کوچ شد امیرزاده کانئہ شوربا بر دست یک سواری
فرستاد که برای حضرت شیخ ببر[2] سوارند کو شیخ دہلی شیخ دہلی گویان
میگشت یک مغلی مولانا [3] محمود تہانیسری را جبل[4] کرده می برد مولانا آغاز کرد
بندگی مخدوم من فلانم[5] بندگی حضرت مخدوم ایستاده شدند از[6] وی رہانیدند
ہمچنان آن کانئہ شوربا رسید بندگی حضرت مخدوم فرمودند این کانئہ
بمولانا بدہید که او مستحق است علمی که او دارد ما را آن مقدار نیست روزی
مغلی معتقد مہمانی کرده بود یاران ما را دعوت کرده آن مغل را در خاطر
افتاد تا این درویش حاضر نہ شود کندوری فراز نکنید[7] ناچار رفته شد
در محل نعال نشسته آمد و سید کمال الدین در صدر نشسته بود نفس در کار شد
خاطر[8] جوشید سید را چون نشاید که در نظر درویش در صدر نشسته بماند
برفور برخاستیم و در خیمہ مغلی دیگر مقام کردیم دو سه روز گذشته در مقامی[9]
که این درویش بودی زوار بسیار می آمدند سید لاامیر حسین معذرت
کرد و گفت سید ایا شیخ را این جا بیار یا تو هم برو سید برین درویش
آمد گفت مغل ما را ماندن نمی دہد و تا ہمچنین میگوید با سید اتحاد بسیار بود

۱ ح= ندارد ۲ ح= پیر، ک= پر ۳ ح= ندارد ٤ جیل = ح، جبل = ک
۵ ک= ندارد ٦ ک= از ۷ ک= میکنید ۸ ک= حاضر ۹ ک= مقام

قصه آن مجلس گفته شد که شما را کجا روا باشد که همچنین بکنید سید در حال
قسم یاد کرد که بندگی حضرت مخدوم بالله العظیم هر بار در دل آمد که ای
فلان ترا چه اندازه باشد که در نظر ایشان نشستی اما از دحام بسیار بود بر خاستن
میسر نشد سید را دست گرفته هم در وثاق اول رفته آمد شبی یک
مغلی میزری بالا پوشیده و میزری فرو بسته پیدا شد آغاز کرد هندوستان
چنین و هندیان چنین سخنها بی وضع گفتن گرفت گفتیم ای عزیز همین آموخته
یا علمیت هم داری که مسئله از ما پرسی جواب تو گویم گفت شما چه مجتهد اید
گفتیم فیض منقطع نیست آغاز کرد پیغامبر صلی الله علیه وسلم چون معصوم بودند اطلاق
ذنب بروی در آیة لِيَغْفِرَ لَكَ اللّٰهُ مَا تَقَدَّمَ مِنْ ذَنْبِكَ وَمَا تَاَخَّرَ اط
چگونه جایز باشد گفتیم اکنون وجوه بشنو چند وجه گفتند وجه آخرین این بود
که اطلاق ذنب مراو ترا جائز نباشد اما اگر مولی پیغامبر اطلاق ذنب
بر پیغامبر کند شاید روزی ناگاه امیر حسین مذکور را محلی روان کردند
امیر حسین سبب تنهائی ما متعلق[1] شد در عین کوچ مغلی امیر اینک
نام دیدیم[2] که با خیل و تبار میرود آغاز کرد بندگی حضرت مخدوم شما ن صحبت
این مغل نگذارید هم صحبت ایشان در سمرقند خواهید[3] رفت امیر اینک سا
گفت حضرت شیخ بسیار مردی بزرگ اند باید که شما از حال حضرت شیخ

۱ح= تعلق ۲ح= ندارد ۳ح= خواهند

غافل نباشند و در صحبت [خود] تا سمرقند برسید چون کوچ فرموده آمد[1]
شخصی بملاقات این درویش آمد چهار نابات آورد امیر اینک را
دادیم امیر اینک برخاست گوسپندی ذبح کرد و بر آشنایان خود قسمت
کرد ما را یاد نه کرد و باز پرسی نه نمود قضا را در ولایت غوریان در آمدیم
نفران [امیر][2] اینک مذکور[3] از دیهی چیزی نمک و جز آن ستدند خلق دیه فریاد بر آوردند
و غوریان از هر طرف بیرون آمدند نفران او را گرفتند جامه و رخت و اسلحه
ستدند شخصی بر اینک آمد کیفیت گفت این درویش [بر][4] حوضی بجهت وضو
فرود آمده بود و تحیت وضو میگذارد[5] [امیر] اینک زن را سوار بر درویش گذاشت
تا اسپ الاغ ما را نگاه دارد خود اسپ چوب کرد و بر[6] ان غوریان رسید[7] [غوریان] امیر اینک
را بستند و تیغ بند و کمربند و جامه و اسپ بردند و کشاله کرده ببستند
چون زن بر ایشان رسید بدست[8] اشارت کرد که بروی تیغ باید راند[9] در نظر
غلام افتاد چون این درویش رسید چه بیند غوریان بجماعت عظیم
غوغا میکنند[10] این درویش بر رئیس ایشان گفت ای رئیس کافران[11] این چه
ظلم ست که می کنانی رئیس گفت بندگی مخدوم چنانچه ایشان دهلی را
غارت کردند[12] دید ما را هم غارت کنند[13] یک نفری از ایشان در آمد بزور
هر چیزی از دیه ما ستد این درویش گفت یک کس ستده است نه همه[14]

١ح = فرود آمد ٢ح = ندارد ٣ح = مذکور را ٤ح = کردند ٥ح = ندارد
٦ح = ندارد ٧ح = ندارد ٧ز = ندارد ٨ک = بد ٩ک = راند ند
١٠ح = میکند ١١ح = کافر ١٢ک = ندارد ١٣ح = کنند ١٤ک = ندارد

شما همه را غارت کردید این چه مسلمانی است این درویش فرود آمد بند امیر[1]

اینک را بدست خود کشاد رئیس مذکور برعایت این درویش تمام اسباب

امیر اینک و نفران او را انیده تسلیم کردند بعد هم[1] امیر اینک معتقد شده

غلامی اشارت زن را دیده بود[2] مانا که[1] امیر اینک را گفت و این هم گفت که این عورت

یا فلان سرخیل[3] سرکاری دارد امیر اینک در حال تیغ بران سرخیل کشید

سرخیل گریخت در پناه این درویش آمد امیر اینک خواست که[4] تیغ بر سرخیل گریخته[5]

بزند این درویش حائل شد که آدمی را بگمان کشتن کجا روا باشد بگذار[1] امیر

اینک گذشت چون سمرقند رسیدیم و بلده[1] امیر اینک عورتی شنا ایستاده[6] [illegible]

بود بسیار رعایت و تعظیم کرد و گفت بندگی حضرت مخدوم

نفری دارم که از خوردگی باز[7] پیش من تربیت یافته است و اصطلاح

و رسوم این دیار را حاوی است خادمی او را فرمایند و هرچه او عرض دارد

مسموع نمایند این درویش قبول کرد ایشان ضیافتی عظیم کردند

دنبه گان[8] و سپیان فربه را ذبح کردند علماء و اکابر را طلبیدند دانشمندی

با این درویش مباحثه میکرد امیر اینک او را گفت برین عبارت که[9] ای فلان

من چندین تکلیف از برای ایشان کرده ام که[10] حضرت شیخ چیزی بخورند

تو یک ساعت شیخ را مزاحمت مده و آن خادم عارف لقب داشت

۱ح = ندارد ۲ک = زن رادید که اشارت بود ۳ح = سرخیذ ک = سرختل
۴ز = ندارد ۵ح = گذارکند ۶ح = ندارد ۷ح = تا این زمان ۸ک = دنبگاه
۹ح = ندارد ۱۰ک = ندارد

موزہا خوب دوختی و در سمرقند ہر کہ نام دار است از اکابر او در ہنر از ہمہ
اہل صناعت فائق تر است جامہ[1] تقطیع کنانیدہ بودیم عورات[2] بزرگ بارزو[3]
التماس نمودند ہر یکی گفت کہ من بدوزم و ہر روز از بازار کانہا
خریدی تا چاشت فروختی دو تنکہ حاصل کردی چون برین درویش آمدی
زایران را معذرت کردی کہ عزیزان وقت قیلولہ است شما ہم استراحت
نمائید[4] بعدہ زایران می خواستند[5] پیش ما[6] از ہر جنسی طعام پختی و سکاک
و بریان و نان و حلوا کشیدی خورانیدی و شب را محافظت بازار[7] کردی
شبے در بازار آتش گرفت رخت دو کانہا سوختہ تند تر رگ[8]
آتش در چشم عارف رسید گل در چشم از ان افتاد اما بہیچ مکافات[9]
اونتد اسپے داشتیم بہ نیت[10] کار خیر دختر او در خانہ او فرستادیم باز فرستاد
کہ بدین قدر کار خیر نشود گفتیم دیگر چیز خواہیم داد و ما فہم نکردیم کہ او از
علو ہمت نہ گرفت بعدہ گفت کہ بعدہ برای سواری شما ناچار
اسپے باید ہمین از من[11] خدمتی باشد[12] گفت[13] در ین مقام خواجہ عبد الاول
مردے بزرگ است و در فقہ بسے غالب است تا او در استفتا کتبہ نکند
کسے نکند اکثر فتاوی ضبط دارد نبیرۂ صاحب ہدایہ[14] است و ضابط
از سخن او تجاوز نکند با او ملاقات باید کرد و ہر چند [با] عارف جہد کردہ

١ ح= جامع ٢ ک= عورت ٣ بارز= ک ٤ ح=نمایند ٥ ک= خواستند کہ
٦ ح=ندارد ٧ ک= باران ٨ ح=شرشک، ک= شک ٩ ح=از ہیچ
مکافات، ک= از باہیچ بمکافات ١٠ ح= نیت ١١ ک= ما ١٢ ح= ندارد
١٣ ح= در ١٤ ک= ہدایت

شد که بار بر دیوار[1] کسی نه رفته ایم نشنید بضرورت رفتیم بر در خواجه نشستیم خادم خواجه بیرون آمد عارف تعریف کرد خادم را تا نکه مصلحت نیفتاد که بگذارند[2] چند بار بیرون آمد مبالاتی نکرد و مارا لباس از آنها نه بود فوطه چرکین و پیشوازی کلمین[3] در بر و کلاهی رمگین[4] بر سر بود خادم دانست که این بچه[5] سخت است بگذارند[6] باز عارف او را گفت که ای خادم بندگی حضرت شیخ مردی بزرگ اندرین دیار مخصوص از دہلی برامیر آمده اند تا امر معروف کنند شما بر خواجه خبر کنید ہم علم نداد[7] درویش این مصرعه بلند خواند مصرع

"آن کیست که تقریر کند حال گدا را" در حضرت شاہی بسمع خواجه رسید در حال طلبیدند خادم رسید شتاب این درویش را غصه در کار شد خواست که طپانچه بروی آن خادم زند تا تحمل کرد چون بر خواجه رفت خواجه دو زانو نشسته مصافحه کرد گفتیم برخیز ای خواجه[8] بے ادب دست گرفته خواجه را بر کردیم[9] خواجه گفت من[10] نمیدانم که شما کیانید[11] گفتیم نشنیں خواہی دانست خواجه را در کنار زیلوچه نشاندند خود بر زیلوچه نشستند نظر بر کتاب خانه افتاد تمام جماعت خانه پر کتب بود خواجه را فرمودند چیزی ازین کتب بفرمایند خواجه گفت ما را از ہیبت تیمور ہیچ یاد نمی آید تسبیل کنایت خلق دہلی این درویش گفت پس چندین تحمل چیست بیا تا ما و شما در حج برویم

---

۱ ح = ندارد ۲ ک = بگذارید ۳ کذا در ہر دو نسخه احتمالاً لفظ اینجا گلین باشد
۴ ک = رنگین ۵ ح = ہمه ۶ ک = بگذرانید ۷ ک = ندارد ۸ ک = ندارد
۹ ح = بر کردند ۱۰ ک = ندارد ۱۱ کیانند

خواجه گفت شما تنها اید و من خلق بسیار دارم این درویش گفت
آن همه[۱] از مال تیمور جمع کرده اید[۲] همه بگذارید[۳] روان شوید خواجه ساکت شد
بعده در کتاب حسامی در آغاز اَمّا بَعد دو حاشیه افتاده است یکی
از تحقیق شرح حسامی و دوم خاصه مولانا معین الدین عمرانی رحمة الله علیه
درمیان آن که دو معارضه است گفتیم خواجه راجح کدام قول است خواجه حامی سنند[۵]
هر دو حاشیه مطالعه کرد بشنیدن این درویش ترکیب نخواند که نبایدد[۶] ر
ترکیب این درویش دخلی کند و جوب نه گفت گفت بندگی مخدوم
از تیمور یک ساعت قرار نیست هر بار گوش در دهلیز میداریم چون آواز
بلند می شنوم گمان می شود مگر کسے از در رسید که بگیرد در اثنا و حکایت
از زبان خواجه صادر شد که غریب از غرابت خود گفتیم از غریب خواجه هم غریب
گفت چنانچه[۷] گاهی گفته بودیم عَلیٰ بفتح لام عَلِیٌ بکسر و این فرق اصلی نیست اصطلاحی
است[۸] بعده متعلق مسئله برسید جواب او گفتیم خواجه گفت
این روایت کجاست گفتیم در فتاوی سراجی است خواجه گفت فتاوی سراجی
تصنیف این دیار نیست ناگاه بچه گریان آمد خواجه او را بر زانو نشاند این
درویش گفت خواجه حالیا[۹] علمی که این بچه دارد بعد بزرگ شدن
فراموش خواهد کرد موجب فراموشی چیست خواجه گفت گویم بچه بکسے داد

۱ ح= هم ۲ ح= اند ۳ ح= بگذرید ۴ ک= ندارد ۵ ک= سند
۶ ک= شاید این درویش دخلی کند ۷ ح= ندارد ۸ ح= این است
۹ ح= والیاً، ک= حالیان

جواب گفت لا اُسلّم گفت چرا وجہ بیان کردیم دیگر خواجہ ہم چہ سبب آن گفت تا اگر مفسد ما اعتماعی افتند دران دخل کنند گفتیم خواجہ شما بعلم را تعلق بروح مید ہید یا بتن اگر تعلق بروح مید ہید روح لطیف است صلاحیت نسیان ندارد و اگر تعلق بنفس مید ہید نفس کثیف است صلاحیت علم ندارد خواجہ جوابی کہ گفتہ در دلیش آن را رد کرد و وجہ منع ہم ہمیان کرد بعدہ خواجہ بر سبیل تشمودست پیش آمد کہ این جواب توان گفت گفتیم ہم گفت چرا گفتیم از ین جہت بعدہ خواجہ گفت جواب این بندگی حضرت مخدوم بفرمایند گفتیم گوئیم دل را خاصیتی است کہ جز یک چیز نگیرد و دل بہ یکے توجہ کند از دوم پشت نمود خواجہ جواب را پسند کرد و تعظیم نمود خواستیم کہ باز گردیم خواجہ گفت آرزو داریم کہ نماز با شما بگزاریم نماز عصر بیک جا گزاردیم و مصافحہ کردیم زیرا کہ مصافحہ را نیز سنت است تا پیغامبر صلی اللہ علیہ وسلم بعدہ خواجہ گلہ پادشاہ تیمور آغاز کرد کہ روزے برخواہر تیمور گفتیم کہ چندین خدمتی شما را بکنم اگر گاہے مذاکرہ افتد عرض دارید کہ خواجہ دوست شما است خواہر شش روزی ہم چنین گفت تیمور جوابی داد کہ او دشمن ما است چون شنید ہم خدمتی دیگر قبول کردم تا بپرسد چہ دشمنائگی است باز خواہر پرسید چہ دشمنانگی است گفت اگر خواہد در یک روز

۱ ک = گفتیم ۲ ح = ندارد ۳ ک = کسیف ۴ ک = نمود ۵ پشت = ک
۶ ح = دیداریم ۷ ح = ندارد ۸ ک = گلہاء ۹ ح = ندارد ۱۰ ح = ندارد
۱۱ ک = جواب

ملک عالمگیر دبینی ہمہ خلق با او اطاعت دارند بعدہ باز گشتیم عارف گفت کہ ملک العلما برادر زادہ خواجہ است شیخ حسام الدین نام دارد سجادہ او ست سجادہ از خواجہ عبد الملک بر زنو گرفتہ است زیارت او ہم باید کرد خانہ او نزدیک بود چون رفتیم ملک العلما از دور بر ما افتاد برخاست درون خانہ رفت ما بزیارت خواجہ عبد الملک کہ قبر ایشان متصل خانہ ایشان بود رفتیم وقت بازگشت بر در نہ بود دیگر[1] در مسجد جمعہ کہ رفتیم خطیبی فصیحی با لہجہ ظریف و الحان لطیف خطبہ خواند چون از ستایش بادشاہ کہ الحامی لبلاد اللہ الراعی بعباد اللہ وکذا وکذا فارغ شد گفت استغفر اللہ العظیم این درویش گفت اے خطیب استغفار بر محل ادا کردی چون خطیب بعد جمعہ بر خواجہ عبد الاول رفت کیفیت استغفار گفت خواجہ ہم تحسین کرد این درویش اسپے را کہ امیر اینک پیش آوردہ بود[2] پشت او بر آمدہ بود برائے نمودن نفس لطف فرستاد خطیب سوار از پیش مسجد واز اسپ فرود آمد عارف گفت خطیب برائے تعظیم شما از اسپ فرود می آید ملاقات شدیم خطیب گفت آنچہ بندہ گ حضرت مخدوم فرمودند کہ استغفار بر محل ادا کردی در وہم وفہم بندہ نبود

۱- ک = ندارد ۲- ح = شست

بعده شیخ عبدالاول را مصلحت افتاد که پیش سلطان محمد بهادر
بادشاہ سمرقند که نبیسۂ تیمور بود و تیمور بادشاہ[1] خود را بطریق وزیر
ساخته بود علم داذند[2] که شیخ دهلی این چنین محقق است ملک سیف الملک
وزیر از بادشاه بازگشته[3] میرفت میان راه ملاقات شد
خواجه کیفیت ملاقات کردن با[4] با بادشاه بروی گفتن گرفت زهی دولت
وسعادت همین زمان عنان گردانید متوجه بدر[5] سری شد گفتیم
این زمان غیر محل شده باشد بعده ملک سیف الملک بادشاه را علم داد
فرمان شد سبب رضا را میر تیمور زیارت نمی توان رفت بندگی حضرت
شیخ را بگویند همین جا گرم فرمایند دوم روز با بادشاه ملاقات شد.
گفتیم التواضع فی شرفک احسن من شرفک پس تواضع کرد و دریافت
که این درویش مستعد و مستقل است حکایت روزی بادشاه همه
علماء سمرقند را جمع کرد تا ما را امتحان کنند ما و سلطان بر چبوتره
نشسته بودیم که مرد و ار بود دانشمندی را فرود چبوتره چپا آما آوردند[6]
ایستاده کردند و ما را ازان علم نه و علماء سمرقند را عجب علمی بود
که بر آینده ابتداء سوال نمیکردند هم[7] دران وقت شخصی فریاد کرد که در
باغ او اسپان فلان در آمدند ضرر نمودند فرمان شد از خصم قدر نقصان

۱ بعدازیں درنسخۂ 'ح' تیمور بادشاہ آمده که "بی ربط می باشد ۲ ح = دهند
۳ ح = گشت ۴ ک = ندارد ۵ ح = بدار ۶ ح = ندارد ۷ ک = ندارد

بدہانند حضرت شیخ این حدیث فرمودند کہ عَدلُ ساعةٍ خیرٌ مِن عِبادةِ سِتّین سَنةٍ آن دانشمند اینجا سوال کرد مِن عِبادة مَن بندگی حضرت شیخ بر بدیہہ فرمودند مِن عِبادَتِہٖ وروی بطرف او بمزاج گرم کردند آن دانشمند بزبان ترکی بر سلطان عرض کرد کہ درین دیار در علم بندگی حضرت شیخ را کسے بس نیاید حضرت بغایت مستعد اند سلطان معتقد شد طعام طلبید وکاسہائی نانخورش بدست خود می ستد بنیں امید انشت خواجہ الیاس نام وزیری بود بترکی بر سلطان گفت کہ شیخ بہ تنگ از دست بادشاہ کانہ نمیگرد چون بازگشتند عارف را محزون دیدند گفتند چہ سبب محزونی گفت الیاس خواجہ بر سلطان بترکی ہم چنین گفت فرمودند چہ تعلق است گفت خیر مصلحت آن است کہ او را بہ بینند صباح بروی رفتیم ملک العلماء ہم رسید سلام کرد حجیب نشدیم گفتیم اینجا اخیر آمدی عمل بر حدیث نکردی کہ اَلقادِمُ یُزارُ گفت بندگی حضرت مخدوم سہو شد اما بندگی حضرت مخدوم این قدر لطف نکردند کہ من[1] درویش زادہ این دیار باشم در جماعت خانۂ بندہ بجز[2] نزول نفرمودند گفتیم اَلغَرِیبُ کَالاَعمٰی الیاس خواجہ محل راست کرد دو جا ببالا زیلوچہ[3] دو نہالچہ فراز کنانیدہ وحاجب را فرستاد کہ ہر دو بزرگوار را بدو دست تعظیم و[4] تاخیر نشود وحاجب ہمچنان کرد الیاس خواجہ بسیار چنانکہ تقدیم

۱ ک= ندارد ۲ ک= ندارد ۳ ک= زلیچہ ٤ ح= ندارد

استقبال کردم بر[1] نہا لجہ تا نذ کنند وری پیش[2] ما ابتدا نمود گفتیم لے
ترک باز احسان تو ما را ہمین پیش[3] است یک طرف خود نشست دوم
طرف ملک العلما گفتیم شما بخورید[4] کہ حدیث است مَنْ اَکَلَ مَعَ مَغْفُوْرٍ
غُفِرَ لَہٗ و بندگی حضرت مخدوم را نیت صوم بود نخوردند الیاس خواجہ گفت
معنی این حدیث چیست ملک العلما گفت اینکہ شما با ما طعام
می خورید سبب آمرزش چیست شما است معنی این است بندگی
حضرت مخدوم خواستند کہ نزاع کنند اما سبب آنکہ پیش ازین رنجانیده
بودند او بعد ازین پیش آید[5] بود چیزی نگفتند دیگر جمعہ بندگی حضرت مخدوم
قدس اللہ سرہ العزیز منبر بودند قریب ممبر در مقامی کہ دو نفر شہزاده
ساغرچیان نشستند[6] در آن مقام ہمان قدر بود کہ دو نفر بیش نگنجد
یک برادر آمده بود دوم ہنوز نرسیده بود ما خالی ذہن مقام برادر دوم
خالی دیده رفتیم نشستیم برادر چون آمد پس نشست ما نشست یک برادر
سوال کرد[7] وَمَا الرُّوْحُ ما گفتیم شیئ لطیف دوم برادر آیت خواند وَیَسْئَلُوْنَکَ
عَنِ الرُّوْحِ قُلِ الرُّوْحُ مِنْ اَمْرِ رَبِّیْ این درویش گفت ما ماہیت کے
بیان کردیم بیان وصف کردیم سوال علماء آن دیار برین وضع بود
کہ آیت خواند نگفت لَا نُسَلِّمُ و ما بر سر دستار سیاه داشتیم

۱ح=ندارد ۲ک=از پیش ۳ک= ندارد کذا در نسخہ 'ح' ظاہراً محل "پس" یا "پسنده" میباشد۔ ۴ح=بخورند ۵ح= آمد ۶ح= میشد ۷ح=ندارد

یک برادر گفت بندگی حضرت مخدوم سیاه را این مغلال نامبارک میگیرند حالیا بادشاه که بیاید بی شبه بر مزاج او بیفتد[ع۱] با بندگی مخدوم اختلاف نماید[ع۲] دستار بنده سفید است بر سر به بندید تا از شر او ایمنی باشد بندگی مخدوم فرمودند که شیخزاده ما سر خود بر پای خویش آورده ایم ما را تعلق نیست همدرین کلمات خویش[ع۳] [؟] بودند که سلطان محمد بهادر مذکور رسید تمام جماعت بآمدن[ع۴] وی برخاستند ما برنخاستیم گفتیم قال النبی صلی الله علیه وسلم لَا تُعَظِّمُونِی فِی بَیْتِ رَبِّی سلطان گفت بندگی مخدوم اینجا بیایند یعنی در صف سلطان نزدیک او ما رفتیم سلطان گفت دستار سیاه چه پوشیده اید ملک العلما میگفت خطبای پوشند سلطان گفت خطبا می پوشیدند[ند] ما منع فرمودیم تا نپوشند بندگی حضرت مخدوم روایت خواند که قَدْ بُ لَبِسَ السَّوَادِ ملک العلما گفت لباس عباسیان است سلطان برخاست علما جمع شدند صفوف کرد[ع۵] نزدیک این درویش آمدند در بحث لَا تُعَظِّمُونِی فِی بَیْتِ رَبِّی هریکی چیزی می گفت غوغا شد طریق گوسفندان گفتیم چندین غوغا چیست یکی را اختیار کنید که با ما بحث کند جواب بگوئیم دانشمندی گفت ابوسعید اخوی خواهد[ع۶] گفت

۱ ک= بیفتد ۲ ح= نماید ۳ ک= ندارد
۴ ح= ندارد ۵ ح= کرد ۶ ک= خواهر

گفتیم خواه لغوی[۱] ابوسعید گفت در روایتها افتاده است که
بنشستن استاد جائز است و بہچو شما بزرگی چون بپایند[۲] چگونه نخیزند
گفتیم پیغامبر با وجود عظمت خود گفت مرا تعظیم مکنید دیگر را چه
مرتبه است مردے دور نشسته بود دستار در حلق اقتعاط کرده به
آواز بلند گفت بشنوید بشنوید ما نیز دوزانو نشسته گفتیم بگوئید بگوئید
همه دانشمندان خندیدند او گفت این برخاستن[۲] با دفعاً للشر باشد ما
دوزانو نشسته گفتیم اے جاهل برائے چه آنجا بنشینی که ترا شری لاحق
شود بعده گفتند که آں روایتی که بندگی حضرت مخدوم[۳] خواندند کجا است
گفتیم در کنز است کنز آوردند در کتاب الحظر والاباحت تفحص کردند نیافتند
یکے گفت غیر مشروع مگوئید[۴] گفتند پیغامبر دوام پوشیده است
شما دوام می پوشید[۵] گفتیم پیغامبر گاہے سر تراشیده است
شما دوام چرا سر می تراشید گفتند این تردید است جواب نیست گفتیم[۶]
کنز مرا بدهید روایت نمایم شما را در کنز روایت نیست کنز را
کشادیم همان روایت مذکور در مسائل نشستن افتاده است
همه خجل شدند دریا ے افتادند هجوم چندان بود که در اثنای
مصافحه وقت نماز عصر تنگ[۷] شد برخاستیم سوار شدیم در مجلسی[۸] دیدیم متعلمان

۱ح=ندارد، ک= نیایند ۲ برخاستند ۳ح=ک ۳ ح=ندارد ۴ح=بگوئید
۵ح=پوشند ۶ح=ندارد ۷ح وک=تنگچه ۸ک=ہر مجلسی

بحثها را تکرار میکنند[1] فلان چنین گفت، حضرت شیخ چنین فرموده[2] متعلمان
که بازگشتند بر شیخ عبد الاول رفتند، بحثها اندکو عرض میکردند چون
خطیب یعنی خواجه خطیب را پرسیدند شما درین مجلس حاضر بوده آید[3]
گفت من اوله[4] تا آخره[5] بوده ام[6] هیچ بزرگی از سمرقند از آنجا نگفت که امکانات
حضرت شیخ شود شیخ عبد الاول فرمودند افسوس در دیارها آوازه
خواهد رفت که پیش یاب دهلوی همه علمای سمرقند مانند دیگر چون تیمور
در شهر رسید ما مسجد جمعه برای نماز رفتیم شخصی درویشی[7] گفت
شیخ چون تیمور شما را کنار گیرد محکم خواهند[8] گرفت شما هم محکم بگیرید[9] و چون
طرف شما نظر تیز ببیند شما هم طرف او تیز ببینید بعد نماز ملاقات
شد کنار محکم گرفت ما هم محکم[10] گرفتیم گفت شیخ قوت میکنند[11] بعده چون نشسته
طرف ما تیز میدید ما هم طرف او تیز میدیدیم خواست با ما وحشت کند
بعنایت[12] ربانی قاصدی از تبریز رسید که یوسف قرا[13] تبریز را نهب
کرده و داماد تیمور را که در تبریز متعلق کرده گذاشته بود کشت و آن ولایت را
گرفت مغلان بزبان ترکی چیقیق کردند تیمور پادشاه در خانه بازگشت[14] هم از
مسجد جمعه روی به تبریز نهاد این درویش چون امر معروف کردن بروی
نیت بود دنبال او سوار شده برفت ناگاه خواجه عبد الاول را دید

1 ک = میکردند 2 ح = فرمود 3 ح = ندارد 4 ک = اوّل 5 ک = آخر 6 ح = بود
7 ک = درویش 8 ک = خواهید 9 ح = بگیرند 10 ح = ندارد 11 ح = میکنند
12 ک = بعنانی 13 ح و ک = فرع 14 ح و ک = گشتت

که[1] از تیمور وداع کرده بازگشته[2] می آمد این درویش[3] و بد گفت بندگی
حضرت مخدوم شما کجا می روید گفتیم برای امر معروف کردن
بر آن اعرج[4] متروک عنان اسپ ما را گرفت و باز گردانید گفت سگی[5]
در غضب شده می رود این چه وقت امر معروف بر وی است امر
معروف بر کسی باید کرد[6] که او بد[7] آنند که ظلم میکنند گفتیم امر معروف باید کرد داند[7]
نمی داند و عنان اسپ ما را خواجه نگذاشت گفت بندگی مخدوم
حالیا دو نفر را بحضور من گردن بزد سر هر یکی جدا شد در خواندن سورة[8] یسین
هنوز او در جنبش بود گفت حکم[10] خدای تعالی چنین بود شما را من باز میگردانم
مصلحت در رفتن نیست **حکایت**[11] وقتی سید علی همدانی که یکی از کبار
آن دیار بود نزدیک بسمرقند رسید ملوک و علما بر تیمور گذرانیدند
که سید علی همدانی مردی بزرگ است استقبال او می باید کرد سوار شد
سید علی از پیش رسید و نشست سید طرف قبله بود و تیمور از مغرب
مقابل وی رفت روی طرف قبله داشت تیمور گفت که سید چرا
قبله را پشت داده ملاقات کردی سید گفت ای امیر[12] تا پشت بقبله
ندهند روی تو نه بینند ناخوش شد هم در غصه سید را در خانه آورد
با سید قدری نشست و سید را جامهای سیاه بود تیمور گفت جامهائی سیاه

۱ک=ندارد ۲ح= گشت ۳ح= ندارد ۴ک=ندارد ۵ک= این وقت امر معروف است ۶اضافه قیاسی = ندارد = ح ۷ح= نداند ۸ک= ندارد
۱۰ک= ندارد ۱۱ک= ندارد ۱۲ک= میر

برای چه پوشیده اید[1] سید گفت برای ماتم نفس تیمور گفت نفس دوست یا دشمن سید گفت دشمن[2] تیمور گفت ای سید ماندہ ماتم دشمن کسی ندارد در دیار ما[3] من نمانی سید گفت فیروز دیار خود نهمای که آنجا روبم بدین سخن خوش شد گفت در فلان کوه بروید بمانید حکایت[4] روزی در خانه مغلی مهمانی بود سید شریف را طلبیده بودند این درویش را هم بردند سید بتعظیم و تکریم ما را بسیار نواخت و پیش آمد و[5] بر زانوی[6] ادب نشست بحثی نکرد این درویش گفت سیدا[7] واقعه که اهل دهلی را افتاده حمل بر ابتلا کنید[8] یا بر استدراج سید گفت بندگی مخدوم این چنین واقعه شیخ نجم الدین دایه را افتاده بود در دیباچه مرصاد العباد که تصنیف ایشان است ذکر کرده است و آن دلالت بر ابتلا کند[9] اما سید تعین نکرد و بنا بر آن که شاید این درویش در تعیین دخلی کند حواله بکتاب کرد یا سبب تعظیم این درویش حکایت[10] مغلی[11] دیگر ضیافت کرده بود اکابر سمرقند حاضر شده بودند شخصی این درویش را پرسید سماع چگونه ست گفتیم علماء نشسته اند جواب خواهند فرمود یکی گفت حرام است سائل را گفتیم بپرس که علت حرمت[12] چیست سائل گفت[14] ما یوجب[15]

۱ک = ندارد ۲ح = دشمن است ۳ک = و ۴ک = ندارد ۵ک = ندارد ۶ح و ک = زانو ۷ک = سید ۸ح = ابتداکند ۹ح = ابتدا ۱۰ک = ندارد ۱۱ک = معلی ۱۲ح = ندارد ۱۴ح = حرمت مجیب گفتیم ۱۵ک = موجب

حرمت السماع گفت[1] لهو وطرب اگر نباشد همه ساکت شدند

بعده ربابی[2] رباب زد گفتیم این نیک است یا بد گفتند بد گفتیم بد باید

زد اشارت کرد[3] قوالان شروع کردند **حکایت**[4] روزی عارف خادم

گفت دانشمندی است این جا گوشه نشین و نیز مستعد

و ظریف اوصاف شما[5] شنیده است[6] ملاقات شما

بباید[7] ما را دل کشید رفتیم[8] در بسته بود شخصی بیرون آمد او خبر کرد

ما را درون طلبید دیدیم چند نفر حلقه کرده[9] بغار بزرگ بالیده[10]

نرم می خوردند ما دو نفر[11] جای دادند و این درویش را نیت صوم بود یکی

از جماعت آن لقمها بزرگ همچنان میبکرد[12] در دهان نمی گنجد

این درویش گفت عدل ساعة خیر من عبادة ستین سنة آن

بر سر نشد بلکه روی ترش کرد که اوصاف حضرت شیخ جنید

میگفتند اما این حدیث مناسب حال نیست بعده[13] لقمه

هم بران هیچ کرد گفتیم[14] عدل یا[15] اخی آن بزرگوار از خنده بیهوش

شد گفت حضرت شیخ در سالها ما را مرهم کردی ما نترسم این را

نمی گفتیم حدیث شما برمحل بود ما برسر نشدیم او گفت خادم شیخ

هم تقصیر میکند گفتیم او دو حصه برمیدارد یک حصه خود دوم[16] حصه

١ح= ندارد ٢ک=بعد بابی ٣ک= کرده شد ٤ک= ندارد ٥ک=شما
٦ح=ندارد ٧ح= بیانید ٨ک= ندارد ٩ح= ندارد ١٠ح= برمالیده
١١ح=مادونفررا ١٢ح=میگیرد ١٣ح= ندارد ١٤ک=ندارد ١٥ک=را ١٦ک= یک

ازانِ من آن بزرگوار بدین لطیفه ہم منشرح شد گفت این جا دانشمندی
ظریف نابینا اما از روایت[ء] منکر است گفتیم حسابی منکر است
یعنی چون چشم ندارد لابد منکر شد[۱] این لطیفه ہم پسند بگفت
بندگی مخدوم چنانچه [ازرا] شنیده بودیم اضعاف[۲] آن یافتیم دیگر [در][۳] مجلس
سلطان محمّد بہادر ذکر این درویش افتاد که این درویش
دہلوی میگوید که امیر تیمور دہلی را که[۴] خراب کرده است ظلم و تعدی کرده
و علمای این مقام علم ندارند ازان مانع نشدند الیاس خواجه وزیر دست
این درویش گرفته نزدیک[۵] سراپرده رفت و گفت بشنوید که چه میگوید[۶]
فرمان شد چون شیخ ہمچنین میگوید فردا علما را جمع کنند[۷] و شیخ را ہم
فرمان برسان[۸] که در محضر حاضر شوند آن فرمان در تمام شہر منتشر شد
که فردا با شیخ محضر خواہد شد تا بچه انجامد بیشتر خلق غمگین شدند الیاس
خواجه گفت بندگی حضرت مخدوم شما چون حاضر شوید باید که ساکت
باشید[۹] ابتدای بحث نکنید[۱۰] من جانب شما خواہم بود کسی را مجال بحث
با شما نخواہد شد شخصی که بر ما بے لطفی داشت و پیش سلطان بدگوئی
میکرد ملاقات شد او را گفتیم الیاس خواجه کجا است[۱۱] گفت
الیاس خواجه را چه میکنند[۱۲] امیر از شما بے مزه است[۱۳] فردا[۱۴] علماء

۱ کذا در ہر دو نسخه احتمالاً "رویت" میباشد ۲ ح=شود ۲ ک= اصعاف
۳ ح= ندارد ٤ ک=ندارد ۵ نزدیک ترز ٦ ک=چه میگویند ۷ ح=کنند
۸ ک=برسانند ۹ ح= باشند ۱۰ ک= ندارد ۱۱ ک= ندارد ۱۲ ح= میکنند
۱۳ ک= مز ۱٤ ک=کیفیت

باشما بحث نخواهند کرد و اوراگفتیم ما را پندے دہ تلقین خوبی کرد[1]
کہ در صحنِ دیوان بروید[2] تا حالان شما را بر گیرند و گذارا کنند زیرا چہ بزرگی
اگر می آید ویرا حالان اگر ہمچنین میکنند[3] ہجوم شود بغیر علم یا دت، برین طریق
ببرند[4] در آن محلت آمد[5] تا بودیم عورات و مرد محزون شدند عورتی دران محلت
شب را خواب دید[5] کہ ہم حضرت شیخ را بر اسپ خنگی[6] سوار دیدیم کہ از ہوا[7] در
بالا[8] میرود آن عورت آمد بشارت داد کہ شیخ شما را حج خواہید[9]
بود امشب ہمچنین خواب دیدیم پگاہ بدر سرا ے رفتیم حالان ہیچ[10] مزاحم نہ
شدند بر چبوترہ بر آمدیم نشستیم ملک العلما حاضر شد شخصے گفت بندگی
حضرت شیخ شما چہ بحث خواہید کرد بفرمائید[11] تا باز گردانیم ما جوابی
ندادیم باز دیگر گفت گفتیم بالا چبوترہ بیا تا بگویم بحث را کفایت
باید بعد ازان اورا گفتیم این معنی کہ[12] تیمور بر خلقِ دہلی کرد حلال است
یا[13] حرام او خفتہ شد[14] اگر حرام گوید ملزم می[15] شود و اگر حلال گوید کافر می شود
ملک العلما گفت[16] زود جواب بگو ترا چہ مجال است، کہ درین مقام درآئی
او را[17] از اینجا کشیدند بقا ے راز دہلی اسیر کردہ مسلمان کردہ آوردہ بودند
او را حاضر کردند تا او گواہی دہد کہ در دہلی بیع خمر و[18] فواحش آنکارا
بود او را بزبانِ ہندوی گفتیم کجا آمدہ[19] می خواہی کہ ہم مقام آبا و اجداد خود را

[1] ک = تلقینی [2] ح = روند [3] ح = میکند [4] نبرند = ح [5] ح = ندارد [6] ک = خنگ
[7] ح = ندارد [8] ح = باراہ [9] ح و ک = خواہید [10] ک = ازلاء گذر کردند
[11] ح = بفرمایند [12] ک = ندارد [13] ک = با [14] ک = خفہ [15] ک = ندارد
[16] ک = گفت [17] ح = ندارد [18] ک = ندارد [19] ح = آمد

فضیحت کنی علال زادگی نباشد آن بقال بعنایت اللہ

آن مجلس گذاشت علماؤ اتراک جمع شدند ہمہ روی برین درویش

داشتند سلطان رسید بر چبوترہ نشست ملک العلماؤ الیاس خواجہ

گفتند شیخ شما ہدایت مکنید ہر بار ہمیں میگویانید[1] ند شیخ

بکر نام مردی بود کہ او را سلطان تعظیم بسیار نمود[2] او را می گفتیم!

فرمان شد شیخ چہ میگویند ما زانو باطرف سلطان گردانیدہ

گفتیم شاہا روزے چند در سایہ دولت آسودہ بودیم اگر اجازت شود

سوے حجاز سفر کنیم فرمان شد ہوا برف است و شما نازک تاب[3]

آور دن نتوانید[4] روزنامہ زیچ طلبید[5] ند حساب دیدند[6] ہنوز دوازدہ

یا سیزدہ روز برف باقی است گفتیم تا آنکہ فرمان تمام شود[7] چند روز

خواہند گرفت فرمان شد سید خطاط بندگی حضرت شیخ را فرمان

نبشتہ بدہ سلطان ہمیں قدر گفت و محل درون رفت ہمہ ملوک مبارکباد

کردند[8] فتوح فرستادند زن شحنہ شوہر[9] را گفت ہر کسے براے شیخ مبارکباد و فتوح

فرستادہ از خانہ ما چیزے نرفت شحنہ گفت مرا دیوان مصادرہ کردہ

است از کجا بفرستیم امروز زرینہ قسط التسمر جدا کن ہر چہ زیادہ

ماند بر بندگی حضرت ببر[10] کم زن تسمر دہ[11] تنکہ زیادت شد شحنہ

---

۱ ک= میگوید ۲ عظیم بسیار بود=ح ۳ ح= ندارد ۴ ک= توانید
۵ ح= طلبید ۶ ح= ندارد ۷ ک= ندارد ۸ ح= برسانیدند
۹ ک= شوہرم ۱۰ ح= ببرم ۱۱ ک= دو

در تعجب شد گفت بیا تا من بشمرم[1] نسخه بشمرد بست تنگه زیاده

شد باز عورت شمرد سی تنگه زیاده شد قسط در دیوان دادند و سی تنگه برین

درویش آوردند گفتند بندگی حضرت مخدوم این قصه

بو العجب است کرامت آنحضرت ظاهر است[2] ما یقین میدانستیم[3]

که قسط اگر تمام باشد[4] عجب بود سه بار گردانیدیم[5] شمردیم هر بار

ده تنگه زیاده شد از جمله[6] سی تنگه زیاده شد آن[7] (زیادت) من الله تعالی

برای بندگی حضرت مخدوم است ورنه ما در تدبیر

قسط شبه بود **حکایت**[8] روزی در مجلس سلطان محمد بهادر

ذکر این درویش افتاد یکی از ملوک بر سلطان گفت شیخ دهلی

دانشمند است بزرگی دیگر گفت شیخ دانشمند و[9] صاحب وقت اند

و تکیه این درویش در سمرقند بخانه عورتی پاکی معتقده بود[10]

دختری داشت نام او مراد بر آور[11] بود روزی از غایت سرما در آفتاب

آمده نشسته بودیم دختر کی آغاز کرد[12] که خلق هندوستان سیاه فام[13]

چرا باشند گفتیم یک ساعتی را[14] منشوش حال ما چرا می شوی[15] میهمانی

(و تا اکنون مرا معلوم نیست که قلتاق)

یا برخیزیم مادرش ملامت کرد که قلتاق[16] چه باشد ترا یارای[17] آن باشد

که بحضور حضرت شیخ تکلم کنی خیس کن و همه عورات سمرقند معتقده بودند

---

۱ ح= بشمرد ۲ ک= ندارد ۳ ک= میدانستیم ۴ ک= شود ۵ ح و ک= گردانیدم
۶ ک= آنجمله ۷ ک= ندارد ۸ ک= ندارد ۹ ح= ندارد ۱۰ ح= بودی
۱۱ ک= درياور ۱۲ ک= ندارد ۱۳ ک= وام ۱۴ ک= ندارد ۱۵ ح= شود
۱۶ ح= ندارد و درنسخه "ک" بجای قلتاق 'فلناف' ضبط شده ۱۷ ک= بار

چنانچه وقتی عورتی را شکم درد شد در تکیه ما آمد و ما با مغلی
در محل درون بحثی مشغول بودیم او را در[1] زور آورد و آن مغل
نمی خاست از فرود نعلین ما خاکی برد[2] و در آب انداخت و خورد
بعنایت الله تعالی همان زمان شفا شد" سید خطاط
چون فرمان نبشت داد ما روان شدیم همه عورات محلت زاری
و عریو[3] بعضی سرها برهنه کردند و نعرها برآوردند که ای نعمان ما و ای
عالم ربانی و شیخ حقانی بعده چون در بلخ رسیدیم خاوندزاده
مقطع بود و لب آب آمو[4] از بلخ گروهی دو سه باشند در گذار او
اجازت شحنه میخواهند خاوندزاده را ملاقات کردیم فرمان نمودیم
فرمان برین جمله نبشته بود هو الغنی سلطان محمود خان بن سعید[5] بن محمد سلطان
بهادر سورونیزد[6] درین وقت شیخ احمد اعظم[7] دهلوی رخصت خواست (اعازم د
و بعزم زیارت بیت الله الحرام احرام بسته[8] توجه نمود هرچند
صحبت او مغتنم است و ظاهر و باطن آراسته او چنانکه دل خواسته
و غیبت او جایز نمی فرمایم اما چون عزم ادراک دولتی عظیم شرفنا
الله وایاه بها جزم کرده منع نتوانستیم نمود و جواز[9] دادیم تا روانه شود
داروغگان و حکام ممالک و[10] محافظان راه و قولها و ایلچیان

١ ک= در دروازه ٢ ک= بود هر ٣ ک= ندارد ٤ ح= آموزک = آمون
٥ ح وک= سعند ٦ ک= سوروسیر ٧ کذا در هردو نسخه ٨ ح= بسته داشت
٩ ک= جوار ١٠ ح= روایات ک= روان و

و آیندگان و روندگان باید که وظیفهٔ رعایت و مراقبت[1] بتقدیم رسانند
به هیچ وجه از وجوه مانع و معترض نگردند و پنج نفر مرد[2] و یک اسپ و یک سر
درازگوش که همراه دارد جواز داده بسلامت بگذرانند و در راه[3] گذار
تشویش اوقات او نفرمایند ایلچیان باید که او و الاغ او نگیرند و مزاحم
نشوند و چون بتوقیع رفیع موشح و موضع گردد اعتماد نمایند کتب بالامر العالی
اعلاه الله تعالی و حکم بنفاذه فی الثانی عشر من جمادی الاولی
اثنین و تسعمائة خاوندزاده فرمان مطالعه کرد اما چندانی مبالات
نکرده امیر سلیمان نام مردی زرادی زره‌های[4] تیمور را جلا میداد نیز
بروی گفتیم او هم چیزی نگفت سوار شد از دیوان بیرون رفت
ما با او عقب شده رفتیم جائی که زره‌ها را جلا میداد تند ایستاد
گفت شما را که آورد گفتیم شمان آوردید[5] خندید بازگشت
در دیوان آمد گفت شما[6] برابر من نیائید[7] بعد بیائید[8] تا او گمان
به بر من نکند ما بعده رفتیم هیچ التفاتی نکرد دوم روز خاوندزاده
سوار شده در حوض خود رفت حوض نو کاویده بود و در آن حوض آب
از چشمه می‌خواست ببرد که از آن چشمه خلق آب در کشتهای خویش
سالها بازمیدهند میان خلق آن نواحی و میان خاوندزاده

۱ ح = مراتبت ۲ ح = کس هرد ۳ ح = راه و ٤ ح = زینهاء
۵ ح = آوردند ٦ ک = سما ۷ ح = می آیند ۸ ح = می آیند

گفت بسیار شد همچنان این درویش رفت خلق استقبال کرده [1]

آمدند ما را حکم ساختند که شرعاً چه می آید چه [2] گفتیم شرعاً اول

کشتها آب بنوبت [3] دهند بعده در حوض برند خاوندزاده را غصه

بر ما زیادت شد خلق گفت [4] بندگی حضرت شیخ شما دنبال این

چه می گردید در سر آب شحنهٔ دگر است شخصے را بر وے فرستادند که شیخ

دهلی فرمان پادشاه آورده [5] الله او مردے بزرگ است تعظیم او می باید کرد

و استقبال باید نمود ما روے بر لب آب نهادیم امیر سلیمان حایل شد

که امروز مهمان من باشید گفتیم همین مهمانی شماست که امروز گذارا [6] نشویم

امیر سلیمان چابکی خوبی از آستین خود کشید که بندگی حضرت مخدوم

این یادگار من بخدمت شما باشد ما را پند و [7] دادم گفت یک حکایت

از من بشنوید ما دو برادران بودیم دو سر دراز گوش داشتیم در تکابوی [8] روزگار

میگذرانیدیم در منزلی فرود آمدیم یگان پای از هر دو دراز گوش

در یک زنجیر بستیم تا دزد نبرد [9] دزد اما استاد تر بود زمینی و بیشتر دیده [10]

بریده [12] را برد چون بیدار شدیم [دیدیم که] [13] بیچاره دراز گوش

دست [11] یک دراز گوش دست بریده از درد دست هر طرفی لنگان میگشت

بندگی حضرت مخدوم باید که شما هشیار در راه بمانید غفلت

نه کنید و بازگشت شحنهٔ آب با نفران خود استقبال ما کرده ملاقات کردیم

١ ح = ندارد ٢ ح = می گفتیم ٣ ک = بنویت ٤ ک = گفتند ٥ ح = آوردند
٦ ک = گذار ٧ ح = ندارد ٨ ک = تکابوی ٩ ح = ندارد ١٠ ح = دید
١١ ک = است ١٢ ح = ندارد ١٣ ک = ندارد

تعظیم بسیار کرد کشتی[۱] آراسته اول رخت و مراکب فرود آورد وندبار
دوم این درویش را هم گذارا کردند نماز شام دیهی رسیدیم باران بود
مقام نیافتیم در پناهِ دیواری ماندیم مارا و چارپا[۲] را طعامی و علفی نه
صباح را سوار شدیم در مقامی[۳] آمدیم که آنجا درویشی بود بملاقات
او رفتیم در خانه نبود امّا زنی نیک بختی داشت محلی خوبی فرود آورد
مارا سردی باران سخت زور آورده گفتیم ای صبیه[۴] آتشی داری مارا گرم
کنی بگفتن ما آتش[۵] کرد همچنان شیخ رسید شیخ مارا هر چیزی
از مسائل شرعی پرسیدن[۶] گرفت و شیخ را عمل بر توره چنگیز خان
بود ما بر دین محمد رسول الله صلی الله علیه وسلم جواب میگفتیم
[۷] که ایشان چه می فرمایند خادم میگفت
شیخ بر سر نمی شد خادم را میگفت موجه میفرمایند دین محمد رسول
الله صلی الله علیه وسلم برین است شیخ هر مسئله دستهای مالید
[۸] میگفت
وای ولی خادم دانا بود تفهیم میکرد شیخ ضیافت نیکو کرد
گفتیم ای شیخ صبیه[۹] تست که مارا بآتش زنده کرد که الشیخ یحیی و یمیت
صباح را چون روان شدن[۱۰] گرفتیم خادم خبر داد که شیخ را
فکر این شده است که[۱۱] شما را بدارد و دختر کی بدهد حالیا که می آید
شما را به بهانه وداع خواهند[۱۲] برد و خواهند داشت هوشدارید[۱۳]

۱ ک= کستی ۲ ک= اسپ ۳ ک= مقام ۴ ک= سنه ۵ ح= گرم؟ آتش
۶ ک= پرسیدند ۷ ح= ندارد ۸ ح= ندارد ۹ ک= سنه ۱۰ ک= شدند
۱۱ ح= ندارد ۱۲ ک= خواهدکرد ۱۳ ک= هوشدار باشید

چون شیخ آمد ع۱ مهمان کرد گفت عورات بجمال شما می خواهند که ع۱ مشرف
شوند همه منتظر شما اند و ما سوار درون خانه رفتیم هرچند
عورات گفتند فرود آیند بنشینند گفتیم ما روان می شویم
چون سوار شدیم فرود ع۲ نیائیم بسیار کوشیدند راه ندادیم
روان شدیم شیخ ع۳ خادمی ع۴ را گفت راهی دیگر بنمای او بفرق دو سه
کروه راهی نمود دران راه درآمدیم غلط کردیم در جنگلی ع۵ افتادیم
که تنگ ع۶ بوده نه آبادانی نه آب یافتیم تا میانه ع۷ وقت
شد حیرت پیش آمد تشنه در ع۸ جنگل وها بودن میرفتیم ع۸ نه آدمی درو می ع۸ نه پرنده رنج عجیب
گرفتیم مرکب تیز راندیم بیگاه شده بود راهی یافتیم دیهی پیش آمد
یکی ملاقات شد ع۹ گفت ازین رنج چگونه آمدید ع۱۰ گفتیم راه غلط
کرده بودیم گفت کرامت شما بود که رنج عجیب گرفتید ع۱۱ درین
بیابان بسیار تلف شده اند در قصبهٔ رسیدیم بانگ نماز
شام شنیدیم برای نماز در مسجد درآمدیم امام بعد نماز
بحث در مسئله کردن گرفت جواب گفتیم بیرون شدیم اسپ
نیافتیم امام آوازی کرد که در ع۱۲ دروازه ببستند بندگی حضرت مخدوم
تعلق مکنید حالیا اسپ می آید ناگاه شخصی اسپ آورد

١ ح = ندارد ٢ ک = ندارد ٣ ح = ندارد ٤ ک = خادم ٥ ح = جنگل
٦ ک = سنگ ٧ ح = میان ٨ ح = ندارد ٩ ک = کرد ١٠ ح = آمدند
١١ ح = گرفتند ١٢ ح = ندارد

بو العجب ضابطه آن قصبه دیدیم از آن جا روان شدیم در دیه
شیخ مودود چشتی که سرچشمهٔ چشتیان[1] دران وقت او بود
رسیدیم و شیخ مودود دامادی داشت سرباک با شیخ نمردی
ورزیده در بیابانی[2] تنها گوسفندان بسیار گرفته مانده بود
هرکه بروے میرفت او را تیز زدی گفتیم یک نفر برابر ما بیاید
او را از دور بنماید یکے پیش شد دران بیابان رفتیم از دور نمود
بازگشت چون با با نظر دوچار[3] شد گفتیم این چه ساز است این چنین
و چنین نرم شد گفت بندگی حضرت مخدوم ایشان با من بے
وضعی میکنند[4] شیخ پشتی دختر میکنند و من تاب آوردن نمی
توانم گفتیم تو سخن ما رد[5] نکنی بیا با ایشان آشتی بدهانم مطیع شد
برابراین درویش بازگشت آشتی دادیم دهقانیان در تعجب
شدند که زہے قوتی که بندگی حضرت مخدوم را هست[6] آن ترک
به کسے سبب فرود نمی آورد بندگی حضرت مخدوم[7] او را موم کردند از آنجا چون روان
شدیم شیخ مودود برائے رسانیدن[8] ما یک روز برابر بود هر چیز
از آداب[9] مشائخ میگفتیم حکایت[10] چون شیخ مودود
از شیخ[11] وداع کرده روان شد از موضع ساتیج[12] داماد خود را

١ ح= چشتیانست ک= چشتیاتست ٢ ک= بیانی ٣ ک= دوچهار نظر
٤ ح= میکشد ٥ ک= در ٦ ک= راست ٧ ح= ندارد ٨ ح= رسیدن
٩ ح= ادب ١٠ ک= ندارد ١١ سلطان در هر نسخه که صحیح بنظر نمی رسد۔ ظاهراً سهو کاتب نسخهٔ منقول عنه است۔ ١٢ ک= ساتیج

اسمٰعیل امیر فرستادہ بود برین درویش فرستاد یک جفت کارد آورد وگفت شیخ مودود خدمت رسانیده است وگفته است مارا جنگل وکتل راه می باید مالید کوه وکوه ساری باید گذشت فاتحه درخواست کرده اند که بر حال ما کنید مسکین چون در¹ حرغزار غیرے درآمد وبے ملاقات رفت سفر مبارک شد درمیان راه بقضاء الله تعالی یسری² شد چون بت هر برات آمدیم شیخ شهاب الدین خیلوانی³ را ملاقات کردیم شیخی کامگارے یافتیم در راه مشیخت آراسته ومقامات سلوک دریافته پیر معمر بود وبسیار مشائخ را دیده وعقبات درویشی را عبور کرده تا دیری در صحبت ایشان بوده ایم چون بازگشتیم پسران را گفت بر بنده گی حضرت شیخ احمد دهلوی بر وید⁴ بملاقات مشرف شوید تا آنکه بر ما نشسته بود حضور داشتیم شیخزادگان آمدند ملاقات کردند وکیفیت مذکور گفتند که والد اوصاف شما بسیار میکرد با ایشان وداع کرده روان شدیم ملکت⁵ آغاز آن امیر⁶ شهرخ شنید که شیخ جهان قطب زمان شیخ احمد دهلوی بر شیخ شهاب الدین خیلوانی⁷ آمده بود⁸ ندا مارا علم چرا نه دادید⁹ بر ما صحیفه نبشت¹⁰

شیخ را گفته فرستاد که⁹ شیخ

۱ک= ندارد ۲ح= بسری ۳کذا در هر دو نسخه ولی "خلوتی" یا "جلوانی" صحیح بنظر می رسد ۴ح= ندارد ۵ح و ک= ملکت ۷ح= خیلواتی ۸ح= بود ۹ح= ندارد ۱۰ک= نوشت

که مدفن امام فخر الدین در هرات است بندگی حضرت مخدوم

زیارت نکرده اند و بنده تنهاملک[۱] آغا هم تا سنف بسیار کنند[۲]

دیگر[۳] بزیارت امام مشرف شویم ملک[۴] آغا هم آمد فتح[۵] ملاقات کرد

ساعتی نشست گفتیم:

ملکهٔ[۶] عشق ملک نه از کرم الهیم . نیست من و پلاس[۷] غم اینست قبای[۸] بادشاهیم

همان مصرع اول خواندیم ملک آغا حکایت[۹] چهل چهار

طبقات مشائخ تمام گفت گفتیم آنچه ما را می باید گفت

شما میفرمائید لعبدهٔ ملک گفت اگر بندگی حضرت[۱۰] مخدوم

در هرات بمانند یک مدرسه بنا کنم خلق از برکات[۱۱] شما

بسیار نفع گیرند ما قبول نکردیم ملک نقرهٔ[۱۲]

بسیار پیش آورد باز گشت ما نقرهٔ مذکور برای حاضران مجلس را

قسمت کردیم ملک[۱۳] شنید همان مقدار نقره بر ما فرستاد و گفت

شما را دور دست می باید رفت بضرورت ستده شد[۱۴] چون

بقندهار رسیدیم امیر سیفل[۱۵] مقطع بود و بر ما اعتقادی داشت

گفت بندگی حضرت مخدوم در بلندی[۱۶] باغی دارم هزار درهزار قبول

کنند و با ما موافقت فرمایند درویشی آن را قبول نکرد و

بلند نام موضع ایست در جوار قندهار و منکوحهٔ امیر سیفل

۱ح وک = ملکت ۲ ح = کرد ۳ ک = ندارد ٤ ح وک = ملکت ٥ ح = ندارد
٦ ح وک = ملکت ٧ ح = بداس ٨ ح = ندارد ٩ ک = آغا آغاز ١٠ ح = ندارد
١١ ک = برکت ١٢ ح = ندارد ١٣ ح وک = ملکت ١٤ ک = ستد شده
١٥ ح = سفل ١٦ ح = بلند

را شاهزاده امیر تیمور خواهر[1] می خواند چون روان شدن[2] گرفتیم
امیر سیفل او را گفت بندگی حضرت مخدوم[3] روان می شوند تو چه پیشکش آری
او گفت هرچه تو پیش[4] بیاری امیر سیفل بسیار خواست[5] که ما را باز دارد
اما بهول قبر بابا اسحاق نماندیم چون در قصبه اُج[6] رسیدیم در برج ماموں
فرود آمدیم دوم روز وقت استوا بالاء برج سید السادات
سید را جو میزری بر سر انداخته رسیدند کسے را نگفتند که خبر کنید
و فرمودند یا الله مخدوم را[7] امروز علم شد گفتیم ای میران شما
علم دو جهانی مطلوب است هژده تنکه یا کم[8] علوفه پیش[9]
آوردند بعده در ملک واهن آمدیم گفتند شیخ را در خانه طرب
فرود آرند در خاطر نگران شدیم چون رفتیم خانه خوبی خالی دیدیم[10] فرود
آمدیم عورتی زال صالحه مصلیه محافظت می نمود[11] و ما را ماندگی راه زور آورده
بود نماز عشا کهتر گذاردیم خفتیم میان شب برای تهجد خاستیم
گزاردیم و چشم پیش کردیم عورت مصلیه بود[12] آغاز کرد این چه درویشی چه شیخی
است که وقت صباح شد هنوز بیدار نمی شود[13] پسر شر گفت
شیخ بیدار شده بودند[14] نماز بسیار گزارد[15] و شما بیدار
نه شدید آن عورت عورتی دیگر را که مصلیه بود خبر کرد او برای ملاقات

۱ح= خواهرش ۲ح و ک= شد ۳ح= شیخ ۴ک= ندارد ۵ک= ندارد
۶ک= اج ۷ک= مرا ۸ک= وکم ۹ پیش علوفه =ح ۱۰ دیدم در هر دو نسخه
۱۱ح= بود ۱۲ح= شیخ ۱۳ک= نمیشوید ۱۴ح= بود ۱۵ح= گزارد

ما آمد هر چیزی از مسائل پرسید[1] تنبیهه کردیم آن عورت ساختگی توشته
کرد ما شنیدیم که[2] شتر سواری از جبلپور[2] آمده است روان می شود
با سوار شدیم از عقب شتر سوار مذکور عورات مذکوره نفر فرستاده
که آن شتر سوار راه زن است اسپ شما را خواهند ستد در صحبت
او رفتن مصلحت نیست گفتیم چون سوار شدیم چگونه باز گردیم بر
سر حوضی رسیدیم برای وضو فرود آمدیم شتر سوار مذکور کرتی خود برای
ما آورد و خدمت کرد لگام از دهن اسپ کشید چرانیدن گرفت
در دل قصه[3] عورات یاد آمد گفتیم خدای تعالی کافیست وضو کردیم
سوار شدیم شتر تیز میرفت اسپ ما کره بود[4] با این بهم فرق افتاد[5]
او از جهت ما وقفه میکرد ما میرسیدیم دوم روز شتر سوار گفت
مرا فرصت وفا نمیکند از ینجا جبلپور یک روز راه است و در
میان خوف نیست شما وقفه کرده بیایید شتر سوار رفت
ما نماز شام بر سر چاهی رسیدیم پیری[6] معمری بود نیمی از دستار
خود پاره کردیم او را دادیم تا دیگر طعامی کند پیر گفت شیخ غله نایافت
است زن او آمد در خانه بر و کیفیت دیار گفت که قحط مهلک افتاده
است قافله چند گردون اینجا رسیده بود از بی آبی دبی کاهی[7]

۱ ک = پرسیدند ۲ ح = ندارد ۳ ک = قصد ۴ ک = ندارد
۵ ک = میافتاد ۶ ک = پیری و ۷ ح = بی دبی وبی گاهی

ستوران سقط شدند آدمیان گرد و نها گذاشته رفتند
درین گفتار شب بسیار رفت بعد دیر دو نانی پیش آورد بگاه
از آنجا روان شدیم در جیسلمیر رسیدیم شتر سوار مذکور رای که بمقدم
جیسلمیر را خبر کرده بود که این چنین بزرگی می آید او استقبال کرده در خانه
فرود آورده برهمنان را[1] طلبیده[2] گفت با[3] شیخ بحث کنید
برهمنان گفتند ما را چیزی بپرسید گفتیم ما در علم شما خویتی[4] نداریم
اما میدانیم که شما اوتار میگویند[5] یعنی تناسخ قائلید[6] ایشان
گفتند بغیر اوتار بقاء عالم ممکن نیست ما گفتیم بسرگ و نرک
مقر اید[7] یا نه گفتند چون گنهگار[8] را میگویند که موشی شود کرمی گردد
بسبب شامت[9] گناه و نیکوکار را آدمی کنید[10] برین تقریر عملها را جزا[11]
هم درین جهان باشد کس در بهشت و دوزخ که سرگ و نرک
است که برود[12 چون] این مقدمه باطل[12 شد] پس تناسخ هم باطل شد
برهمنان ملزم شدند رای که منصف شد برما[13] تحسین کرد که شیخ
برحق اند ما از آنجا روان شدیم برهمنان تا دو سه گروه رکاب ما آمدند
هر چیزی می پرسیدند جواب ایشان می گفتیم بعده باز گردانیدیم

١ح= ندارد ٢ک= طلبید ٣ح= یا ٤ک = حویتی ٥ح= رامیگویند
٦ک= قالید ٧ح= اند ک = آید ٨ک= نی (بی) گناه ٩ح و ک = شامیت
١٠ک= می کنید ١١ک= چرا ١٢ح= ندارد ١٣ح= مارا

فصل پانزدهم[1]

در کیفیت رسیدن بندگی حضرت شیخ جهان قطب زمان از خراسان در گجرات در حیات مظفرشاه سلطان۔ بندگی حضرت شیخ جهان قطب زمان میفرمودند تا[2] ماه رجب سنه اثنین و ثمانمائه در موضع بیلی[3] جوار شهر نهرواله دیدیم[4] در شهر در[5] آمدیم ایوب قوال[6] شیخ ملاقات شد برادر سید محمد گیسودراز رفت مولانا خانو محتسب را گفت که بندگی حضرت مخدوم شیخ احمد در فلان محلت فرود آمده اند مولانا مذکور بسید محمد گفت سید گفت بر سید شنیده میگویند یا دیده گفت بچشم خود دیدم انعام یافتم[7] دوم[8] روز سید روان شد در کنبهایت رفت در دیتابان دو سه روز[9] در خانه مسلمانی قرار گرفتند با او آشنائی شد هر سالے در سر کهیج می آمد ملاقات می شد مراعات بسیار میکردند بعده اتفاق شد که در دکهن بیروم[7] در دهولقه رسیدیم[8] از دهولقه گردونی کرایه[9] نشد گردونبان بعد سوار شدن گفت که مرا اول باید رفت نه گفتیم که در کهنبایت[10] می رویم ملک گفتم و را اول بران میرفتیم ناگاه گردونی از پیش پیدا شد گردونبان[11] او را گفت که بندگی حضرت مخدوم را عزیمت کهنبایت است وے گفت زہے دولت بر گردون او[12] کرایه داده نشستیم[13] قاضی معین

١ ک=یازدهم ٢ ک=در ٣ ک=برلی ٤ ک=دید ٥ ک=ندارد ٦ ح=کوسج
٧ ح=یافتیم ٨ ح=در ٩ ک=ندارد ٧=بروند ٨ ک=رسیدند ٩ ح=کری
١٠ ک=کهمایت ١١ ک=گردونیان ١٢ ح=اوراکراه ١٣ ح=نشستم

پسرِ قاضی فخر الدین حاکم کھٹو برابر بود گفتیم قاضی معین الدین شما
را اتفاق کجا است گفت او در زادگان من در کھضیایت اند صاحبان
عمل اند بر ایشان میرویم در خاطر گرانی آمد سید کرم الله پسر سید رحمة الله
ناگوری شنید در حال برین درویش آمد گفت مقامی ظریف دارم
در خانه[1] بنده فرود آیند هرچند که عذر کرده شد نشنید در خانهٔ خود بر[2] در دروازه
بزرگی دیگر را فرود آورده بود او را مقامی دیگر داد ما را بران دروازه داشت
قاضی نظام الدین با پسران که اقربای قاضی معین الدین مذکور اند بجهت ملاقات
ما آمد[3] گفت ما بندگان قدیم ازان شما باشیم ما را گذاشته محل دیگر
چگونه فرود آیند ما سخت بیدل می شویم روز جمعه قاضی نظام الدین
با جماعت خود بر ما آمد گفتیم قاضی شما در مسجد بر وید قاضی گفت سید محمد
گیسو دراز و شیخ رکن الدین چشتی با گرد و فر در مسجد خواهند آمد من کی روا دارم
که شما تنها در مسجد روید ما دیانی[4] با زین خدمتی پیش آورد خود با پسران
در رکاب شد نفس را گفتیم تو دل شکسته چرا میکنی که ما کجا فرود خواهیم آمد خاطر جمع
دار مولی ترا باد قرمید[5] ادا بعده به قاضی معین الدین ملاقات شد گفت
او در خدمت شما مادیان خدمتی آورد مرا یک کهنه گی[6] داد گفتیم
مقدر[7] شما همان بود و مقدر[8] ما این بیت[9]

[1] ح= ندارد [2] ح= ندارد [3] ک= آمدند [4] ک= مادر بانی [5] کذا در هر دو نسخه احتمالاً "وقار" باید باشد۔ [6] کذا در هر دو نسخه مراد "از قسمی" از سواری" است [7] ح= مقصد، ک= مقدار [8] ک= مقدار [9] ک= ندارد

مقسمت ندهد روزئی که ننهاده است	اگر بپای بپوئی و یا به سر بدوی

بعده در کناره آب[۱] نربدا رفتیم ملاحان را نیز گذار نکردند گفتند کسی که در سمع [اعظم] همایون ظفرخان رسانیده است که بندگی حضرت شیخ احمد در دکهن می روند ملاحان را اشارت رسیده[۲] است که خدمت بندگی حضرت مخدوم را فرود نیارند ملک برهان الملک تاتارخانی را اشارت شده است که بخدمت بندگی حضرت شیخ احمد بروعرض دارکه متقدم نادوت سرکشی کرده است من بجهت گوشمال او در موضع راتپور[۳] مانده ام مرا فرصت نیست واگر نه خود بیایم خدمت کنم بلطف در لشکر بیاینه تا بیمن قدم ایشان[۴] این مهم هم بکفایت رسد ملک برهان الملک مذکور رسید پروانه نمود سبب آشنائی قدیم که در مسجد خانجهان آمد شد برما داشت در لشکر رفته شد[۵] خان رخت لعل[۶] در جوار سرای خود بجهت ما برآورده آنجا فرود آمدیم سلطان محمد تاتارخان گفته فرستاد که بنده را اشتیاق[۷] غالب است اگر اشارت شود[۸] سبقت کنم گفتیم هم بمصاحبت بدرخوتر باشد بعد نماز ظهر ظفرخان از راه نیز[۹] پیدا شد گفت کجا خوند کار شما شده[۱۰] گفتیم مگر ما را نمیدانی[۱۱] ملزم[۱۲] شد گفت من خدمتگار قدیم زایر شما ایم چگونه ندانیم[۱۳] در مسجد خانجهان بسیار ملاقات مشرف شده ایم

۱ح = لبیاء ک = لب آب ۲ ک = رسانیده ۳ ح = خوانده نمی شود احتمالاً صحیح "رتنپور" میباشد۔ ۴ ک = شما ۵ ک = ندارد ۶ ح و ک = نعل تصحیح قیاسی ۷ ح = آشنائی ۸ ح = باشد ۹ ک = شرز ۱۰ ک = ندارد ۱۱ کذا در هر دو نسخه احتمالاً اینجا محل "نمیدانی" هست۔ ۱۲ ک = گرم (نرم؟) ۱۳ ک = ندانم

گفتیم که[1] با این استعداد و پیلان دهلی را مددی نکردی[2] گفت بندگی
حضرت مخدوم آن پسرک یعنی بجلی خان را با چوندا[3] مفسد مقابله که
افتاده ولایت ناگور خراب ماند راه با مخالف گشت و لشکر در محصرهٔ
مندور مشغول شد تیر آن[4] کافر را بکفایت رسانیده بودیم اما از موضعی
آن پسرک که ناگفته از لشکر بازگشت وداع هم نه کرد دل شکسته شد
نهایت او ولایت ناگور گم خواهد کرد بضرورت در شهر پٹن بازگشتیم دیدیم
اگر مدد دهلی میکنیم گجرات مطلق از دست برود ضرورتا راضی بقضاء حق تعالی
شده ماندیم بعده طعام با تکلف موازنه صد رخت بر دست کارکنان
فرستاد و گفت هم برین نهج هر روز دو وقت ببرند گفتیم ما تنها ایم چندین
تکلف چراست ظفر خان گفت شما وقتی تنها نباشید زائران را
کار آید بعده سلطان محمد تاتار خان با برادران دیگر آمدند دو تبچه جامه
ظفر خان[5] بر دست ایشان فرستاد یکی از آن[6] صوف و سقلاط
و دوم از آن بهیرم و سالو با سلطان محمد تاتار خان بر خان گذرانید
که بندگی حضرت شیخ را یک[7] دیهی خوبی باید داد[8] تا خرج مطبخ ایشان شود
اشارت شد پیش در بر دیهی قابل را تتبع کن و[9] بیار بر در سرای[10]
آمد او دهرن نام تاکی بود مقطع دهولقه برو گفت اگر بزرگی از آشنایان تو

١ ک = کی ٢ ک = ندارد ٣ ک = چوندان ٤ ح = او ٥ ح = مظفر خان
٦ ک = از ٧ ح = ندارد ٨ ح = ندارد ٩ ح = ندارد ١٠ ح = شیخ سرای

ببایدچه نوع رعایت کنی بندگی حضرت شیخ احمد کهتو بزرگوار از آشنایان

قدیم ما آمده اند اشارت شده است دیهی قابل بدهند[1] در پرگنه دهولقه

که محصول اورا اندک باشد و حاصل بسیار بکنش او در حصن گفت

موضع اوتیلیه نام دیهی است[2] آنجنان اما در وجه بو بوبڈی بدو هزار تنکه

کرده، داده اند[3] کیفیت مذکور پیش خان گذرانند[4] خان فرمودند بوبو بدی

را دیهی بزرگ باید داد آں دیهه بندگی حضرت شیخ احمد را بدهند پروانه

دیهه مذکور تسلیم ما باشد و برای ملک بدر علا دامادو[*] نایب

غیبت نبشتند که بندگی حضرت شیخ را خانه خوبی[5] هر کجا که اختیار

کنند[6] برای سکونت بدهند و قاضی خان و محتسب را برابر فرستاد

در سرکهیج که رسیدیم مقامی خوبی کناره لب آب گوشه دیدیم همیں جا

اختیار افتاد که بسازیم ملک بدر علا خانه بدابو هره خوب و بزرگ

بود تسلیم ما کرد زن بدابو هره آمد و گفت شما مقتدا[7] مشائخ باشید در

خانه ما فقیران چرا می مانید ما را دستگاهی جز[8] ایں خانه نیست گفتیم

ما مقامی دیگر خواهیم گرفت اما سبب مصلحت تو دریں خانه مانده ایم ناگاه

ایں کیفیت در دیوان رسید خانه غیرے را بدهانند از دست تو ابر[9] و داز هر

سالی چندین علوفه کرایه[10] بستانی بعده عمارت خانه دوم کردند که در جوار آن خانه

---

۱ ح = بدهند ۲ ک = ندارد ۳ ک = دادند ۴ ک = گذرانید ☆کذا در هر دو نسخه احتمالاً "دامادو" باشد ۵ ک = ندارد ۶ ح = کنند ۷ ح = مقرر ۸ ح = نه جز، ک = به جز ۹ ح = ندارد ۱۰ ح = غله کری

بود اختیار کردند همسایگان را که دعوی آن مقام میکردند مال داده خوشنود کردند میان چهار ده روز بجای آن مزبله[۱] خانه ظریف ساختند دران خانه سکونت کردند[۲] در خانه بدابوهره بعضی خدمتگاران را داشتند[۳] وکرایه[۴] آن هر سالے بر عورت می رسانیدند و در سالی که موضع[۵] او تیلیه در خرج مطبخ بندگی حضرت شیخ جهان قطب زمان بود[۶] گندم بسیار شده بود چنانچه خبر آمد که هیچ[۷] بلندی و نشیبی بی گندم نیست سال دوم متصل مقدم موضع مذکور را اجازت دادیم اودهرن را خوش نیامد برخان کیفیت مذکور نبشت[۸] ومقدم مذکور در دادن وجه اجازت بر ما[۹] دغا کرد و حاصل بسیار شده بود پروانه خان بر اودهرن رسید محصول موضع مذکور را از پوته[۱۰] بده و بعد ازان تصرف کن آخر کار از شامت[۱۱] بیوفای مقدم با این درویش اودهرن مذکور سر مقدم مذکور ببرید در دیه تصرف کرد محصول بر مقدم ماند سال سیوم اودهرن معماری کرد شصت تنکه کاهید خواجه بده مقدم سرکیع را به خان فرستادیم فرمان شد بندگی حضرت مخدوم خوش اند و نه گفت برای چه آمدی و بچه مصلحت فرستاده اند مدتی خواجه بده در لشکر بود بازگشته[۱۲] آمد دو سر اسپ خریدیم کسے برخان رسانید که بندگی حضرت مخدوم دو سر اسپ خریده اند[۱۳] تا در دکهن بروند[۱۴] اودهرن را اشارت شد کیفیت دیه چیست

۱ ک= مزیله ۲ ح= کردم ۳ ح= داشتم ۴ ح= کراء ۵ ک= موضعی ۶ ح= وفا ۷ ک= ندارد ۸ ک= ندارد ۹ ک= برو ۱۰ ح= یوته ۱۱ ح و ک = شامیت ۱۲ ح و ک = گشت ۱۳ ح= است ۱۴ ح= برود

گفت سلطان از موضع محصول کاہیہ اشارت شد ز انچ[1] محصول از
خانۂ خود برسان دیہہ بستدی و بندگی حضرت شیخ را رنجانیدی
و خواجہ خاصہ حاجب[2] را اشارت شد بانصد تنکہ از خزانہ بر بندگی حضرت
شیخ ببرد داد کہ من زندہ ام مرا مگذارید خواجہ خاصہ بر بندگی حضرت
شیخ جہان قطب زمان آمد و بحث کرد کہ قریب یک لکہ تنکہ شما را
از خان رسیدہ است جواب آن[3] بگوئید[4] بعدہ روان شوید بندگی
حضرت مخدوم فرمودند جواب دو لکہ تنکہ بگوئیم[5] اما نمانی[6] مانم خواجہ عرض
داشت کہ من سخن برعایت مزاج خان گفتہ ام اما اشارت شدہ بود[7] کہ
چون بہ ہیچ نوع نمانند بگوئی تا من زندہ ام مرا مگذارید برین سخن غصۂ بندگی
حضرت مخدوم فرود آمد بانصد تنکہ خدمتی پیش نہاد و پروانہ دیہہ مذکور
بہ سہ ہزار تنکہ کردہ آورد در[8] مضمون آنکہ باسمی ورسمی فرمایش دیوان در موضع
مذکور نباشد واو دھرن یعنی دیسائی مبلغ دو ہزار تنکہ محصول نقد فرستادہ[9]
خدمتگاران بندگی حضرت مخدوم کرد خان از ناددوت باز گشت در درون گنجد شستہ بود[10] سلطان
دیہہ مذکور تسلیم نخستند تا تار خان ویل یافت خان را گرفت در بھروچ
فرستادہ بعد در تخت نشست نزیارت بندگی حضرت مخدوم
آمد بندگی حضرت مخدوم را از گرفتن[11] ظفر خان خوش نیاید[12] فرمودند
چہ کردی آن شیخ غریبان را گرفتہ در بھروچ او را زود باز گردانند[13]
در نادوت رفت تاخت بسیار کرد ہمان جا سر نہاد ظفر خان از بھروچ باز گشت

۱ک= ندارد ۲ک= صاحب ۳ک= او ۴ح= بگویند ۵ح= بگویند
۶ح= نمانند ۷ح= ندارد ۸ح= ندارد ۹ح= فرستاد ۱۰ح= ندارد
۱۱ح= گرفتی ۱۲ک= نیاید ۱۳ح= گردانیدند

وملک گرفت بر[۱] بندگی حضرت مخدوم آمد و عرض کرد بندهٔ خود در
یاد کرده بودند که چه کردی آن شیخ غریبان را ازان روز باز دل را اطمینان
شد که ما را هنوز حیات باقی است دیگر درآنکه شور ملاعین در گجرات افتاد
وخلق در ساحل دریا رفت[۲] بندگی حضرت شیخ جهان قطب زمان هم[۳] خدمت گاران
را در جهایم فرستادند بعده خود هم رفتند یک روز ماندند ملک عثمان ملاقات
کرد دوم روز بازگشتند شیخ شمس الدین که ملازمت ظفرخان داشت چند
کرت گفت که بندگی حضرت شیخ احمد هم در ساحل رفت ظفرخان بر سخن وی
هیچ ملتفت نه شد ناگاه ملکی[۴] که اساول گذاشته رفته بود[۵] بر ظفرخان رفت
اشارت شد کسی را دیده آمده[۶] گفت بر بندگی حضرت شیخ احمد در سرکهیچ مقیم
طعام خورانیدند وداع کردم و متوجه رکاب شدم و دران وقت شیخ
شمس الدین شکایت کرده بود پیش خان اعظم و قاضی خان نائب حاضر بود خان
اعظم گفت [او]☆ بر قاضی خان بحضور شیخ شمس الدین مذکور فرمود قاضی خان گفت هر که
می گفت که بندگی حضرت شیخ احمد در ساحل هم رفتند[۷] او چنین و چنین می خورد با شیخ داشت[۸] مشهور گشت حکایت وقتی سلطان
مظفر از لشکر بازگشته[۹] آمد بندگی حضرت شیخ جهان قطب زمان را ملاقات کرد
چون بازگشت دستها بر چوب در نهاده ایستاده قاضی منصور و شیخ
تاج الدین و شیخزاده احمد کرمانی پیش در حاضر بودند حاجب را بر بندگی حضرت شیخ

۱ک= ندارد ۲ک= دریافت ۳ک= همه ۴ح وک= ملکی را ۵ح وک= بودند
۶ک= آمدی ۷ح= ندارد ۸ک= داشته ۹ح= گشت ☆اضافه قیاسی

فرستاد[۱] که پیش ازین معتاد بود که سبب فقرا شفاعت میکردند این بار نه کردند سبب چیست بندگی حضرت مخدوم[۲] فرمودند چند نفرے حاضراند ایشان را چیزی تعیین شود اشارت شد نفرے را بست گان تنکه نقد[۳] و بست کان بیگه زمین از موضع چورانبلی[۴] برسد بعد سه چهار[۵] روز[۶] خان باز پیش[۷] بندگی حضرت مخدوم رسید فرمودند عنقریب چیست که مشرف کردید[۸] گفت برائے تفرج[۹] درآب آمده بودیم در خاطر شد که چه دلها شد که بمفاصله اندک بدیدار مبارک مشرف نکردند"

فصل شانزدهم

در سفر آخرت بندگی حضرت مخدوم ادام الله برکاته بالرحمة والرضوان چون عید فطر سنه تسع واربعین وتمانمائة گزارده بازگشتند طعام عود کرد آب لعل[۱۰] شکل از[۱۱] نبول افتاد[۱۲] متفکر شدند طعام گذاشتند زائران را هم از بیرون تبرک داده باز میگردانیدند[۱۳] از عالم انقطاع گرفتند و سخن اندک بود[۱۴] ملازمان را اشارت شد هم در دهلیز شب را قرار گیرند بعضے مخلصان را که دم در شغل و ترک میزدند در وقت ارشاد ایشان را نفس می شد که چنین باید بود چنان باید ماند و لیپا بچه بارانی مرحمت کرده بودند و هم افتاد که حجاز گردانیده اند شتاب شتابند[۱۵] و میان خلق

۱ ک = فرستادند ۲ ک = ندارد ۳ ک = ندارد ۴ ح = چورانبلي ازان، ک = جوارنیلی
۵ ح = درجهان ۶ ح و ک = روزی ۷ ح = ندارد ۸ ح = کردند، ک = کردیدید
۹ ک = تفرح ۱۰ ح = لال ۱۱ ک = ندارد ۱۲ ح = افتاده ۱۳ ح = میکردند
۱۴ ح = بودند ۱۵ ح = شدند

آشکارا کردن گرفتند چنانچہ بعضے ملوک آمدند از بندگی حضرت مخدوم
استفسار کردند یکی ہم از ایشان آمد گفت آرے کیفیت برین جملہ است
بندگی حضرت مخدوم سخت ناخوش شدند ما بارے ہنوز زندہ ام بعدہ
ملک نظام جہجو[1] رسید کیفیت تمام کہ در دیوان مذاکرہ شدہ بود عرض
داشت بندگی حضرت مخدوم[2] فرمودند استغفر اللہ استغفر اللہ این معنی از ما نبود
جواب بندگی حضرت مخدوم کہ استغفر اللہ فرمودند دلالت میکند کہ اگر فرض
کنیم اجازت کردہ باشند ہم رجوع کردند[3] و رجوع از اجازت جایز است
زیرا چہ پیغامبر صلی اللہ علیہ وسلم یکی را از صحابہ رضوان اللہ علیہم در مقام[4]
امارت میفرستادند چون بجہت وداع یا کارے[5] آمد یکے امیر المومنین حسن
یا[6] حسین رضی اللہ عنہما پیش آمد پیغامبر صلی اللہ علیہ وسلم بر پیشانی او از مہر
بوسہ زد صحابی گفت مرا دہ پسر است ہیچ یکے را گاہے بوسہ نہ زدہ ام پیغامبر
صلی اللہ علیہ وسلم او را باز گردانیدند و فرمودند کہ بے مہر است لائق امارت
نیست بر فرزندان خود گاہے شفقت نہ کرد[7] بر رعیت کے کند بدیگری
حوالہ کردند پس قیاس برین حدیث توان کرد کہ اگر شیخی از اجازت
مریدے رجوع کند مقبول باشد چون ملالت غلبہ کرد بندہ مؤلف
حکایتی[8] در خیر المجالس ملفوظ بندگی شیخ نصیر الدین محمود دیدہ بود عرضداشت

۱ح و ک = جہجو ۲ک = ندارد ۳ک = ندارد ۴ح و ک = مقامی
۵ک = بکارے ۶ک = و ۷ح = کردند ۸ک = حکایت

درویشی را چون سفر آخرت پیش آمد و[1] سجاده حواله به کسی نه کرده بود درویشی
دیگر شنید که[2] سجاده خالی می گذارد گفت فرستاد که سجاده خالی "
گذاشتن سنت مشایخ نیست گفت فیروز[3] را بنشانند و همان زمان آسوده
شد بعد تجهیز و تکفین و تعزیت خدام تفحص کردند از مریدان نام فیروز کسی نبود
نیافتند بعده در شهر تفحص کردند که باشد کسی را که او را فیروز نام بود نیافتند
جز یک[4] سبوکشی را در میخانه بردی کیفیت نصیحت شیخ گفتند وی گفت
مرا غسل داده نزدیک قبر شیخ ببرید از آنجا چه کشاید خدام هم بران نهج بر سر قبر
بردند گفتند فیروزی دیگر در شهر نیست جز[5] این آواز برآمد فیروز فیروزتر
خدام او را بر سجاده نشاندند یکی از واصلان[6] حق شد چون بنده مؤلف
این حکایت[7] تمام کرد اشارت شد ملان تو متشرع[8] باشی آواز از تربت آمدن
چگونه قبول کنی این حکایت بر ما کسی نگوید که ما بر سجاده کسی را بنشانیم[9] زمانه دیگرگون
شده است خلق را هوس جاه و طلب دنیا و هوا نفس سخت
غالب شده اگر امروز این درویش[10] کسی را اجازت[11] دید هرچه[12] او کند فردای
قیامت جواب این درویش پرسند که اینچنین کسی را مجاز گردانیدی
و آنک بندگی حضرت مخدوم فرمودند که این درویش هنوز زنده است
این سخن هم دلالت کرد که بندگی حضرت مخدوم شیخ جهان قطب زمان از آن

۱ك= که ۲ك= ندارد ۳ك= ندارد ۴ك= سبوکسی ۵ك= جزین
۶ح= واصل آن ۷ك= ندارد ۸ح= ندارد ۹ك= دیگر گونه
۱۰ح= درویشی ۱۱ح= ندارد ۱۲ك= وهرچه

اجازت پشیمان بوده اند و بندگی حضرت شیخ جهان قطب زمان را[1] در قصبه
کهتو قاضی نیکو عالم بجهت خدمت تعین بود و در مسجد خانجهان
قاضی حاکم و در خراسان عارف[2] و در قصبه سرکهیج آغاز چند روز سید
حسام الدین و امیر حاجی بعدهٔ قاضی عبدالحی منصور موازنه بیست سال
بود اما بغایت مزاج دان و مقبول بود بعدهٔ برادر[3] بزرگ او قاضی عبدالعزیز
دو بی[4] بعده عبدالباقی پسر او چهار سال[5]
سال در خدمت بود بعده برادرم بر آمد غلام خاص بود[5] بعدهٔ شیخ صلاح الدین
در خدمت بودند[6] و شیخ صلاح الدین اگرچه خورد بود اما کارهای بزرگ کردی
مزاج دان و نیک خواه[7] برادر بر آمد بر مزاج نماند همین شیخ صلاح الدین خدمت
کردی اینچنین منظور شد که اگر دیگری برای یاری دادن او برخاستی خوش نیامدی
بلکه میفرمودند که همین خوردک خواهد کرد ما را هوا خواه است بعدهٔ سلطان محمد
بن احمد را حضرت شد که بندگی حضرت مخدوم[8] سخت ملالت دارند در آستانه
مبارک آمد بندگی حضرت شیخ جهان قطب زمان از پلنگ فرود آمدند برای
تعظیم سلطان بر نهالچه غلطیدند و تکلم اندک بود سلطان برخاست گریه کنان
در دهلیز آمد هزار تنگه زر فرستاد شیخ صلاح الدین را اشارت شد بدار ترا
کار خواهد آمد حضار مجلس هم بدین سخن استدلال کردند که بعد رحلت خدمت روضه
منوره متبرکه هم حواله[9] شیخ صلاح الدین شد بعدهٔ ملک عماد الملک و خواجه

١ح= ندارد ٢ک= ندارد ٣ک= ندارد ٤ح= ندارد ٥ح= ندارد
٦ک= ندارد ٧ک= نیکوخواه شد ٨ح= حضرت مخدوم را ٩ک= ندارد

چهجو[1] علیهما الرحمة برادر طالب و شیخ صلاح الدین و عبدالله هر دو خضر[2] را
بحضرت بندگی مخدوم آوردند عرض[3] کرده داشتند که اگر بفرمایند ایشان را پیش تخت
اعلی بگذرانیم تا[*] هم آستانه باشند بدست مبارک اشارت شد شیخ
صلاح الدین را ما[4] بدارند و دیگران را بگذرانند بعده سلطان محمد بن احمد عرض داشت
کنانیده که ما را از دنیا هیچ[5] آرزو نیست حق سبحانه و تعالی بکرم خویش خود
بسلطنت رسانید از بندگی حضرت شیخ[6] جهان قطب زمان این توقع است که
در بهشت ما را برابر خود ببرند بندگی حضرت شیخ جهان قطب زمان انگشت مبارک
بر چشم ها خود نهادند که بالعین والراس سلطان بازگشت بعده برادرم طالب
بحضور ملازمان براین بنده پروانگی رسانید که چون آن وقت رسد باید که
فلان کلمه بگوید و او را از دست نگذارد[7] شب چهاردهم ماه شوال سخت بیهوش
شد ند بعده ساعتی بهوش باز آمدند برخاستند باز غلطیدند دو سه بار همچنین میکردند
چون دیر[8] شد عزیزان گفتند شما را اشارت است[9] چرا کلمه نگوئید[10] این غریب را در خاطر
گذشت که بندگی حضرت مخدوم در حضرت باریتعالی همه وقت چیست و چالاک
و ثابت قدم بوده اند و همیشه در حضرت حق استغراق داشته اند[11] تو مبادا اگر دم
زنی در آخرین دم[12] بر مزاج نیفتد خوب نباشد بنده ساکت بود مخلصی با واز بلند
گفت اَشْهَدُ اَنْ لَا اِلٰهَ اِلَّا اللّٰهُ وَحْدَهٗ لَا شَرِیْکَ لَهٗ وَاَشْهَدُ اَنَّ مُحَمَّدًا عَبْدُهٗ

۱ ک= جهجو ۲ ک= ندارد ۳ ح= ندارد ☆ کذا در هر دو نسخه احتمالاً محل "یا" باشد ۴ ح= بدارید ۵ ح= یکی ۶ ک= ندارد ۷ ح= نگذارند ۸ ک= ندارد ۹ ح= نیست ۱۰ ح= نگویند ۱۱ ک= داشتند ۱۲ ک= ندارد

و در سؤله طبندگی حضرت مخدوم چشم بازکردند[1] و فرمودند این کیفیت در دهلیز[2] بر وید
بنشینید بنده مؤلف شکر خدای تعالی بجا آورد که سکوت عین مصلحت
بود بعد فجر ملک رضی الملک رسید بندگی حضرت مخدوم برخاستند نشستند
برادرم شیخ صلاح الدین را دستار بندانیده طلبیدند دعا کردند پسران را و
نبیره از غلام[3] را مرید کردند غلطیدند بعده ملک عمدة الملک رسید[4] و قدرخان آمد
بدست مبارک اشارت کردند که بنشینید بعده دم بالا شد چند دمی معدود[5] زدند لب
زیرین مبارک قدری جنبید آسودند بنده مؤلف غسل داد برادرم قاضی بده مبارک
و نوالجی[6] آب میریخت بر پالکی کرده در روضه بردند سلطان محمد شاه بن احمد شاه
در آن وقت حاضر شدند بنده مؤلف بجهت امامت بر سلطان گفت[7] السلطان
احق بالامامة[8] فرمان شد مولانا محمد قاسم شما درحیات برامامت کرده[9] اید شما پیش شوید مؤلف بحکم[10]
سلطان سعادت[11] امامت جنازهٔ شیخ جهان قطب زمان[12] قدس الله سره العزیز یافت[13] و
مستفید شد و بحضور مریدان و معتقدان کرده اول قبر در آمد[14] و ریگ پاک
فراز کردند سر آن[15] این بنده بود و پایان قبر قاضی بده مبارک بود[16] بعده فرود آوردند
اِنَّا لِلّٰهِ وَاِنَّا اِلَیْهِ رَاجِعُوْن این[17] رباعی از آن[18] مؤلف است. رباعی[19]

افتاد در جهان چه بلا عظیم دردا قطب زمان احمد کهتو که نقل کرد
روز خمیس چهاردهم ماه[20] عید فطر در هشتصد و چهل[21] نهمین سال فصل برد
روز پنجشنبه چهاردهم ماه شوال ۸۴۵ هـ تسع اربعین و ثمانمایه بنیاد زوال[22]

١ح= ندارد ٢ح= دهلی ٣ح= غلام میر ٤ح= رسیدند ٥ک= معدودی
٦ح= والوالجی ٧ک= ندارد ٨ح= بامامة ٩ح= ندارد ١٠ح= برحکم ١١ح= ندارد
١٢ح= ندارد ١٣ح= مستعد ١٤ک= برآوردند ١٥ک= ندارد ١٦ک= ندارد
١٧ح= ندارد ١٨ح= ندارد ١٩ک= ندارد ٢٠ح= ندارد ٢١ح= ندارد ٢٢ک= ندارد

کاتب فقیر حقیر محمد ولد محمود خطیب ولد اسمعیل خطیب ولد صدیق خطیب

ولد یوسف خطیب ولد محمود خطیب غزنوی

غفر الله له ولوالدیه اجمعین ـ مالکه

دولت محمد ذاکر ولد حاجی محمد

ولد شیخ جی

ولد حسن

بتاریخ بست و هفتم رجب المرجب سنه ۱۱۲۸ھ یک هزار و یک صد

و بست و هشت هجری از مطالعه این کتاب مستطاب

که فصل الخطاب مقوله ازین باب است مستفیع

و بهره مند گردید کمترین مریدان آستانه

ملک آشیانه سید المحبوبین و خاتمهم

السید محمد بن عبد الله الملقب

بنا هیعالم من عبد الله

حیات منهجهن

سلهی

کاتب نسخه هذا عبد المغفور غفر الله له ناظم کتب خانه درگاه شریف